Disarming the Church

12/17/18

Sarah,

I'm so glad our paths
crossed here at Messiah College.
It has been a pleasure getting to know
you. You have many gifts to offer the
world and the church. I pray God's richest
blessing on you as you continue to follow Jesus.
I really hope you enjoy this book. Keep in touch!

Peace,

Eric

Disarming the Church

Why Christians Must Forsake Violence
to Follow Jesus and Change the World

Eric A. Seibert

CASCADE *Books* · Eugene, Oregon

DISARMING THE CHURCH
Why Christians Must Forsake Violence to Follow Jesus and Change the World

Cascade Books
An Imprint of Wipf and Stock Publishers
199 W. 8th Ave., Suite 3
Eugene, OR 97401

www.wipfandstock.com

PAPERBACK ISBN: 978-1-62032-887-3
HARDCOVER ISBN: 978-1-4982-8783-8
EBOOK ISBN: 978-1-5326-5277-6

Cataloguing-in-Publication data:

Names: Seibert, Eric A.
Title: Disarming the church : why Christians must forsake violence to follow Jesus and change the world / Eric A. Seibert.
Description: Eugene, OR: Cascade Books, 2018. Includes bibliographical references and indexes.
Identifiers: ISBN 978-1-62032-887-3 (paperback) | ISBN 978-1-4982-8783-8 (hardcover) | ISBN 978-1-5326-5277-6 (ebook)
Subjects: LCSH: Nonviolence—Religious aspects—Christianity. | Jesus Christ—Teachings. | Violence—Biblical teaching. | Title.
Classification: BT736.6 .S60 2018 (print) | BT736 (ebook)

Manufactured in the U.S.A.   APRIL 6, 2018

New Revised Standard Version Bible, copyright 1989, Division of Christian Education of the Churches of Christ in the United States of America. Used by permission. All rights reserved.

Permissions

Excerpts from *Violence in Families: What Every Christian Needs to Know*, by Al Miles, copyright © 2002 Augsburg Fortress, is used by permission of the publisher.

Excerpts from *Engaging the Powers: Discernment and Resistance in a World of Domination*, copyright © 1992 Augsburg Fortress, *The Powers That Be*, copyright © 1998 by Augsburg Fortress, and *Jesus and Nonviolence: A Third Way*, copyright © 2003 Augsburg Fortress, by Walter Wink are used by permission of the publisher.

Excerpt from *A Farewell to Mars* by Brian Zahnd. Copyright © 2014 Brain Zahnd. *A Farewell to Mars: An Evangelical Pastor's Journey Toward the Biblical Gospel of Peace* is published by David C Cook. All rights reserved.

Excerpt from an assignment written by a student in my "Issues of War, Peace and Social Justice in Biblical Texts" course, January 2007, is used by permission of the student.

Excerpts reprinted from *Choosing Against War* by John D. Roth by permission of Good Books, an imprint of Skyhorse Publishing, Inc.

Copyright © 1984 by the Christian Century. "Bless you, Mrs. Degrafinried" by William Willimon is reprinted by permission from the March 14, 1984, issue of the *Christian Century*.

Excerpts from Chuck McKnight's blogpost, "How One Church Reacted to the Threat of Violence—and the Questions It Forces Us to Ask," is used by permission of the author.

Excerpts from "Soul Repair" by Gabriella Lettini, Rita Nakashima Brock. Copyright © Rita Nakashima Brock and Gabriella Lettini. Reprinted by permission of Beacon Press, Boston.

Excerpt from *Waging Peace: Global Adventures of a Lifelong Activist* by David Hartsough, copyright © 2014 PM Press, is used by permission of the publisher (www.pmpress.org).

Excerpts from "How Personal Forgiveness Created a Platform for Global Peace-making" by Lisa R. Gibson and "Where We Have Been—and Where We Go from Here" by Jim Wallis in *Evangelical Peacemakers: Gospel Engagement in a War-Torn World*, copyright © 2013 Wipf and Stock Publishers, is used by permission of Wipf and Stock Publishers. www.wipfandstock.com.

To Hannah Katherine Seibert,
my youngest child
who brings great delight to our family,
with hope that the world you come to know
will be far less violent than the one that exists today

Table of Contents

Acknowledgements

FINISHING A BOOK IS always a time for great celebration and expressions of gratitude. This book has been many years in the making and countless people have contributed to it in big ways and small. My thoughts about violence and nonviolence have been shaped by lots of people: family and friends, pastors and professors, authors and activists. I am especially grateful for those who have written about peace, spoken about peace, and embodied a life of peace in word and deed. People like Walter Wink (whom I never met) and Daniel Buttry (whom I know personally) have inspired me and influenced my thinking. I gladly acknowledge my debt to individuals like these and am profoundly grateful both for their lives and for the rich treasure trove of resources they have produced. The footnotes throughout the book bear witness to the way I have benefitted from their insights and stories.

Specific words of thanks are due to a number of individuals. Thank you, Rich and Kathy Stuebing, for taking time to be interviewed about a personal story included in this book. Thank you, Kimberly Steiner, for securing items for me via interlibrary loan. Thanks to all the students who took my first year seminar class "Alternatives to Violence" since this is where some of the ideas in this book were first tested. Your ability to grapple with new perspectives and your openness to considering nonviolent options was encouraging. Thanks are also due to all the students who have taken "Issues of War, Peace and Social Justice in Biblical Texts" with me. Your active engagement with the material and your good conversation not only enriched the classroom experience immeasurably, it forced me to think more deeply about the topics we addressed.

A number of individuals read a draft of this manuscript in 2016 and provided valuable feedback: Harriet Bicksler, Terry Brensinger, Michelle Curtis, Michael Gingerich, Tom Kaden, Jay McDermond, Dan Schmidt,

Elisa Seibert, and Chris Wenger. Thank you one and all for reading what I wrote and for offering comments. The book is much improved because of you! Of course, all remaining shortcomings are mine alone. Harriet, I deeply respect the way you live out your convictions in the real world. You inspire me. Terry, you have left a huge imprint on my life. I hope you hear your voice in some of these pages, especially in the postscript. Michelle, your feedback was so helpful at many points. This book has more grace and less "oughts" because of you. Michael and Tom, your friendship has been a special gift. Thank you for reaching out to me, listening to me, and encouraging me along the way. Jay, thanks for being honest and giving good counsel about content to eliminate from the book. Most of it is gone! Dan, thank you for stopping by my office periodically to see how I was doing. Thanks also for sharing your lunch with me when I forgot mine. Chris, your enthusiastic response to the manuscript was so very encouraging. Thank you for this and for your helpful comments throughout.

I owe a special word of thanks to Elisa Joy Seibert, my wife of twenty-six years and my best friend. You have been excited about this book from the very beginning. That has been a real blessing to me. Thank you for being interested in what I write and for having such passion around this topic. It is wonderful to journey through life with you, and I consider myself ridiculously fortunate to be married to someone who is equally committed to living nonviolently. I deeply appreciated your many insightful comments and critiques along the way. Thanks also for caring so beautifully for our three wonderful children, Nathan, Rebecca, and Hannah, and for providing time and space to write. I love you!

I also need to thank my parents, Laverne and Kathy Seibert, for spending countless hours in child care and for helping with chores around the house. This freed me to write, and I am grateful for the many, many hours of work on this book that were made possible by your help in these ways. I appreciate all the sacrifices you have made for me and love you both very much. I hope you enjoy the final product.

I am especially grateful for my co-workers in the Biblical and Religious Studies Department: Mike Cosby, Richard Crane, Stephen Gallaher, Drew Hart, Jake Jacobsen, George Pickens, Emerson Powery, Sharon Putt, Shelly Skinner, Brian Smith, and David Weaver-Zercher. It is hard to imagine a better group of colleagues. Thank you for the ways you affirm my scholarship and what I do in the classroom. Thanks also for lots of laughter. You make me glad to come to work.

Toward the end of the project I received a boost of much needed energy from a college student named Max Whitehead who, without complaint, engaged in the very tedious business of checking many quotes for accuracy.

Thanks also to George Pickens for "lending" Max to me for this task. I also wish to express my gratitude to Sharon Berger for taking the time to help me with questions related to formatting certain items. It was much appreciated. Thanks also to Paula Holtzinger for doing a fantastic job of preparing both indexes for the book.

Finally, I want to express my sincere appreciation to the good folks at Wipf and Stock for taking on this project and seeing it through to completion. Special thanks are due to K. C. Hanson for meeting with me in Chicago in the fall of 2012 and for accepting this book for publication. I am also grateful for the early assistance offered by Christian Amondson and later by Matthew Wimer. Thank you, Matt, for granting multiple extensions and for being so very patient with me while I finished this manuscript. Thanks also for all your assistance with my many questions in the final stages of working on this book. It was a huge help! I would also like to express my appreciation to Rodney Clapp for his editorial work and to Heather Carraher for typesetting the manuscript.

To all who read this, I hope you find the book enjoyable and transformative. May it disarm each of us as we strive to live more faithfully in the way of Jesus.

Prologue

What If Jesus Meant What He Said?

Sadly, most American evangelicals have been quicker to vote for war than to wage peace. We say that not as accusation but as confession. For four decades God has trusted us with Christian leadership, but only in recent years have we opened our eyes, minds, and hearts to the biblical call to peacemaking and reconciliation. God, forgive us.

—BILL AND LYNNE HYBELS[1]

IN HIS NOVEL *BENEDICTION*, Kent Haruf describes a sermon that does not go well for Reverend Rob Lyle, the newly arrived minister of the Community Church in Holt, Colorado.[2] On this particularly hot Sunday in July, the sermon text contains familiar words of Jesus from the Gospel of Luke.

> Love your enemies, do good to those who hate you, bless those who curse you, and pray for those who mistreat you. . . . You will then have great reward, and you will be sons of the Most High God. For He is good to the ungrateful and the wicked. Be merciful just as your Father is merciful.[3]

As Reverend Lyle begins his message, he gives voice to what many people in the congregation are already thinking—Jesus did not really expect his

1. Hybels and Hybels, "Foreword," 10, emphasis original.

2. Haruf, *Benediction*, 138–45. My thanks to Harriet Bicksler for bringing this to my attention.

3. Ibid., 139, quoting Luke 6:27–28, 35–36 from Today's English Version (first edition).

followers to live this way. "Oh, that was a nice idea Jesus had," says Lyle. "That was a pretty notion, but you can't love people who do evil. It's neither sensible nor practical. . . . There is no way on earth we can love our enemies. They'll only do wickedness and hatefulness again. And worse, they'll think they can get away with this wickedness and evil, because they'll think we're weak and afraid. What would the world come to?"

But then Lyle abruptly switches tactics and pursues a different line of thinking, one that reveals his true intentions and convictions. He engages in a thought experiment by asking the congregation some rather challenging questions. "But . . . what if Jesus wasn't kidding?" Lyle muses. "What if he really did mean what he said two thousand years ago? What if he was thoroughly wise to the world and knew firsthand cruelty and wickedness and evil and hate? Knew it all so well from firsthand personal experience? And what if in spite of all that he knew, he still said love your enemies? Turn your cheek. Pray for those who misuse you. What if he meant every word of what he said? What then would the world come to?"

Lyle ponders what would happen if "we [the United States] tried it." What would happen if we told our enemies about all the harm we *could* do to them but instead said:

> We are going to spend the great American national treasure and the will and the human lives that we would have spent on destruction, and instead we are going to turn them all toward creation. We'll mend your roads and highways, expand your schools, modernize your wells and water supplies, save your ancient artifacts and art and culture, preserve your temples and mosques. In fact, we are going to love you. And again we say, no matter what has gone before, no matter what you've done: We are going to love you. We have set out hearts to it. We will treat you like brothers and sisters. We are going to turn our collective national cheek and present it to be stricken a second time, if need be, and offer it to you. Listen, we—

At this point Lyle is unable to continue. Even though he is not even half-way through the sermon, someone in the congregation has begun shouting angrily at him. "Are you crazy? You must be insane." The distraught man hastily ushers his wife and young boy out of the church in protest. Another congregant calls Lyle "a damn terrorist sympathizer," stands to his feet and says, "We never should of let you come out here. You're an enemy of our country." Other hostile words are spoken and more people leave the church. One even stops at the back of the sanctuary, turns around, and shouts, "You go to hell!"

Although more than half the congregation still remained after the most disgruntled members had exited the sanctuary, the atmosphere was no longer right for a church service. After beginning—but finding it impossible to finish—the final hymn, the service comes to a sputtering halt.

But for Lyle, the ordeal is not over yet. After the rest of the congregation has gone and the usher is locking the church, Lyle is left standing outside with his wife and son, John Wesley. John is furious with his Dad and expresses his displeasure in no uncertain terms before bolting for home a couple blocks away. Lyle's wife then says to her beleaguered husband:

> "You've ruined this too . . . haven't you. What did you think people would do? Did you actually think they'd agree with you? Be convinced by your eloquence and passion? My God."
>> "No, No, I didn't think that. I had to say it anyway."
>> "Why? For what earthly reason?"
>> "Because I believe it."

1

Introduction

Getting Beyond an Eye for an Eye

Violence is not the way that Christians bring about change in the world, but by being faithful to Christ and bearing witness to him, we become change agents.

—JUSTIN BRONSON BARRINGER[1]

AMONG CHRISTIANITY'S MOST NOTABLE teachings are commands to forgive wrongdoers (Col 3:13), love enemies (Matt 5:44), and serve others (Matt 20:20–28). Christians, empowered by God's Spirit, should exhibit "love, joy, peace, patience, kindness, generosity, faithfulness, gentleness, and self-control" (Gal 5:22–23).[2] Retaliation, retribution, and revenge are forbidden (Matt 5:38–42). Believers are never to "repay anyone evil for evil" (Rom 12:17) but rather are to "overcome evil with good" (Rom 12:21). Love is the quintessential virtue of Jesus' followers and the identifying mark by which the world will recognize them as his disciples (John 13:35; 1 John 3:11–24; 4:7–12). Christians are to love their neighbors (Matt 22:39), treat others as they wish to be treated (Matt 7:12), and be merciful (Luke 6:36). They are to live such exemplary lives that others see their "good works" and glorify God (Matt 5:16).

1. Barringer, "What about Those Men and Women?," 100.

2. All Scripture references are from the New Revised Standard Version (NRSV) of the Bible unless otherwise noted.

In its better moments, the church has embodied these commitments, living out its calling with faithfulness, courage, and conviction. Thousands of stories could be told of Christians who have lived extraordinary lives serving the poor, working for justice, resolving conflict, and making peace. In the United States, for example, the church played a pivotal role in the abolition of slavery, the struggle for women's right to vote, and the civil rights movement. And around the world, Christians have been instrumental in such things as the removal of Filipino dictator Ferdinand Marcos, the fall of the Berlin wall, and the cessation of violence in Liberia after years of civil war. At its best, the church has improved the lives of countless individuals and has been an incredible blessing to the world.

But here's the rub: the church has not always been at its best. Throughout history, far too many Christians have behaved violently, tarnishing the reputation of the church and doing immeasurable harm.

A Spotted Past

The church's long and ugly history of violence is well documented and indisputable.[3] The record shows that Christians, claiming to follow the "Prince of Peace," have often been anything but peaceful. Rather than rejecting violence, the church has often sponsored it. And rather than loving enemies, the church has often killed them. Christians have waged wars, executed "witches," brutalized children, oppressed women, enslaved Africans, massacred Muslims, and exterminated Native Americans. During its 2,000-year history, the church has been responsible for unspeakable atrocities and massive amounts of bloodshed. "It is an undeniable historical fact," writes Lee Camp, "that people who claim the lordship of Jesus . . . have killed or participated in the killing of thousands and thousands of civilians in acts of horrid violence."[4] Camp supports this claim by citing the Crusades, the religious wars of 16th- and 17th-century Europe between Catholics and Protestants, the massacre of Native Americans, and the firebombing of European cities along with the use of the atomic bomb in World War II. It is a tragic irony that the very people called to model the nonviolent love of Jesus have engaged in precisely the kind of behavior they were to reject.

On many occasions, Christians have taken up arms against their fellow Christians. Take, for example, the American Civil War, in which thousands

---

3. As Mark Noll writes, "For anyone who makes the effort to study history carefully . . . the role of Christians in promoting the destruction of others . . . cannot be denied" ("More Harm Than Good?," 83).

4. Camp, *Who Is My Enemy?*, 11.

of Christians on one side killed thousands of Christians on the other. Watching this was deeply disturbing to David Lipscomb, namesake of Lipscomb University in Nashville, Tennessee.

> Lipscomb witnessed the Battle of Nashville, in December 1864, in which 1,500 Confederates and 3,000 Union soldiers died in a two-day period. . . . How, Lipscomb wanted to know, could southern Christians slaughter their northern Christian brothers? How could northern disciples make widows out of their southern sisters in Christ? Over the course of the war, six hundred thousand men were slaughtered—most of whom claimed Jesus as Lord. Brothers in Christ, on opposite sides of the battle lines, seeking to kill one another, their battles bathed not only in blood but in prayer—and witnessing this, Lipscomb knew that there was some agenda other than the kingdom of God at work.[5]

How could Christians justify such behavior? How could they read their Bible, attend church, pray to God, and then go out and slaughter fellow believers?

If all this were in the past, water over the dam, so to speak, that would be bad enough. The church would still need to confess its sins, seek forgiveness, and try to make amends wherever possible. But this is not ancient history. The church continues to condone—and sometimes even participate in—various forms of violence.[6] Many Christians support warfare, approve of torturing suspected terrorists, and endorse capital punishment. And Christians routinely express hostility toward certain groups of people such as atheists, Muslims, and members of the LGBTQ community. Unfortunately, it is precisely this kind of *un*christian behavior that leads people to doubt the integrity of the church and its message of peace and goodwill.

Surprised by Nonviolent Christians

Given the church's complicity with violence, it is unremarkable that many people do not regard nonviolence as a hallmark of the Christian faith. The astonishment some have upon meeting Christians committed to nonviolence is reflected in the following conversation recounted by David Augsburger:

> After my colleague Nancey Murphy delivered an address in London, two Muslim men sought her out to ask, "Did we hear correctly? You are a Christian and you believe in nonviolence?"

5. Camp, *Mere Discipleship*, 18.

6. This point will be explored at length in chapter 2.

"Yes, I come from a long tradition, Anabaptism, which, like Jesus did, refuses violence."

"And you would not kill, even to protect your family?"

"I've told both my husband and my son that I would gladly die for them, but I will not kill for them."

"This is part of the Christian tradition?" they asked, surprised. "This is not the Christianity we know about."[7]

Many people are similarly surprised when they see Christians loving their enemies and forgiving those who have harmed them. The reaction some people had to the forgiveness so beautifully offered by the Amish after the events at Nickel Mines, Pennsylvania, is an excellent case in point. The story is well known and has been thoroughly discussed in the book *Amish Grace*.[8] On October 2, 2006, Charles Roberts entered the Nickel Mines schoolhouse, barricaded himself inside, and shot ten Amish schoolgirls (aged six to thirteen), five of whom died, before killing himself. Almost immediately, various members of the Amish community announced their forgiveness for the man who had committed this atrocity. But they did more than that. They reached out to Amy Roberts, the shooter's widow. They befriended her, attended the burial of her husband—the man who had killed their children—and offered tangible gifts of peace and reconciliation.[9] This response was profoundly consistent with their Christian convictions. Yet, the world was dumbfounded. Even many Christians were amazed. As Tripp York recalls, "Think of the reaction that so many Christians had to the Amish response. They were shocked, baffled, and confused. What made bigger news—the killing of the children or that Christians would forgive a killer—is difficult to determine."[10]

Why was the world, including many within the church, shocked by this response? Were they unaware that forgiveness is one of the basic tenets of Christianity? Perhaps. But I suspect the reason for their astonishment lay elsewhere, in the simple fact that *they rarely see Christians acting this way*. They were caught off guard by the extravagant mercy and unconditional love the Amish extended to the Roberts family after the shooting since this kind of behavior is seldom exhibited by Christians today.

Stories like these indicate the church has a serious problem on its hands. Something is clearly wrong when people are *surprised* to see Christians living nonviolently and refusing to retaliate. This is what they should

7. Augsburger, *Dissident Discipleship*, 129.

8. Kraybill, Nolt, and Weaver-Zercher, *Amish Grace*.

9. Ibid., 43–52.

10. York, "Conclusion," 225.

expect. Moreover, when Christian acts of love, grace, and forgiveness become a major news story, it suggests this sort of behavior is far too uncommon among believers today.

Why I Wrote This Book

I wrote *Disarming the Church* because I am troubled by how much violence Christians condone—and sometimes participate in—and by how much violence the church sanctions and sometimes actively supports. I do not believe this is what God intended. God does not want people to be victims of violence—and certainly not at the hands of those who claim to be following God! In fact, one of the central claims I will make, and one I believe is borne out by a careful reading of the Gospels, is that *Jesus lived nonviolently and taught his followers to do the same.* Condoning or participating in violence, even for the most noble reasons, runs contrary to the teachings of Jesus. Therefore, I have written to encourage Christians to reject all forms of violence as they strive to follow Jesus.

As noted above, Christians hold a wide range of views about violence. Many approve of things such as capital punishment, torture, and war, and many more would have no qualms about personally engaging in acts of violence for self-defense or to protect others. Maybe this describes some of your own beliefs. Perhaps you may regard violence as appropriate and even necessary in certain situations. If so, I'm glad you are reading this book. It has been written with you in mind. While the pages that follow will undoubtedly challenge some of your assumptions, they will offer you new perspectives to consider as you reflect on the life and ministry of Jesus and the nature of Christian faith. I am hopeful you will be convinced by what you read and will embrace the nonviolent way of Jesus in all its fullness.

I have also written *Disarming the Church* for those who are already committed to nonviolence, especially those who wish to deepen that commitment and live it out more fully. Unfortunately, the church does not always offer much help in this regard. Though we are told to love enemies, forgive offenders, and overcome evil with good, we are seldom given much guidance about how to put these things into practice. In order to embody the teachings of Jesus, we need to know what living nonviolently looks like in the real world. Specifically, we need to be aware of creative nonviolent alternatives we can use to deal with situations of conflict, warfare, and injustice. Although this book is not primarily a "how-to" book for engaging in nonviolent action, we will discuss many practical nonviolent strategies that can be used to respond to everything from a personal assault to global terrorism. Along the way, additional resources will be noted for those wanting to learn more and to consider these strategies in greater detail. As we'll discover, violence is *never* the only option, much less the best one.

Ultimately, I wrote this book because I care deeply about the church and want the church to look more like Jesus. I want Christians to do all they can to make the world a *much less violent* and *much more peaceful* place. Rather than perpetuating endless cycles of retaliation, violence, and bloodshed, the church can show the world a better way by modeling peacemaking, justice, and reconciliation. I want Christians to recognize that *all* people are created in God's image and to treat *all* people with dignity and respect: black and white, rich and poor, gay and straight, Muslim and Christian, young and old—everyone! When this happens, when the church makes known the love of God to people everywhere in large and small ways, the kingdom of God comes among us. This is the kind of world I want for myself, my family, my friends, and even my enemies. If this book is of some help in creating that kind of a world, writing it will have been well worth the effort.

A Brief Overview

The book is divided into four sections. The first part (chapters 1–4) examines the problematic relationship between violence and the church. Chapter 2 explores various ways the church has been—and continues to be—complicit in acts of violence and killing. The picture that emerges is sobering, to say the least, and should cause the church to do some serious soul-searching. In particular, it should prompt us to ask *why* so many Christians find certain forms of violence unproblematic. We take up this question in chapter 3. There we identify several reasons that begin to help us understand why Christians frequently condone the use of violence in certain situations. Then, in chapter 4, we lay bare the truth about violence by exposing its destructive, harmful, and unredemptive nature. This supports a major assumption operative throughout the book, namely, the belief that violence is inherently bad.

The second section of the book (chapters 5–9) makes a case for Christian nonviolence primarily from New Testament texts. Chapter 5 discusses key passages from the Gospels that support the claim that Jesus was nonviolent. This includes stories in which Jesus explicitly rejects violence and sayings that contain Jesus' teachings about nonviolence. Of course, not everyone is convinced that Jesus was nonviolent, and various objections are often raised from the New Testament. These include things such as Jesus' behavior in the temple, his comment about not coming to bring peace but a sword, and his favorable interaction with a Roman centurion. Chapter 6 responds to these objections (and others), none of which are judged to be insurmountable. The next chapter explores the nonviolent nature of discipleship by discussing what followers of Jesus were to do, namely, serve rather than dominate, forgive rather than retaliate, suffer harm rather than inflict it, repay evil with good rather than more evil, and love rather than hate. Chapter 8 considers some of the implications of living nonviolently, specifically, whether it is permissible for a Christian to participate in warfare and killing. The just war theory is considered, as are biblical arguments routinely made by Christians who appeal to Scripture to support war. The final chapter in this section, chapter 9, moves beyond the New Testament in an effort to illustrate what forsaking violence and following Jesus looks like in the real world. This chapter contains true stories of how Christians have followed the nonviolent way of Jesus faithfully in a wide range of contexts and situations.

The third part of the book (chapters 10–12) explores many practical alternatives to violence. This is vitally important since many Christians will not completely rule out violence until they are convinced there are viable alternatives for resolving conflict and confronting evil. The chapters in this section provide these alternatives along with numerous stories of people who have used them to great effect. How might you respond to someone threatening to harm you without harming them? Chapter 10 includes true stories of people who did just that. These stories illustrate the kind of nonviolent actions that can be used to get through dangerous situations like these. Chapter 11 considers a related, albeit somewhat different, kind of scenario. What should we do if we come upon *somebody else* being harmed? How can we help them without resorting to violence? Again, true stories are included and various alternatives that can be used in situations like these are discussed. Chapter 12 takes this to a whole new level and considers how nonviolence can be used on a large scale. This chapter includes a basic primer on the principles of nonviolent struggle and highlights some of the amazing stories of how nonviolence has been successfully used to resolve conflict, stop oppression, and correct injustice around the world.

In the final section of the book (chapters 13–17) we explore various ways to live nonviolently in the daily grind of our everyday lives as we interact with family members, friends, co-workers, churchgoers, and others. Chapter 13 lays the groundwork for this by discussing what is involved in cultivating a nonviolent mind-set. How we view others, particularly those who differ from us in significant ways, greatly influences how we think about them and interact with them. Chapter 14 provides some guidance for how to resolve interpersonal conflict nonviolently. Since many people find it difficult to handle conflict constructively, it is important to develop some good skills for doing so.

The next two chapters focus more specifically on living nonviolently at home. Chapter 15 is devoted to nonviolent parenting. It explores various ways parents can shape, guide, and correct their children without resorting to violent forms of discipline. It also offers some suggestions for talking about violence with your children. The following chapter addresses the problem of domestic violence. This form of violence is particularly dangerous and quite widespread. Sadly, it happens just as frequently in Christian homes as elsewhere. Chapter 16 contains heartbreaking stories of abuse and suggestions for how the church can respond more effectively.

The final chapter in the book is written specifically for church leaders—pastors, priests, Sunday school teachers, worship leaders, youth workers, and others who play a significant role in planning and facilitating what happens in the life of the church. The chapter offers many practical suggestions for disarming the church such as training Christians to live nonviolently, developing a comprehensive peace education program, infusing worship services with nonviolent emphases, telling stories of Christian peacemakers, and challenging all forms of prejudice, bigotry, discrimination, and exclusion. The goal here is to provide specific things church leaders can do to form people of peace who reject violence and follow Jesus.

The book concludes with a brief postscript describing the importance of imagination for deepening our commitment to nonviolence. This is followed by a discussion guide that contains questions based on each chapter of the book. These questions provide an excellent starting point for people who plan to discuss the book with others in a small group or Sunday school class. They are also helpful to individuals who read the book without the benefit of such a group since they provide prompts for deeper reflection and exploration.

Finally, a brief word about footnotes is in order here. Though many people prefer to ignore these, I would encourage you to glance through them since they sometimes support the argument being made or offer alternative perspectives. The footnotes also provide additional sources to consult if you wish to read more about a particular topic under discussion. Many of the issues raised in this book deserve far more space and attention than I could devote to them. Sometimes they merit a book all their own. The footnotes will point you in helpful directions if you wish to pursue these topics further.

A Special Focus on Stories

As you may have gathered from the overview, this book gives special attention to stories. Stories appear throughout the book, and one chapter is devoted entirely to them. Why? Because stories are powerful. Stories engage our affect, and affect is critical for storing things in our brain and moving us to action. Stories have the power to form us, shape our assumptions, and excite our imagination.

Stories demand our attention and call us to a deeper response as we enter into them. They engage us on a personal level and invite us to consider what we would do, or how we might respond, in similar circumstances. Stories sneak around our defenses and force us to ask questions, sometimes uncomfortable ones, we might otherwise avoid. What would I have done in that situation? Would I have made the same decision? Been that courageous? Sacrificed that much?

So much of what we remember in life is the stories we have heard, told, and lived. When many words have been forgotten, stories remain. This is especially true of great sermons or speeches we hear. While we may remember the gist of the message, it is often quite difficult to recall the specific words that were spoken. But if stories were told—and told well—during a sermon or speech, they linger on. Stories have a way of working themselves deep into our souls, refusing to let go. They challenge and confront us, and we continue to mull over them long after we hear them.

Many of the stories included in this book demonstrate how people took Jesus' words to heart and made choices to behave in nonviolent ways. My hope is that these stories will stick with you, inspiring you to go and do likewise.

Defining Violence and Nonviolence

Before proceeding, it is necessary to offer some working definitions of violence and nonviolence. *Violence* is a notoriously difficult word to define. Part of the challenge relates to how broadly or narrowly the term is understood. Should the definition be limited to physical acts, or expanded to include behavior that causes psychological and emotional trauma as well? Can animals and forces of nature be violent, or should violence only be understood as something human beings do? Is violence primarily defined by motivation (the desire to harm), the end result (someone or something is hurt or destroyed), or some other metric altogether? Moreover, while some forms of violence are overt and easily recognizable, other forms are less obvious and more difficult to see. Everyone knows rape, murder, and terrorist attacks are violent acts. But what about buying clothing made in a sweat shop, or eating chocolate harvested by unfairly paid workers? How do the purchases we make and the foods we eat make us complicit in acts of violence?

Questions like these illustrate the challenge and complexity of defining violence. Yet the way we define violence is important since it determines what kind of behavior is—or is not—classified as being violent. And this, in turn, is often what determines whether we regard such behavior as "right" or "wrong."

While no definition is perfect, allow me to offer a slightly adapted version of one I have used elsewhere as a point of reference. Violence is *physical, emotional, or psychological harm done to a person by an individual(s), institution, or structure that results in serious injury, oppression, or death.*[11] Some definitions of violence, like the first one given in the Oxford English Dictionary—"the deliberate exercise of physical force against a person, property, etc.; physically violent behavior or treatment"—tend to restrict violence to a *physical* act.[12] This seems too narrow given the enormous amount of emotional and psychological harm that can occur in the absence of *physical* violence. Also, an adequate definition of violence needs to acknowledge that violence is not limited to what one person does to another. Institutions and structures can—and unfortunately often do—perpetuate all sorts of violence. Considerations like these inevitably make my definition of violence rather broad.

An even more expansive definition might also include harm done to animals and creation. Many people would want these elements included in a comprehensive definition of violence.[13] While I recognize the great importance of animal ethics and creation care, I have chosen to limit my discussion of violence to harm done to people in order to keep the book more manageable and to provide some focus to an already broad topic.

Defining nonviolence also presents a number of special challenges. What people mean by nonviolence varies considerably depending upon whether it is being defined in secular or religious terms. Those who primarily see nonviolence as a political philosophy, or a strategy to address social injustice, often define it in reference to power. It is a means to achieve certain goals by eroding the power of your opponents (see chapter 12). On

11. Adapted from Seibert, *Violence of Scripture,* 9. While the harm done is often intentional, it can be unintentional as well.

12. Oxford English Dictionary Online, s.v. "violence."

13. For helpful collections of essays addressing the issue of nonviolence toward animals and creation, see York and Alexis-Baker, eds., *Faith Embracing All Creatures* and *Faith Encompassing All Creation,* respectively.

the other hand, Christians, especially those who understand nonviolence as a way of life and believe Jesus taught his followers to live nonviolently, tend to define it more in terms of how we treat one another. Although these two understandings are not mutually exclusive, a Christian view of non-violence—rooted in the life and teachings of Jesus—will include ideas not necessarily embraced by other nonviolent practitioners.

One could simply define *non*violence as the opposite of violence, but that leaves much unsaid and does not really give the full picture. I find it more useful to define nonviolence positively, by what it is, not merely by what it is not. To that end, I define Christian nonviolence as *a way of life modeled after Jesus, one that completely rejects violence, actively confronts evil, and unconditionally loves others by practicing gracious hospitality, radical forgiveness, and deep compassion.* Put simply, nonviolence is love in action.

The emphasis on nonviolence being active is especially important since people often (erroneously) equate nonviolence with passivity. While it is true that a Christian commitment to nonviolence involves refusing to retaliate, nonviolence should not be understood as "doing nothing." On the contrary, a fully formed understanding of Christian nonviolence involves a commitment to *help* others, not just a refusal to *harm* them. That is why I have included the notion of *actively* confronting evil in my definition. Love for others requires us to help people in need, those who are oppressed and experiencing injustice. As Christians, we must do everything within our power to stop oppression and correct injustice—and we must do this with-out resorting to violence. This is because loving all people unconditionally means we care about both the oppressed *and* the oppressor, the one *being* harmed and the one *doing* harm. Christian nonviolence emphasizes the sacredness of *all* persons and the need to treat *everyone* with respect, even those who seem most terrible and unlovable. We will have the opportunity to reflect on these ideas later in much greater detail.

Conclusion

As you read this book, I trust it will take you on a journey that leads toward Jesus and away from violence, one that encourages you to put down the sword and pick up the cross. Christians are called to look like Jesus and live like Jesus. Though the church has often failed in that regard, we need not re-peat mistakes of the past. Rather, as we forsake violence and follow Jesus, we can show the world a better way, one that is not mired in the endless cycles of violence that separate us from one another and from God. By embracing the nonviolent way of Jesus and putting love in action, we bring hope and healing to a broken world. This is what the church is called to do.

Yet before we can say more about that, we need to step back and take a look at the uglier side of the church. We need to explore both how and why the church has often failed to look like Jesus. Diagnosing the problem is an important first step in moving us toward a solution. As we begin to understand what is wrong, we will be in a better position to offer suggestions about making things right.

2

A Violent Church

Believers Behaving Badly

The historical record demonstrates that [Christian] believers have acted violently, made unholy alliances, conquered enemies, discriminated against others, and vilified pagans and each other. The love and peace that God promises through Jesus has been, it appears, compromised through the lives and words of many believers.

—Kenneth Chase[1]

Throughout my life, the church has been very important to me and has played a very positive role in my life. As a child, I was at church each week my family. We regularly attended Sunday school, the Sunday morning worship service, and Sunday evening services (when they had them) at Morning Hour Chapel, a small Brethren in Christ church located a few miles outside of East Berlin, Pennsylvania. For a time, I also went to Wednesday night prayer meetings with my mom. In the summer, I participated in Vacation Bible School and on a couple occasions, spent a week at Kenbrook Bible Camp. I was baptized at the age of nine and was subsequently received into church membership. Needless to say, I was well churched.

I have many happy memories of my childhood church experiences, and I am grateful to have been raised in the church. Growing up in the

1. Chase, "Introduction," 9.

church was very formative for me, and it nurtured my faith in more ways than I can remember. I think fondly of the many Christian women and men who invested so much in me over the years. Indeed, it is difficult to imagine where I would be today without their influence or the church community of which we were a part.

Early in life, I sensed God calling me into ministry, and over the years I had the privilege of ministering in various ways. I served as assistant to the chaplain at a local nursing home, as interim pastor at an independent Bible church, as youth director in an inner-city mainline church, as a chaplain in state parks and private campgrounds, and briefly as a pastoral assistant in what is now my home congregation.

I have also served the Brethren in Christ Church at the denominational level in a number of official capacities. I was part of the denomination's Equipping for Ministry Team, I taught one of four core courses required by the church for ministerial credentialing, and I represented the church on the editorial council of the Believer's Church Bible Commentary series. In addition, I was a licensed minister in the denomination for over fifteen years. Currently, I serve on the Missions, Peace and Service Commission at the Grantham Church, the local congregation where I am an active member.

Why am I telling you all this? To indicate that I am a friend of the church and to make it clear that my intentions in this chapter are not sinister. I am about to tell stories and quote statistics that cast the church—or at least significant portions of it—in a very bad light. In doing so, I have no interest in impugning the church or trying to minimize the great good it does in the world. Rather, I write as one who loves the church and is concerned about its spiritual health and vitality. I want the church to be all God intends it to be: salt and light, a city on a hill, a spotless bride, an alternative community of faithful disciples. I care deeply about the church and want God's best for it. Therefore, when I see the church behaving violently, in ways that are often indistinguishable from the rest of the world,[2] I feel compelled to speak out—much like a good friend would upon seeing someone they love making a series of bad choices. My hope is that confronting these difficult issues will persuade the church to change course, to reject violence and to follow Jesus more faithfully. This is what frames my critique.

Jesus Comes in Third

In 1978, Michael Hart published an intriguing book in which he ranks the one hundred most influential people in history from his perspective.[3]

2. Cf. Sider, *Scandal of the Evangelical Conscience*.
3. Hart, *The 100*.

Scientists, explorers, inventors, philosophers, and musicians populate the list, along with notable religious and political leaders, both ancient and modern. Hart devotes several pages to each person, explaining their significance and his rationale for their placement on the list. Among the top ten are many familiar names, including such luminaries as Buddha, St. Paul, Johann Gutenberg, and Albert Einstein.

Obviously, with a list like this, people are naturally curious about who takes first place. Who does Hart regard as the most influential person in all of human history? Is it Jesus? As the founder of Christianity (and God incarnate!) we might assume that Jesus must certainly be the most influential person of all time. But Jesus is not first on Hart's list. Jesus does not even place second. Instead, Jesus comes in third. He is outranked by Isaac Newton in the number two spot and the Prophet Muhammad who tops the list. Why is this? "The impact of Jesus on human history is so obvious and so enormous," writes Hart, "that few people would question his placement near the top of this list. Indeed, the more likely question is why Jesus, who is the inspiration for the most influential religion in history, has not been placed first."[4] Exactly!

Hart answers this question at the end of his essay about Jesus. After referencing Jesus' teachings from the Sermon on the Mount about turning the other cheek, loving enemies, and praying for persecutors (Matt 5:39, 43–44)—which many believe to be Jesus' clearest and most direct teaching about nonviolence—Hart offers this explanation for Jesus' third place finish:

> Now, these ideas—which were not a part of the Judaism of Jesus' day, nor of most other religions—are surely among the most remarkable and original ethical ideas ever presented. If they were widely followed, I would have had no hesitation in placing Jesus first in this book.
>
> But the truth is that they are not widely followed. In fact, they are not even generally accepted. Most Christians consider the injunction to "Love your enemy" as—at most—an ideal which might be realized in some perfect world, but one which is *not* a reasonable guide to conduct in the actual world we live in. We do not normally practice it, do not expect others to practice it, and do not teach our children to practice it. Jesus' most distinctive teaching, therefore, remains an intriguing but basically untried suggestion.[5]

Considering the violent history of the church, Hart is on to something. Though he somewhat overstates his case—there are *many* examples

4. Ibid., 17.

5. Ibid., 20–21, emphasis original.

of people who have taken the teachings of Jesus seriously and tried to follow them—the sad truth is that the *majority* of Christians have *not* been guided by Jesus' directive to love their enemies. Instead, they have routinely justified all sorts of violence, often against the very enemies they were supposed to love. Numerous books and articles have been written describing the way the church has harmed others and behaved violently over the past two thousand years. They make for difficult reading.[6]

While it is important to learn from the church's past mistakes in order to avoid repeating them in the future, my intention is not to provide that sort of historical overview here. Instead, the purpose of this chapter is to identify particular forms of violence that are frequently condoned by the church *today*. If we hope to *dis*arm the church, we need to begin with a clear understanding of how deeply implicated it is in the violence all around us.

Violence and the Church Today

What follows is a broad sampling of some of the ways contemporary Christians sanction, support, and participate in various forms of violence. This is meant to be illustrative rather than exhaustive, highlighting some of the more troubling expressions of the church's accommodation to violence. Although there is no particular significance to the order in which these categories are discussed, some forms of violence—like war—obviously carry far greater consequences.

Participating in Warfare and Condoning Torture

Ever since the fourth century, most of the church has regarded warfare as an acceptable course of action to take for any number of reasons: to stop aggressors, to maintain order, to defend borders, and so on. Historically, the church has been guided by the just war theory and this continues to be the case.[7] Hence, it comes as no surprise that many Christians have participated in war through the years. Although it is difficult to quantify with precision, the number of people who have died at the hands of Christian soldiers in the

6. See, for example, Ellerbe, *Dark Side*. A number of books consider how the Bible itself has been used to perpetuate all sorts of violence and evil. Examples include Hill and Cheadle, *Bible Tells Me So*; Thatcher, *Savage Text*, especially 135; Spong, *Sins of Scripture*.

7. There are signs that support for the just war theory may be waning in the Catholic Church. See Berger, "Game Changer?" See also Pope Francis's marvelous statement on nonviolence for the 50th annual World Day of Peace and the work being done through the Catholic Nonviolence Initiative (nonviolencejustpeace.net).

twentieth century alone would easily be counted in millions.[8] Sometimes the slain have been people of other faiths (e.g., the Crusades); sometimes they have been brothers and sisters in Christ (e.g., the American Civil War).

Today, the majority of Christians continue to believe warfare is a legitimate way to deal with conflict, at least in some circumstances. In fact, many see war as the only effective way to respond to certain forms of evil and injustice in the world. Some continue to adhere to the just war theory and believe war is *only* justified when it meets a specific set of very stringent criteria (more on this later).[9] Others believe war is permissible when it is deemed necessary for national security, regardless of whether or not it actually meets any such predetermined "criteria." Whatever the reason, many within the church support warfare and are not categorically opposed to participating in it. Pacifism is a decidedly minority view in the church today.

Many Christians in the United States are in the armed services and many more support the military in various ways. Typically, these individuals see no contradiction between their Christian faith and military service.[10] In fact, those who are enlisted often regard their military service as a faithful expression of their Christian convictions. Yet war is inherently violent. Even when people go to war for incredibly noble reasons, the sad reality is that war destroys communities, fractures families, and results in enormous bloodshed, grief, and death. This should give Christians great pause, especially in light of Jesus' command to love enemies and to treat others the way they want to be treated. At the very least, it should cause Christians to be more reluctant to sanction warfare than those who do not profess to follow Jesus and his teachings. But that has not always been the case.

Surveys are one way to gauge the church's support for war—and the results here are not particularly encouraging.[11] In churches where you would expect to find some of the strongest opposition to war, you find precisely the opposite. In a 2006 survey called the Church Membership Profile (CMP), the attitudes and beliefs of Christians from three historic "peace churches"— the Brethren in Christ (BIC), the Church of the Brethren, and the Mennonite Church USA—were explored.[12] Each of these denominations opposes

8. This claim would seem to be self-evident given the significant number of Christians engaged in many of the wars of the twentieth century (consider World War II alone) and the fact that over one hundred million people died as a result of war in the twentieth century (Wink, *Powers that Be*, 157).

9. See chapter 8.

10. This point is discussed more fully in chapter 3.

11. This paragraph and the next is adapted from Seibert, "Pacifism and Nonviolence," 198–99.

12. Full survey results for the Brethren in Christ church in North America are found in the Brethren in Christ Member Profile 2006.

Christian participation in war as a combatant. In this survey, participants were asked questions about a wide range of topics, including some related to peacemaking and participation in war. While it was reassuring to discover that 88 percent of church members surveyed within my own denomination, the BIC Church, agreed that "peacemaking is a central theme of the Gospel," it was alarming to discover that over 75 percent *disagreed* that "it is wrong for Christians to fight in any war" and that over 64 percent disagreed that "all war is sin."[13] Given the BIC church's official position "that preparation for or participation in war is inconsistent with the teachings of Christ," one would have expected far less disagreement with these statements.[14]

It was also distressing to discover that many individuals within my own denomination were even *more* supportive of the Iraq War than the general population. A full 61 percent of those surveyed from the Brethren in Christ church agreed that "the U.S. did the right thing by going to war against Iraq." Yet, a 2004 Princeton University poll asking the same question reported only 46 percent of Americans surveyed saying the United States had done the right thing, and a 2005 ABC News poll indicated that just 48 percent said the United States had done the right thing.[15] What makes this especially striking is that these two polls were conducted earlier than the CMP, at a time when the war was *more* popular (presumably, these percentages would have been even lower had they been taken at the same time as the CMP). Moreover, they reflect the attitude of the general public, not just that of Christians. Something is surely wrong when Christians are more enthusiastic about war than the population at large.

The church, in general, did not fare much better in a survey taken a few years later that explored the way people felt about torture. In April 2009, the Pew Research Center asked 742 adult Americans the following question: "Do you think the use of torture against suspected terrorists in order to gain

13. Somewhat more encouraging are the results from the Global Anabaptist Profile (GAP), a more recent survey in which the BIC church in the United States participated. When asked to indicate their level of agreement/disagreement with the statement, "It is OK for Christians to fight in a war," only 43.7 percent of the BIC responding agreed, with 20.0 percent indicating they were unsure (Burwell, "Results," 369). There are some issues with the sample, however, that may skew this data to some degree (Burwell, "Results," 336–39).

14. It was also disheartening to discover that 58 percent said they would comply "if faced with a military draft." More specifically, 31.2 percent said they would engage in regular military service and 26.8 percent said they would engage in non-combatant military service. Once again, the results of the GAP were a bit more encouraging here. When a similar question was asked, only 15.6 percent respondents indicated they would engage in regular military service, and 25.7 percent said they would participate in non-combatant military service (Burwell, "Results," 370).

15. Scovell, "Church Member Profile 2006," slide 46.

important information can often be justified, sometimes be justified, rarely be justified, or never be justified."[16] The results were very unflattering for the church. As it turned out, people who attended church at least once a week were *more* likely to say that torture is often or sometimes justified than those who attend less frequently. Moreover, among the religious groups surveyed, white evangelical Protestants were the *most* likely to say that torture can often (or sometimes) be justified. In contrast, those unaffiliated with any religious group were *least* likely to say torture can be justified.[17]

That Christians give any measure of support to the use of torture is deeply troubling. Inflicting that kind of torment and pain on another human being violates the Golden Rule, to treat others as we want to be treated, and the law of love. But the fact that churchgoers are *more* supportive of torture than those not affiliated with any religious group is even more worrisome. Christians, the very people who should be the most vocal opponents of warfare, killing, and torture, are sometimes its strongest supporters. If we are to disarm the church, we must radically rethink our attitudes about warfare and torture in light of the life and teachings of Jesus.

Using Violence for Self-Defense

It is not uncommon to find Christians who approve of the use of violence for self-defense. In spite of Jesus' clear teaching to "turn the other cheek" and Paul's directive to overcome evil with good, many would not hesitate to use violence to defend themselves or those they love. A recent survey (2013) conducted by the Barna Group in their "FRAMES" series asked 1,000 adults living in the United States to indicate whether they agreed with the following statement: "I have the right to defend myself, even if it requires violence."[18] Among "practicing Christians" who were surveyed, nearly 3 in 5 agreed that it would be acceptable to defend themselves with violence if necessary. Although one might expect practicing Christians to be very reluctant to use violence in these circumstances given Jesus' instructions about loving enemies and non-retaliation,[19] this does not appear to be the case.

Interestingly, Christian attitudes about using violence for self-defense closely mirror those of the general population. The percentage of practicing

16. Pew Research Center, "Religious Dimensions."

17. For similar results, see *The Washington Post*, "Majority Says CIA Harsh Interrogations Justified," for discussion of a Washington Post–ABC News poll conducted in December 2014.

18. Merritt and Wigg-Stevenson, *Fighting for Peace*, 55, 76.

19. See Matt 5:38–45.

Christians who believe it is acceptable to use violence in self-defense (57 percent) is only slightly lower than that of all participants in the survey (60 percent).

What makes the survey results pertaining to this question even more striking is the fact that only one in ten of those surveyed (11 percent) thought Jesus himself would have agreed with the statement. In other words, the survey data revealed a huge disparity between what *Christians* believed and what they thought *Jesus* would have believed. This same disparity was evident in numerous survey questions related to violence, not just this particular one. As Tyler Wigg-Stevenson comments:

> The most unsettling section of the FRAMES data was the difference between practicing Christians' attitudes to violence and what they thought Jesus would think. In question after question—from self-defense and gun ownership to the death penalty and nuclear weapons—Christians said one thing while admitting they thought Jesus would answer differently. . . .
>
> In summary, *Christian opinions about violence look more like those of nonbelievers than what they think are the views of Jesus.*[20]

This is problematic. In chapter 3, we will attempt to understand some of the factors that have led to this undesirable state of affairs. As we will discover, one of the reasons for the disconnect between what Jesus taught and what Christians believe—at least as it relates to something like self-defense—is a lack of faith in the effectiveness of nonviolence. Many Christians simply do not believe nonviolent alternatives can really work in situations like these, and some are unaware of the nonviolent alternatives they have at their disposal. Therefore, they are ready to resort to what they know—violence—even though they recognize this puts them at odds with Jesus.

In chapters 10 and 11, we explore several nonviolent ways to respond when threatened with harm or when coming to the aid of someone being harmed. Being aware of these alternatives to violence, and hearing stories of how people have used these strategies with great success, challenges the assumption that violence is the only reasonable response in situations like these.

Mistreating Jews and Muslims

Even though Jesus said the second greatest commandment is to love your neighbor as yourself, Christians have frequently struggled to put this into

20. Merritt and Wigg-Stevenson, *Fighting for Peace*, 53–54, emphasis mine.

practice. The church has often had a poor track record when it comes to loving others, especially when those others are Jews or Muslims. Anyone with even a cursory knowledge of church history is aware of the church's long history of anti-Semitism. It is at once both shameful and appalling. Episcopal bishop Shelby Spong regards the violent and hateful way Christians have treated Jews over the centuries as "the darkest and bleakest side of the Christian faith."[21]

Some of the most revered leaders in Christian history were brazenly anti-Semitic and guilty of terrible calumnies against the Jews. The great Reformer Martin Luther was particularly notorious in this regard. He regarded Jews as liars and blasphemers, and he advised Christians to burn down synagogues and destroy Jewish homes, to confiscate their sacred texts, and to forbid rabbis from teaching.[22]

Tragically, the antipathy Christians have felt toward Jews has often manifested itself in ugly and very lethal ways over the years. The church's complicity in the Shoah (Holocaust) is case in point. According to Victoria Barnett, "The anti-Judaism in the Christian Churches . . . gave theological legitimation to racial anti-Semitism, which . . . led some church leaders to publically defend the Nazi measures against the Jews."[23] The failure of the church at this critical moment in history is damning.

Even today, many Christians harbor negative attitudes and deep prejudice toward their Jewish brothers and sisters.[24] This is often the result of bigotry and hatred that begins in the church. As Bishop Spong recounts from his own childhood:

> When I was a child attending an Evangelical Episcopal (Anglican) Sunday school in North Carolina, I was taught that it was okay to hate Jews. If I doubted that, the Bible was quoted to validate that negativity. I never met a good Jew in all of my prepared Sunday school material. Jews were those evil people who were always out to get Jesus—and get him they did, I was told.[25]

Portraying Jews like this is extremely dangerous. Moreover, it is never right to hate others, and the Bible should not be used to encourage prejudice. When the church behaves like this, it has clearly lost its way.

21. Spong, *Sins of Scripture*, 183. For a fuller discussion, see 183–210.

22. Luther, "The Jews and Their Lies."

23. Barnett, "Beyond Complicity," 98. Obviously, there were exceptions. There were Christians who resisted the Nazis and worked courageously to save Jews, and there were church leaders who worked behind the scenes to oppose Hitler.

24. Cf. Spong, *Sins of Scripture*, 12.

25. Ibid., 193.

Christian attitudes toward Muslims today are also very worrisome. Since the attacks in the United States on September 11, 2001, a lot of Americans—and American Christians—have developed very negative views of Islam. The rise of ISIS and other expressions of Islamic extremism have only added to the fear, prejudice, and hatred many feel toward Muslims. Many perceive Islam as a threat and believe Muslims must be watched carefully—or else!

These negative views of Muslims are reflected in a recent survey conducted by the Pew Research Center. In 2014, the Center conducted a survey of 3,217 Americans to ascertain their attitudes toward eight religious groups: Atheists, Buddhists, Catholics, Evangelicals, Hindus, Jews, Mormons, and Muslims.[26] Participants were instructed to rank these groups on a "feeling thermometer" that had a scale of 0 to 100. The groups they felt warmest toward and most positive about were ranked at the high end of the scale, while those they felt coldest toward and most negative about were assigned values at the lower end. The results were very revealing. Of the eight groups under consideration, Muslims were ranked the lowest. They received a chilly 40 on the feeling thermometer, edging out atheists by a point.

When you analyze how *Christian* respondents among those surveyed ranked these eight groups, the results are very similar. Like the general population, Christians ranked atheists and Muslims at the bottom of the list, the only difference being that Christians ranked atheists slightly lower than Muslims. Protestants gave Muslims a frigid 36 on the feeling thermometer (atheists were at 32), and Catholics ranked Muslims at 40 (atheists were at 38). These results are especially telling when you consider that non-monotheistic religions, like Buddhism and Hinduism, were viewed more warmly than Islam, even though Islam shares much in common with Christianity.

One of the reasons some Christians view Muslims so negatively is because they (mistakenly) believe Muslims are intent on world domination and will do anything necessary to achieve it. Professor Lee Camp received a flood of concerned responses after a lecture he gave encouraging "peaceful coexistence" between Christians and Muslims unexpectedly grabbed front page headlines the following morning.[27] One email from a Christian real estate developer claimed, "There will be no peace with Muslims because that is not what they want. Muslims want one of three things—converts, dhimmis, or death."[28] These sentiments were typical of many responses Camp received, responses that were clearly driven by fear. Many believe "there can

26. Pew Research Center, "How Americans Feel about Religious Groups."
27. See Camp, "Theological Ground for Peaceful Co-existence."
28. Camp, *Who Is My Enemy?*, 4.

be no dialogue with Muslims, no parley with the enemy, no trusting conversation, because the enemy simply wants to convert you, kill you, or make you submit."[29] Viewing Muslims this way legitimates, and even encourages, acts of violence against them.

In recent years, notable Christian leaders have sometimes made incendiary comments which fan the flames of anti-Islamic sentiment and endanger Muslims. The words of Jerry Falwell, Jr., president of Liberty University, come to mind as one particularly distressing example. Falwell's remarks, spoken at the close of a convocation service at Liberty in December 2015, were made in reference to a massacre that had taken place in San Bernardino, California when Syed Rizwan Farook and Tashfeen Malik, both Muslims, entered the Inland Regional Center and opened fire. By the time their rampage ended, there were fourteen people dead and over twenty wounded. Though the motive of their attack has never been determined, many regarded the shooting as an act of terrorism inspired by Islamic extremism.

A few days later, Falwell said to a packed auditorium, "I always thought that if more good people had concealed carry permits, then we could end those Muslims before they walked in and killed." Falwell went on to urge students to get their concealed carry permits, saying, "Let's teach them a lesson if they ever show up here."[30] Such violent rhetorical swagger is a long way from Jesus. It is dangerous and irresponsible, *especially* when it comes from the president of the largest Christian college in the world.[31]

Falwell's words reinforced negative stereotypes about Muslims and encouraged Christians to prepare themselves to engage in acts of violence. His comments were especially unfortunate given the fear and vulnerability many Muslims in America were already feeling in the immediate aftermath of the San Bernardino shootings. Instead of using his powerful position to encourage Christians to stand in solidarity with their Muslim friends and neighbors, Falwell further aggravated an already tense situation. Rather than disarming the church, Falwell did precisely the opposite.

What I found most disturbing about this whole incident was not just Falwell's unapologetic endorsement of violence. Rather, it was how the student body reacted. Thousands of young Christian men and women cheered and applauded, clearly resonating with Falwell's bravado. Seeing an auditorium full of Christian students enthusiastically embracing such violent rhetoric was disconcerting, to say the least. It serves as a poignant example

29. Ibid.

30. A video of Falwell's remarks can be found at Bailey, "Jerry Falwell Jr."

31. Liberty University boasts nearly 15,000 residential and nearly 100,000 online students.

of how terribly disconnected some Christians are from the nonviolent way of Jesus.

Hating Atheists

Like Jews and Muslims, atheists have also experienced a considerable amount of hostility from churchgoers. Christians have often been very uncharitable toward atheists over the past few hundred years, and this shows no signs of abating. Randal Rauser convincingly demonstrates this in his excellent book, *Is the Atheist My Neighbor?* Rauser begins the book by quoting part of a sermon preached by pastor John Hagee to his congregation of over 20,000. "Atheism is bankrupt and empty," proclaims Hagee. "It's brain dead!" On another occasion Hagee says, "To the atheist watching this telecast, if our belief in God offends you . . . move! There are planes leaving every hour on the hour going every place on planet earth. *Get on one.* We don't want you and we won't miss you, I promise you."[32] So much for Christian hospitality.

Of course, Hagee is not alone. Rauser surveys a number of prominent Christians in the twentieth century who have spoken or written against atheism with considerable derision.[33] This includes people like Grant Jeffrey, Ray Comfort, D. James Kennedy, Dan DeHaan, Ron Rhodes, R. C. Sproul, and James Spiegel. Some of these individuals, like Ray Comfort and James Spiegel have written books with very uncomplimentary titles such as *You Can Lead an Atheist to Evidence but You Can't Make Him Think* (Comfort) and *The Making of an Atheist: How Immorality Leads to Unbelief* (Spiegel). To further illustrate the aggressive posture many Christians have toward atheists, Rauser also cites the amazing popularity of the recent film *God's Not Dead* (2014) which has an astounding 15,462 reviews on Amazon.com with a 4.4/5.0 rating even though it reinforces very negative stereotypes about atheists.[34]

Christians routinely mischaracterize atheists, portraying the whole lot as God-haters who deny the truth so they can live the kind of godless lives they supposedly really want to live.[35] This is far from the truth. Christians who think this way should take time to get to know more atheists. Even if

32. Rauser, *Is the Atheist My Neighbor?*, 1–2, emphasis original.

33. Ibid., 22–31.

34. Statistics as of June 2016.

35. Rauser calls this the "Rebellion Thesis" and defines it as follows: "While atheists profess to believe that God does not exist, this disbelief is the result of an active and culpable suppression of an innate disposition to believe in God which is born of a hatred of God and a desire to sin with impunity" (*Is the Atheist My Neighbor?*, 6).

this characterization were accurate, it would still not justify hurling invectives at atheists or viewing them as intellectually and morally deficient. We are called to love others unconditionally, without exception. The animus Christians direct toward atheists is not only unchristlike, it is counter-productive. It creates walls rather than bridges, and denies us the opportunity to get to know, love, and learn from people who see the world differently than we do but who share much in common with us as well.

Expressing Hostility toward Members of the LGBTQ community

The debate over same-sex attraction and same-sex marriage continues to be one of the most contentious issues in the church today, with people lining up on either side of the aisle.[36] While some churches have offered a warm welcome to members of the LGBTQ community, the church, on the whole, has a rather dismal record when it comes to loving individuals who identify this way. As researchers David Kinnaman and Gabe Lyons concluded after conducting a three-year study investigating attitudes young Americans have about the church: "Outsiders say our hostility toward gays—not just opposition to homosexual politics and behaviors but disdain for gay individuals—has become virtually synonymous with the Christian faith."[37] Regardless of what Christians think about the morality of same-sex sexual expression, the church has an obligation to welcome these individuals and to treat them with the same compassion and kindness they would extend to anyone. Unfortunately, rather than experiencing this kind of love and acceptance, many in the LGBTQ community have experienced just the opposite, often at the hands of pastors and other prominent church members.

Though most Christians typically do not threaten these individuals with *physical* harm,[38] they routinely respond in ways that are violent just the same. In her book *Hate Thy Neighbor*, Linda Patterson writes about hurtful things church leaders like Jerry Falwell, Pat Robertson, James Dobson, and Rick Warren have said about people who are gay or lesbian.[39] She also comments on official statements from the Catholic Church and the Southern

36. For a recent—and very civil—entree into this debate, see Sprinkle, ed., *Two Views of Homosexuality*. The book contains contributions from four authors, two holding the affirming view, and two holding the traditional view.

37. Kinnaman and Lyons, *Unchristian*, 92. Cited in Lee, *Torn*, 3

38. Though sadly, there are stories where this has been the case (Spong, *Sins of Scripture*, 116).

39. Patterson, *Hate Thy Neighbor*, 9–22.

Baptist Convention that have been very harmful. Patterson understands that our words matter. She writes:

> We are all familiar with the saying "sticks and stones may break my bones, but words will never hurt me." Growing up, I believed in the wisdom of this adage. Now, having been on the receiving end of hateful homophobic rhetoric, I know that words can actually attack the heart and soul of the target. I also know that such vitriol has encouraged gay-bashers to attack—and in some cases even kill—with sticks and stones, and guns and knives. So now I agree with philosopher Jean-Paul Sartre that "words are loaded pistols."[40]

Tragically, many in the LGBTQ community experience the church as a place that is armed and dangerous, one they find harmful to them in many ways. This is especially true when the church encourages, and sometimes even pressures, these individuals to try to change their sexual orientation,[41] or when it restricts them from meaningful opportunities to serve the church. This results in people feeling even more marginalized, isolated, and unloved. As Dale Martin observes, "There can be no debate about the fact that the church's stand on homosexuality has caused oppression, loneliness, self-hatred, violence, sickness, and suicide for millions of people."[42]

In light of this, it comes as no surprise to discover that many people in the LGBTQ community no longer want anything to do with the church. Disarming the church will require Christians to rethink their attitudes toward the LGBTQ community, especially if they want to imitate Jesus' inclusive embrace of people from all walks of life.[43]

Committing Domestic Violence

Although "Home Shouldn't be a Place that Hurts," as a brochure on domestic violence puts it, that's exactly what it is for millions of people who are abused by members of their own family. Domestic violence is an epidemic

40. Ibid., 9.

41. Efforts to change sexual orientation, sometimes called conversion therapy or reparative therapy, are ineffective and have been thoroughly discredited. See Gushee, *Changing Our Mind*, 24–27, and Lee, *Torn*, 70–96.

42. Martin, *Sex and the Single Savior*, 50.

43. For a powerful example of this kind of rethinking from a prominent evangelical ethicist, see Gushee, *Changing Our Mind*. For an alternate perspective, one that affirms gay Christians but believes they should remain celibate, see Hill, *Washed and Waiting*.

in the United States and around the world—and Christian homes are not immune. As Al Miles observes:

> Hidden deep within the community of believers worshiping in churches around the globe is an ugly secret: domestic violence occurs among Christian couples just as it does among couples in every other corner of society. There are men who identify themselves as followers of Jesus Christ who beat, curse, rape, and violate their wives and girlfriends. There are Christian women (and their children) who live . . . under the constant horror of being tortured emotionally, physically, psychologically, and sexually by males calling themselves "men of God."[44]

Sadly, it appears that domestic violence is just as common in Christian homes as it is among the population at large. Drawing upon a number of studies, Ron Sider concludes that "theologically conservative Christians . . . commit domestic abuse at least as often as the general public."[45] This is highly concerning. Likewise, Catherine Kroeger and Nancy Nason-Clark point out "that researchers in the field of family violence have consistently argued that abuse crosses all religious boundaries and that the rates inside and outside the walls of the church are similar."[46]

In his recent book, *Corporal Punishment in the Bible*, William Webb tells a story that illustrates how common and acceptable domestic violence is in certain Christian communities. Webb speaks of his friendship with an Ethiopian student named Fanosie who persuaded him to spend a couple months teaching in Ethiopia one summer.

> As I was preparing for the Ethiopia trip, I gave Fanosie several chapters of this book on corporal punishment, asking for his feedback. More specifically, I asked if I should take this material to Addis and teach some of it there. About a week or two later, I bumped into Fanosie in the foyer of our seminary and asked him what he thought about the chapters. I still remember his vivid answer. He said nothing, nothing at all. Instead, Fanosie bent down his head and showed me a series of welts, scars and ugly disfigurations. He is a tall man and his dark curly hair hid these marks fairly well. He explained to me that he could take off his clothes and show me more marks from beatings he had as a child. He described *being raised in a typical Christian home,*

44. Miles, *Violence in Families*, 50. Of course, there are also wives who abuse their husbands, but this is less common.

45. Sider, *Scandal of the Evangelical Conscience*, 27.

46. Kroeger and Nason-Clark, *No Place for Abuse*, 50.

and how, not infrequently, his father beat him with a stick. In
fact, Fanosie told how *it was still acceptable for many Christian
husbands in Ethiopia to beat their wives* as an act of corrective
discipline.[47]

For such abuse to happen anywhere is tragic. For it to happen in a
Christian home and be regarded as acceptable *Christian* behavior is scandal-
ous. Behaving violently toward another family member is neither a mark of
Christian discipleship nor a sign of spiritual maturity.

As this story reminds us, domestic violence not only affects women,
it impacts children as well. Some Christian parents believe certain kinds
of physical violence, like spanking or smacking, are appropriate forms of
Christian discipline. In fact, some believe God *commands* them to discipline their children this way (more on this later). Other Christian parents
behave violently toward their children out of frustration, impatience, or
anger. Whatever the reason, the result is the same: children are victims
of violence. Christian parents who behave violently toward their children
through abuse, neglect, or ill-conceived notions of what constitutes "Christian discipline," are not following the nonviolent way of Jesus. If we hope to
disarm the church, we need to pay attention to how Christians treat their
own family members. Domestic violence has no place in God's family.

Other Examples of Christians Behaving Violently

There are many other ways that the church condones violence—and that
Christians behave violently—that could be discussed here. Space only allows
brief mention of a few. For example, while large segments of the Christian
population oppose abortion, a significant percentage of Christian women
with unplanned pregnancies often feel pressured from *Christian* family and
friends (and others) to terminate the pregnancy. Realizing they may well
be ostracized at church if their situation becomes known, and frequently
lacking any support from their partner to keep the child, many women with
limited options make the excruciating and very personal decision to have
an abortion even though it often violates some of their most fundamental
beliefs. Tragically, this too is a form of violence, one that destroys the most
vulnerable lives.[48]

---

47. Webb, *Corporal Punishment in the Bible*, 18–19, emphasis mine.

48. I realize this is an incredibly complex issue, one I cannot adequately address
here. Suffice it to say, my point is *not* to condemn women who make this very difficult
choice. If we (the church) are serious about being "pro-life," we need to develop the social, emotional, and financial supports necessary for women to continue the pregnancy,

The church also condones violence when it supports capital punishment. Sadly, white Protestants and Catholics in the United States support the death penalty at *even higher* rates than those with no religious affiliation.[49] As Shane Claiborne puts it:

> We Christians are the biggest champions of executions in this country. In fact, the regions where the death penalty has flourished are precisely the areas where Christians are most concentrated. Eighty-five percent of all executions since 1976 have happened in the Bible belt. Other studies confirm that the group that supports capital punishment most fervently is evangelical Christians—much more so than secular people.[50]

The church also has a long and shameful history of sexual violence that cannot be denied. While this problem cuts across various Christian traditions and denominations, the Catholic Church has come under intense scrutiny in recent years. The sex abuse scandal among Catholic priests and the church's cover-up have made headline news, and subsequent investigations have exposed just how pervasive sexual violence has been in the church.[51]

The violence of racism is also alive and well in many churches across America. According to Michael Emerson and Christian Smith, this is especially problematic among evangelical Christians. In their book, *Divided by Faith: Evangelical Religion and the Problem of Race in America*, they conclude that "white evangelicalism likely does more to perpetuate the racialized society than to reduce it."[52] While the church has certainly made great strides in reducing some of the most blatant forms of racism, racist attitudes and perceptions are still far too prevalent among churchgoers, and these

---

to care for themselves and their newborn upon arrival, and to insure their well-being every step of the way thereafter. For a beautiful example of what this looks like, see Boyd, *Myth of a Christian Nation,* 144–45. Unfortunately, this comes at a cost and sacrifice most churchgoers are unwilling to render. For women who have had abortions and are looking for hope and healing, see http://hopeafterabortion.com/.

49. Pew Research Center, "Shrinking Majority of Americans Support Death Penalty."

50. Quoted in Mommsen, "Building the Jesus Movement," 27. Claiborne's recently published book, *Executing Grace,* calls upon the church to work for the abolition of the death penalty.

51. Although this has come to light more recently, it is a problem that spans the entire history of the church. For an exposé, see Doyle, Sipe, and Wall, *Sex, Priests, and Secret Codes.*

52. Emerson and Smith, *Divided by Faith,* 170. Cited in Sider, *Scandal of the Evangelical Conscience,* 26.

sometimes manifest themselves in ugly words and deeds. The following story told by Pastor Rob Schenck illustrates this all too well.

> Sitting at a dining-room table full of fellow evangelical pastors, I asked how many were "carrying" (a euphemism for being armed with a concealed handgun). They all raised their hands. Then I asked, "What determines when you draw your gun and prepare to shoot another human being?" There was awkward body language and mumbling. After a few seconds passed, one older man said, "I'll tell you what determines whether I draw the gun or not. It's the man's skin color."
>
> I was left speechless by the pastor's jarring, blatant racism. Still, as respectfully as possible, I asked him to please clarify what he meant.
>
> "Well, we got a big city nearby, and, you know, the black people there are always killin' people. Now, if a colored man comes into this county, I know he means trouble because he knows he doesn't belong here. That makes him more dangerous than a white man. That's why I'd pull my gun."
>
> The man who was speaking, and the others nodding their heads in agreement, are my colleagues. I am one of them when it comes to a statement of faith—but not when it comes to race and guns.[53]

Stories like this reveal how much work the church has to do to eradicate racism and how hard this is to accomplish when some of those leading the church harbor such racist attitudes and beliefs. Moreover, even those of us who are shocked by such a story and consider ourselves free from such racial bias, often think, act, and behave in ways that reveal just how racialized we actually are, whether we realize it or not.[54]

To cite one final example of how Christians sometimes behave violently toward others, consider what happens in the plethora of church conflicts that plague believers.[55] These internal disputes among church members arise over issues ranging from the frivolous to the extremely serious. Church conflicts pit Christians against Christians and often get quite nasty, leaving many people verbally and emotionally wounded in the process. The number of books specifically devoted to addressing church conflict bears witness to

---

53. Schenck, "Should Christians Own Guns?," 14, 16.

54. For an excellent recent treatment along these lines, see Hart, *Trouble I've Seen*.

55. Obviously, not all church conflict is bad. Nor does it always turn violent. But far too often, church conflict is not handled well and results in serious harm to those involved.

just how prevalent and problematic these disputes tend to be.[56] Suffice it to say, we have a lot work to do.

The Church Is Not All Bad

As this chapter has demonstrated, the church has a real problem with violence. Too often, Christians harm rather than help, hate rather than love, and retaliate rather than forgive. This behavior causes significant pain and suffering to countless individuals, families, and communities. It damages the credibility of the church and compromises the good news of the gospel.

Yet lest we despair, it is crucial to emphasize that the church's violent legacy is but one part of a much larger, and more hopeful, story. As historian Mark Noll reminds us, "Any indictment of Christianity for the damage it has done in human history is dishonest to the core if it does not also pay attention to the good done by Christians. That good has been very consistent and very considerable throughout history."[57] Noll is absolutely right. Christianity has made a positive impact upon the world in countless ways and continues to do so to this day.[58] The church does tremendous good by working for justice, caring for the "least of these," and confronting all sorts of evil and oppression. As Noll puts it, "Without denying that the religion originating in Jesus has been used for many nefarious purposes, the historical record fairly bulges with instances where the followers of Jesus really did follow him in deed as well as word."[59] We will have occasion to hear some of this stories later in the book. Thus, in stressing what is wrong with the church, we dare not lose sight of all that is right.

Moreover, even though Christians have been responsible for an enormous amount of violence, it is important to remember this is not because violence is part of the church's DNA. Violence is an aberration, a deviation from what the church is supposed to be and do. In fact, some (myself included) would argue that behaving violently is completely incompatible with living faithfully as a Christian. But if that is true, why do so many Christians approve of so much violence?

56. To cite just a few titles, see Barthel and Edling, *Redeeming Church Conflicts*; Brubaker, *Promise and Peril*; Gench, *Faithful Disagreement*.

57. Noll, "Have Christians Done More Harm Than Good?," 91.

58. See, for example, Schmidt, *How Christianity Changed the World*.

59. Noll, "Have Christians Done More Harm Than Good?," 87.

3

Why Do Christians Condone So Much Violence?

The culture we live in assumes that violence and war are acceptable solutions to aggression, and the majority of the Christian church basically agrees.

—HARRIET BICKSLER[1]

There is something profoundly unsettling about watching those who follow Jesus, the Prince of Peace, use weapons of warfare to kill others and still think they are somehow following Jesus.

—SCOT McKNIGHT[2]

GIVEN THE NEW TESTAMENT'S clear directives to love enemies, repay evil with good, and reconcile rather than retaliate, it is fair to ask why large numbers of Christians condone so much violence against others. Why do so many churchgoers support capital punishment, approve of using violence for self-defense, sanction torture, and justify warfare? Why do they mistreat Jews and Muslims, hate atheists, and express hostility toward members of the LGBTQ community? What accounts for this? Although there is no simple answer to these questions, we can begin to make sense of

1. Bicksler, "Pursuing Peace," 130.
2. McKnight, "Foreword," 19.

this perplexing (and unfortunate) state of affairs by considering a number of factors.

Why the Church Condones Violence

Before we can disarm the church, we must first understand why Christians believe violence is sometimes necessary and even virtuous. That is the purpose of this chapter. In the pages that follow, we will explore several reasons why Christians approve of so much violence. While some of these reasons are unique to Christians, others apply to a broad range of people regardless of any religious affiliation. Though what follows is not meant to be exhaustive, it highlights some of the most significant factors that help us understand why the church condones certain forms of violence.

We Believe Violence Stops Evil and Saves Lives

One of the key reasons many Christians are open to the use of violence is because of the good they expect it to accomplish. As they see it, violence stops evil and save lives. For example, it is an indisputable historical fact that the violence of the Allies in World War II stopped the evils of Nazi Germany and saved the lives of many Jews (and others) imprisoned in concentration camps. In the minds of many, these good ends justified the means. Since violence brought about the end of the war, and the liberation of thousands of individuals, many Christians believe it was justified and morally acceptable. This view is strengthened by the commonly held belief that violence was the *only* way to bring about these desired ends. When viewed from this perspective, the violence used to defeat Germany and the Axis powers is regarded as both necessary *and* noble.

The idea that violence is sometimes indispensable, and that it is precisely what is needed to eliminate evil, rescue the innocent, and reestablish order, is what Walter Wink refers to as "the myth of redemptive violence."[3] This myth declares that violence is sometimes the *only* way to stop warfare and killing and to deal effectively with injustice and oppression. Many people, including many Christians, wholeheartedly agree. To use Wink's language, they believe "violence saves."[4] When violence is used to protect or rescue someone, it is regarded as redemptive and therefore positive.

3. Wink, *Engaging the Powers*, 13–31.
4. Wink, *Powers that Be*, 42.

Jim Forest describes the same idea as "the Gospel according to John Wayne."[5] He writes:

> At the core of the Gospel according to John Wayne is a good man with a gun killing bad men with guns. . . .
>
> The Gospel according to John Wayne is also the Gospel according to Luke Skywalker and the Gospel according to Batman. The moral is the same in any case: We are saved by deadly weapons plus the courage and skill of those community defenders who wield them.[6]

Both Wink and Forest recognize that people often regard violence as an effective (and efficient) way to combat evil, and they condone it for that purpose. If someone threatens to harm my family, and I use violence to neutralize or eliminate the threat, my violence is judged approvingly since it was used to protect them from harm.

This idea that violence saves and is virtuous when used for a "greater good" is reinforced in countless ways. For example, in the United States we are conditioned to believe that the only way to achieve peace is through war, and the only way to have security is through military strength.[7] Our country was founded on bloodshed. We gained our freedom from the British by killing them. We celebrate it. We sing songs about it. We honor those who gave their lives for it. It is part of our national identity and an integral part of how we think about ourselves. We believe violence is a prerequisite for freedom and accept the notion that some must die so others might live.

We see this same narrative played out ubiquitously in movies and television shows. Time and again, violence is presented as the only real option. The villain is portrayed as being malicious, merciless, and unstoppable, hell-bent on wreaking as much havoc as possible. Violence appears to be the only reasonable response. As Forest observes:

> How rare is the movie in which the hero or heroine is allowed to aim for the legs or, rarer still, find a bullet-free, nonviolent solution. In film after film, the implicit message is that, in confrontations with evil, there are no nonlethal—still less nonviolent—solutions. It's a kill-or-be-killed world. Period. Next subject.[8]

---

5. Forest, *Loving Our Enemies*, 21–25.
6. Ibid., 23.
7. Cf. Wink, *Engaging the Powers*, 17.
8. Forest, *Loving Our Enemies*, 25.

Movie makers present this so skillfully that even people who oppose violence may find themselves hoping the "evildoer" is utterly destroyed by whatever means necessary.

Yet, the message of redemptive violence is not only communicated through our historical narrative and popular culture. We find it all sorts of places. As Wink observes, "The myth of redemptive violence is played out in the structure of children's cartoon shows (and is found as well in comics, video and computer games, and movies). But we also encounter it in the media, in sports, in nationalism, in militarism, in foreign policy, in televangelism, in the religious right, and in self-styled militia groups."[9] We are constantly bombarded with messages like "might makes right," peace comes through war, and violence is just the way of things.[10] We are told time and again that violence is good when used against those who seek to harm us or limit our freedom. As National Rifle Association Executive Vice President Wayne LaPierre said after the deadly December 2012 shooting at Sandy Hook Elementary School in Newtown, Connecticut that left twenty-six dead: "The only thing that stops a bad guy with a gun, is a good guy with a gun." Saturated by messages like these, it is little wonder many Christians do not even think to question the legitimacy of violence in certain situations.

We Have Been Desensitized to the Horror of Violence

Part of the problem with violence being portrayed positively in movies, novels, music, art, and drama is that we become desensitized to it. When "virtual" violence is glamorized and presented as something attractive and advantageous, we forget how awful and devastating it really is. This causes people to view violence more favorably than it deserves.

The sheer quantity of violence we are exposed to in the news media also tends to desensitize us to it. Stories of murder, killing, warfare, and gun violence are so common they have lost their shock value. We have grown so accustomed to violence in the real world that sometimes we are no longer even troubled by it, or at least not to the same degree we once were. Many acts of violence no longer grab our attention unless they are *really* dramatic. In fact, they sometimes seem like little more than background noise. We are aware of their presence but seldom reflect on the terrible human drama they represent.

Our desensitization to the horror of violence is compounded by the fact that many of us have little firsthand experience with certain forms of

9. Wink, *Powers that Be*, 49.
10. Ibid., 42.

violence. Take war, for example. Although we can easily learn about war through books and documentaries, most of us have never fought in the trenches. We have not been pinned down in a firefight or seen our comrades staggering around the battlefield in a desperate, albeit futile, search for their severed limbs. Nor have we heard people crying out in agony on the field of battle as they lay bleeding and dying from shrapnel that has ripped through their body. We know things like this happen, but we have no lived experience of these realities.

Since most of us have never experienced combat, we are often unaware of the terrible psychological, emotional, and relational toll war exacts on survivors and perpetrators alike. For example, it is not uncommon for individuals who have been through the horrors of war to experience nightmares, flashbacks, crippling anxiety, suicidal ideation, and relational difficulties.[11] When we live a safe distance from the front lines, we don't often think about these things and are sometimes not even cognizant of the massive trauma that results from war and persists for years to come. This makes it far easier to support warfare and killing uncritically, without really stopping to consider all it entails.

This is poignantly illustrated by a story evangelical pastor Brian Zahnd tells about himself in his compelling book, *A Farewell to Mars*.

> It was January 16, 1991. I was busy and excited. As the pastor of a rapidly growing nondenominational church, I was busy with all the sorts of things pastors do. But that day, I kept a radio on in my study to stay abreast of the big news: America was going to war! That was what I was excited about. The real fighting of the Gulf War was about to begin—Operation Desert Storm. The bombing of Baghdad. A real shooting war. And it was going to be on TV! That evening I hurried home, so terribly excited. This was going to be a first—a war was on, and CNN would be there to bring it live into my living room! Like the Super Bowl! And that's how I treated it. Friends were invited to the viewing party. We ordered pizza. We watched a war. On TV. America won. CNN had huge ratings. Wolf Blitzer became famous. I was entertained. . . .
>
> And I didn't think about it again for fifteen years. I promise you, my pizza-eating, war-watching evening of entertainment didn't cross my mind for fifteen years. Then, one day in 2006, while I was in prayer, for no apparent reason this whole scene from a decade and half earlier played back in my mind. I had

---

11. I am indebted to Dr. Elisa Joy Seibert for the insights at the beginning of this paragraph.

forgotten all about it. But there it was, played back in my memory like an incriminating surveillance video. Then I heard God whisper, "That was your worst sin." That whisper was a devastating blow. I wept and repented and wept. Had I been so shallow, so *desensitized*, so lacking in Christlikeness that I could think of war and violent death as a kind of entertainment? Of course, that was part of the problem: televised war carried out by cruise missiles and smart bombs launched from a safe distance seemed like a video game . . . except that the points scored were human beings killed.[12]

Like Zahnd, many Christians have become desensitized to the horror of war and the devastating effects it has upon countless individual lives. Even though they claim to follow Jesus, the prince of peace and the giver of life, they support various forms of violence—sometimes with great enthusiasm—and fail to consider the human tragedy it causes.

We Are Unaware of Viable Alternatives to Violence

Another reason many in the church condone violence is because they are not aware of other alternatives. In the United States, this lack of awareness can be traced, in part, to our educational system. Many of us have been shortchanged. Elementary school, middle school, and high school taught us little—if anything—about the great peacemakers of the twentieth- and early twenty-first centuries. Instead, we were led to believe the only way to resolve serious conflict or gain freedom was through warfare and military confrontation. But this is far from true. Unlike the American colonists, the people of India, for example, gained their independence from Britain peacefully, *without* going to war. Violence is not the only—or arguably even the most efficacious—way to gain freedom from colonial rule.[13]

Many individuals have little knowledge of the fact that throughout the twentieth century, millions of people were able to bring about sweeping social and political changes through nonviolent struggle.[14] Entire books have been written to tell these amazing stories. These powerful stories are hopeful and inspiring—but they are rarely taught. We will discuss some of these stories and the principles of nonviolent struggle in a later chapter.[15]

12. Zahnd, *Farewell to Mars*, 25–27, emphasis mine.

13. For an interesting discussion of nonviolent options available to the American colonists, see Juhnke and Hunter, *Missing Peace*, 37–53.

14. For a helpful overview, see Buttry, *Christian Peacemaking*, 39–102.

15. See chapter 12.

In his book *Peacemaking Christians*, Michael Duffey describes how large numbers of Christians (and others) in places like Poland, East Germany, and the Philippines effected significant change *without* resorting to violence.[16] In each of these places, people used nonviolent means to confront the Powers that Be. This enabled them to secure labor reforms (Poland), defeat Communism (East Germany), and overthrow a corrupt and violent dictator (Philippines). After reading these stories, one of my students wrote the following response:

> It was encouraging to read these examples of nonviolence. More often than not in school systems, we tend to learn about the wars and the violence, but I can honestly not remember a specific time where we learned about the nonviolent struggles that succeeded. It was just never given as an option.[17]

The twentieth century is full of compelling stories about courageous men and women who made great sacrifices to resolve conflict and do justice without resorting to violence. Yet, most of us have not learned very much about these amazing moments in history. Most secondary schools in the United States provide very little instruction about the effectiveness of nonviolence or about the great peacemakers of the twentieth century apart from a general introduction to Gandhi and Martin Luther King Jr. As Walter Wink observes:

> What young people learn in schools is largely a chronicle of kings and dynasties, wars and empires. . . . Even where nonviolent resistance was successfully used, it tends to be neglected. *A people kept ignorant of the existence of the history of nonviolence will naturally believe that it is impractical and unrealistic.*[18]

People who have never heard how nonviolent action has been successfully used to remove dictators, stop oppression, and bring about social change can hardly be faulted for thinking that violence is the only viable option. They simply do not have other alternatives at their disposal.

16. Duffey, *Peacemaking Christians*, 113–42.

17. A student in my "Issues of War, Peace and Social Justice in Biblical Texts" course (J-term 2007).

18. Wink, *Engaging the Powers*, 243, emphasis mine.

We Do Not Believe Nonviolence Will Work in Certain Situations

A related reason why Christians (and others) sometimes support violent "solutions" is because they are unconvinced that nonviolence will work in certain situations. Even people who know something about the history of nonviolence and its success believe there are some circumstances in which nonviolence is simply not a realistic option. World War II is frequently cited in this regard. What chance could nonviolent efforts have of stopping the brutal Nazi regime? Or how effective could nonviolence have been against those intent on committing genocide in places like Bosnia, Rwanda, or Darfur? Many people are convinced that violence is the only effective response to evil of this magnitude.

Similarly, many people think violence is absolutely essential in the "war on terror." The only effective way to combat terrorism, they believe, is to kill terrorists. In a speech to the West Point graduating class of 2003, former Vice President Dick Cheney said, "With such an enemy [terrorists], no peace treaty is possible; no policy of containment or deterrence will prove effective. The only way to deal with this threat is to destroy it, completely and utterly."[19] Many Christians would concur. In an interview on CNN's "Late Edition" in Fall 2004, the late Rev. Jerry Falwell said as much: "But you've to kill the terrorists before the killing stops. And I'm for the president to chase them all over the world. If it takes ten years, blow them all away in the name of the Lord."[20] While some Christians might be reticent to put it quite so bluntly, they too condone killing terrorists. Why? Because they do not believe nonviolence is an effective way to respond to religious extremists. Even if nonviolence might work in some circumstances, they are convinced it is not a realistic option in others. As they see it, lethal violence is the only way to win the "war on terror." Later in the book, we will challenge this perspective by discussing nonviolent responses to terrorism.[21]

Thus far, the reasons given to explain why churchgoers are often so accommodating toward violence are the same reasons that explain why many Americans—churched or not—believe violence is not only justifiable, but sometimes absolutely necessary. We are now ready to consider some additional reasons that are more specific to Christians and the church.

19. Cheney, Graduation Speech.
20. Blitzer et al., "CNN Late Edition."
21. See chapter 12.

We Misapply Sacred Texts that Sanction Violence

Anyone who has spent even a little time in the Bible, particularly the Old Testament, quickly realizes it contains a considerable amount of violence. Though some acts of violence are clearly condemned by the writer (e.g., Cain murdering Abel), others are not. In fact, much of the violence in the Old Testament is described as being divinely sanctioned. On numerous occasions, God is said to have commanded Israelites to smite, slaughter, and slay. The people of Israel are to kill all the inhabitants of Canaan (Deut 7:1–2; 20:16–18) and utterly annihilate every last Amalekite (1 Sam 15:1–3). In other cases, God is portrayed as being directly engaged in acts of violence, destroying entire cities (Gen 19:24–25) and wiping out thousands of people in single acts of divine destruction (2 Kgs 19:35). These examples of "virtuous violence"—a phrase I use to describe any violence sanctioned in Scripture—include, but are not limited to, acts of divine violence (violence God *commits* in the Old Testament) and accounts of divinely sanctioned violence (violence God *commands* in the Old Testament). Passages containing divine violence and/or divinely sanctioned violence appear with great frequency throughout the Old Testament.[22]

The presence of all this "virtuous" violence in the Bible leads some Christians to conclude that certain forms of violence, like war, must be acceptable under certain circumstances. If warfare was used for divine purposes in the ancient world, they reason, it seems logical to conclude that warfare can be used for divine purposes in the modern world. This way of thinking is extremely persuasive for many believers. As one student quipped, "If killing was good enough for Joshua, then it's good enough for me!"[23]

While most Christians would not state it so baldly, many agree with the underlying assumption: killing in times of war is okay today, because killing in times of war was okay back then. In short, they condone warfare and killing because the Bible does. This argument is put forward every time there is a debate about whether it is acceptable for Christians to participate in warfare, and it helps us understand why some Christians are prepared to condone so much violence. Since this line of reasoning presents a significant challenge to the main thesis of this book—that Christians must *reject* violence to follow Jesus faithfully—we'll consider it more carefully later.[24]

---

22. Raymund Schwager claims there are approximately 1,100 passages (*Must There Be Scapegoats*, 55, 60).

23. Cited in Brensinger, "War in the Old Testament," 23.

24. See chapter 8.

We Rarely Hear the Church Calling Us to Love Enemies and Live Nonviolently

Many Christians receive virtually no instruction—biblical or otherwise—from the church about peacemaking and nonviolence. It is rare to hear sermons preached from key texts like Matt 5:38–48 or Rom 12:14–21, and rarer still to hear a strong case for Christian nonviolence made from the pulpit. Most churches do not emphasize the importance of living nonviolently, and fewer still provide people with practical ways to live out this calling. While these churches undoubtedly teach many other good things, they often fail to emphasize that followers of Jesus are never to hate, hurt, or kill others.

Even historic peace churches don't always do a very good job of helping people develop a commitment to nonviolence. Many Christians from these traditions are unaware of the church's strong opposition to violence and its commitment to creative, nonviolent peacemaking. In fact, it is not at all unusual for someone to be raised in a peace church without ever being taught the church's official position on violence and war. Yet, the church should play a central role in shaping our convictions about peace and nonviolence. When it fails to teach the nonviolent way of Jesus, it abdicates its responsibility, leaving Christians on their own to figure out what they believe. When this happens, many Christians unfortunately take their cues from the surrounding culture which often glorifies and glamorizes violence and killing.

Many Christians are unlikely to be persuaded to reject all forms of violence without first hearing a strong case against violence that is rooted in Scripture, particularly in the life and teachings of Jesus. When the church fails to make this case—as it often does—there is little hope that Christians will commit themselves wholeheartedly to living nonviolently. After all, if the church does not persuade its members to live nonviolently, who will?

We Receive Mixed Messages about Violence from the Church

To make matters worse, the church frequently sends mixed messages about violence. The church often soundly condemns certain forms of violence (e.g., rape and murder) while approving of others (e.g., capital punishment and war). This gives people the impression that some violence is "bad" while other violence is "good." Mixed messages like these are not only confusing, they are counterproductive.

When the church fails to uphold an unwavering commitment to nonviolence, and blesses various forms of violence, it compromises its message and its mission. For example, when the church celebrates the decision of young men and women in the congregation who enlist in the armed forces, it signals the approval of warfare and killing in certain situations and discourages people from raising questions about the compatibility of military service and faithful Christian discipleship. This leads to mixed messages about the role of violence in the life of the Christian. Similarly, how will congregants be encouraged to embrace nonviolence fully if one week the pastor urges them to love their neighbors and the next week uses the sermon to ridicule atheists or condemn people who are gay or lesbian? Mixed messages like these are deeply problematic and help explain why many Christians are not fully committed to nonviolence.

We Confuse the Demands of the State with the Will of God

One of the most significant reasons many Christians in the United States endorse so much violence—and arguably *the* most significant reason—is because they are fiercely nationalistic and patriotic. It is quite common to meet Christians in America who are deeply committed to the values and ideals of the nation state. They are passionate about our national narrative and believe our way of life, and the freedoms we enjoy are worth celebrating and defending. This love of country manifests itself in many ways, even during church services. For example, it is not at all unusual for churches in America to celebrate national holidays such as Memorial Day and the Fourth of July on the Sundays closest to them. A Baptist church in Florida advertised its fourth of July service this way:

> First Baptist Church of Fort Lauderdale will host its annual "Faith, Freedom and Fireworks" patriotic celebration THIS SUNDAY, July 2 [2006], at 10:30 a.m. This is one of our most well-attended events of the year, so we encourage you to arrive early! The Celebration will include patriotic favorites from our 200-voice Chancel Choir and Orchestra, indoor fireworks, hundreds of balloons, a military tribute, an Honor Color Guard and more.

The person who sent me this advertisement added, "For the finale, the choir is singing a rousing arrangement of Battle Hymn of the Republic, coordinated to the fireworks (60-some rockets and 40-some flares), a confetti and balloon drop, rappellers coming down from the ceiling in fatigues, and a flag processional."[25] Patriotic church services like this communicate strong

25. Personal email correspondence from Jeff Spotts, July 4, 2006.

support and appreciation for the military and those serving in uniform. But it also raises crucial questions about the relationship between church and state. Is this blend of God and country appropriate for the church? Or, to put the question differently: Can Christians faithfully follow Jesus as Lord while also pledging their allegiance to the state?

Here is where things get messy. As Christians, we have dual citizenship. We are citizens of a particular nation, typically the country of our birth, and we are *also* citizens of the kingdom of God. Thankfully, the demands of these two kingdoms often coincide nicely. Many times, we can obey both the laws of the land *and* the laws of God simultaneously. But not always.

When these two kingdoms collide, we are faced with a real dilemma. How should we respond when the state requires us to do one thing, and our Christian faith calls us to another? Which kingdom takes priority? The answer would seem obvious. We are Christians first and citizens of the state second. Therefore, to quote Peter, "We must obey God rather than any human authority" (Acts 5:29). Since our primary loyalty is to God's kingdom, those demands *should* take precedence over the state's.

Of course, some don't believe any real tension exists between these two kingdoms in the first place. Such individuals often have difficulty discerning where being an American ends and being a Christian begins, so closely are the two intertwined (at least in their own minds). As John Roth puts it, "Many Christians would be surprised to think that faith in Christ or membership in his church could ever be at odds with their loyalty to the nation, so sure are they that patriotic citizenship and faithful Christianity are one and the same thing."[26] One reason for this is the notion of American exceptionalism, the belief that America is a "Christian nation" through which God works in special and unique ways. Christians who view America this way are apt to support the state and to interpret its policies and behavior as compatible with Christian faith. This is particularly true when it comes to the issue of war.

Many Christians in the United States not only believe it is morally acceptable for Christians to participate in war, they are often its most enthusiastic supporters. At the beginning of the Iraq War, for example, Charles Stanley, the well-known pastor of First Baptist Church Atlanta declared: "We should offer to serve the war effort in any way possible."[27] Pastor Stanley apparently saw no conflict between serving God and serving the state in this instance. He believed that following Jesus and fighting others was fully

---

26. Roth, *Choosing Against War*, 131.
27. Quoted in Hughes, "A Vision for Christian Leaders," 537.

compatible. But is it? Do the values of the United States and the values of the kingdom of God so nearly align?

Richard Hughes thinks not. As he trenchantly argues in his book *Christian America and the Kingdom of God*, "The notion of Christian America and the notion of the kingdom of God are polar opposites whose values could not be further apart."[28] He writes:

> The kingdom of God relies on the power of self-giving love while nations—even so-called "Christian" nations—rely on the power of coercion and the sword. For that reason, nations—even "Christian" nations—inevitably go to war against their enemies while the kingdom of God has no enemies at all.[29]

When Christians prioritize the demands of the state over the demands of discipleship, they risk behaving in ways that are violent and destructive and that ultimately don't look much like Jesus.

This is why the church must be very careful to avoid mixing God and country and stirring up patriotic fervor. While certain forms of patriotism are harmless enough—there is certainly nothing wrong with feeling a sense of pride in the natural beauty of one's country or in its unique customs and traditions—patriotism rooted in militarism is particularly dangerous, especially since a Christian's primary loyalty is to the kingdom of God.[30] Roth explains it this way:

> The subtle and cumulative effect of patriotic sentiments is to nurture a deep, primal loyalty to the nation and its leaders that in times of crisis can very quickly trump our claims to trust in God or our bonds of fellowship with Christians in the worldwide church of Jesus Christ.
>
> When we repeat the Pledge of Allegiance with our hands over our hearts, or when we stand with thousands of others before a sporting event to sing the national anthem, or when we prominently display flags from our porches, we are giving public testimony to our loyalty. If not stating so explicitly, we are certainly implying that the nation can count on us to defend it—to kill on its behalf—in times of war. Patriotic emotions lead us to believe that the principles embodied in our nation are, like God, actually transcendent and therefore worthy of the ultimate sacrifice entailed by killing and dying in their defense."[31]

28. Hughes, *Christian America*, 3–4. Cf. Boyd, *Myth of a Christian Nation*, 17–49.
29. Hughes, *Christian America*, 3.
30. See Roth, *Choosing Against War*, 132–33.
31. Ibid., 135.

If Roth is right, if "patriotic emotions" really do cause people to think that national values, such as freedom and democracy, are "transcendent" and worth killing for, then such emotions should be strongly *dis*couraged by the church. As Roth puts it, "Christians should think more carefully about the meaning of patriotic allegiances in light of the international body of Christians. Should, for example, those believers living in Canada or Zambia or China or Saudi Arabia be pledging allegiance to *their* nations as well, promising to die in defense of *their* national ideals and borders?"[32] The answer would seem self-evident.

When the church mixes God and country and behaves as though no tension exists between being a good Christian and a good American, churchgoers are apt to believe the demands of the state are fully compatible with the demands of faithful Christian living.[33] Once that happens and people no longer see any real distinction between being an American (or Belgian, or Russian, or Canadian) and being a Christian, it is all too easy for Christians to justify acts of violence sanctioned by the state. Thus, this "fusion" of church and state in so many churches (especially in America) goes a long way toward explaining why so many Christians condone so much violence.[34]

Conclusion

As we have seen, numerous factors contribute to the church's acceptance of violence. It has been useful to examine these to help us understand why Christians often seem so comfortable supporting, and sometimes participating in, various forms of violence.

Before turning our attention to the New Testament to consider what Jesus had to say about these matters, we need to explore a very important question about the nature of violence itself, namely, what's wrong with it? What makes the use of violence so problematic, particularly for the church? And are there exceptions, times when violence is unproblematic and "right"? We'll take up these questions in the next chapter.

32. Ibid., 136, emphasis original.

33. As Adolf Hitler put it, "One is either a good German or a good Christian. It is impossible to be both at the same time." Cited in Camp, *Mere Discipleship*, 137.

34. Boyd warns against this "fusion" (*Myth of a Christian Nation*, 11, 14, 90.)

4

The Truth about Violence

It's All Bad

*The ultimate weakness of violence is that it is a descending spiral,
begetting the very thing it seeks to destroy. . . . In fact, violence merely
increases hate. . . . Returning violence for violence multiplies violence,
adding deeper darkness to a night already devoid of stars.*

—MARTIN LUTHER KING JR.[1]

Can Violence Ever Be Good?

Violence comes in multiple shapes and sizes, and takes many different
forms. We often classify these various forms of violence on the basis of
things such as the kind of weapon used (gun violence), the group affected
(elder abuse), or the nature of the violation (ethnic cleansing).[2] Though
people have very different opinions about the morality of violence, some
forms of violence are widely condemned all around the world. Murder, for
example, is typically considered to be wrong, and most countries have laws
against it.[3] Likewise, child abuse, domestic violence, and rape are routinely
condemned by the vast majority of people. Even though many individu-

---

1. Quoted in Enns and Myers, *Ambassadors of Reconciliation*, 3.

2. For an extensive discussion of many different forms of violence, see Barak, *Violence and Nonviolence*, 19–136.

3. According to the Oxford English Dictionary, to murder is "to kill (a person) unlawfully, *spec.* with malice aforethought."

als engage in these very harmful and violent behaviors—using all sorts of twisted logic to justify their actions—such violent acts are almost never sanctioned publically.[4] It is hard to imagine people rallying around slogans like "support domestic violence," "endorse child abuse," or "make rape legal."

Yet there are other forms of violence that are regarded much more positively. For instance, many people approve of using violence in self-defense. This is the basis of the controversial "stand your ground" laws that have been adopted by many states in America. These laws permit people to use lethal force to protect themselves if they believe they are in imminent danger. Many people also view violence positively when it is used to enhance national security or protect innocent people. This is why many regard violent measures such as drone strikes, torture, and targeted assassinations as an appropriate way to deal with terrorists. Additionally, when violence is used to end genocide, remove dictators from power, or stop violent offenders (such as an armed gunman on a shooting spree), it typically enjoys wide approval. In fact, people who use violence to deal with war lords, dictators, and violent offenders are often celebrated as heroes, which reinforces the belief that violence is acceptable and even praiseworthy in some circumstances. In short, people are inclined to regard violence as "good," or at least acceptable, when it is used to stop oppression, punish evildoers, or protect those in harm's way. Even though these people may wish there had been a different way to respond, they believe it is morally right to harm—and even kill—some in order to save others. The ends (protection, security, freedom, justice) ultimately justify the means (torture, harm, violence, death), which brings us back to the question: Can violence ever be good? To answer that question in an informed way, we must first consider the truth about violence.

The Truth about Violence

Many Christians (and others) who justify various acts of violence don't always consider the full ramifications of these acts. Instead, they focus more on the immediate and desired outcome: a terrorist plot has been averted (because the would-be terrorists were killed), an active shooter is no longer a threat (because he was gunned down), and so forth. What often goes unnoticed are the negative—and typically long-term—consequences that result when people fight violence with violence. These consequences should

---

4. That is not to say public officials always prosecute individuals who engage in these law-breaking activities. Far too often, police officers, judges, and others in power turn a blind eye to the plight of those who have been victimized in these ways.

be considered very carefully before deciding whether certain forms of violence can be good

Violence Breeds More Violence (Violence's Dirty Little Secret)

As discussed previously, one of the reasons so many people approve of violence in certain situations is because they are convinced it works. They believe violence can prevent terrorism, resolve conflict, and end wars. And there is some truth in this. As noted earlier, the enormous amount of violence used by the Allied forces in World War II did, indeed, end the war. It prevented further atrocities from German and Japanese soldiers, and put an end to the unspeakable evils occurring in concentration camps in Germany and Poland. Since shutting down these camps and ending the war were both desirable outcomes, many believe the violence used to achieve them was justified.

Yet, anyone who thinks the Allied victory brought an end to the violence unleashed during the war is sorely mistaken. Rather than ending violence, World War II led directly to the Cold War, a disturbing chapter in human history which resulted in millions of deaths at the hands of communist leaders. Josef Stalin alone is thought to be responsible for the death of 20 million people—and this may be a low estimate.[5] And herein lies violence's dirty little secret: *violence breeds more violence.*

Rather than "settling the score" or "making things right," one act of violence inspires another. We see this all the time. A child who is pushed on the playground pushes back. A gang member gunned down by a rival is avenged by fellow gang members who retaliate with deadly force. Religious extremists who kill and terrorize others become targets themselves. And one war sows the seeds of the next. Violence has a boomerang effect.

Even those who use violence with the best of intentions—to stop a dictator from oppressing people or to prevent terrorists from carrying out their deadly plans—inevitably discover that their efforts to reduce violence have precisely the opposite effect. For example, while killing terrorists may seem like a reasonable way for states to deal with the threat of terrorism, it is actually counterproductive. Targeting and killing terrorists plays to their advantage and serves as a marvelous recruiting tool for new initiates. Rather than reducing the threat of terrorism, the use of violence actually increases it, making us less safe, not more.[6]

5. Ghosh, "How Many People Did Joseph Stalin Kill?"

6. For further discussion and support of this point, see the discussion on terrorism at the end of chapter 12. See also Germanos, "CIA Chief Just Confirmed 'War on Terror' Has Created a Lot More Terrorists."

Trying to fight violence with violence is as effective as trying to put out a wildfire by dumping gasoline on it. It simply doesn't work. Violence cannot ultimately bring an end to violence. It just brings more of the same. As Walter Wink observes:

> We want to believe in a final violence that will, this last time, eradicate evil and make future violence unnecessary. But the violence we use creates new evil, however just the cause. It inculcates the longing for revenge, and for what the losers call "justice." And they will have learned from our example how to use violence more efficiently. *Violence can never stop violence because its very success leads others to imitate it.* Paradoxically, violence is most dangerous when it *succeeds.*[7]

Those who use violence—for whatever reason—often find themselves in its cross hairs. They perpetuate a never-ending cycle of violence from which there is no easy escape.

Violence Escalates Dangerous Situations
(Violence Makes Things Worse, Not Better)

As discussed, many people would not think twice about using violence to protect themselves, or those they love, from someone trying to hurt them. If someone threatens to harm you, or those around you, conventional wisdom says we should not hesitate to use violence—even lethal violence—to save yourself and others. Popular books, movies, and TV shows routinely portray this kind of behavior as honorable and good. It is how we are expected to behave in situations like these. Why? Two reasons can be given.

First, people often assume violence is the only *realistic* option in situations like these. Nothing else will do. Second, people assume violence will work. But are these assumptions well-founded? Is using violence really the only viable option in situations like these? Later, we will consider a number of true stories in which people being threatened used creative nonviolent alternatives to escape unharmed without harming others.[8] Stories like these challenge the assumption that violence is the only practical option.

Similarly, the assumption that violence will be "successful" in situations like these is far from certain. Will it eliminate the threat? Possibly. Violence can be effective. You might be able to use violence to prevent an unwanted intruder from harming you. Then again, you might not. There

7. Wink, *Engaging the Powers*, 216, emphasis original.
8. See chapters 10 and 11.

are no guarantees. What if you shoot and miss? What if you reach for your baseball bat only to find a gun pointing at your head? What if you start trading punches and are knocked unconscious? Then what? There are just too many variables to know for sure whether violence will work the way you hope and keep you safe.

In fact, there is a good chance that resorting to violence in situations like these might actually make things worse and put you at greater risk. It may prompt someone to act *more* aggressively than they had intended. Perhaps the intruder in your home only planned to steal some jewelry and petty cash and had no intention of harming anyone. But now that you are charging at him with a crowbar, he feels compelled to fight back, if only to save himself. Our decision to use violence, or to threaten someone with violence, is likely to aggravate the situation. It may even get us killed. A couple of stories help to illustrate this point.

Later in the book, I tell the story of five inmates who escaped from Fort Pillow State Prison a number of years ago, one of whom was a man named Riley Arzeneaux. Arzeneaux made his way to the home of Nathan and Louise Degrafinried, an elderly Christian couple living in Mason, Tennessee, and threatened them with a gun. Without giving away too much of the story, let me just say the Degrafinrieds do not respond violently, and things end well.

But later that day, a very different scenario played itself out when two of the inmates who had escaped with Arzeneaux approach another couple. As William Willimon tells it:

> That afternoon, two of the prisoners who had been separated from Arzeneaux earlier entered a suburban backyard where a couple were barbecuing. The husband went into his house and came out with a gun. The escapees shot and killed him and took his wife hostage. They released her the next day.[9]

Presumably, this man went into his house to get a gun for protection. Maybe he thought he could use it to force the inmates off his property. Or perhaps he planned to shoot them. Whatever his intentions, his actions had disastrous consequences. His decision to brandish a gun was a fatal mistake. It cost him his life and seriously endangered his wife. Rather than protecting himself and the woman he loved, his actions had precisely the opposite effect. A story like this reminds us that we run the risk of making things worse when we use violence, or the threat of violence, in an effort to defend ourselves or others.

9. Willimon, "Bless You, Mrs. Degrafinried," 270.

To reflect further on this point, consider what happened in a small church in North Carolina on New Year's Eve. Pastor Larry Wright was holding a New Year's Eve service at his church on December 31, 2015, when an armed gunman entered the sanctuary.[10] The man was holding the gun in one hand and some ammunition in the other. Pastor Wright approached him and asked, "Can I help you?" The gunman asked for prayer, and Pastor Wright ministered to him, talking with him and praying for him. He then instructed the man to sit in the front row so he could finish the New Year's Eve sermon. When the sermon ended, Pastor Wright gave an altar call, and the gunman came forward to commit his life to the Lord.

The gunman then asked to speak to the congregation. He apologized to the people there, telling them he had "intended to do something terrible that night." It takes very little imagination to envision what that would have looked like. But thankfully, due to Pastor Wright's nonviolent and compassionate response, nobody in the church was harmed.

But let us consider what might have happened if someone had responded violently to this man. As blogger Chuck McKnight asks, "What would have happened if Wright had responded to violence with violence? Or what would have happened if a church member had pulled out a concealed weapon and started shooting?"[11] McKnight imagines two possible scenarios. In what he calls the *"best-case scenario,"* he believes *"the armed church member would have successfully taken out the gunman."*[12] Yet, as McKnight insightfully observes:

> A man would have died needlessly—right before he otherwise would have accepted salvation. . . .
>
> Furthermore, a man [the person who killed the gunman] would have blood on his hands. It doesn't matter if the cause is just; you can't kill a man and remain unscarred. The church member who took this man's life would have had to live with that for the rest of his own life.
>
> Let's also not forget the trauma that all the other church members would have experienced having witnessed a man shot to death.
>
> And this is still assuming the best-case scenario.[13]

10. Hassan and Almasy, "During Sermon on Violence, N.C. Pastor Confronts Man with Rifle."

11. McKnight, "How One Church Reacted to the Threat of Violence."

12. Ibid., emphasis original.

13. Ibid.

McKnight then ponders what might have happened *"if the armed church member wasn't successful?"*[14]

> What if he missed, potentially shooting another member? What if he hit the gunman but didn't take him out—angering him enough to fire rounds into the congregation when he wouldn't have otherwise?
>
> Of course this is all speculation. We can't possibly know what will happen when people start shooting. . . .
>
> *We won't ultimately be any more secure because of it. All we'll do is increase the potential for something to go wrong.*[15]

Fighting violence with violence is risky business. Those who approve of using violence in self-defense, or in the defense of others, typically assume their violence will be effective. They do not always consider other possible outcomes or the very real possibility that using violence might actually make things worse.

Violence Harms Countless People (The Dark Side of Violence)

People who justify the use of violence routinely emphasize the good they believe will result from it—innocent lives will be saved, ruthless dictators stopped, terrorist plots thwarted, civilians protected, and so forth. While that may (or may not) be the case, this much is certain: *it is only part of the story.* Whatever good violence might achieve for some people, it inevitably causes tremendous harm to many others. People get hurt, and some are killed. Families are shattered, children are traumatized, livelihoods are ruined, and all sense of security is lost. In fact, long after the violence ends, those negatively affected by it often continue to suffer for months or years to come.

What is dangerous about a myopic focus on positive results is that it prevents us from considering the full impact and destructive force of violence. We are led to believe that what really matters is that oppressed people have been liberated, a despot is no longer in power, and the country is at peace. Pay no attention to the fact that thousands of civilians were killed in the process, millions displaced, and countless others scarred for life. And do not be overly concerned that the country's infrastructure has been destroyed, its land ravaged, and its public institutions left in shambles. These unpleasant realities are rarely part of the conversation.

14. Ibid., emphasis original.
15. Ibid., emphasis mine.

If we want to know the truth about violence, we have to be brutally honest about it. Violence is traumatic, terrifying, and terrible. *Thus, we dare not speak about the evil violence stops without also discussing the evil violence starts.* Violence is, after all, inherently destructive. It destroys communities, sows fear, and impoverishes people. It causes physical, emotional, and psychological trauma, creating wounds that are hard to heal.

This explains why some who justify its use are so keen on sanitizing it. This is especially true with regard to war. Those responsible for making war rarely speak honestly about the human costs of war, particularly as it concerns casualties on the other side. Rather than speaking about the number of people killed, injured, or displaced, political and military leaders speak euphemistically about "targets" and "collateral damage." They talk about "degrading" the enemy and "neutralizing" the threat. All such language sanitizes violence and obscures the human tragedy of war. It discourages us from contemplating the horrors of war and the calamity of so much blood spilled and so many human lives lost.

Many of us do not often consider the devastating and long-lasting effects of violence, whether that be the violence of war or some other form. For example, we do not follow the wounded victim through months and years of rehab. We do not see the brokenhearted mother whose grief is inconsolable because her little girl got caught in the crossfire. We do not look into the eyes of the young boy struggling to make it on his own after his parents were killed by a drone strike. If we listened to these stories and felt the pain they express, I suspect many of our attitudes about violence and war would be quite different.

Violence Wounds Those Who Use It (The Corrosive Nature of Violence)

Something else we don't always stop to consider is that violence harms both the victim *and* the perpetrator. People who engage in acts of violence are often deeply hurt by their own violent behavior. Veterans, for example, often carry around the wounds of war. There has been growing recognition of the devastating psychological effects combat has upon soldiers. Many return from active duty with post-traumatic stress disorder (PTSD), and an alarming number commit suicide after coming home. In fact, the suicide rate among soldiers far exceeds that of the general population, highlighting the traumatic impact violence has had upon these individuals. According to one recently published study surveying more than one and a quarter million US soldiers "who served in active-duty units between 2001 and 2007," the suicide rate among veterans was 50 percent higher than people who had not served in the military.[16]

Many soldiers also suffer "moral injury." Brock and Lettini explore this idea in their excellent and troubling book *Soul Repair*. Moral injury occurs when soldiers engage in activities that violate their conscience and their "core moral beliefs."[17] It can be triggered by "killing, torturing prisoners, abusing dead bodies, or failing to prevent such acts."[18] Soldiers who partici-pate in (or are complicit with) these acts of violence are prime candidates for this kind of injury. Recovering from moral injury is a very long, and very hard road to travel. As Brock and Lettini observe:

> The consequences of violating one's conscience, even if the act was unavoidable or seemed right at the time, can be devastat-ing. Responses include overwhelming depression, guilt, and self-medication through alcohol or drugs. Moral injury can lead veterans to feelings of worthlessness, remorse, and despair; they may feel as if they lost their souls in combat and are no longer who they were. . . . When the consequences become overwhelm-ing, the only relief may seem to be to leave this life behind.[19]

"Fortunately," writes Robert Meagher, "not all combat veterans return from war with wounds to their bodies or to their souls. But many do, too many."[20]

In their book, Brock and Lettini discuss the devastating impact war had on four veterans. One of these veterans, Camilo Ernesto Mejía, talks about the day he killed a man, something that changed him forever.

> As I observed that young man through the sight of my rifle, when he was still alive, there was something inside me, a voice one could say, that was telling me not to squeeze the trigger. And I knew, without a shred of doubt, that I should not disobey that voice, and that if I did, there would be serious consequences to face.[21]

As Camilo reflects further on this experience he says, "I was staring at a point of no return, the very Rubicon of my life, and I crossed it. My moral injury is the pain I inflicted upon the very core of my being when I took

16. Zarembo, "Detailed Study Confirms High Suicide Rate."
17. Brock and Lettini define moral injury as "the violation of core moral beliefs" (*Soul Repair*, xiii; cf. xiv).
18. Ibid., xv.
19. Ibid., xv–xvi.
20. Meagher, *Killing from the Inside Out*, 1.
21. Brock and Lettini, *Soul Repair*, 88.

something I could never give back. It is a pain that redefined my life."[22] Another veteran describes the personal toll war takes this way: "No one truly 'recovers' from war. No one is ever made whole again. . . . I strive each day to forgive and absolve myself of guilt, and to live with the wounds of war that will never heal."[23] As these individuals testify, engaging in violent acts can be psychologically shattering and spiritually devastating.

This is certainly *not* how many of us typically conceive of violence. In the movies, people who use violence to "fight evil" look strong and sexy. They appear powerful and in control. Their violent acts are portrayed as moments of heroic greatness. This is especially common with superheroes who routinely resort to violence to overcome evil and rescue those in distress. By utilizing their special powers, they defeat the forces of darkness and restore peace and order to the universe. In these scenarios, violence plays an indispensable role in their success and seems to leave them none the worse for using it. This is misleading at best. It promotes the fiction that people can use violence without being harmed by it. But it does not work that way in the real world. People who use violence to harm others are often harmed themselves in the process.

Unfortunately, this often has unintended consequences for those around us. The psychological trauma we are experiencing is likely to have a negative effect on our relationships with others. Inevitably, family members and friends will be impacted by our suffering. We may become more irritable and abusive and less communicative and compassionate. We may even become suicidal. People will notice something has changed in us, and they will realize the change is not for the better. We are not the same people we were before, and others will be hurt by our brokenness. This, too, is the truth about violence.

Violence is Unnatural (We Were Not Created to Kill)

The reason using violence, particularly lethal violence, "messes us up," is because human beings were not designed to kill. Killing others is not part of our collective DNA, so to speak. Therefore, it comes as no great surprise to discover that many people throughout history, even soldiers, have often been very reluctant to kill others.

One way to demonstrate this is by considering the low firing rate among soldiers in various conflicts in the nineteenth and twentieth centuries. Contrary to what we might suspect, many soldiers actually refused to

22. Ibid.
23. Ibid., 75.

fire their weapons in combat situations. Others shot over the heads of their enemies in order to avoid killing them. In his landmark book *On Killing*, Lt. Col. Dave Grossman cites various kinds of evidence to support these claims (e.g., first person accounts, the presence of thousands of fully loaded weapons discarded on the Gettysburg Battlefield, the work of Brigadier S. L. A. Marshall on firing rates). Grossman argues there were many "nonfirers" in the Civil War, World War I, and World War II. For example, during World War II, it appears that only about 15–20 percent of American soldiers who were engaged in combat actually fired their weapons.[24] As Grossman sees it, the evidence suggests "the vast majority of combatants throughout history, at the moment of truth when they could and should kill the enemy, have found themselves to be unable to kill."[25] Why? According to Grossman, it is because "there is within most men an intense resistance to killing their fellow man. A resistance so strong that, in many circumstances, soldiers on the battlefield will die before they can overcome it."[26]

To compel soldiers to obey orders, which sometimes involves killing others, this natural resistance to killing must first be overcome. This is why a crucial part of basic training involves breaking down these barriers by conditioning new recruits to kill instinctively. One way the army does this is by requiring recruits to repeat some rather chilling phrases over and over again:

> DS [Drill Sergeant]: What's the spirit of the bayonet?
> US: Kill, kill, kill. Kill without mercy!
> DS: What makes the grass grow?
> US: Blood, Blood, Bright Red Blood![27]

Exercises like this are designed to "help" soldiers overcome their natural and innate aversion to killing others. They are conditioned to respond instantaneously and unreflectively. The fact that this kind of training is needed further underscores the point being made here: killing is not natural.

Another way to lower a soldier's reluctance to kill is to demonize the "enemy." Demonizing enemies paves the way for killing them by ignoring their humanity and portraying them as irredeemably wicked. The kind of language used to dehumanize others is particularly telling in this regard. For example, during World War II, the Nazis frequently referred to Jews as vermin, and in 1994, during the Rwandan genocide, Hutus spoke of Tutsis

24. Grossman, *On Killing*, 3–4.
25. Ibid., xviii.
26. Ibid., 4.
27. Cited in Mann, *To Benning and Back*, 49.

as cockroaches. Describing people as pesky rodents and undesirable insects not only dehumanizes them, it reinforces the notion that exterminating them is both necessary and desirable. In short, it makes killing much easier.

One of the problems with demonizing others is that it is ultimately dishonest. To be sure, some of our enemies have done very bad things. Some have committed gross moral atrocities. Still, for all the wrongs they have committed, nobody is "pure" evil, and nobody is beyond redemption. Like it or not, we are all a mixture of good and bad. As Aleksandr Solzhenitsyn famously wrote:

> If only there were evil people somewhere insidiously committing evil deeds, and it were necessary only to separate them from the rest of us and destroy them. But the line dividing good and evil cuts through the heart of every human being. And who is willing to destroy a piece of his own heart?[28]

The considerable effort often made to dehumanize others in order to justify killing them further illustrates how unnatural this is. Human beings are not hard-wired to kill. When we take someone's life, we violate our very nature, harming ourselves and others in the process.

Violence is Extremely Costly (We Can't Afford to Do Violence)

One final truth about violence: it is very expensive and extremely costly. This is especially true of militarism and war. In addition to the cost in human lives, staggering amounts of money are spent each year to manufacture weapons, train and equip soldiers, transport troops and equipment, run the day-to-day operations of maintaining a standing army, and support war efforts around the world. The financial cost of the Iraq War (2003–2011) alone is a mind-boggling two trillion dollars—and rising, even though the war officially ended years ago.[29] The United States spends an outrageous amount of money on military spending, budgeting 640 billion dollars in 2015, more than half the federal budget.[30]

What makes the financial cost of war especially distressing is the fact that it diverts badly needed funds from other essential areas of need like education, healthcare, the environment, and housing. This prevents resources from getting into the hands of those who most desperately need them. As former President Dwight D. Eisenhower famously said: "Every gun that is

28. Solzhenitsyn, *Gulag Archipelago*, 75.
29. Trotta, "Iraq War Costs U.S. More Than $2 Trillion."
30. National Priorities Project, "Discretionary Spending."

made, every warship launched, every rocket fired signifies, in the final sense, a theft from those who hunger and are not fed, those who are cold and are not clothed."[31] It seems immoral to spend so much money on things designed to harm people when it could be used to help so many Americans (and others) in desperate need.

Of course, military spending is only one way to assess the high cost of violence. Every year billions of dollars are spent in healthcare costs to assist those who have been physically harmed by acts of violence. Staggering amounts of money are also spent on therapists, inpatient programs, and medications to help victims of violence recover and heal. And then there is the cost of processing and institutionalizing violent offenders, a very expensive undertaking indeed. It takes large amounts of money (much of this borne by taxpayers) to maintain our justice system and to operate correctional facilities.

To look at this from yet another angle, consider what Gary Haugen and Victor Boutros describe as "the locust effect." They persuasively argue there is an unmistakable connection between poverty and violence. Specifically, they demonstrate how the good efforts of people trying to help the poor and raise them out of poverty are being sabotaged by acts of violence (like locusts coming to eat a crop). This, they contend, is a crucial point often overlooked by those trying to bring an end to poverty.

> When we think of global poverty we readily think of hunger, disease, homelessness, illiteracy, dirty water, and a lack of education, *but very few of us immediately think of the global poor's chronic vulnerability to violence*—the massive epidemic of sexual violence, forced labor, illegal detention, land theft, assault, police abuse, and oppression that lies hidden underneath the more visible deprivations of the poor.[32]

This "chronic vulnerability to violence" makes it difficult for the poor to ever get ahead. Until this is addressed, the poorest of the world will continually struggle in poverty, seeing whatever gains they are able to make taken away in acts of "predatory violence."[33]

However you look at it, violence is extremely costly: physically, relationally, emotionally, financially, societally, and in many other ways. Whether it's because money spent on bombs can no longer be used to buy bread, or because violence against the poor away takes what little they have,

---

31. Quoted in Larson and Micheels-Cyrus, eds., *Seeds of Peace*, 62.

32. Haugen and Boutros, *Locust Effect*, xii, emphasis mine.

33. Ibid., xi. The authors propose effective law enforcement that is able to hold this violence at bay as a solution to this undesirable state of affairs (ibid., xiii–xvii, 241–75).

or because lives are lost and communities shattered, violence impoverishes us all.

Conclusion

Regardless of the benefits that may result from using violence, the truth about violence is simply this: violence is always harmful. And though the use of violence is certainly more understandable in some cases than others, it should never be seen as good or "virtuous." As one United States veteran put it:

> The biggest lie I have ever been told is that violence is evil, except in war. . . . My government told me that. My church told me that. My family told me that . . . I came back from war and told them the truth—"Violence is not evil, except in war . . . violence is evil—period."[34]

When we talk about violence we need to tell the truth. We need to be honest about the harm it does, both to those who use it and those who experience it. When we do so, it becomes much more difficult to justify the use of violence, and it prompts us to redouble our efforts to find other ways to respond to conflict, injustice, and oppression in our world.

Throughout this chapter, I made my case against violence without appealing to the Bible or distinct Christian beliefs. The truth about violence is something that should be evident to everyone, regardless of any faith commitment they may—or may not—have. But since the purpose of this book is to address *the church's* problematic approval of so much violence, it is important to consider what the Bible might contribute to this conversation. What does the Bible, particularly the New Testament, say about how followers of Jesus should relate to violence? While the reasons given in this chapter should be enough to cause anyone to think twice before resorting to violence, the life and teachings of Jesus provide the strongest reason for Christians to forsake it altogether.

---

34. Claiborne and Cohen, *Jesus, Bombs, and Ice Cream*, 33.

5

The Nonviolent Way of Jesus
Providing a Model for Christians to Follow

There is no unambiguous evidence that Jesus ever used or advocated violence against another person. Jesus lived, taught, and practiced a way of nonviolence.

—SIMON JOSEPH[1]

IN HIS BOOK, CHRISTIAN *Peacemaking*, Daniel Buttry tells an interesting story about a pivotal conversation he had with a friend many years ago while a student at Wheaton College.[2] It was a conversation that changed the course of his life forever.

> "But what did Jesus say?" Christie persisted. She was sitting across from me in the college dining hall. We were arguing about the war in Vietnam. I was making the case, and making it quite well, that the Christian position is that of allowing just wars. Furthermore, Vietnam was a just war for the United States. I had argued that point on my high school debate team, so I was well armed with statistics, historical data, and brilliant quotes. Christie didn't have a chance, except for that one question: What did Jesus say? Having grown up in a military family, many of

1. Joseph, *Nonviolent Messiah*, 38.
2. Portions of this chapter are adapted from Seibert, "Pacifism and Nonviolence."

my dreams and ideals were shaped by the images of glory won on the battlefield or in dogfights in the skies. Christie's question threatened not only my debating points but the entire construct of values on which my political opinions were based.

What did Jesus say? I had recently made a decision to become a Christian, to follow Jesus as Lord. Christie was in the small Bible study group in which I was participating, and she kept bringing me back to that commitment. "If you really are serious about following Jesus," she said, "what does he say about our involvement in war?" Shaken, I went back to my dorm room and read the Gospels with new eyes and fresh questions. That night I had a second conversion experience, turning from values that glorified participation in war to following the path of this one called the Prince of Peace. I had no idea where that path might lead, but I had a guiding light in that simple question: What did Jesus say?[3]

The purpose of this chapter is to explore "that simple question," not just in regard to war, but also with respect to all forms of violence. What did Jesus say about violence and killing? How did Jesus expect his disciples to live and behave? To answer these questions, we need to look carefully at a number of key passages in the Gospels where we find Jesus' teachings on these matters.

Before doing so, it is helpful to consider what the Old Testament has to say in this regard since these were the Scriptures Jesus cherished and utilized in his own ministry. It goes without saying that the Old Testament contains many violent passages. While not all of these passages bless the violence they contain, many do. Time and again, we read about God killing people (sometimes lots of people) and commanding Israel to go to war. As we noted earlier, texts like these have often been used to justify Christian participation in war and other acts of violence.

Yet, nestled among Old Testament passages that sanction—and sometimes even celebrate—violence, are texts that speak with a different voice. These texts critique violence and offer alternatives to bloodshed and killing. While it would take us far beyond the scope of this book to do justice to all the Old Testament has to offer in this regard, it is important to highlight some of these passages since they seem most consistent with Jesus' own thinking about these issues, as we shall see.

3. Buttry, *Christian Peacemaking*, 7.

Old Testament Foundations for Peace

Many people fail to realize that the Old Testament contains many resources for peace. Yet, as David Leiter writes in his book *Neglected Voices: Peace in the Old Testament*, "The notion of peace rings out consistently and continually in various ways in the broad spectrum of the Old Testament."[4] Numerous Old Testament passages can be used to encourage people of faith to make peace and to seek alternatives to violence. To illustrate this very briefly, consider the following examples.

The opening chapter of Genesis describes people being created in the image of God (Gen 1:26–27). This says something wonderful about the intrinsic value of humanity. It underscores the enormous worth each person has and reminds us to be very careful about how we treat each another. This is an extremely important point, and we will explore it in greater detail later.[5] Incidentally, in contrast to other ancient creation stories, Genesis 1 portrays God creating *without* violence. This also has profound ethical implications for human beings created in God's likeness.[6]

A number of Old Testament narratives describe people dealing with conflict without resorting to violence. Examples include the story of Joseph, the man who forgave his brothers (Gen 45:1–15; 50:15–21); the story of Abigail, the woman who prevented a massacre (1 Sam 25:2–43); and the story of Elisha, the prophet who fed his enemies (2 Kgs 6:8–23), among others. These narratives, which demonstrate the resolution of conflict without bloodshed, encourage us to seek alternatives to violence as well.

The Old Testament also contains a number of specific verses that condemn, or at least seriously constrain, violence and killing. The sixth commandment prohibits killing (Exod 20:13),[7] the Psalmist declares that God's "soul hates the lover of violence" (Ps 11:5), and the writer of Proverbs 3 says not to "envy the violent" or "choose any of their ways" (Prov 3:31), to cite just a few examples.

In addition, the prophets instruct people to avoid violence and to live peaceably with others. The prophet Jeremiah said, "Act with justice and righteousness. . . . And do no wrong or violence to the alien, the orphan, and the widow, or shed innocent blood in this place" (Jer 22:3), and Ezekiel told

---

4. Leiter, *Neglected Voices*, 15. See further Friesen, *Old Testament Roots of Nonviolence*; McDonald, *God and Violence*, 59–72, 193–214; Wenham, *Story as Torah*, 17–43, esp. 37–41.

5. See chapter 13.

6. See Middleton, *Liberating Image*, 235–69.

7. The verse is often too narrowly translated "you shall not murder." See Bailey, *"You Shall Not Kill."*

Israel's leaders to "put away violence and oppression, and do what is just and right" (Ezek 45:9). More strikingly, the prophets dared to dream of a world without war. Isaiah envisioned a day when weapons would be transformed into agricultural tools and military academies would close their doors forever. On that day, people "shall beat their swords into plowshares, and their spears into pruning hooks; nation shall not lift up sword against nation, neither shall they learn war any more" (Isa 2:4; cf. Mic 4:3). Similarly, the prophet Hosea spoke of a time when God "will abolish the bow, the sword, and war from the land" (Hos 2:18).

These Old Testament passages, and others like them, can be viewed as an invitation to pursue peace and to find ways to deal with differences that do not involve warfare and killing. They illustrate some of the rich resources that were available to Jesus as he taught his disciples how to live in a violent world. While it is difficult to know how directly these texts influenced Jesus' thinking about violence and nonviolence, even a cursory reading of the Gospels makes it clear that Jesus' teaching about how we should treat one another is more in line with the peaceful parts of the Old Testament than the violent ones. When Jesus commands his followers to reject violent retaliation and to concentrate on loving others, for example, he echoes themes that first appear in the Old Testament, even if only in whispers. As we turn to the New Testament, we will see how Jesus develops and amplifies some of these crucial themes and ideas.[8]

Jesus Teaches Nonviolence in the Sermon on the Mount

As noted earlier, many believe Jesus' most direct teaching about nonviolence is contained in the Sermon on the Mount (Matt 5–7). This sermon also appears in Luke's gospel, albeit not on a mountain and in much shorter form (Luke 6:17–49). In Matthew, the Sermon on the Mount is the first of five major sections of teaching in the book (Matt 5–7; 10; 13; 18; 23–25). Some have suggested Matthew intentionally included *five* sections of teaching to mirror the Torah, the first *five* books of the Old Testament. For Jews, the Torah is the most important part of the Hebrew Bible since it contains God's laws and describes what life with God should look like.[9]

8. The reason for privileging the words (and deeds) of Jesus is rooted in the conviction that Jesus is the fullest and clearest revelation of the moral character of God. In other words, we most clearly see who God is, and how God wants us to live, when we look at Jesus. Therefore, obeying the teachings of Jesus—not least of which his teachings related to living nonviolently—is of paramount importance for all Christians. See Seibert, *Disturbing Divine Behavior*, 183–207.

9. Matthew's description of Jesus giving this sermon on a mountain (Matt

Similarly, the Sermon on the Mount contains key instructions about how followers of Jesus are to live. It is, as New Testament scholar Richard Hays describes it, "Jesus' basic training on the life of discipleship."[10] Its placement as the first of these five sections of teaching suggests its foundational importance for followers of Jesus. The Sermon on the Mount serves as "Jesus' programmatic disclosure of the kingdom of God and of the life to which the community of disciples is called."[11] In other words, Jesus is not simply moralizing or discussing random ethical principles about how to live a better life. Rather, in this sermon, Jesus is describing the *essential* nature of this new community his followers would embody. As Hays describes it, this is a community in which "anger is overcome through reconciliation (5:21–26), lust is kept under discipline (5:27–30), marriage is honored through lifelong fidelity (5:31–32), language is simple and honest (5:33–37), retaliation is renounced (5:38–42), and enemy-love replaces hate (5:43–48)."[12]

One of the most distinctive aspects of this new community of followers is that it would be characterized by nonviolence. This is especially evident in three places in the sermon where Jesus speaks about being peacemakers (Matt 5:9), loving enemies (Matt 5:38–48), and treating others nonviolently (Matt 7:12).

Be Peacemakers (Matt 5:9)

Jesus begins the Sermon on the Mount with the beatitudes, a series of short sayings which highlight various attitudes and actions that are blessed by God. Peacemaking is one of these. "Blessed are the peacemakers," says Jesus, "for they will be called children of God" (Matt 5:9). As Perry Yoder points out, the Greek word for peace (*eirene*) "is used in much the same way as [its Hebrew counterpart] shalom—for material and physical well-being, good relationships, and moral character."[13] Like *shalom*, the word *eirene* "points to a positive state of affairs where things are as they should be."[14] When people are disadvantaged, peacemakers work for justice. When people are oppressed, peacemakers work for liberation. When people are estranged,

---

5:1)—rather than on a plain as in Luke's account (Luke 6:17)—recalls God giving instructions to Moses on Mt. Sinai, further emphasizing the importance of this message.

10. Hays, *Moral Vision*, 321.

11. Ibid.

12. Ibid.

13. Yoder, *Shalom*, 19.

14. Ibid., 21.

peacemakers work for reconciliation. Peacemakers engage in the sacred work of restoring damaged relationships and healing broken spirits.

The reason Jesus says peacemakers "will be called children of God" is because people who make peace reflect God's character. They imitate the reconciling work God has done—and continues to do—through Jesus. As the writer of Colossians puts it, "Through him [Jesus] God was pleased to reconcile to himself all things, whether on earth or in heaven, by making peace through the blood of his cross" (Col 1:20; cf. 2 Cor 5:19). Since peacemakers facilitate reconciliation, the same kind of work God does, they bear a "family" resemblance and are aptly called God's children.

As the New Testament describes it, peacemaking is done without hostility or violence. In fact, part of the purpose of making peace is to overcome these very things (Eph 2:13–18). Peacemaking is about uniting people and overcoming barriers that keep them apart. This cannot be achieved by domination or brute force. Instead, it requires love. As we shall see, the peacemaking Jesus envisions is grounded in nonviolent love for others, even those we find most disagreeable.

Love Your Enemies (Matt 5:38–48)

Jesus' most extensive—and arguably most important—teaching about nonviolence in the New Testament is Matt 5:38–48:

> You have heard that it was said, "An eye for an eye and a tooth for a tooth." But I say to you, Do not resist an evildoer. But if anyone strikes you on the right cheek, turn the other also; and if anyone wants to sue you and take your coat, give your cloak as well; and if anyone forces you to go one mile, go also the second mile. Give to everyone who begs from you, and do not refuse anyone who wants to borrow from you. You have heard that it was said, "You shall love your neighbor and hate your enemy." But I say to you, Love your enemies and pray for those who persecute you, so that you may be children of your Father in heaven; for he makes his sun rise on the evil and on the good, and sends rain on the righteous and on the unrighteous. For if you love those who love you, what reward do you have? Do not even the tax collectors do the same? And if you greet only your brothers and sisters, what more are you doing than others? Do not even the Gentiles do the same? Be perfect, therefore, as your heavenly Father is perfect.

Several points require comment here.

First, in this passage, Jesus makes it clear that his disciples are not to retaliate. To make this point, Jesus begins by quoting Old Testament laws of retribution (*lex talionis*) that stipulate "eye for eye, tooth for tooth."[15] These commands are sometimes thought to be mean-spirited and vindictive— whatever harmful things people do to you, do the same to them. But that misses the intent of these laws. Rather than encouraging vengeful violence, they were designed to place limits on how much violence could be done to someone who harmed you. You were permitted to inflict no greater injury than the one you received. If someone broke your nose, the *most* you could do in return would be to break theirs. You were not allowed to draw your sword and slice off their head! Presumably, this was intended to keep things from escalating and to ensure some measure of equity and fairness.

Yet, Jesus forbids his followers from engaging in any form of retaliation and calls them to a higher way. Jesus' disciples are *not* to retaliate when they are harmed. Jesus says, "Do not resist an evildoer" (v. 39). This is better translated, "Do not *violently* resist an evildoer," a point Walter Wink argues convincingly.[16] The Greek word *antistēnai*, which the NRSV simply translates as "resist," most commonly refers to *violent* resistance. Wink notes that in the Septuagint, the Greek translation of the Old Testament, *antistēnai* is primarily used "for armed resistance in military encounters."[17] He also observes that fifteen of the seventeen times the Jewish historian Josephus uses this term in his writings, he uses it to refer to "violent struggle." This evidence leads Wink to conclude that *antistēnai* means "to resist *violently*, to revolt or rebel, to engage in an insurrection."[18] *Violent* resistance is not an option for followers of Jesus and is strictly forbidden.

To illustrate this point, Jesus provides three illustrations: turning the other cheek (v. 39), giving the cloak off your back (v. 40), and going the extra mile (v. 41). Whenever followers of Jesus are smacked, sued, or conscripted, they are not to respond violently or retaliate in any way. Many Christians are bothered by these directives, particularly the one about turning the other cheek. It makes Christians appear passive, weak, and ready for abuse. Should we really just stand there and let people hit us? Is that what Jesus wants? Wink thinks not. He believes all three of these illustrations function in a similar way, namely, to assert the dignity of the one being harmed.

To demonstrate this, let's look more closely at the first of these three illustrations: "if anyone strikes you on the right cheek, turn the other also"

15. Exod 21:22–25; Lev 24:19–20; Deut 19:16–21.
16. Wink, *Engaging the Powers*, 185.
17. Ibid.
18. Ibid., emphasis original.

THE NONVIOLENT WAY OF JESUS

(v. 39). Wink assumes the person doing the hitting is socially superior and likely to strike with the right hand since the left hand was reserved for unclean tasks (like wiping yourself after going to the toilet). The only way for the aggressor to hit the other person on the *right* cheek (an important detail in v. 39) is by using a backhanded slap with their right hand. Wink says this would be "the usual way of admonishing inferiors" and was used "to humiliate, to put someone in his or her place."[19]

But turning the other cheek after being slapped creates a real dilemma for your adversary: it makes it impossible for them to deliver another backhanded slap. There is simply no good way for someone to use their *right* hand to deliver a backhanded slap to someone's *left* cheek (try it sometime—without making physical contact, of course!). While this individual could decide to hit you straight on, that would be tantamount to treating you as an equal, something any self-respecting, socially *superior* individual would be loath to do.

Rather than communicating weakness or a desire to be beaten up, turning the other cheek asserts your dignity and your resistance to oppression. "By turning the cheek," writes Wink, "the 'inferior' is saying: 'I'm a human being, just like you. I refuse to be humiliated any longer. I am your equal. I am a child of God. I won't take it anymore.'"[20] According to Wink, Jesus' instructions about giving your cloak and going the extra mile function similarly.[21] Whatever we take to be the exact meaning of Jesus' illustrations in vv. 39–41, his insistence on nonretaliation comes through loud and clear. (Parenthetically, I would stress that Jesus' emphasis upon nonretaliation and nonviolent resistance to evil should *not* be interpreted to mean that followers of Jesus are supposed to stay in abusive interpersonal relationships. More on this later.)[22]

A second key aspect of this passage is Jesus' command to love enemies and pray for persecutors.

> Love your enemies and pray for those who persecute you, so
> that you may be children of your Father in heaven; for he makes

---

19. Ibid., 176.

20. Wink, *Powers that Be*, 102.

21. See Wink, *Engaging the Powers*, 175–84, for a discussion of Jesus' three illustrations in vv. 39–41. Though not everyone is persuaded by Wink's interpretation, prominent scholars such as Wright, *Jesus and the Victory of God*, 290–91, and Stassen and Gushee, *Kingdom Ethics*, 138–39, follow him here.

22. See the end of chapter 7 and the extensive discussion of domestic violence in chapter 16.

his sun rise on the evil and on the good, and sends rain on the
righteous and on the unrighteous (Matt 5:44–45).[23]

Jesus' command to love enemies is one of several so-called antitheses
found throughout Matt 5:21–48. Six times, Jesus reminds people of something they already know ("You have heard that it was said") and then goes
on to teach them something new ("but I say to you"). The fact that Jesus'
teaching about loving enemies is the sixth and final antithesis may be a way
of emphasizing its great significance and importance by making it climactic.
In any case, the command to love enemies constitutes one of Jesus' strongest
statements against the use of violence. It is central to any understanding of
Christian nonviolence since loving one's enemies would seem to preclude
behaving violently towards them.[24]

For many, the big question here becomes how broadly to define "enemies." Some have argued that Jesus is only referring to personal enemies:
nasty neighbors, contentious co-workers, and the like. Those who adopt this
more narrow view limit the applicability of Jesus' command to individuals
we actually know firsthand. They do not think the command to love enemies is relevant to questions about warfare, international conflict, or global
terrorism, situations which often involve fighting against people we have
never met. How can we decide whether we should adopt this more restrictive understanding of Jesus' command? Is there anything in this passage that
would lead us to believe Jesus was commanding his followers to love certain
kinds of enemies and not others?

Presumably, many of Jesus' listeners would have immediately thought
of their Roman oppressors when they heard Jesus' words. This seems especially likely since Jesus had just alluded to them moments earlier by using
the illustration about going an extra mile when forced to carry the heavy
packs of Roman soldiers. "For a Jewish teacher to talk about 'enemies' to
Palestinian Jews in the first century," writes Greg Boyd, "was to speak first
and foremost about Romans."[25] Boyd explains it this way:

> The very fact that idolatrous and immoral pagans ruled them
> and occupied their God-given land was theologically offensive
> to most orthodox Jews. To make matters worse, however, Ro-
> man rule was often unjust and violently oppressive. . . . It wasn't

23. Cf. Luke 6:27, 35.

24. Some argue that behaving violently toward someone can demonstrate love
for that person in certain situations. I find such reasoning unpersuasive. If someone
harmed me and then claimed they did so out of love for me, I would be very disinclined
to believe them.

25. Boyd, "Does God Expect Nations?," 109.

uncommon for Jews to lose their land, property, and/or freedom because they could not meet their enormous tax obligations. Nor was it uncommon for Jews to witness compatriots being imprisoned, beaten, and/or crucified for an alleged crime, often without a fair trial. To say that most Jews loathed this situation is to make a massive understatement. In fact, it wouldn't be going too far to compare the animosity that many Palestinian Jews felt toward their Roman oppressors to the animosity felt by most Americans toward Al Qaeda and other terrorist groups after 9/11—except that in the case of first-century Jews, the terrorists weren't simply *threatening* their country; they were already *ruling* it.[26]

When Jesus taught about loving enemies, it seems inevitable that some Jews would have understood him to be talking about their political enemies, not just about their nasty next-door neighbor. In light of this, and seeing no good evidence to the contrary, it seems best to interpret enemy-love in the broadest possible terms.[27]

It is instructive to note that Jesus' teaching about enemy-love is grounded in an understanding of God's gracious nature. In Luke's version of the sermon, Jesus reminds us that God "is kind to the ungrateful and the wicked" (Luke 6:35). In Matthew's version, Jesus emphasizes that God's goodness extends to everyone, including enemies. God "makes his sun rise on the evil and on the good, and sends rain on the righteous and on the unrighteous" (Matt 5:45). This suggests that God gives good gifts to everyone indiscriminately. God is not nice to the righteous and mean to the unrighteous. No, God's gracious provisions are lavished upon all of us, however worthy or unworthy we may be. In this way God's behavior serves as an example for our own. When we treat our enemies lovingly, we are, in fact, treating them as God does. This is why Jesus tells his disciples that loving enemies and praying for persecutors makes them "children of your Father in heaven." Just like peacemaking, when we love enemies we bear a striking resemblance to God.

Behaving this way testifies to the goodness and grace of God and to the truth of the gospel. As Hays puts it:

> The community of Jesus' disciples is summoned to the task of showing forth the character of God in the world. That character is nowhere more decisively manifest than in the practice of loving enemies (Matt 5:44–45), a practice incompatible with killing

26. Ibid., emphasis original.

27. For a fuller discussion of this issue, see ibid., 108–12.

them. . . . Peacemakers are to be called "sons of God" (5:9) because, like God, they love their enemies. . . . Thus, the church's
embodiment of nonviolence is—according to the Sermon on
the Mount—its indispensable witness to the gospel.[28]

When we treat our enemies with love and respect, we bear witness to a nonviolent, enemy-loving God. A more powerful witness is hard to imagine.

Treat Others Nonviolently (a.k.a. The Golden Rule—Matt 7:12)

One of the most well-known sayings of Jesus, the so-called Golden Rule, can
easily be understood as a call to live nonviolently despite the fact it is not
often heard that way. Jesus says:

In everything do to others as you would have them do to you;
for this is the law and the prophets (Matt 7:12).

One of the most striking things about this command is its compre-
hensiveness. "In *everything* do to others as you would have them do to
you." Whatever the command means, it relates to everything we do to everyone. Moreover, Jesus claims that obeying this command "is the law and
the prophets." To sum up two-thirds of the Hebrew Bible is one concise
command is no small feat.[29] Clearly, Jesus is saying something very, very
important here.

Yet far too often, we gloss over this command and fail to take it seriously. We domesticate the "Golden Rule" and miss its full import by reducing it to a maxim about being "nice" to one another. We use it in Sunday
school to teach children how to behave, saying things like, "Since you would
not want someone to say unkind words to you, you should not say unkind
words to others," and, "Since you want people to share their toys with you,
you should share your toys with them." While using and applying the command this way is certainly not wrong or inappropriate, it only begins to
scratch the surface of what is implied by Jesus' words.

This command requires us to reject *all* forms of violence and any
kind of behavior that would violate, harm, or oppress another. Indeed, as
Wink sees it, the Golden Rule may be "the most fundamental statement of
nonviolence."[30] It is one of the clearest and most direct commands of Jesus
about how his followers are to treat others. And it would seem that obeying

28. Hays, *Moral Vision*, 329.

29. The Hebrew Bible is divided into three parts: the law, the prophets, and the
writings.

30. Wink, *Engaging the Powers*, 127.

it requires us to abandon violence completely and absolutely. Do you want someone to behave violently toward you? If not, then the Golden Rule says you cannot behave violently toward them. We are to treat everyone—friends *and* enemies, family members *and* strangers, people like us *and* those very different from us—the same way we would like to be treated.

By issuing this command, Jesus once again calls his followers to a higher standard. If people treat us badly, we are not supposed to treat them badly in return. We have no right to demand an eye for an eye or a tooth for a tooth. Instead, we must treat others the way we want to be treated, *regardless* of how they behave toward us. Since nobody in their right mind wants to be a victim of violence, we should not behave violently toward others. Instead, we should treat people with compassion, mercy, and love, the same way we ourselves would like to be treated. Once we hear the Golden Rule this way, and realize its depth and breadth, its relevance for discussions about living nonviolently become immediately obvious.

As we have seen, in various ways throughout the Sermon on the Mount, Jesus calls upon his followers to forsake violence. Therefore, if we desire to follow Jesus, we cannot retaliate, seek revenge, or harbor hate in our hearts. Rather, we are called to make peace, to love our enemies, and to treat people with the same dignity and respect we want for ourselves.

Jesus Forbids his Disciples from Behaving Violently: Two Teachable Moments

We have no record of how the original audience responded to the Sermon on the Mount that day. It would be interesting to know what people in the crowd, especially Jesus' disciples, thought about the things they had heard. To what extent did they agree with Jesus' nonviolent message? Did they find it attractive? Offensive? Disorienting? It is difficult to say with certainty. What we do know is that not all the disciples were fully persuaded. Some continued to believe violence was permissible, and even desirable, in certain situations.

On two separate occasions, the disciples ask Jesus if they should behave violently. In one instance, the disciples appear eager to exact retribution on Samaritans. In the other, they are ready to wield swords to prevent Jesus' capture. The way Jesus responds in both situations is instructive. It confirms his commitment to nonviolence and his expectation that the disciples behave likewise.

Fire from Heaven? (Luke 9:51–56)

In a story told only in Luke's gospel, Jesus and his disciples suffer a grievous breach of hospitality at the hands of some Samaritans.[31]

> When the days drew near for him [Jesus] to be taken up, he set his face to go to Jerusalem. And he sent messengers ahead of him. On their way they entered a village of the Samaritans to make ready for him; but they did not receive him, because his face was set toward Jerusalem. When his disciples James and John saw it, they said, "Lord, do you want us to command fire to come down from heaven and consume them?" But he turned and rebuked them. Then they went on to another village (Luke 9:51–56).

Given the animosity that existed between Jews and Samaritans, their response is not entirely unexpected, though it is rather surprising given the enormous importance placed on hospitality in ancient Mediterranean cultures.

Of the many issues dividing Jews and Samaritans, one of the most contentious was a disagreement about the proper place to worship. Samaritans believed it was Mount Gerizim; Jews insisted it was Mount Zion (Jerusalem). Therefore, when these Samaritan villagers realized Jesus and his entourage were heading to Jerusalem, they refused to offer food and lodging, basic hospitality, because of their fundamental theological differences. This insult prompts James and John, two of Jesus' closest disciples to ask whether they should respond with violence. "Lord, do you want us to command fire to come down from heaven and consume them?" (v. 54). James and John apparently thought this would be an appropriate way to punish these inhospitable Samaritans.

The idea of calling down fire from heaven to destroy people was inspired by an Old Testament story featuring the prophet Elijah (2 Kgs 1:1–16). As the story goes, the Israelite king Ahaziah is injured and sends messengers to inquire whether he will recover. There is just one problem with this. Rather than sending his messengers to inquire of Yahweh, the god of Israel, he instead sends them to Baal-zebub, the god of Ekron. When Elijah is informed of this, he confronts these messengers and chastises them. He also tells them to inform King Ahaziah that he will not recover.

---

31. The Samaritans were descendants of Jews who intermarried with foreigners brought into the land after the northern kingdom of Israel fell to the Assyrians in 722 BCE. Many Jews viewed Samaritans with disdain, seeing them as mongrels. As this story clearly illustrates, feelings of animosity ran deep between these groups.

After the royal messengers relay this unwelcome news to the king, Ahaziah decides to send a delegation of fifty men, with their captain, to ask Elijah to come and meet with him. The meeting is brief and goes badly for all the king's men. "Then fire came down from heaven, and consumed him and his fifty" (2 Kgs 1:10). A second delegation is sent but meets the same fate. When a third delegation arrives on the scene, the captain begs for his life and the life of his men. They are spared, but Elijah's message remains unchanged: the king will die from his injury.

This extremely violent story, in which over one hundred men are killed when "the fire of God" comes down from heaven, lies behind the disciples' request. Should they behave like the great prophet Elijah? Should they call down fire from heaven to slaughter these sinful Samaritans and teach them a lesson they would not soon forget? Is that what Jesus wanted? Apparently not since we are told Jesus "turned and rebuked them" (Luke 9:55). Some versions of the story include Jesus' rebuke to his violence-prone disciples: "You do not know what spirit you are of, for the Son of Man has not come to destroy the lives of human beings but to save them."[32] The disciples' problematic proposal is swiftly rejected. Retaliatory violence is not the way of Jesus.

Violence in the Garden? (Matt 26:47–56; Luke 22:47–53)

The disciples were also prepared to use violence in the garden of Gethsemane on the night Jesus was betrayed.

> While he [Jesus] was still speaking, suddenly a crowd came, and the one called Judas, one of the twelve, was leading them. He approached Jesus to kiss him; but Jesus said to him, "Judas, is it with a kiss that you are betraying the Son of Man?" When those who were around him saw what was coming, they asked, "Lord, should we strike with the sword?" Then one of them struck the slave of the high priest and cut off his right ear. But Jesus said, "No more of this!" And he touched his ear and healed him (Luke 22:47–51).

If there was ever a moment when violence must have seemed justified, this was it.[33] Think about it. You have been following Jesus all over Galilee for

32. For a listing of the manuscripts containing this rebuke, and for a brief discussion of evidence for and against the authenticity of this saying, see Marshall, *Gospel of Luke*, 407–8.

33. I first heard the line of reasoning in this paragraph suggested (and rejected) by John Dear.

months. It has been the most exciting and exhilarating time you've ever had. You are convinced Jesus is more than just a prophet—you believe he is the messiah. You have seen Jesus feed the hungry, heal the sick, and even raise the dead! And now you see a large group of armed people coming to take Jesus away. Shouldn't you fight to keep Jesus from being arrested? Isn't this the perfect opportunity to draw your sword? Peter thinks so. He unsheathes his sword and slices off the ear of the high priest's slave.[34]

Jesus' response to this violent act is immediate and unequivocal. He says, "No more of this!" (Luke 22:51). Jesus answers the disciples question about whether to strike with a sword with a resounding "No!" Jesus does not want his disciples to use violence even for such a noble cause. Instead, Jesus commands Peter to put away his sword, "for all who take the sword will perish by the sword" (Matt 26:52; cf. John 18:11). Jesus understood how violence works. He knew that violence breeds more violence and that using it is dangerous and sometimes deadly.

After Jesus finishes admonishing Peter, he heals the slave's ear, the one Peter just detached from his head. In this brief incident, Jesus not only prevents a bloodbath, he demonstrates that his mission—and that of his disciples—involves *helping* people, not *hurting* them.

Jesus Rejects Punitive Violence: The Case of the Adulterous Woman (John 7:53—8:11)

The way Jesus restrained his disciples' violent inclinations in these two episodes aligns with what he taught in the Sermon on the Mount. It is also consistent with the way he acted on other occasions. Jesus regularly rejected violence throughout his ministry, even in situations where violence might seem justified. To look at another example of this, consider how Jesus responds when he is confronted with a question about what should happen to an adulterer.

> Early in the morning he [Jesus] came again to the temple. All the people came to him and he sat down and began to teach them. The scribes and the Pharisees brought a woman who had been caught in adultery; and making her stand before all of them, they said to him, "Teacher, this woman was caught in the very act of committing adultery. Now in the law Moses commanded us to stone such women. Now what do you say?" They said this to test him, so that they might have some charge to bring against him. Jesus bent down and wrote with his finger on the ground.

34. John 18:10 identifies Peter as the sword-wielding disciple.

> When they kept on questioning him, he straightened up and said to them, "Let anyone among you who is without sin be the first to throw a stone at her." And once again he bent down and wrote on the ground. When they heard it, they went away, one by one, beginning with the elders; and Jesus was left alone with the woman standing before him. Jesus straightened up and said to her, "Woman, where are they? Has no one condemned you?" She said, "No one, sir." And Jesus said, "Neither do I condemn you. Go your way, and from now on do not sin again" (John 8:2–11).

As this passage indicates, the scribes and Pharisees bring this woman before Jesus to entrap him, not because they are particularly concerned about what should be done to her (vv. 5–6).

Jesus' response is brilliant: compassionate, clever, *and* nonviolent. Jesus says, "Let anyone among you who is without sin be the first to throw a stone at her" (v. 7). Rather than getting caught in their trap, Jesus' redirects their question, taking the focus away from the woman's sin and turning it upon their own. Needless to say, no stones were thrown that day.

Jesus refuses to condone the use of violence to punish this woman even though the law mandated it (see Deut 22:22). Jesus' response seems to set a new precedent for dealing with sinners, even those who have committed serious infractions of the law. Since none of us is without sin, none of us has the right to throw stones. Strictly followed, that would effectively eliminate lethal violence as a legitimate form of punishment.

After her accusers depart, Jesus speaks directly to the woman. He says he does not condemn her, and sends her on her way with the admonition to sin no more. Once again, in this story we see Jesus rejecting violence *even though* its use was sanctioned by Scripture and stipulated by law in this case.

Jesus Inaugurates a Kingdom without Violence

One of the primary reasons Jesus routinely rejects violence, and neither wants nor needs his disciples to use violence, is because his kingdom is completely different from all the rest.[35] This is stated most directly in an intriguing interchange between Pilate and Jesus.

> Then Pilate entered the headquarters again, summoned Jesus, and asked him, "Are you the King of the Jews?" Jesus answered,

---

35. For an excellent discussion of how the kingdom of God differs in essential and fundamental ways from all kingdoms of the world, see Boyd, *Myth of a Christian Nation*, 17–49.

"Do you ask this on your own, or did others tell you about me?" Pilate replied, "I am not a Jew, am I? Your own nation and the chief priests have handed you over to me. What have you done?" Jesus answered, "My kingdom is not from this world. *If my kingdom were from this world, my followers would be fighting to keep me from being handed over to the Jews. But as it is, my kingdom is not from here.*" (John 18:33–36, emphasis mine)

If Jesus had been trying to establish an earthly kingdom, similar to one of the kingdoms of this world, it would have made sense for him to arm his disciples and to instruct them to fight (and kill) on his behalf. But that was not the kind of kingdom Jesus came to establish. Instead, Jesus came to inaugurate a completely different kind of kingdom, one that was unlike any other earthly kingdom, and one that was, therefore, not dependent upon violence in any way. Jesus referred to this kingdom as the "kingdom of God" and spoke frequently about it in many parables and sayings.[36]

The kingdom of God is best understood as God's reign of peace and justice over all creation. It is what we ask for when we pray, "Your kingdom come. Your will be done, on earth as it is in heaven" (Matt 6:10). As such, it is not a physical kingdom demarcated by borders and boundaries. Nor is it synonymous with the church or heaven. While the church participates in the kingdom of God, and is called to advance it, they are not one and the same. Likewise, while heaven reflects the priorities of God's kingdom, the kingdom of God is not restricted to some other-worldly reality. It is here and now.

As the Apostle Paul describes it, "The kingdom of God is . . . righteousness and peace and joy in the Holy Spirit (Rom 14:17). Peace (Hebrew *shalom*) connotes well-being, wholeness, and completeness. This is what God desires for every individual. God wants people to have their basic needs met, to be secure, to enjoy healthy relationships with others, and to be in right relationship with God. The good news of the gospel is that we can participate in the kingdom—God's reign of peace and justice—today. When the hungry are fed, the sick are healed, and the oppressed are freed, the kingdom of God is made manifest among us. Likewise, when someone forgives rather than retaliates, loves rather than hates, repays evil with good rather than more evil, and disarms rather than harms, the kingdom of God has come. In response to the Pharisees question about when this kingdom was coming, Jesus replied, "The kingdom of God is not coming with things that can be observed; nor will they say, 'Look, here it is!' or 'There it is!' For, in fact, the kingdom of God is among you" (Luke 17:20–21).

---

36. Matthew's gospel renders this as the "kingdom of heaven."

Obviously, we only experience the reign of God partially and incompletely in this life. We continue to suffer from violence, broken relationships, poverty, disease, and death. But the Christian hope is that when God's reign is fully realized, all these evils will be done away with. Sickness, sorrow, oppression, injustice, violence, war, and death will be no more. Instead, there will only be health and wholeness, peace and love, grace and goodness, security and abundance. This is what God wants for all creation.

Jesus Lived Nonviolently, Healing Rather Than Hurting

Jesus embodied the kingdom of God in his life and ministry, and this validated his identity. When John the Baptist's disciple came to ascertain whether Jesus was "the one who is to come" (Luke 7:19), Jesus said: "Go and tell John what you have seen and heard: the blind receive their sight, the lame walk, the lepers are cleansed, the deaf hear, the dead are raised, the poor have good news brought to them" (Luke 7:22).

Jesus' public ministry was characterized by acts of love, grace, and compassion. Particularly noteworthy is the fact that Jesus never resorted to violence. Indeed, the whole thrust of Jesus' ministry was about *helping* people, not *hurting* them. "One of the remarkable features of Christianity," writes Jim Forest, "is that its founder healed many and killed no one."[37] That's not to say Jesus never got riled up. The Gospel writers make no effort to conceal Jesus' indignation and anger on numerous occasions. Jesus became especially irritated with the religious elite who used Scripture and tradition to oppress others.[38] Yet, even in those moments, Jesus never became physically violent. He never punched a Pharisee or assaulted a Sadducee—though I am certain there were times when he must have been sorely tempted! Still, such violent behavior is completely absent from the life of Jesus.[39]

As Jesus moves about Galilee and elsewhere, he is known for his power to *heal* others, not *harm* them. Large crowds are attracted to Jesus because of this. Near the beginning of Jesus' public ministry, Jesus enters the home of Simon and Andrew and cures Simon's mother-in-law of a fever. Here's what happens next:

> That evening, at sunset, they brought to him all who were sick or
> possessed with demons. And *the whole city* was gathered around

37. Forest, *Loving Our Enemies*, 136.

38. See, e.g., Mark 7:1–13; Matt 23:1–36.

39. See chapter 6 for a discussion of selected New Testament passages (such as the so-called "cleansing of the temple") that people sometimes use to argue Jesus was violent.

the door. And he cured many who were sick with various diseas-
es, and cast out many demons (Mark 1:32–34, emphasis mine).

This scene repeats itself time and again throughout Jesus earthly ministry.
Jesus heals the sick, gives sight to the blind, frees people from bondage, and
sometimes even raises the dead. People flock to Jesus because of his power
to help and heal.

Our familiarity with these stories sometimes causes us to miss their
true significance. We often regard these miraculous healings as random acts
of kindness. While they certainly were acts of kindness and expressions of
deep compassion, they were much more than that. They were evidence that
the kingdom of God had come near in the person of Jesus. The Gospels
routinely portray Jesus healing, forgiving, restoring, and liberating people,
not hurting, condemning, or oppressing them. Why? Because violence has
no place in the kingdom of God. In God's kingdom, people are healed, not
harmed. This explains why Jesus behaves the way he does.

This point is worth stressing since it demonstrates that nonviolence
was characteristic of Jesus' *entire* way of life. It was not *only* evident in what
he taught or how he responded in certain situations, it was representative
of how he lived day in and day out. By proclaiming the kingdom of God
in both word *and* deed in one town after the next, Jesus embodied God's
nonviolent reign of peace and justice and invited others to join in.

Two Final Considerations

Before concluding, we should briefly note two additional pieces of evidence
that further suggest Jesus was nonviolent and taught his disciples to be nonviolent. Both are rooted in history and take us beyond arguments that can
be made from the Bible alone.

Did the Roman Authorities View Jesus and His Band of Disciples as Violent?

One interesting aspect of the story of Jesus that provides at least indirect
evidence that Jesus did not advocate violence concerns the way his disciples
were treated after his arrest and crucifixion. If Jesus was arming his disciples
for violent insurrection, they too would have been regarded as a threat to
the Roman authorities and would have been punished accordingly. But they
are left alone. As Simon Joseph remarks, "The fact that Jesus—but not his
disciples—was arrested by the Temple guards, and that Jesus—but none of

his disciples—were executed by Pilate has rightly been recognized as a major argument *against* seeing Jesus or his movement as nationalistic, violent, or militaristic."[40] This is a fairly compelling line of reasoning.

What Did the Early Church Believe Jesus Taught about Violence and Killing?

Another line of evidence that strongly supports the view that Jesus taught nonviolence is the historical witness of the early church. As Ron Sider rightly observes:

> What the earliest Christians in the first three centuries understood to be the teaching of Jesus on killing surely has some relevance for our understanding of what Jesus taught. We cannot simply assume that the early Christians accurately understood Jesus's teachings. But it seems plausible to suppose that Christians much closer to the time of Jesus . . . would be more likely to understand Jesus's teaching on loving enemies than those who lived centuries later.[41]

So what did Christians in the first few centuries of the early church believe Jesus taught about violence and killing? The most extensive collection of primary sources related to this question is found in Sider's book, *The Early Church on Killing: A Comprehensive Sourcebook on War, Abortion, and Capital Punishment*. In it he provides English translations of "all extant data directly relevant to the witness of the early church on killing."[42] Based on his thorough analysis of this data, he concludes that "until the time of Constantine [fourth century CE], there is not a single Christian writer known to us who says that it is legitimate for Christians to kill or join the military."[43] In fact, these sources suggest "the rejection of killing is comprehensive" and "includes abortion, capital punishment, gladiatorial contests (even watching them), infanticide, and warfare."[44]

A similar conclusion is expressed by Rob Arner in his book, *Consistently Pro-Life: The Ethics of Bloodshed in Ancient Christianity*. Like Sider, he too is interested in examining Christian attitudes toward violence and killing in the pre-Constantinian church. What he finds confirms the nonviolent

---

40. Joseph, *Nonviolent Messiah*, 37, fn. 77, emphasis original.

41. Sider, *Early Church on Killing*, 13.

42. Ibid., 14.

43. Ibid., 190.

44. Ibid., 191.

view of Jesus emphasized in this chapter. "Without exception," writes Arner, "the church strongly condemned the taking of human life in any form whatsoever. Neither homicide nor feticide, nor infanticide, nor suicide, nor capital punishment, nor killing in war were considered acceptable to a church fiercely committed to following the teaching and moral example of the incarnate Lord."[45] The rejection of violence and killing by early Christians is strong *historical* evidence that Jesus had indeed, both lived and taught nonviolence.

Conclusion

Some Christians believe there is no better reason for rejecting violence than the example of Jesus. As Harriet Bicksler puts it:

> The bottom line for me . . . in terms of the biblical basis for peacemaking has always been the example of Jesus. Try as I might, I can't imagine Jesus pushing the button to release a bomb, firing a gun at someone, or engaging in a knock-down, drag-out fistfight with an adversary. This is not to say that Jesus didn't vigorously confront evil and wrongdoing; in fact, he overturned the tables of the moneychangers and condemned the Pharisees for their hypocrisy and self-righteousness. But I just can't imagine him deliberately hurting or killing another human being.[46]

Throughout this chapter, we have considered various pieces of evidence that confirm this view of Jesus. We examined Jesus' key teachings about nonviolence in the Sermon on the Mount and discussed how Jesus explicitly rejected violence on numerous occasions. We also emphasized the importance of Jesus' message about the kingdom of God—God's nonviolent reign of peace and justice—and considered how Jesus embodied this kingdom through his life and ministry by healing people rather than harming them, and by extending compassion rather than condemnation. All this evidence leads us to see Jesus as nonviolent.

Later, we will say more about how this view of Jesus informs Christian discipleship.[47] But first, we need to address a prior question, one that threatens to undermine this nonviolent view of Jesus. The question is simply this: What are we to do with New Testament passages that some people believe portray Jesus behaving violently or encouraging others to behave violently?

45. Arner, *Consistently Pro-Life*, 120.
46. Bicksler, "Pursuing Peace," 132.
47. See chapter 7.

For instance, how should we understand Jesus' actions in the temple, his words about not coming to bring peace but a sword, and his insistence that his disciples buy swords? And what are we to make or Jesus' teaching about eschatological judgment and eternal punishment? Do these things negate a nonviolent view of Jesus, or are there ways of understanding these passages that are consistent with the portrait of Jesus we have developed in this chapter?

6

A Violent Jesus?

Responding to Objections to Viewing Jesus as Nonviolent

The revelation of Jesus in the New Testament is no less violent than the revelation of God in the Old Testament.

—TREMPER LONGMAN III[1]

THOUGH MANY AGREE THAT Jesus was nonviolent, not everyone sees him that way. There are skeptics. Some believe Jesus behaved violently at times and also incited violence among his followers. Such a view of Jesus was recently popularized in Reza Aslan's New York Times best-selling book, *Zealot: The Life and Times of Jesus of Nazareth* (2013).[2] Aslan sees Jesus as "a man of profound contradictions . . . sometimes calling for unconditional peace . . . sometimes promoting violence and conflict."[3] Aslan believes Jesus is best understood as a violent revolutionary when the available evidence is interpreted in light of Jesus' historical context.[4]

1. Longman, "Response to C. S. Cowles," 58–59.
2. For Aslan's now infamous interview with Fox News correspondent Lauren Green, see https://www.youtube.com/watch?v=Jt1cOnNrY5s.
3. Aslan, *Zealot*, xxiv, citing Matt 5:9 and Luke 22:36, respectively.
4. For an older attempt to argue that Jesus was a violent revolutionary—and one that posits a 2,000-year attempt to conceal this fact—see Brandon, *Jesus and the Zealots*. Brandon's views are rejected by most contemporary New Testament scholars (so Desjardins, *Peace, Violence and the New Testament*, 117).

Other scholars, like Professor Michel Desjardins, also associate violence with Jesus and his disciples. "Throughout the New Testament," writes Desjardins, "Jesus and his followers can be found accepting, condoning, and even inciting violence."[5] Hector Avalos would concur. In his recently published book, *The Bad Jesus*, Avalos argues that Jesus was violent and did many things that were unethical and, therefore, "bad." He writes, "Jesus is sometimes portrayed as endorsing violence and as actually committing violence."[6]

So what are we to make of such claims? Did Jesus behave violently at times? Did he call upon his disciples to engage in acts of violence? These are important questions to consider, especially in a book urging Christians to *reject* violence and follow the nonviolent way of Jesus.

Was Jesus Violent?

To determine what merit there is in these arguments that Jesus was violent, we need to investigate some of the New Testament passages routinely used to support this view.[7] That will help us understand why some people believe Jesus was violent and will provide an opportunity to consider alternative interpretations. We will begin by exploring Jesus' so-called "cleansing of the temple," arguably the most often cited passage in discussions about Jesus and violence.

Jesus Cleanses the Temple (Mark 11:15–19)

The story of Jesus' behavior in the temple is sometimes regarded as irrefutable evidence that Jesus sometimes behaved violently. It is not difficult to understand why some people see it that way. After all, Jesus did flip over tables and drive people and animals from the temple precincts while wielding a whip. The incident is recorded in all four Gospels, though certain

---

5. Desjardins, *Peace, Violence and the New Testament*, 66. Cf. ibid., 72.

6. Avalos, *Bad Jesus*, 90.

7. For a convenient look at older scholarship dealing with passages some people believe suggest Jesus was violent or endorsed violence, see Swartley, *Slavery, Sabbath, War, and Women*, 250–55. Swartley identifies twenty-four New Testament passages sometimes used to challenge the legitimacy of pacifism and selects the works of eight individuals who have responded to these challenges, indicating which of the twenty-four passages they address. These writers provide "what they regard to be explanations which show that the texts do not jeopardize the pacifist position, but in some cases even directly support it" (ibid., 250).

details vary from one account to the next (e.g., the whip only appears in John's gospel).[8] Here is Mark's version of the story:

> Then they came to Jerusalem. And he [Jesus] entered the temple and began to drive out those who were selling and those who were buying in the temple, and he overturned the tables of the money changers and the seats of those who sold doves; and he would not allow anyone to carry anything through the temple. He was teaching and saying, "Is it not written, 'My house shall be called a house of prayer for all the nations'? But you have made it a den of robbers." And when the chief priests and the scribes heard it, they kept looking for a way to kill him; for they were afraid of him, because the whole crowd was spellbound by his teaching. And when evening came, Jesus and his disciples went out of the city (Mark 11:15–19).

Should Jesus' actions in the temple be regarded as violent? George Aichele thinks so. He believes this interpretation is strengthened by the fact that the temple "cleansing" is bracketed by the account of Jesus cursing a barren fig tree, a story which both precedes and follows this account (see Mark 11:12–14, 20–24).[9] According to Aichele, both stories—temple cleansing and tree cursing—reveal Jesus behaving violently. "By intercalating these two stories," writes Aichele, "the gospel of Mark highlights the violence at the center of each of them."[10] Likewise, Desjardins believes this story displays "Jesus' apparent willingness to use violence," though Desjardins concedes that "not many of Jesus' actions fall under this category."[11]

Whether you believe Jesus behaved violently in the temple probably hangs on one of two things: 1) your definition of violence, and 2) your understanding of what Jesus did with the whip. Since we already spent some time discussing definitions in chapter 1, I will just focus on Jesus' use of the whip. Since this is arguably the most sensational aspect of the story, it is very important to be clear about what kind of whip this was and how Jesus used it. Here is what we are told in John's account:

> In the temple he [Jesus] found people selling cattle, sheep, and doves, and the money changers seated at their tables. Making a whip of cords, he drove all of them out of the temple, both the sheep and the cattle. He also poured out the coins of the money changers and overturned their tables (John 2:14–15).

8. Matt 21:12–17; Mark 11:15–19; Luke 19:45–48; John 2:13–22.
9. Aichele, "Jesus' Violence," 83–5.
10. Ibid., 84.
11. Desjardins, *Peace, Violence and the New Testament*, 76.

There are several points worth considering with regard to this whip.

First, it is important to note that Jesus made this whip *in the temple* (John 2:15). He was not toting it around with him from place to place to use on people whenever they got out of line. Rather, he crafted it on the spot, implying it was something of a makeshift implement. Second, the whip is made from rope. It is called a "whip of cords." The word for "cords" only occurs twice in the New Testament, here and in Acts 27:32. In Acts, it refers to rope used to moor a boat to a dock. Jesus' whip was made of rope, nothing more. It was *not* like a Roman whip, which often had sharp objects embedded in it to inflict maximum pain and harm. Third, although there is a difference of opinion on this point, it seems Jesus directed the whip toward animals only and not toward people.[12] Moreover, the purpose of the whip was to remove these animals from the temple precincts, not to harm them. Even if you think the text allows for the possibility that Jesus directed the whip toward both animals *and* people, the makeshift nature of this rope whip makes it highly unlikely that buyers and sellers would have regarded it as a weapon. Nor is it likely that people left the temple because they anticipated violence at the hands of Jesus. That sort of behavior would have been inconsistent with everything they knew about Jesus from other contexts. Fourth, we are never told Jesus actually hits anyone or anything with this whip of cords.[13] Nothing in any of the accounts suggests Jesus inflicted bodily harm on anyone. "No one is hurt or killed in Jesus' Temple demonstration."[14] Had they been, I suspect Jesus would have been in serious trouble with the authorities. All this seems to suggest Jesus is not behaving violently in this instance.

To be sure, there is no question that Jesus acts very forcefully in the temple. Any lingering sentimental images of Jesus "meek and mild" fly out the window when reading this text. Still, there is nothing about Jesus' actions that should lead us to regard them as being violent.[15] Jesus behaves in the tradition of the prophets, and prophets sometimes used symbolic acts to get people's attention and to communicate their message in powerful and persuasive ways. For example, Jeremiah wore a yoke on his neck in an attempt to persuade the people of Judah to submit to the Babylonians (Jer 27), and Isaiah walked around naked for three years to discourage the people of

12. This case is strongly made by Croy, "Messianic Whippersnapper."

13. For a sustained argument that Jesus did *not* actually hit people or animals with his makeshift whip, one that examines both the history of interpretation of John 2:13–15 and key exegetical concerns, see Alexis-Baker, "Violence, Nonviolence and the Temple Incident."

14. Hays, *Moral Vision*, 334–35.

15. On the distinction between "force" and "violence," see chapter 11.

Israel from trusting in Egypt for military deliverance from the Assyrians (Isa 20). While these symbolic acts were certainly provocative, they were not harmful. Likewise, while Jesus' actions in the temple were forceful and dramatic (people would be talking about this over dinner), they were not violent or destructive (which is why Jesus was not arrested on the spot).[16]

In fact, rather than viewing Jesus' actions in the temple as an aberration, a violent outburst that casts aspersions on his commitment to nonviolence, it is better to interpret Jesus' behavior as fully consistent with his core message about the kingdom of God. The temple system had become a place of corruption, extortion, and oppression. Jesus acts to set things right. As Willard Swartley describes it:

> The wrong he [Jesus] protests is the use of the temple court for money changing, necessary for Passover pilgrims because only Jewish coins could be used to purchase the animals. . . . Coin exchange, from Roman to Jewish money to purchase an animal for sacrifice, became a gross extortion of the poor. Jesus' action is a *nonviolent* protest against the economic desecration of the temple.[17]

Seeing injustice at work in the temple, Jesus takes decisive steps to confront it. Such behavior comports nicely with the nonviolent image of Jesus explored previously.[18]

Jesus Commands His Followers to Buy Swords (Luke 22:35–38)

The so-called "two swords passage" in Luke 22:35–38 is another biblical text that often comes up in discussions about whether or not Jesus was nonviolent. This passage, which occurs only in Luke's gospel, contains some instructions Jesus gave to his disciples just before he was arrested.

> He [Jesus] said to them, "When I sent you out without a purse, bag, or sandals, did you lack anything?" They said, "No, not a thing." He said to them, "But now, the one who has a purse must take it, and likewise a bag. And the one who has no sword must sell his cloak and buy one. For I tell you, this scripture must

16. This is a significant point, especially since the religious officials were looking for a reason to kill Jesus (Mark 11:18; Luke 19:47). If Jesus was behaving violently in the temple, this would have at least been grounds for arrest.

17. Swartley, *John*, 99, emphasis mine.

18. Bredin argues that "Jesus' action in the temple is exemplary and courageous" and calls Jesus "the nonviolent revolutionary of peace par excellence" ("John's Account," 50. See 44–50).

> be fulfilled in me, 'And he was counted among the lawless'; and
> indeed what is written about me is being fulfilled." They said,
> "Lord, look, here are two swords." He replied, "It is enough"
> (Luke 22:35–38).

Obviously, the big question here is why Jesus tells disciples without a sword
to buy one. Did Jesus want his disciples to have this for self-defense? Was he
equipping the disciples to fight and kill their Roman oppressors? Or is there
another way of understanding what Jesus meant by these words?

One of the most important things to consider when interpreting this
passage is whether Jesus' words were meant to be taken literally or figuratively. We know Jesus often spoke in parables and regularly used various
figures of speech to communicate his message. Sometimes, it is fairly obvious how we should interpret Jesus' words. For instance, when Jesus says
we should tear out our right eye if it causes us to sin (Matt 5:29), we realize
Jesus is speaking figuratively, not advocating self-mutilation.[19] Otherwise,
we would all be blind.

So how should we understand Jesus' instruction to buy swords? At first
glance, it might seem best to take Jesus' words literally. After all, when his
disciples produce two swords on the spot, Jesus says, "It is enough" (*ikanon
estin*).[20] Doesn't that imply Jesus wanted his disciples to have real swords
in hand? It seems that a great deal hangs on how we hear the *tone* of Jesus' reply. When Jesus says "it is enough," perhaps he is saying two swords
are *sufficient*; they are all that is needed. Of course, this begs the question,
needed for what? If two swords are enough, Jesus cannot be encouraging
his disciples to take up arms against the Romans. Two swords against the
Roman Empire are bad odds.

Simon Joseph suggests the purpose of having these swords was more
symbolic than functional. Joseph focuses on the reason Jesus himself gives
for instructing the disciples to buy a sword, namely, that it was necessary to
fulfill scripture:

> For I tell you, this scripture must be fulfilled in me, "And he was
> counted among the lawless"; and indeed what is written about
> me is being fulfilled (Luke 22:37).

As Joseph explains, "Jesus needed to be 'numbered among the lawless' in
order to fulfill Isa. 53:12."[21] Since "criminals were known for being armed,"

---

19. Jesus is commanding people to do whatever is necessary (apart from harming
themselves and others) to eliminate things from their lives that cause them to sin.

20. Why these disciples already possess two swords is unclear.

21. Joseph, *Nonviolent Messiah*, 29.

writes Joseph, "the two swords . . . serve a *symbolic* function: not to justify violence but to fulfill scripture."[22] If this explanation is correct, it also helps us understand why Jesus would command his disciples to buy swords without allowing them to use these swords later in the day when the crowd came to arrest him. The swords were only to serve as symbols, never as weapons.

But maybe we should hear Jesus' tone differently. Rather than conveying his contentment with two literal swords, perhaps Jesus is expressing *exasperation* with the disciples' failure to grasp the true meaning of his words. This is especially plausible when you realize Jesus' response could be translated, "Enough, already!"[23] or "Enough of that."[24] Support for this translation comes from a similar expression found in the Greek translation of Deut 3:26. After recounting his unsuccessful efforts to convince God to allow him to lead the people of Israel into the promised land, Moses says, "But the LORD was angry with me on your account and would not heed me. The LORD said to me, 'Enough from you (*ikanoustho soi*)! Never speak to me of this matter again!'" Apparently, God is tired of Moses asking and wants him to stop making this request. Assuming this is the same tone Jesus used with his disciples, Jesus' response seems to be "an expression of his exasperation"[25] or "impatient dismissal"[26] since Jesus' closest followers still do not get it. As Joel Green observes, "The apostles manifest their dullness when they suppose that Jesus opposes his own extensive and emphatic teaching by encouraging them actually to possess (or to purchase) weaponry."[27] The disciples have not yet grasped the true nature of the kingdom Jesus was inaugurating, prompting them to take literally words Jesus intended figuratively.[28]

If Jesus' words are to be understood figuratively, just what was Jesus trying to say? Context is especially helpful here. Jesus has just reminded his disciples of an earlier time when he had sent them out without purse, bag, or sandals (see Luke 10:1–6). At that time, they were to depend upon the

---

22. Ibid., emphasis original.

23. Hays, *Moral Vision*, 333.

24. Fitzmyer, *Luke*, 1,428.

25. Green, *Gospel of Luke*, 775.

26. Hays, *Moral Vision*, 333. Cf. Marshall who regards it "as a rebuke" (*Gospel of Luke*, 827).

27. Green, *Gospel of Luke*, 775. Similarly, Marshall writes, "The disciples fail to understand; taking Jesus literally, they produce two swords, and Jesus has to rebuke them for their lack of comprehension—a lack that will become even more evident when Jesus is arrested" (*Gospel of Luke*, 823–24).

28. Marshall sees this as the climax of the upper-room discourse where the disciples repeatedly misunderstand what Jesus is saying (*Gospel of Luke*, 823).

hospitality of others—and they lacked nothing.[29] But those days are over. Jesus' betrayal and arrest are imminent, and everything is about to change. By telling his disciples they should now take a purse and a bag, and should buy a sword if they do not have one, he is informing them, albeit figuratively, that grave dangers lie ahead. He is not giving them a laundry list of items to acquire but is letting them know things are going to be different this time around. Now they need to be prepared to suffer and perhaps even die. This is consistent with the nonviolent nature of Jesus' teachings discussed in the previous chapter and with the nonviolent nature of discipleship we will explore in the following chapter.

If there are any lingering suspicions that Jesus' instructions about buying swords were intended to arm his disciples for a fight, they are quickly laid to rest several verses later when the crowds come to arrest Jesus. As discussed previously, the disciples ask Jesus if they should use violence and before Jesus has a chance to reply, Peter starts swinging his sword and manages to cut off the high priest slave's right ear (Luke 22:50). Jesus' response is swift and unequivocal. "No more of this!," Jesus says, and then heals the slave's severed ear (Luke 22:51). In this incident, "literal armed resistance is exposed as a foolish misunderstanding of Jesus' message," as Hays puts it.[30] Whatever Jesus meant when he said his disciples should buy swords, it clearly had nothing to do with purchasing weapons to harm others.[31] That was not the kind of discipleship Jesus had in mind.

Jesus Declares He Has Not Come to Bring Peace, But a Sword (Matt 10:34–36)

On the face of it, the words of Jesus recorded in Matt 10:34 do not sound very nonviolent:

> Do not think that I have come to bring peace to the earth; I have
> not come to bring peace, but a sword (Matt 10:34).

This seems to run counter to all we have been saying about the life and ministry of Jesus. Is Jesus claiming he has come to incite violence? Hector Avalos thinks so. He regards this saying as "the most explicit affirmation that Jesus views himself as coming to bring war, not peace to the earth," and

---

29. Cf. Hays, *Moral Vision*, 333.

30. Ibid.

31. As Green puts it, "The possibility that Jesus' followers are literally to respond to hostility with a sword—that is, with violence—is negated in 22:49–51" (*Gospel of Luke*, 774).

speaks of "Jesus' rhetoric" here as "blatantly violent."[32] Is it? How should we assess these words of Jesus?

Once again, in order to understand what Jesus means, it is very important to pay attention to the context. The disciples are about to embark on a preaching and healing mission, and Jesus is giving them words of instruction and advice. He warns that trials and adversity lie ahead (Matt 10:16–23). Some will be taken to court; others will be beaten and even killed. They can expect to be hated and persecuted, but they are not to fear because they are ultimately under God's care. Thus, while the disciples can expect to be recipients of violence, nothing here encourages them to be perpetrators of it.

This context informs and clarifies the words of Jesus in Matt 10:34, words meant to be understood figuratively rather than literally. Jesus is *not* saying he is on a violent mission rather than a peaceful one. Nor is he suggesting that his disciples are to behave violently toward others. He is simply articulating the effect the gospel will have when some people accept his message and others do not. As Hays explains it, "The 'sword' of verse 34 is a metaphor for the division that will occur between those who proclaim the good news of the kingdom and those who refuse to receive it."[33] This is supported by the parallel passage in Luke which reads, "Do you think that I have come to bring peace to the earth? No, I tell you, but rather division!" (Luke 12:51).

Jesus' words in Matt 10:34 are further clarified in the verses which follow: "For I [Jesus] have come to set a man against his father, and a daughter against her mother, and a daughter-in-law against her mother-in-law; and one's foes will be members of one's own household" (Matt 10:35–36). Jesus recognizes his message will be disruptive to family systems. Since following Jesus demands one's ultimate allegiance, it inevitably stresses certain relationships, especially those not similarly aligned. Ask any Muslim, Hindu, or Buddhist who has converted to Christianity, when the rest of their family has not, and they will be able to verify this. Jesus is simply alerting his disciples to these difficult realities. He is *not* endorsing violence or promoting war.[34]

---

32. Avalos, *Bad Jesus*, 91. Cf. Desjardins who regards this as one of a number of sayings which "present Jesus as intent on disrupting people's lives" (*Peace, Violence and the New Testament*, 73).

33. Hays, *Moral Vision*, 332.

34. "To read this verse as a warrant for the use of violence by Christians is to commit an act of extraordinary hermeneutical violence against the text" (ibid., 333).

Is Jesus Verbally Violent with Scribes and Pharisees?

Admittedly, some of the things Jesus said about the religious leaders of his day do not sound very loving or nonviolent. Take, for example, the way Jesus speaks about the scribes and Pharisees. He compares them to "whitewashed tombs" and calls them a "brood of vipers" (Matt 23:27, 33). Today, such language would be regarded as caustic and cruel. Some might even accuse Jesus of being verbally violent. Yet before we rush to judgment and condemn Jesus for such seemingly inflammatory rhetoric, perhaps we should pause to ask how this language would have been perceived in the ancient world. Is it possible that the rhetoric Jesus uses, though harsh to our ears, may have sounded very different in that ancient culture and context?

There is evidence to suggest that the aggressive (and one might even say abrasive) speech we hear in Matthew 23 and elsewhere in the Gospels was neither uncommon nor unusual in Jewish debates in Jesus' day. "Sharp and inflated language roundly condemning what are judged to be failures or excesses on the part of one's opponents," writes Donald Senior in his commentary on Matthew, "was characteristic of such intra-Jewish debate and has precedents in the Bible and in extracanonical Jewish texts of this epoch."[35] In other words, such speech was regarded as both normal *and* appropriate in that historical-cultural context. Even though some of Jesus' words may appear hostile, ungracious, or even violent to us, it is quite likely they were not regarded the same way in the ancient world.

Obviously, our social context is quite different from the one Jesus inhabited in the first century. In light of this, it comes as no great surprise that certain forms of speech and public discourse that were acceptable in Jesus' day are no longer acceptable today. Even though the kind of rhetoric Jesus used with his opponents is still quite common today, it is no longer regarded as "normal" or "appropriate." We know there are better, more respectful, ways to communicate with one another. This is something we are taught early in life by trusted teachers, parents, pastors, and other authority figures.

Therefore, when assessing Jesus' language, it is crucial to remember the difference between his context and ours. Jesus lived in the *first* century, not the twenty-first. We should not expect Jesus to sound like a contemporary peacemaker or nonviolent practitioner. Nor should we evaluate Jesus' rhetoric by modern ethical standards and use those to accuse Jesus of being verbally violent. Instead, his words must be evaluated by the ethical standards and conventions of his particular time and place, namely, first-century

---

35. Senior, *Matthew*, 31. Quoted in Swartley, *Covenant of Peace*, 70.

Palestine. When this is done, even his most colorful language is much more understandable and far less problematic. [36]

Is Jesus an Apocalyptic Avenger?

Some people question whether it is accurate to speak of Jesus being non-violent given the way the Gospels and the book of Revelation sometimes describe him acting at the end of time. For example, in Matt 13:41–42 we read, "The Son of Man [Jesus] will send his angels, and they will collect out of his kingdom all causes of sin and all evildoers, and they will throw them into the furnace of fire, where there will be weeping and gnashing of teeth." And in the great final judgment scene near the end of Matthew's gospel, the Son of Man separates people into two groups based on their deeds. One group inherits the kingdom of God, the other goes "into the eternal fire prepared for the devil and his angels" (Matt 25:41). To many ears, Jesus' end-time behavior in passages like these certainly sounds violent.

Similarly, many readers believe some portrayals of Jesus in the book of Revelation are anything but peaceful, like the one described in this dramatic passage:

> Then I saw heaven opened, and there was a white horse! Its rider is called Faithful and True, and in righteousness he judges and makes war. His eyes are like a flame of fire, and on his head are many diadems; and he has a name inscribed that no one knows but himself. He is clothed in a robe dipped in blood, and his name is called The Word of God. And the armies of heaven, wearing fine linen, white and pure, were following him on white horses. From his mouth comes a sharp sword with which to strike down the nations, and he will rule them with a rod of iron; he will tread the wine press of the fury of the wrath of God the Almighty. On his robe and on his thigh he has a name inscribed, "King of kings and Lord of lords" (Rev 19:11–16).

Some people believe texts like these suggest Jesus is going to be involved in some serious violence at the end of the age. As Mark Driscoll so colorfully expresses it, "In Revelation, Jesus is a pride fighter with a tattoo down His leg, a sword in His hand and the commitment to make someone bleed."[37]

---

36. It is also possible that not all these words originate with Jesus in the article.
37. *Relevent*, "7 Big Questions." See also Driscoll, "Is God a Pacifist?".

But is this how the author of Revelation meant for us to understand Jesus, as someone intent on making heads roll and bodies bleed? I think not. The book of Revelation is primarily apocalyptic literature, a genre that overflows with symbols not meant to be taken literally. When people fail to realize this, it creates all sorts of interpretive problems and leads them to conclude that Revelation presents a very violent portrait of Jesus. As C. S. Cowles observes:

> By interpreting its highly symbolic language literally, the non-violent Jesus of the Gospels is transformed into a violent warrior. . . . Thus, like Clark Kent emerging from the telephone booth as Superman, Jesus at his return will cast aside his servant garments and will disclose who he really is: a fierce, merciless, and physically violent eschatological terminator who will make the blood of his enemies flow knee-deep as in the days of Joshua.[38]

Those who interpret the book of Revelation this way are surely misreading it. "Revelation is not portraying Jesus returning to earth in the future, having repented of his naive gospel ways," writes Brian McLaren.[39] Commenting specifically on Rev 19:11–16, McLaren says:

> The passage in question isn't telling us Jesus is a prize-fighter with a commitment to make somebody bleed. Nor is it claiming that the Jesus of the gospels was a fake-me-out Jesus pretending to be a peace-and-love guy, when really he was planning to come back and act like a proper Caesar, more of a slash-and-burn guy, brutal, willing to torture, and determined to conquer with crushing violence.[40]

Instead, Revelation portrays Jesus as the one who *was* slain, not as the one who slays. He is the victim of violence, not the perpetrator. The blood mentioned in Revelation 19 is Jesus' *own* blood, not that of his enemies. Likewise, Jesus' "sword" is not a weapon in his hand, but words on his lips. As numerous commentators rightly observe, this passage is not about a physical battle at all. Instead, it refers to a different kind of judgment, one that involves words rather than weapons.

In the book of Revelation, Jesus overcomes—or rather, Jesus overcame—by his death and resurrection. The victory of God over sin, evil, and death is achieved by a slain lamb, not an apocalyptic avenger. This

38. Cowles, "Response to Tremper Longman III," 193.

39. McLaren, *New Kind of Christianity*, 125.

40. Ibid., 124.

demonstrates that God's response to violence is not more violence. Rather, it is suffering love.

But what of Jesus' sayings about eschatological judgment recorded in the Gospels? How are they consistent with a nonviolent view of Jesus? When reading these passages, passages that speak about people weeping and gnashing their teeth, being thrown into fire or outer darkness, or suffering "eternal punishment," there are several things to bear in mind. First, Jesus is speaking metaphorically and symbolically, using potent images to convey the unpleasantness and seriousness of divine judgment. It would be a mistake to interpret these sayings literalistically. Second, when Jesus uses these images, he does so to emphasize the importance of right living here and now. Jesus uses these powerful images about the future to encourage people to make good choices in the present. Third, Jesus does *not* speak about eschatological judgment in order to depict exactly what judgment will look like in the hereafter. The precise nature of the judgment to come is never actually specified in any of these sayings. As I have written elsewhere:

> This lack of specificity is significant since it allows for the possibility of divine punishment that is *not* violent. Since it is easy to envision various forms of punishment that are not inherently violent—consider the many kinds of noncorporal punishment parents use—one cannot simply assume that individuals who suffer eschatological divine judgment necessarily experience eschatological divine violence. We just do not know whether their punishment will—or will not—involve the use of violence.[41]

In fact, given what we do know about God's character revealed through Jesus elsewhere in the Gospels, the possibility of a *violent* eschatological ending for the unrepentant seems very unlikely. As Sharon Baker asks in her gracious and provocative book, *Razing Hell,* "Which vision of hell most coheres with the God revealed in Jesus—the view of hell in which persons suffer for all eternity with no hope for reconciliation with God, or the view of hell in which persons understand the depth of their sins, take full responsibility for them, and reconcile not only with God, but also with their victims?"[42] Finally, it has been suggested that some (or perhaps all) of the sayings about divine judgment attributed to Jesus did not originate with him but rather reflect later attitudes and beliefs of Christians in the early church.[43]

41. Seibert, *Disturbing Divine Behavior,* 253, emphasis original.

42. Baker, *Razing Hell,* 124. For variety of different perspectives on the nature of hell, see Sprinkle, ed., *Four Views on Hell.*

43. See Joseph, *Nonviolent Messiah,* 71–89, *et passim.*

Although a more adequate discussion of these issues lies beyond the scope of this present study, I hope enough has been said to demonstrate the validity of reading and interpreting these sayings about eschatological judgment in ways that do not require us to posit a violent Jesus. In recent years, biblical scholars and theologians have been reassessing these passages, challenging us to rethink more traditional views of hell and what divine judgment does, or does not, entail.[44] This should encourage us to consider carefully how we use these passages to form our beliefs about the final judgment and about the character of Jesus. At the very least, it should prompt us to proceed with caution and to avoid simply assuming Jesus will come in wrath the second time when he came in love the first.

Conclusion

Most people who are unconvinced Jesus was nonviolent generally appeal to a handful of passages to support that view.[45] We have considered a number of these passages in this chapter and suggested alternate ways of understanding them.[46] While some may regard these efforts as little more than hermeneutical sleight of hand, a clever attempt to "explain away" problem passages by conjuring up interpretations that nicely align with preconceived notions of a nonviolent Jesus, that has not been my intent. Instead, I have tried to demonstrate that upon closer investigation, many New Testament passages routinely cited as evidence of Jesus' violent proclivities reveal nothing of the sort. Whether the passage in question concerns Jesus' actions in the temple, his instructions about buying a sword, the statement about not coming to bring peace, or something else, none of these reveals a violent Jesus when rightly understood. There are other ways—and I would argue more accurate ways—of interpreting these passages that do not suggest Jesus condoned violence in any way. While his teaching and actions were certainly disruptive—especially to the status quo—they were not violent.

The approach I have taken in this chapter, to respond to "problem passages" one by one, may obscure a larger, more substantive critique I have of these attempts to "violanize" Jesus. Those who interpret parts of the

44. On hell, see Baker, *Razing Hell.* For an extensive treatment of passages dealing with eschatological judgment, see Neville, *Peaceable Hope.*

45. Though for an extensive and forceful critique of Jesus' behavior and character, see Avalos, *Bad Jesus.*

46. In chapter 8, we will also consider Jesus' positive interaction with a centurion (Matt 8:5–13 a Luke 7:1–10) since some believe this suggests Jesus was not opposed to soldiering and warfare.

Gospels as portraying a violent Jesus regularly fail to engage all the evidence which suggests otherwise. Instead, they highlight a few passages, which they believe show Jesus behaving violently, and use these to disprove Jesus was nonviolent. By focusing attention on isolated passages that seem to support their violent view of Jesus, they miss the forest for the trees.

As demonstrated in the previous chapter—and as we will see in coming one—the overwhelming evidence in the New Testament points in completely the opposite direction. Jesus teaches love and inclusivity, not hate and exclusivity. Jesus calls people to lives of service, forgiveness, and reconciliation, *not* to patterns of domination, retaliation, and revenge. Passages that reveal Jesus' fundamental commitment to help and heal, rather than hurt and harm, are ubiquitous in the Gospels. Moreover, his most frequent talking point, the kingdom of God, emphasizes God's nonviolent reign of peace and justice.

Those who wish to argue that Jesus was violent, and that he taught his disciples to be violent, need to do more than just highlight a few texts they believe support that claim. They need to explain how the full force of Jesus' life and teachings point in that direction. How do Jesus' teachings about serving others, forgiving offenders, and loving enemies imply that his followers are to be violent? How does Jesus' explicit rejection of violence on numerous occasions, along with his willingness to suffer and die on the cross, fit with assertions that he was violent? We dare not allow a few apparent outliers to dictate our view of Jesus, especially when these passages can reasonably—and I would argue most accurately—be interpreted in ways that are consistent with the nonviolent view of Jesus that dominates the New Testament.

7

Why Followers of Jesus Must Forsake Violence
The Nonviolent Nature of Christian Discipleship

To the extent that we pick up the sword, we put down the cross.
—GREGORY A. BOYD[1]

Nonviolence is right not because it works but because it is the way of Jesus.
—DAVID AUGSBURGER[2]

IF YOU WERE RANDOMLY to survey people on the street and ask them what it means to be a Christian, you would certainly get a wide range of answers. Some might define a Christian as someone who believes in God, goes to church regularly, and is basically a good person. Others might say something about being "born again," asking Jesus into their heart, or trusting in God's mercy to forgive their sins. Still others might emphasize a willingness to affirm historic Christian creeds, like the Apostles' Creed or the Nicene Creed. So what is it that makes a person a Christian?

An interesting anecdote told by Amir Hussain is helpful in thinking through this question. Hussain recounts an interchange between Wilfred

---

1. Boyd, *Myth of a Christian Nation*, 95.
2. Augsburger, *Dissident Discipleship*, 138.

Cantwell Smith—who was both his mentor and one of the foremost Canadian scholars of religion—and an interlocutor:

> Someone asked Wilfred, "Professor Smith, are you Christian?"
> If the question had been "are you *a* Christian", the answer would
> have been a very simple "yes", a member of the United Church of
> Canada. Instead, Wilfred did what he always did when asked a
> question. He paused, repeated the question, and thought about
> his answer. "Am I Christian", he said. "Maybe, I was, last week.
> On a Tuesday. At lunch. For about an hour. But if you really
> want to know, ask my neighbor."[3]

Smith's rather unusual answer underscores the fact that our words and deeds are ultimately the true test of our Christian character and commitment. While our salvation is not contingent upon the good deeds we do, *being* Christian involves *living* a certain way. To be more specific, being Christian means being like Christ. And being like Christ requires being his disciple. Therefore, being (a) Christian is fundamentally about being a disciple of Jesus. Yet, this does not seem to be how many people in the church view it today.

Is Discipleship Really Necessary?

Dallas Willard, a highly regarded author and speaker on Christian spirituality, makes this dramatic observation in his book *The Great Omission: Reclaiming Jesus' Essential Teachings on Discipleship*:

> For at least several decades the churches of the Western world
> have not made discipleship a condition of being a Christian.
> One is not required to be, or to intend to be, a disciple in order
> to become a Christian, and one may remain a Christian without
> any signs of progress toward or in discipleship. Contemporary
> American churches in particular do not require following Christ
> in his example, spirit, and teachings as a condition of member-
> ship—either of entering into or continuing in fellowship of a
> denomination or local church. I would be glad to learn of any
> exception to this claim, but it would only serve to highlight its
> general validity and make the general rule more glaring. So far
> as the visible Christian institutions of our day are concerned,
> *discipleship clearly is optional.*[4]

3. Hussain, "Building Faith Neighbors," 32.

4. Willard, *Great Omission*, 4, emphasis original. While I generally agree with Willard, he somewhat overstates the case. There are some expressions of Christianity—like

Willard regards the church's decision to behave as though discipleship is optional as the "great omission" from the "great commission," the final words of Jesus recorded in the Gospel of Matthew:

> Go therefore and make disciples of all nations, baptizing them in the name of the Father and of the Son and of the Holy Spirit, and teaching them to obey everything that I have commanded you (Matt 28:19–20).

Discipleship is the prime directive of the church.

Throughout the Gospels, Jesus' closest followers are referred to as his "disciples." This is an apt description since a disciple is "a person who follows . . . another in order to learn from him or her,"[5] one who "subscribes to the teachings of a master and assists in spreading them."[6] This is precisely what Jesus' disciples were to do. They were to imitate Jesus' example and model their lives after his. They were to look like Jesus and live like Jesus—and they were to encourage others to do the same.

As Willard sees it, "Most problems in contemporary churches can be explained by the fact that members have never decided to follow Christ."[7] But claiming to be a Christian without following Jesus is like claiming to be an avid hiker without ever leaving home for a walk in the woods. It misses the whole point of discipleship. As Willard articulates it, disciples are people who have "a *desire*" to be like Jesus in every way and make "a *decision*" to take the necessary steps to ensure that happens.[8] "The disciple," writes Willard, "is one who, intent upon becoming Christ-like . . . systematically and progressively rearranges his [or her] affairs to that end."[9] In short, disciples are people who follow Jesus. It can be no other way. As Jesus himself said, "Whoever does not carry the cross and follow me *cannot* be my disciple" (Luke 14:27).[10]

As we shall see, Jesus called would-be followers to a way of life rather than a set of beliefs. In doing so, Jesus emphasized how we *behave* instead of what we *believe*. This is not to suggest our beliefs don't matter or are unimportant. On the contrary, what we believe matters a great deal. After all,

---

Anabaptism—that do prioritize discipleship. On the importance of following Jesus in thought, word, and deed within an Anabaptist perspective, see Murray, *Naked Anabaptist*, 51–70.

5. *Oxford English Dictionary*, "Disciple."

6. *American Heritage Dictionary*, 2nd college ed., s.v. "disciple."

7. Willard, *Great Omission*, 5.

8. Ibid., 7, emphasis original.

9. Ibid.

10. Emphasis mine. Cf. Luke 9:23.

our beliefs can, and do, shape our behavior in countless ways. We should be diligent to use our mind to the best of our ability to think deeply about the biblical text, historic Christian doctrines, and contemporary issues of faith. The church should encourage and equip its members to be biblically literate, intellectually curious, and theologically astute.[11]

Still, being a disciple is not essentially about having all of our theology straight or believing all the "right things" about God. Being a disciple means following Jesus, and *following Jesus means living like Jesus lived and obeying what he taught.* Unpacking what that looks like will be our task in the coming pages.

What Followers of Jesus Do

We have already considered some of Jesus' teachings related to violence and nonviolence in our discussion of the Sermon on the Mount in chapter 5. This chapter expands that conversation by considering five key characteristics of faithful discipleship that can be derived from the teachings of Jesus and the New Testament more generally. Followers of Jesus are to 1) *serve* rather than dominate, 2) *forgive* rather than retaliate, 3) *suffer harm* rather than inflict it, 4) *repay good for evil* rather than evil for evil, and 5) *love* rather than hate. While these five characteristics do not exhaust all the ethical demands of Christian discipleship, they are among the most important, especially in light of our particular interests in this book. By exploring each of these more carefully, here descriptively and later through stories,[12] we obtain a fuller picture of what it means for Christians to follow Jesus faithfully.

Followers of Jesus serve rather than dominate

The idea of being a servant was a difficult one for Jesus' disciples to grasp. They seem preoccupied with their own status and importance, and on more than one occasion had conversations about who was the greatest.[13] In one instance, James and John, two of Jesus' closest disciples, asked Jesus for the honor of sitting at his right and left when he came in glory, apparently regarding themselves worthy of such special recognition[14] Their pre-

11. For an indictment of evangelicals who have often failed to pay sufficient attention to the life of the mind, see Noll, *Scandal of the Evangelical Mind.*

12. See especially chapter 9.

13. See Matt 18:1–5 // Mark 9:33–37 // Luke 9:46–48; Matt 20:20–28 // Mark 10:35–45 // Luke 22:24–27; cf. Matt 23:1–12.

14. In Matthew's account, their mother makes the request (Matt 20:20–21).

sumptuous request understandably irritates the other disciples. Seizing this teachable moment, Jesus said:

> You know that among the Gentiles those whom they recognize as their rulers lord it over them, and their great ones are tyrants over them. But it is not so among you; but whoever wishes to become great among you must be your servant, and whoever wishes to be first among you must be slave of all. For the Son of Man came not to be served but to serve, and to give his life a ransom for many (Mark 10:42–45).

Jesus draws a sharp contrast between the way people generally conceived of greatness and the way he wanted his disciples to understand it. Turning conventional wisdom on its head, Jesus says greatness is not determined by one's ability to dominate, but by one's capacity to serve: "Whoever wishes to be great among you must be your servant."[15]

Since Jesus himself came "not to be served but to serve," he expected no less of his disciples. Jesus' willingness to serve is displayed with special power and poignancy by washing the feet of his disciples on the night he was betrayed. Richard Foster imagines the scene this way:

> Gathered at the Passover feast, the disciples were keenly aware that someone needed to wash the others' feet. The problem was that the only people who washed feet were the least. So there they sat, feet caked with dirt. It was such a sore point that they were not even going to talk about it. No one wanted to be considered the least. Then Jesus took a towel and a basin and redefined greatness.[16]

Even though Jesus had every right to ask one of his disciples to care for this basic matter of hospitality, he used this as an opportunity to demonstrate how his followers should behave toward one another. To be sure they got the point, Jesus followed his actions with these instructions, "If I, your Lord and Teacher, have washed your feet, you also ought to wash one another's feet. For I have set you an example, that you also should do as I have done to you" (John 13:14–15).

When Elisa and I got married over twenty-five years ago, we did something rather unconventional during the wedding ceremony: we washed each other's feet. We did this to symbolize the commitment we were making to serve one another from that day forth. We wanted to put servanthood at

---

15. For a fuller exploration of this theme, see Kraybill, *Upside-Down Kingdom*, 231–55, and Foster, *Celebration of Discipline*, 126–40.

16. Foster, *Celebration of Discipline*, 126.

the forefront of our relationship, and we regarded this as a meaningful way to demonstrate that desire.

A number of years later, when I had the privilege of performing a wedding ceremony for two former students of mine, I used my message to emphasize the importance of serving one another:

> Sam, how will you serve Kristen? And Kristen, how will you serve Sam? When there is a job to be done, what will your attitude be? Will you consider the other as better than yourself? Will you look to their interests and not your own? Will you each jump at the chance to serve the other? When the bathroom needs to be cleaned, which one of you will be the first to arrive there with toilet brush in hand and declare, "I will serve!" And when the trash can is overflowing, which one of you will seize the opportunity to serve the other by secretly gathering the garbage and whisking it away to the garbage can outside. This is the stuff that servanthood is made of.[17]

Following Jesus involves serving others.

Though Jesus' command to serve others certainly includes our close circle of family and friends, it does not end there. We are called to serve our enemies as well.[18] Jesus emphasizes this in the parable of the Good Samaritan (Luke 10:30–37). Despite the enormous enmity that existed between Jews and Samaritans, Jesus tells a story in which a Samaritan (of all people!) cares for a Jew who had been beaten and left for dead. Jesus' scandalous instructions: "Go and do likewise" (v. 37).

Jesus' emphasis on serving others raises a very important question: Is it possible to serve others while behaving violently toward them? It would seem not. Violence is, after all, essentially an act of domination. When you behave violently toward someone, you force your will upon them. You do things to them they do not want done. Serving, on the other hand, is precisely the opposite. Serving is not about imposing my agenda or my will upon someone else. Rather, it is about putting the needs of others before my own and doing what is in their best interests (see Phil 2:4). Since violence is a form of domination, and since followers of Jesus are clearly instructed to serve and not to dominate, it appears that obeying Jesus on this point requires us to reject violence. Acts of service, it seems, necessarily preclude acts of violence.

17. Names have been changed.
18. See Rom 12:19–20. Cf. Prov 25:21–22.

Followers of Jesus forgive rather than retaliate

Followers of Jesus are also commanded to forgive, not retaliate. Previously, we discussed key verses from the Sermon on the Mount in which Jesus forbids retaliatory violence. Instead of striking back, seeking revenge, or settling scores—acts that perpetuate cycles of violence—followers of Jesus are to *love* their enemies, *pray* for their persecutors, and *forgive* their offenders.

> You have heard that it was said, "You shall love your neighbor and hate your enemy." But I say to you, Love your enemies and pray for those who persecute you, so that you may be children of your Father in heaven (Matt 5:43–45).

Part of what is means to love our enemies is to forgive them for the wrong(s) they have done to us. Otherwise, we will find it very hard to love them.

Minimally, forgiving someone means we decide not to "get even" with them, or to make them pay for what they did to us. It also means deciding to treat them with love and respect *in spite of* the way they have treated us. This is a practical application of the Golden Rule (Matt 7:12), which reminds us that forgiveness is a profoundly *non*violent act. Indeed, there is no violence in forgiveness. On the contrary, "forgiveness helps to break the cycle of violence."[19] Forgiveness stops the never ending series of paybacks and revenge and makes a new future possible.

Forgiving others is such an important part of discipleship that Jesus included it in what we call the Lord's Prayer, the brief prayer Jesus taught his disciples when they asked him how to pray. "Forgive us our sins, for we also forgive everyone who has wronged us" (Matt 6:12, Common English Bible). In this prayer, Jesus predicates the disciples' request for divine forgiveness upon their forgiveness of others.[20] Or, to look at this the other way around, in the book of Colossians Christians are admonished to forgive others since they have been forgiven by God: "Just as the Lord has forgiven you, so you also must forgive" (Col 3:13). Forgiving others is a central characteristic of Christian discipleship.

The forgiveness we offer others is to be unconditional and unlimited. "How often should I forgive?" Peter asked Jesus. "'As many as seven times?' Jesus said to him, 'Not seven times, but, I tell you, seventy-seven times'" (Matt 18:21–22). Nothing should qualify or restrict our willingness to forgive. Following Jesus involves forgiving freely and frequently.

19. Bicksler, "Pursuing Peace," 135.

20. See also the parable of the Unforgiving Servant in Matt 18:23–35. The parable stresses the extreme importance of forgiving others, especially considering all we ourselves have been forgiven.

The beautiful thing about forgiveness is that it can be offered regardless of whether the offender asks for it, acknowledges the wrong, or shows any signs of remorse or repentance. While such things are certainly desirable, none are necessary for us to forgive. Rather, forgiveness is an act of sheer grace that returns good for evil and creates the space for reconciliation to take place. Even if reconciliation ultimately proves impossible, forgiveness frees the one who offers it from being controlled by feelings of anger, bitterness, and hate.

Followers of Jesus suffer harm rather than inflict it

One of the more challenging aspects of following Jesus is that it inevitably entails suffering. As Dietrich Bonhoeffer wrote in his classic book *The Cost of Discipleship*, "Suffering . . . is the badge of true discipleship."[21] Being a disciple of Jesus means being ready to experience persecution, suffering, and death—just as Jesus did. "For to this you have been called," says the writer of 1 Peter, "because Christ also suffered for you, leaving you an example, so that you should follow in his steps" (1 Pet 2:21).

Although all four Gospels include an account of Jesus' suffering and death, the Gospel of Mark emphasizes Jesus' suffering more than the other accounts. In three consecutive chapters, Jesus tells his disciples that he must suffer (Mark 8:31; 9:31; 10:33–4).

> Then he began to teach them that the Son of Man must undergo great suffering, and be rejected by the elders, the chief priests, and the scribes, and be killed, and after three days rise again. He said all this quite openly. And Peter took him aside and began to rebuke him. But turning and looking at his disciples, he rebuked Peter and said, "Get behind me, Satan! For you are setting your mind not on divine things but on human things" (Mark 8:31–33).

Peter's response here is completely understandable. At that time, many Jews expected the messiah to be a conquering king, not a suffering servant. They thought the messiah would be a military leader who would free them from Roman oppression. They certainly did *not* anticipate the messiah being yet another victim of the Roman Empire. Therefore, Jesus' talk about suffering, rejection, and death just did not make sense to them. It disrupted their expectations of what the messiah was to be and do. They believed the

---

21. Bonhoeffer, *Cost of Discipleship*, 100. Quoted in Camp, *Mere Discipleship*, 99.

messiah was supposed to deal a fatal blow to the Romans, not suffer and die at their hands.

But Jesus had not come to meet people's expectations. Jesus came to meet people's needs. His mission was to save, not to kill; to help, not to harm. Therefore, Jesus rejected the way of violence and took the way of the cross. And Jesus expected his followers to do the same. Immediately after announcing that he must suffer and die:

> He (Jesus) called the crowd with his disciples, and said to them, "If any want to become my followers, let them deny themselves and take up their cross and follow me. For those who want to save their life will lose it, and those who lose their life for my sake, and for the sake of the gospel, will save it" (Mark 8:34–35).

If you want to follow Jesus, you too must take up your cross. This means you must be prepared to die. In addition, taking up the cross requires laying down the sword. Followers of Jesus must reject violence and accept suffering. This is taught throughout the New Testament. As Richard Hays observes, "From Matthew to Revelation we find a consistent witness against violence and a calling to the community to follow the example of Jesus in *accepting* suffering rather than *inflicting* it."[22] Followers of Jesus should be willing to suffer harm for the sake of the gospel, but they should never harm others in the process of living out their faith. As Bruxy Cavey likes to say, "It's always okay to die for your faith, it's just never okay to kill for it." This is the way of Jesus.[23]

Followers of Jesus Repay Evil with Good rather than More Evil

Jesus calls his followers to repay evil with good. In Luke's version of the Sermon on the Mount, Jesus tells his disciples to "do good to those who hate you, bless those who curse you, pray for those who abuse you" (Luke 6:27–28). The Apostle Paul says much the same in one of the most important and challenging passages in the New Testament:

> Bless those who persecute you; bless and do not curse them. . . .
> Do not repay anyone evil for evil, but take thought for what is

---

22. Hays, *Moral Vision*, 332, emphasis original. Hays discusses Matt 5:38–48 at some length and refers to passages such as Rom 12:14–21; Heb 10:32b–34; 1 Pet 2:21, 23; Rev. 12:11, and others (*Moral Vision*, 319–32).

23. Throughout the history of the Christian church, many followers of Jesus have given their lives for the truth of the gospel. Examples can be found in Foxe, *Foxe's Book of Martyrs*, and van Braght, *Bloody Theater*.

noble in the sight of all. If it is possible, so far as it depends on you, live peaceably with all. Beloved, never avenge yourselves, but leave room for the wrath of God; for it is written, "Vengeance is mine, I will repay, says the Lord." No, "if your enemies are hungry, feed them; if they are thirsty, give them something to drink; for by doing this you will heap burning coals on their heads." Do not be overcome by evil, but overcome evil with good (Rom 12:14, 17–21).

Christians are *never*, under any circumstances, to repay evil for evil (Rom 12:17). "Do not repay evil for evil or abuse for abuse," says the writer of 1 Peter, "but, on the contrary, repay with a blessing. It is for this that you were called—that you might inherit a blessing" (1 Pet 3:9). Followers of Jesus should not avenge themselves but should treat their adversaries with dignity and respect (Rom 12:19). Specifically, they are to bless, and not curse, their persecutors (v. 14). Like the good Samaritan, they are to care for their enemy's basic needs, providing food and water when they are hungry and thirsty (v. 20).

At first glance, the reason Paul gives for behaving this way may seem odd and not very peaceful. Paul says treating our enemies with kindness and compassion "will heap burning coals on their heads." Earlier interpreters understood this expression metaphorically and believed it referred to the final judgment these "enemies" will experience at the end of the age. But this does not make much sense. How could showing kindness to your enemies be the catalyst for such terrible eschatological judgment? Moreover, this very negative—and punitive—interpretation of this verse does not fit the context very well since the passage stresses repaying evil with good.

Many scholars today interpret the statement about "heap(ing) burning coals on their heads" more positively. It may be related to an Egyptian ritual in which a penitent person carried coals in a dish on their head as evidence of their genuine repentance.[24] If that is what is in view here, then Paul seems to be suggesting that treating one's enemies with kindness creates an opportunity for them to have a change of heart, an interpretation that seems more in keeping with the overall tenor of the passage.

However we understand this particular expression, the main thrust of the passage is clear enough: followers of Jesus are called to overcome evil with good (v. 21). Once again, this seems to rule out the possibility of using violence. Violence is *not* good. In fact, as we argued at some length in chapter 4, the truth about violence is precisely the opposite: it's all bad. Violence

24. Dunn, *Romans 9–16*, 751. This also seems to be confirmed by the Targum, which either reads "'and God will hand him over to you' or 'will make him your friend'" (ibid.).

is harmful and destructive. It breeds more violence and harms countless people. Therefore, while Christians are called to overcome evil, they must reject efforts to do so through violence and killing. Instead, they must find ways to overcome evil with good. This is how we follow Jesus faithfully. In chapter 9 (and beyond), we will look at some stories that help us envision what this looks like and how it can be done.

Followers of Jesus love rather than hate

Finally, followers of Jesus are called to love, not hate. In fact, Jesus says the command to love neighbor as self is second only to the command to love God—it is that important. Love is to be the defining characteristic of Christ followers. It is what identifies us as Christian. As Jesus said to his disciples: "By this everyone will know that you are my disciples, if you have love for one another" (John 13:35). Disciples of Jesus are to be notorious for the way they love each other.

Although Jesus does not spell out all that it means to "have love for one another," the Apostle Paul elucidates this with his helpful description of love in 1 Corinthians 13. Although this passage was written in the context of how spiritual gifts should be exercised in the church, it has much broader applicability.

> Love is patient; love is kind; love is not envious or boastful or arrogant or rude. It does not insist on its own way; it is not irritable or resentful; it does not rejoice in wrongdoing, but rejoices in the truth. It bears all things, believes all things, hopes all things, endures all things. Love never ends (1 Cor 13:4–8).

It is easy to see that violence does not measure up very well to this description of love. Violence is neither patient nor kind, but impatient and cruel. Moreover, contrary to love, violence *does* insist on its own way, the way of the one who wields it. *Love is not violent*, and violence is not love. Anyone who has ever been a victim of violence can readily testify to that.

In his letter to the church at Galatia, Paul wrote, "The fruit of the Spirit is love, joy, peace, patience, kindness, generosity, faithfulness, gentleness, and self-control" (Gal 5:22–23). When talking about the fruit of the Spirit, it comes as no surprise that love tops the list and that violence is absent from it. Violence is *not* a fruit of the Spirit. In fact, Paul contrasts the fruit of the Spirit to "the works of flesh," which includes things such as "enmities, strife, jealousy, anger, quarrels, dissensions, factions"—things that often have a close relationship with violence (Gal 5:19–20). Christians are to exhibit the fruit of the Spirit and avoid the works of the flesh. We are to embody love, not engage in violence.

As "imitators of God," Christians are to "live in love, as Christ loved us and gave himself up for us" (Eph 5:1–2). As Greg Boyd writes:

> There is no greater power on the planet than self-sacrificial love. . . . When God flexes his omnipotent muscle, it doesn't look like Rambo or the Terminator—it looks like Calvary! And living in this Calvary-like love moment by moment, in all circumstances and in relation to all people, is the sole calling of those who are aligned with the kingdom that Jesus came to bring.[25]

In light of that, Boyd asks this very important question, "What would happen if the ultimate criteria we used to assess how 'successful' or 'unsuccessful' our churches were was the question, *are we loving as Jesus loved*?"[26] That is *the* question. As Rick Warren put it in his best-selling book *The Purpose Driven Life*, "The point of life is learning to love—God and people. Life minus love equals zero."[27] Without love, nothing else matters very much.

The church is to be a community of individuals who love one another. But loving those who love us is not enough. We are to extend that same love to people outside the walls of the church, to those who are most unlike us, to those we find terribly disagreeable, and to those we consider our enemies. Returning to what Jesus said in the Sermon on the Mount:

> For if you love those who love you, what reward do you have? Do not even the tax collectors do the same? And if you greet only your brothers and sisters, what more are you doing than others? Do not even the Gentiles do the same? Be perfect, therefore, as your heavenly Father is perfect (Matt 5:46–48).

There is nothing spectacular or uniquely Christian about loving those who love you. Doing that makes us no different from the rest of the world.

Jesus calls us to a higher standard. Jesus says, in effect, "Don't just love your family and friends. Love those who care nothing for you. Love those who ridicule you. Love those who oppose and oppress you. Love those who make your life miserable. Love those who hate your guts." Jesus calls us to a love that knows no limits. The command to love enemies comes with no exception clauses. Jesus does not say, "Love your enemies, unless they hurt you deeply." Or, "Love your enemies, unless they are truly unlovable."

25. Boyd, *Myth of a Christian Nation*, 32.

26. Ibid., 45, emphasis original.

27. Warren, *Purpose Driven Life*, 125. Quoted in Jacobsen and Sawatsky, *Gracious Christianity*, 22.

The command is unconditional and absolute. Followers of Jesus should be known for their capacity to love others. This is at the very core of what is means to be one of Jesus' disciples.

Admittedly, loving enemies is one of the hardest things followers of Jesus are called to do. Such love does not come easily or naturally, especially when people are antagonistic toward us. Therefore, when it comes to obeying this particular command, we are reminded of how desperately we need divine empowerment. Only the Spirit of God can enable us to love those we would rather hate. The good news, of course, is that God is eager to help us. As we open ourselves to God, we discover that the God who commands us to love enemies equips us for that very same task.

Another thing that makes obeying this command difficult is a lack of clarity about what it actually requires of us. What does it really mean to love enemies? Does it mean we must have warm feelings toward them? Regularly spend time with them? Learn to enjoy being around them? I don't think so. Rather, loving enemies involves making a series of decisions about how we are going to treat them, regardless of whether or not we are ever able to like them. Minimally, loving enemies means deciding not to retaliate against them *regardless of what they have done to us*. We can forgive them and refuse to get back at them without feeling warm fuzzies toward them. Second, loving enemies also means treating them with dignity and respect, *even if they do not reciprocate*. This is hard, I know. But if we truly believe every person is created in God's image and loved unconditionally by God, we must take great care how we treat others, despite what they have done to us. Finally, whenever possible, we should attempt to convert our enemies into friends through acts of hospitality and gestures of goodwill. Obviously, these efforts may, or may not, be successful. For various reasons, it is not always possible to convert an enemy into a friend. Yet when we do, we demonstrate love for our enemy in the most radical way possible.

In the chapters that follow, we will have opportunity to hear some true stories of people who loved their enemies in very concrete and tangible ways. These stories not only help us better understand what this command involves by displaying enemy love in action, they inspire us to go and do likewise. So hang tight and keep reading!

Following Jesus Involves Living Nonviolently

In this chapter and the previous two, I have attempted to build a case for Christian nonviolence based on the life and teachings of Jesus. We are now ready to take stock of the evidence considered along the way as we draw some conclusions that will be important throughout the remainder of this book.

In chapter 5, we explored various stories and sayings of Jesus that are suggestive of his commitment to nonviolence. Specifically, we noted how Jesus taught nonviolence in the Sermon on the Mount, and we observed how Jesus rejected violence on a number of different occasions throughout his ministry. We also stressed that Jesus' public ministry was characterized by helping and healing people, not harming them, and we emphasized how the kingdom of God (God's reign of peace and justice) was central to Jesus' message and mission. All this warrants viewing Jesus as nonviolent in both word and deed, in what he taught and how he behaved.

Chapter 6 addressed common objections frequently raised by those who are not convinced that Jesus was completely opposed to violence. We looked at Jesus' behavior in the temple, his instruction to buy swords, his saying about not coming to bring peace, and his seemingly harsh rhetoric with religious leaders. In each case, we concluded that when these passages are rightly understood, they present no barriers to understanding Jesus as nonviolent. We also raised questions about the claim that eschatological judgment must be understood violently. There are other—and arguably better—ways to understand these passages. Ultimately, none of these objections seemed persuasive enough to merit overturning the overwhelming evidence in the Gospels that Jesus was nonviolent.

In the present chapter, we emphasized the idea that being a disciple means following Jesus, and that following Jesus means living like Jesus lived and obeying what he taught. We then considered some of Jesus' key teachings by exploring five characteristics of Christian discipleship: serving, forgiving, suffering, overcoming evil with good, and loving others. All of these are profoundly nonviolent acts. This confirmed what we learned earlier, namely, that Jesus was committed to nonviolence and that he taught his disciples to live nonviolently as well.

At this point, we are now able to draw a very important conclusion, one that will be assumed throughout the rest of this book. That conclusion, simply stated, is this: *following Jesus involves living nonviolently*. This is at the heart of what it means to be a disciple of Christ. As Glen Stassen and David Gushee put it, "The point is to be faithful to the way of Jesus, and Jesus clearly taught nonviolence and exemplified it in his life and in his death on the cross."[28] Since violence is antithetical to the way of Jesus and to the nature of Christian discipleship, it is not an option for his followers.

28. Stassen and Gushee, *Kingdom Ethics*, 166.

If we want to be faithful to Jesus, we need to live nonviolently, just like Jesus. Here it might be helpful to recall the definition of nonviolence developed in chapter 1. There we defined Christian nonviolence as *a way of life modeled after Jesus, one that completely rejects violence, actively confronts evil, and unconditionally loves others by practicing gracious hospitality, radical forgiveness, and deep compassion*. Or again, to put is most simply, nonviolence is love in action. This is the kind of behavior that should characterize all who strive to follow Jesus faithfully.

Hopefully, the evidence we have considered thus far has convinced you that Jesus was nonviolent and that he expected his followers to be nonviolent. Going forward, these claims will no longer be defended but will simply be assumed. Our interest now is to explore their practical implications. What does Christian nonviolence look like in the real world? How can we use nonviolence to respond effectively to all the conflict, warfare, and oppression people experience? And what does it really mean to live nonviolently in all our relationships—with family, friends, co-workers, church members, and others? These are important questions. I believe they are worthy of careful exploration *even if* you are not fully persuaded that Christians must reject all forms of violence. Every follower of Jesus should strive to reduce violence and "live peaceably with all" (Rom 12:18). Learning to live nonviolently goes a long way toward helping us achieve that goal.

A Very Important Caveat: Living Nonviolently Does Not Mean Staying in Abusive Relationships

While the ideas discussed in this chapter help us understand what it means to follow the nonviolent way of Jesus, they have sometimes been distorted and inappropriately applied in harmful ways. For example, some Christians have taken the New Testament's emphasis on serving, forgiving, suffering, and loving and have used these ideas to control others and keep them in abusive situations. A batterer beats his wife and convinces her to stay with him and to keep silent about the abuse by telling her she needs to "forgive" him and "love" him. A young man is repeatedly molested by a family member and believes this is his cross to bear because he has been told that suffering is a natural part of Christian discipleship. I hope it is obvious that this is *not* what I am suggesting here. Christians who behave violently toward family members or others, and then attempt to justify their behavior from the Bible, are twisting Scripture in the most egregious way. *Any* interpretation of

Scripture that legitimates violence is an illegitimate interpretation. The Bible should never be used to harm others.[29]

Living nonviolently like Jesus lived means treating others as you would like to be treated. It involves respecting people and acting toward them in ways that communicate genuine love, care, and concern. It does *not* mean letting people do whatever they want to do to you. Moreover, while a commitment to nonviolence sometimes requires sacrifice and hardship, it is not an invitation for abuse or mistreatment. The teachings of Jesus and the demands of discipleship support healthy relational connections, not oppressive ones. For this reason, living nonviolently *never* requires you to remain in an abusive relationship. Anyone who tries to convince you otherwise, and who does so by appealing to the Bible, is certainly wrong. People who find themselves in abusive relationships should take the necessary steps to insure their own safety and well-being and should be supported by the church as they do so.

Conclusion

We have explored what it means to be a follower of Jesus by identifying a number of practices that are to be characteristic of all Christians. We observed that all of these practices—serving, forgiving, suffering, repaying good for evil, loving—are incompatible with violence, and concluded that living nonviolently is central to Christian discipleship. We have discussed all this in rather general terms, but have yet to discuss how this gets worked out in specific circumstances. For instance, what does living nonviolently look like when it comes to parenting, resolving conflict, or responding to a personal assault? Or, how does a commitment to follow the *nonviolent* way of Jesus affect the way we respond to issues such as gun violence, warfare, and political oppression? In other words, what are the implications of embodying these practices in all we say and do? These are important questions for followers of Jesus, and they will occupy our attention throughout the remainder of the book.

Since warfare is arguably *the* dominant issue in discussions about Christians and the appropriate use of force, it will be the focus of the next chapter. How should the teachings of Jesus inform our thinking about Christians and war? Are there some circumstances in which fighting and

---

29. Seibert, *Violence of Scripture*, 2, *et passim*.

killing in wartime *is* our Christian duty and obligation, or do the nonviolent teachings of Jesus rule out any possibility of Christian participation in war?

8

Can Christians Go to War?

Some Implications of Living Nonviolently

*But how will a Christian man go to war? Indeed, how will he serve in
peacetime without a sword which the Lord has taken away? For even
if soldiers came to John [the Baptist] and received advice on how to
act, and even a centurion became a believer, the Lord in subsequently
disarming Peter disarmed every soldier.*

—TERTULLIAN[1]

NEW TESTAMENT PROFESSOR PRESTON Sprinkle tells a story about a
non-traditional student named Bob Armstrong he once had in class.
Bob was a veteran. He had served in three wars and received a Purple Heart
for wounds sustained in combat. Professor Sprinkle was teaching an ethics
course, and a significant portion of it was devoted to addressing the issue
of war. Understandably, Sprinkle was apprehensive about how Bob, a deco-
rated combat veteran, might respond to his teaching on this subject. What
he discovered surprised him.

> I [Sprinkle] tried not to come down too hard against war be-
> cause I assumed that he believed war was justified. But I was
> pleasantly shocked at his view. "War is evil. There should be no

1. Tertullian, *On Idolatry*, 19. Quoted in Driver, *How Christians Made Peace with
War*, 41.

war," Bob declared in his candid style. He even protested my use of a "four views on war" book that I assigned the class. "There's only one *Christian* view on war. War is wrong."[2]

Bob had recently become a Christian, and this had transformed his views about warfare and killing. Over breakfast one morning, Sprinkle questioned Bob about his views:

> I asked Bob, "Do you think Christians should join the military?"
> "No!" Bob blurted out. "Jesus Christ said, 'Thou shalt not kill.'"
> "But," I pushed back, "what if a Christian wanted to serve his country?"
> "You can serve your country in many ways, but in war you have to shoot people. And *Christians shouldn't shoot people.*"[3]

Christians and War

Over the centuries, Christians have held a variety of positions on the morality of war and the role followers of Jesus can—or cannot—play in such conflicts.[4] Even today, there is a wide range of differing views about the appropriateness of Christian participation in war. For many Christians, this is a particularly sensitive matter because it often affects them personally. Many Christians are serving (or have served) in the military, and many more have close family members or friends who are serving (or have served) in the military. For these individuals, military service and participation in war are not just random "issues" that Christians sometimes discuss and debate. It hits much closer to home.

Among Christians, this conversation is often framed as a debate between pacifism (the belief that it is morally wrong to participate in war as a combatant) and just war (the belief that it is morally right to participate in war *if* the war meets certain predetermined criteria).[5] Unfortunately, framing the debate this way tends to obscure how much common ground there is between Christians who hold differing views on these issues.[6] Both "sides" oppose violence and would prefer to find nonviolent alternatives to warfare and killing. And there are many ways pacifists and just war theorists can

2. Sprinkle, *Fight*, 245, emphasis original.
3. Ibid., emphasis mine.
4. See, e.g., Clouse, ed., *War*, and Bainton, *Christian Attitudes*.
5. See, e.g., Clough and Stiltner, *Faith and Force*.
6. See especially Wink, *Engaging the Powers*, 209–29.

work together, side by side, to reduce violence, resolve conflict, and make peace. Therefore, great care should be taken to avoid giving the impression that these two "camps" are at opposite ends of the spectrum with no common ground between them. Nothing could be further from the truth.

Obviously, there are significant differences between these positions. Adherents of the just war theory believe it is appropriate for Christians to enlist in the armed forces and to fight and kill in wars that meet the strict demands of the just war theory. Pacifists disagree. While some pacifists believe it is acceptable to serve in the military as a noncombatant (e.g., as a medic or military chaplain), all pacifists believe it is wrong to fight and kill in war.

Pacifism is a decided minority view in the church today. The vast majority of Christians around the world accept the just war theory or some variation of it. They believe there are situations in which it is appropriate—and perhaps even necessary—for Christians to go to war. If they are right, how does this fit with the nonviolent teachings of Jesus we have been discussing? The purpose of this chapter is to think through this question by first evaluating the just war theory itself and then considering some of the biblical evidence that is often used to support Christian involvement in war.

The Just War Theory

The origins of the just war theory are typically traced back to two early church fathers, namely, Ambrose (340–396 CE), who was the bishop of Milan, and Augustine (354–430 CE), who was converted under the ministry of Ambrose and who became one of the most significant figures in church history. Although neither of these individuals believed it was appropriate for Christians to use violence in self-defense, both believed it was "*the obligation of Christian love* to defend and protect the *innocent third party*."[7] As they saw it, participation in war was not simply a matter of personal conviction. It was not just something each individual could develop an opinion about based on their own conscience. Rather, they believed it was the duty of Christians to rise up and fight when innocent people were being oppressed.

Since the days of Ambrose and Augustine, many influential Christian thinkers have adopted, developed, and applied what we now call the just war theory. The basic premise of the theory is that some wars are just and some are not. For a war to be considered just, it must meet a set of predetermined criteria. If all of these criteria are met, just war theorists believe the war is just and Christians are free to participate in it. If even one of the criteria

7. Charles, *Between Pacifism and Jihad*, 41, emphasis original.

is unmet, the war is not considered just, and Christians have no right to engage in it. The basic criteria used to determine whether a war is just, as articulated by Walter Wink, are as follows:

1. The war must have a *just cause*.

2. It must be waged by a *legitimate authority*.

3. It must be *formally declared*.

4. It must be fought with a *peaceful intention*.

5. It must be a *last resort*.

6. There must be reasonable *hope of success*.

7. The means used must possess *proportionality* to the end sought.[8]

Then, when the war is actually being waged, the following criteria also come into play and dictate certain rules of engagement.

1. *Noncombatants* must be given immunity.

2. *Prisoners* must be treated humanely.

3. *International treaties and conventions* must be honored.[9]

Even a quick glance at these criteria reveals that many elements of the just war theory are highly commendable. For instance, the idea of war being fought to address an injustice or to stop oppression is certainly more desirable than sanctioning war fought to expand one's territory or for reasons of national pride. Likewise, resorting to war as a last resort, after all other reasonable efforts to make peace have failed, is better than going to war at the first sign of provocation. If these criteria for going to war were rigorously applied, it would effectively limit warfare since the criteria are very stringent and few wars are able to satisfy them all. In addition, this theory has the advantage of limiting the negative effects of war itself. If a war is declared just, and you decide to participate in it, then waging war according to just war principles is greatly preferable to waging war without them. The just war theory limits the use of force to only what is necessary, disallows targeting civilians, and requires the humane treatment of prisoners of war. These are all admirable parameters within which to wage war.

In theory, this all sounds very good. But here's the problem. Regardless of how good it sounds in theory, it doesn't work very well in practice for various reasons. Though space only allows for a brief evaluation and

---

8. Wink, *Powers that Be*, 132–33, emphasis original.

9. Ibid., 133, emphasis original.

critique, what follows highlights some of the weakness of this particular approach, especially as it relates to *Christians* trying to use and apply it.[10]

What's Wrong with the Just War Theory?

As already noted, for a war to be considered just, it needs to meet every single one of the just war criteria. Otherwise, it does not qualify. But many times, it is quite challenging to determine whether a particular armed conflict meets certain criteria. Many questions need to be asked when trying to discern whether an armed struggle is "just," and some are extremely difficult to answer in certain circumstances. For example, consider these questions proposed by Wink:

> What constitutes a legitimate authority in a guerrilla insurgency aimed at overthrowing a dictator? Are wars of national liberation against colonial powers just, even if they use violent means? How do we distinguish between "offensive" and "defensive" war? How do we determine who really started it? Who are noncombatants in an age of total war? What happens when *both* sides believe they can construct a valid case for a just war? Do some criteria outweigh others? Are they still applicable in the nuclear age, or in the face of the unparalleled firepower now available to assailants? And why should these criteria be regarded as authoritative in the first place?[11]

To these questions one might add: How do we know all reasonable alternatives have been exhausted? Who gets to decide whether or not the war is just? And how do these criteria apply when considering a response to terrorism? The difficulty of answering questions like these in any sort of definitive way significantly undermines the usability of such a theory.

Part of what is also troubling about the just war theory—and this troubles rigorous just war theorists as well—is the way people often *mis*use it to justify all sorts of wars, regardless of whether the war actually fulfills all of the just war criteria. In fact, many Christians who claim to be adherents of the just war theory know very little about it, and most would be hard pressed to name even a handful of the criteria. As Wink observes:

> Many Christians assume that any war that they *feel* is just *is* just. Excusing themselves from both the rigors of nonviolence and

---

10. For a recent and extended critique of the theory, see Meagher, *Killing from the Inside Out*. Meagher regards the just war theory as "a dead letter" (ibid., 129).

11. Wink, *Powers that Be*, 133, emphasis original.

the demands of just-war theory, Christians have, since Constantine, fallen upon one another and others with a ferocity utterly at odds with their origins.[12]

This should be deeply troubling to Christians of all stripes.

A related challenge of implementing this theory is the simple reality that nationalistic sentiments tend to preempt a dispassionate examination of the just war criteria. Since many Christians closely align themselves to national priorities and ambitions, if their country goes to war, they believe it is the right thing to do.[13] This causes many Christians in America, for example, to be largely uncritical of wars waged by the United States. In fact, as noted earlier, Christians in America are sometimes *more* supportive of the country's warmaking than the general population.[14]

But what happens when Christians on both sides of a conflict believe the war is just and enter into it assuming God is on *their* side? What happens is that Christians from one country slaughter Christians from another, both convinced they are fighting and killing with divine blessing. German Christians in World War II, for example, went into battle sporting belt buckles that read, "*Gott mit uns*" (God with us), while Christians from the United States and elsewhere entered the fray quite certain God was with them. In such cases, national loyalties take precedence over our most basic Christian duty to love one another, the act by which people will know we are followers of Jesus (John 13:35).

This is vividly illustrated by a disturbing story from World War II involving two Christian soldiers, one German and one American. This story, which I have adapted slightly here for the sake of clarity and flow, is told by Tony Campolo. It recounts a conversation Philip Yancey had with a World War II veteran.

> He [Philip Yancey] was having dinner with a man who had been in World War II. The man was talking about the fact that he was in the Battle of the Bulge and was part of a special unit that was sent out every morning to kill the wounded German soldiers. The Battle of the Bulge was so chaotic that taking prisoners became impossible. So this unit was sent out each morning to look for wounded Germans and blow their brains out.
>
> He comes upon this German soldier who was sitting with his back against a tree, completely dissipated. He is not

12. Ibid., 132, emphasis original.

13. As Wink puts it, "Christian moral discrimination tends to follow the flag" (ibid.).

14. See chapter 2.

wounded. He's just too tired to move. He's just completely spent, and he's there, just hanging, limp.

Philip said, "My friend came up to him and raised his gun and was about to shoot him and the man said, 'Wait a minute,' in perfect English. 'Give me just a moment to pray.'"

The guy with the gun said, "Are . . . are you a Christian?"

He said, "Yes."

He said, "I'm a Christian too." And they sat down together.

The man said, "We opened the Scriptures and actually shared some Scripture with each other and prayed with each other. He showed me his family pictures and I showed him my family pictures, and we prayed for each other's families. It was a beautiful time."

And Philip kept on pressing him saying, "And what did you do? And what did you do?"

He said, "I stood up. I looked at him, and I said, 'You're a Christian, and I'm a Christian. I'll see you in heaven.' And I blew his brains out."[15]

Campolo then concludes:

When I tell that story, there's always a stunned reaction because the sense is that the guy's going to say, "Oh, I can't kill you because you are my Christian brother."

Oh no. That's what militarism is. You forget your spiritual values. You forget that you're shooting a Christian brother. You forget that Jesus Christ is in that person and that what you do to that person you are doing to Jesus Christ himself. That's what militarism does. It makes nationalism more important than being a citizen of the kingdom of God.[16]

If people are supposed to know we are Jesus' disciples by the love we show for each other, what are they going to think when they see us killing one another? Perhaps that's why, in 1984, John Stoner and M. R. Zigler offered what they considered to be "a modest proposal for peace." Their proposal? "Let the Christians of the world agree that they will not kill each other."[17] That would be a good start! What makes it modest, of course, is the simple fact that Christians should not kill anyone—Christian or otherwise. Whether in war or for any other reason, killing is incompatible with the

---

15. Cavey, *Inglorious Pastors*, disc 2, part 4, slightly adapted.

16. Ibid.

17. Quoted in Murray, *Naked Anabaptist*, 133.

nonviolent nature of Christian discipleship, it violates the law of love, and it does irreparable harm to witness of the church in the world.

For some Christians, this inherent conflict with the teachings of Jesus is the just war theory's fatal flaw and what makes it ultimately untenable. Regardless of how beneficial or noble the criteria might be, and regardless of how carefully you analyze wars in light of these criteria, at the end of the day, the just war theory sanctions killing. Even if it does so under the most carefully circumscribed conditions, this theory says there are times when it is right for Christians to kill. Yet, based on what we have seen in the Gospels, Jesus does not give us that option. Followers of Jesus do not kill. Ever. For any reason.

Is There Biblical Support for War?

Although the just war theory is not derived from the Bible, and none of the criteria are dependent upon it, Christians who embrace this theory, or believe war is justified for various reasons, routinely use the Bible to support their position. How should we evaluate these arguments?

Old Testament War Narratives

Throughout history, many in the church have found support for Christian participation in war from the pages of the Old Testament. In particular, they appeal to passages where God commands the people of Israel to fight and kill in war:

> But as for the towns of these peoples that the LORD your God is giving you as an inheritance, you must not let anything that breathes remain alive. You shall annihilate them—the Hittites and the Amorites, the Canaanites and the Perizzites, the Hivites and the Jebusites—just as the LORD your God has commanded (Deut 20:16–17).

> Thus says the LORD of hosts. . . . "Now go and attack Amalek, and utterly destroy all that they have; do not spare them, but kill both man and woman, child and infant, ox and sheep, camel and donkey" (1 Sam 15:2–3).

Many believe texts like these play a crucial role in evaluating the morality of war and in determining whether or not it is right for Christians to go to war. As Martin Luther wrote hundreds of years ago:

If the waging of war and the military profession were in themselves wrong and displeasing to God, we should have to condemn Abraham, Moses, Joshua, David, and all the rest of the holy fathers, kings, and princes, who served God as soldiers and are highly praised in Scriptures because of this service.[18]

More recently, professor George W. Knight III expressed a similar view:

The God and Father of Abraham, Isaac, and Jacob, and of our Lord Jesus Christ, instructed his people of old to wage war when necessary and to slay the enemy. . . . These explicit instructions by God make it impossible to maintain that God prohibits the believer from engaging in war under any circumstances.[19]

Many Christians agree. Since the Old Testament claims God initiated, sanctioned, and sometimes even participated in warfare and killing, many believe war cannot be inherently wrong or immoral. Just as God used warfare in the past, they believe God sometimes uses warfare today to liberate the oppressed and to punish evildoers. This is what kept New Testament scholar Richard Hays from completely renouncing warfare earlier in life. He writes: "I, as a young Christian during the Vietnam War era, found myself unable to justify claiming conscientious objector status because I could not claim that I would never fight; God might command me, as he had commanded [King] Saul, to slay an enemy."[20]

In his book, *When God Says War is Right*, professor Darrel Cole emphasizes God's "warlike character" in the Old Testament and believes it has direct relevance for the question of Christian participation in war.[21] Since the Old Testament claims that God sometimes uses lethal force for the sake of justice, Cole believes Christians must do likewise in certain circumstances since they are to imitate God's behavior. Cole argues that God's expression of this warlike character through the "use of force" is to be understood as "a product of His justice, mercy, and love."[22] These are the principles Cole believes should also govern Christian participation in warfare.[23] Since God "uses force to check evil and to bring justice," Cole believes Christians should "fight for justice" and "use force to restrain evil because God is like that."[24]

18. Luther, *Whether Soldiers*. Quoted in Harstad, *Joshua*, 265.

19. Knight, "Can a Christian Go to War?," 4. Quoted in Swartley, *Slavery, Sabbath, War, and Women*, 97.

20. Hays, *Moral Vision*, 336.

21. Cole, *When God Says War Is Right*, 28.

22. Ibid., 36.

23. Ibid.

24. Ibid., 48.

All this raises a very important question: Is it legitimate to draw such far-reaching conclusions about the appropriateness of a Christian's participation in war based on Old Testament texts portraying God as warrior? I think not. Assuming, for the sake of argument, that God actually did command Israelites to fight and kill as the biblical text claims, it is a huge hermeneutical leap to suggest this somehow legitimates Christian participation in warfare today. In fact, rather than justifying Christian participation in warfare, some Christian pacifists, like Elmer Martens, believe God's warring suggests precisely the opposite. He contends God's violence is what motivates and sustains a Christian commitment to nonviolence.[25] "That God is a warrior," writes Martens, "means . . . that his people need not be warlike."[26] Since God will settle the score, so to speak, Christians do not need to retaliate.

Other scholars, even those who may not share Martens' commitment to pacifism, see these texts as *descriptive* of how God called ancient Israelites to live, not *prescriptive* for how Christians are to behave today. While some of these individuals believe it is appropriate for Christians to participate in war, many caution against using the Old Testament to justify war in the modern world. Eugene Merrill, for example, emphasizes the unique relationship God had with Israel as a theocracy and emphasizes that God no longer works primarily through one particular nation. Thus, he believes Christians should *not* "be guided . . . by the Old Testament principles and practices of Yahweh war, for they were relevant to the Israelite theocracy only."[27] Since the church is transnational, the need to defend borders "in the name of God" no longer prevails. Approaches like Martens's and Merrill's—along with others that assume God sanctioned warfare in the ancient world—are not without problems. They can—and should—be critiqued in various ways.[28] Still, one can appreciate their efforts to dissuade people from simplistically using the Old Testament as justification for participation in war today.

An even stronger case can be made against using Old Testament war narratives to justify Christian participation in war by those who challenge the idea that God sanctioned these wars in the first place. Despite how God's involvement in war is portrayed in the Old Testament, many scholars do not believe God commissioned or participated in warfare in the way the Bible

---

25. See Martens, "Toward Shalom," 33–57, especially 50–56. Compare Volf, *Exclusion and Embrace*, 301–304.

26. Martens, "Toward Shalom," 53.

27. Merrill, "Case for Moderate Discontinuity," 92.

28. See, e.g., Seibert, *Disturbing Divine Behavior*, 69–88; Davies, *Immoral Bible*.

describes. Rather, they believe Israel's depictions of God's participation in war reflect views about divine involvement in warfare that were common in the ancient world. While these views make perfect sense given Israel's historical context, they do not necessarily reflect what God actually did in time and space.

Those who take this approach—myself included—emphasize that people in the ancient world viewed war theologically.[29] They believed the gods were intimately involved in their experience of war.[30] They routinely conceived of God as a warrior, and were convinced that God/the gods commissioned war, participated in it, and determined the outcome of it. These assumptions about God's involvement in war are evident in *many* texts from the ancient world.[31] These texts, along with the witness of the Old Testament, make it unmistakably clear that God's involvement in war was a theological given in the ancient world.

In such a context, one would expect Israel's understanding of God's involvement in war to be quite similar to that of the surrounding nations—and it was.[32] Like other people in the ancient world, the Israelites believed God sanctioned their wars, sometimes fighting for them, sometimes against them. They also shared the common belief that victory in battle was a sign of divine favor while defeat in battle reflected divine displeasure. These assumptions about the theological significance of war and God's role in it are evident in numerous Old Testament passages. All this leads many scholars to conclude that Israel's portrayals of God's involvement in war reflect the historical context from which they emerged, yet do *not* serve as reliable indicators of what God actually said and did in the past. If they are correct, if God did not actually command the Israelites to engage in warfare, it makes no sense to use these texts as the basis for Christian participation in warfare today.

Regardless of whether one thinks God did or did not actually commission warfare in the ancient world, using Old Testament war narratives to justify the horrors of warfare today—and Christian participation in it—is irresponsible. It is also contrary to the purpose and goal of Scripture which is to encourage life and peace rather than death and war.[33]

29. See Seibert, *Disturbing Divine Behavior*, 156–60.

30. What follows is adapted from ibid., 160.

31. See, e.g., Kang, *Divine War*.

32. The depiction of the god Chemosh in the Mesha Stele is particularly instructive in this regard, and a number of intriguing parallels could be noted. For a brief discussion, see Seibert, *Disturbing Divine Behavior*, 157–59.

33. For more on how to read Old Testament war narratives in ways that do not justify Christian participation in warfare today, see Lilly, "What about War and Violence

The Treatment of Soldiers by John the Baptist and Jesus

Since neither John the Baptist nor Jesus ever told the soldiers they met that being a soldier was wrong, some Christians regard this as evidence that both Jesus and John approved of soldiering and, by extension, warfare.[34] Is this conclusion warranted?

Prior to the start of Jesus' public ministry, John the Baptist was baptizing people in the Jordan River, warning them of "the wrath to come" and calling them to engage in acts of "repentance" (Luke 3:7–14). Specifically, the text identifies three groups of people—the crowds, tax collectors, and soldiers—who came to John asking what they should do. Each is given a different answer that is uniquely relevant to their particular group.

> And the crowds asked him, "What then should we do?" In reply he said to them, "Whoever has two coats must share with anyone who has none; and whoever has food must do likewise." Even tax collectors came to be baptized, and they asked him, "Teacher, what should we do?" He said to them, "Collect no more than the amount prescribed for you." Soldiers also asked him, "And we, what should we do?" He said to them, "Do not extort money from anyone by threats or false accusation, and be satisfied with your wages" (Luke 3:10–14).

If John the Baptist believed military involvement was wrong, the argument goes, he should have told these men to get into a different line of work. Since John does nothing of the sort, some conclude he had no qualms about soldiering. This line of reasoning has led many people—including theological heavyweights such as Augustine, Martin Luther, and John Calvin—to use this passage to support Christian participation in war.[35]

Like John, Jesus never challenges soldiers to stop being soldiers. The most extensive conversation recorded in the Gospels between Jesus and a solider involves an unnamed centurion whose highly valued slave is deathly ill (Matt 8:5–13).[36] According to Matthew's account, the centurion comes to Jesus and requests healing for his beloved slave. Jesus is willing and plans to travel to the centurion's home. But the centurion replies:

---

in the Old Testament?" and Seibert, "Old Testament as a Problem for Pacifists."

34. Desjardins cites two other passages he believes are also relevant to this point: Mark 15:39, the centurion who witnesses Jesus' death, and Acts 10–11, the conversion of a centurion named Cornelius (*Peace, Violence and the New Testament*, 78–82).

35. See Charles, *Between Pacifism and Jihad*, 51, 54.

36. In Luke's version (Luke 7:1–10), Jesus and the centurion never actually meet, and the entire conversation happens through messengers sent by the centurion.

> Lord, I am not worthy to have you come under my roof; but only
> speak the word, and my servant will be healed. For I also am a
> man under authority, with soldiers under me; and I say to one,
> "Go," and he goes, and to another, "Come," and he comes, and to
> my slave, "Do this," and the slave does it (Matt 8:8–9).

Jesus is amazed at the centurion's faith, performs a long-distance healing, and has nothing but praise for this Roman solider. Nothing in the story
even hints at Jesus' disapproval of the centurion's occupation, and there
certainly is no directive to "put down your sword and follow me." In the
absence of any critique of the centurion for being a solider, some conclude
Jesus did *not* object to soldiering or the violence it sometimes entailed. This
has opened the door for Christians to support various forms of violence
and killing. As Andy Alexis-Baker observes, "This text has been successfully used to legitimate Christian participation in war making and to justify
everything from the crusades to policing, wreaking havoc on innumerable
lives."[37] But can such far-reaching conclusions be drawn from the very limited encounters Jesus and John the Baptist had with soldiers?

Using such passages to argue that Jesus or John approved of soldiering,
warfare, or any other form of violence goes far beyond what the text actually
says. John the Baptist is simply identifying some of the ways people can live
more faithfully to God within their present situation. He is not addressing
the merits of either tax-collecting or soldiering as occupations. With regard
to Jesus, it is important to keep in mind that the conversation he has with
the centurion is precipitated by a major crisis—the life-threatening illness
of the centurion's slave—and is focused on the resolution of that crisis. Discussing the merits of the centurion's line of work is not the point of this very
short and very focused conversation.

To use either of these passages as evidence that Jesus and John the
Baptist were not opposed to war is to make an argument from silence. Such
arguments are often not very compelling. This is especially true in this particular case since the same argument could be used to suggest Jesus (and
John) approved of many things he most certainly did not. As Alexis-Baker
plays this out:

> Since Jesus did not rebuke Pilate for being a governor of an
> occupying force, he [Jesus] must have sanctioned the Roman
> occupation and their right to exploit weaker nations, and by
> extension all colonial and military expansions. Since he did
> not ask Zacchaeus to leave his job as a tax collector, he must
> have approved of Roman tax collection and their right to drain

37. Alexis-Baker, "What about the Centurion?," 171.

resources from an area to the wealthy elite in Rome. Since Jesus did not admonish Pilate for murdering some Galileans in the midst of their sacrifices (Luke 13:3), he sanctioned police brutality and severe repressive measures. Since Jesus did not tell the judges at his own trial that they were wrong for their irregular court proceedings, he sanctions kangaroo courts and dictatorships today. Since Jesus did not reprove the centurion for owning slaves, he therefore condones slavery, even today. These arguments from silence can make Jesus to be the advocate of whatever we want.[38]

This argument from silence is especially unconvincing as it relates to Jesus because Jesus speaks so clearly *against* violence and retaliation elsewhere. Jesus instructs his followers to serve others, love enemies, pray for persecutors, and forgive wrongdoers. These things, rather than arguments from silence, should govern our understanding of Jesus' views on warfare and killing.

The Command to be Subject to Governing Authorities

Two New Testament passages, Rom 13:1–7 and 1 Pet 2:13–14, which instruct Christians to be subject to God-ordained governing authorities, often factor into discussions about Christian participation in war. The beginning of Romans 13 is especially relevant here:

> Let every person be subject to the governing authorities; for there is no authority except from God, and those authorities that exist have been instituted by God. Therefore whoever resists authority resists what God has appointed, and those who resist will incur judgment. . . . But if you do what is wrong, you should be afraid, for the authority does not bear the sword in vain! It is the servant of God to execute wrath on the wrongdoer (Rom 13:1–2, 4).

For those who believe these verses support Christians going to war, the logic goes something like this. Governments are ordained by God to maintain order and are permitted to use lethal force, including warfare, to do so.[39] Since Christians are to be subject to the governing authorities,

38. Alexis-Baker, "What about the Centurion?," 178.

39. Wright notes that "Romans 13 was frequently invoked in support of military action by the United States and its allies against other countries" after the terrorist attacks on 9/11/2001 ("Letter to the Romans," 723).

Christians have an obligation to engage in warfare and killing when ordered by the state.

While space does not allow for a full response to this argument, a few points are worth noting. First, whatever this passage means, it should *not* be interpreted as saying Christians are obligated to obey whatever the state tells them to do. The Living Bible's paraphrase of Rom 13:1, "Obey the government, for God is the one who put it there," is particularly unhelpful here. Yet this is precisely how the passage has sometimes been understood. As New Testament scholar Paul Achtemeier writes about some German Protestants in the twentieth century:

> By means of this passage [Rom 13:1–7] they justified their claim that Christians owed allegiance to Adolph Hitler. For further support, they cited Luther's interpretation of this passage. Luther had written: "Christians should not refuse, under the pretext of religion, to obey men, especially evil ones."[40]

It seems highly unlikely this is what the apostle Paul had in mind when he wrote about being "subject to the governing authorities." Whenever Romans 13 is used to discuss a Christian's responsibility to the state, it should always be read in conversation with passages like Acts 4:19–20 and Acts 5:29. These passages reflect the belief that obedience to God takes precedence over obedience to any other authority. When the demands of the state conflict with the demands of discipleship, allegiance to God must take priority, not the other way around.

Second, it is important to interpret Rom 13:1–7 within its literary context. As discussed earlier, in Rom 12:14–21, the passage which immediately precedes Rom 13:1–7, Paul urges Christians not to "repay anyone evil for evil" but rather to "overcome evil with good." In the passage immediately following Rom 13:1–7, Paul tells his readers to "Owe no one anything, except to love one another; for the one who loves another has fulfilled the law" (Rom 13:8). The placement of Rom 13:1–7 between these two passages, both of which seem about as far away from an endorsement of violence as you can imagine, makes it difficult to believe Paul is writing in favor of Christian participation in war here.

Third, we should keep Paul's historical context in mind when interpreting Rom 13:1–7. Paul is writing a letter to Christians living in first-century Rome, a specific group of individuals living at a particular moment in time. He is encouraging them to obey the laws of the land since he believes God uses civil society, in this case the Roman Empire, to keep order

40. Achtemeier, *Romans*, 204.

and administer justice. As Paul sees it, if you behave and do right, there is nothing to fear. If you disobey, expect to be punished by the state since it is an instrument of divine judgment. Yet, as Luke Timothy Johnson reminds us, "Paul's statements . . . are possible (and tolerable) only in a situation in which the rule of law is in fact basically benevolent. And for all its excesses, the Roman state could be so regarded, particularly at the time Paul was writing."[41] In a different historical context, such as one in which the state was persecuting, torturing, and killing Christians "simply for being Christians," such advice would be inappropriate.[42] Therefore, we must be very careful not to universalize Paul's counsel in Romans 13.

Paul is speaking to Christians living under imperial rule, not to Christians living in a participatory democracy. Therefore, great care needs to be taken in how we apply Paul's words today. Minimally, they remind us that society does not function well without some kind of organizing structure and the means to enforce it. It is easy to see that many laws designed for the public good are also congruent with Christian values and ethics. Christians should readily comply with these. Doing so puts us in good standing with the state and keeps us from being punished. But there are limits to our obedience. When governing authorities require us to do things that violate our conscience, we should resist and should stand with Peter and the apostles who declare, "We must obey God rather than any human authority" (Acts 5:29).

Fourth, we should keep in mind that Romans 13 is talking about how Christians are to relate to civil authorities. As such, it does not directly address the issue of war. As N. T. Wright comments:

> Romans 13:1–7 is about the running of civic communities, and the duty of Christians toward them. It does not mention or allude to the interactions between different civic communities or nations. It was because of this that later Christians developed a theory of "just war," . . . . Romans 13 is sometimes called as a witness in this discussion, but its relevance may be doubted.[43]

Appealing to Rom 13:1–7 to support Christian participation in war claims too much and misses the real point of the passage.

Fifth, rather than suggesting that Christians have a responsibility to wage war when called upon by the state to do so, a more accurate understanding of this passage may suggest precisely the opposite. Some interpreters believe this passage functions as an extension of Paul's call to

41. Johnson, *Reading Romans*, 189.
42. Ibid.
43. Wright, "Letter to the Romans," 720.

nonviolence. Thomas Yoder Neufeld, for example, believes this passage is "intended to reinforce Paul's teaching *against* participation in violence and *for* aggressive overcoming evil with good."[44] Neufeld's reading is based on his understanding of subordination as an act of nonresistance (see Rom 13:1). "Subordination," writes Neufeld, "becomes part of the 'arsenal' of aggressively pursuing the stranger with love and the persecutor with blessing."[45]

The legitimacy of this interpretation is reinforced by the fact that the early church did *not* regard this passage as a justification for Christians to go to war or engage in acts of violence. In fact, as Jon Isaak notes, "Until the fifth century, this text was understood as a call to peacemaking in relation to the government."[46] This represents a fundamentally different way of viewing the text than what is often suggested today, and it should carry some extra weight since it represents how those most familiar with Paul and his time period understood the meaning of what he wrote. According to Isaak, "Only after the rise of imperial Christianity was the text reversed and used as the basis for a Christian theology of the state and as a warrant for the state's use of lethal force in executing justice."[47] In light of this, it seems very likely that the church has grossly misunderstood Paul's words for centuries, using them to justify acts of violence and killing when Paul intended nothing of the sort and was actually trying to encourage peace and nonviolence. All this should give great pause to anyone appealing to this text in support of war.

The Command to Love Your Neighbor

Jesus' command to "love your neighbor" (Matt 22:39) is arguably the most compelling biblical argument used by Christians to support warfare. How can we stand by and do nothing when we see our brothers and sisters around the world being systematically persecuted, tortured, and killed? Doesn't love of neighbor require us to fight, and even kill, on their behalf so they can be delivered from oppression and tyranny? A lot of Christians think so. In fact, Jesus himself said there was no greater love than laying down our life for our friends (John 15:13). Doesn't this imply that going to war to save

44. Neufeld, *Killing Enmity*, 119, emphasis original.

45. Ibid., emphasis original.

46. Isaak, "Christian Community," 42.

47. Ibid. Isaak notes that the sword mentioned in v. 4 is actually a "small dagger used by the police to ensure compliance" (ibid.). This leads him to conclude that "*Paul's reference to the dagger concerns the policing function of the state. It does not legitimize execution or the use of violence in defense of justice. Paul is saying Christians should not take up arms for or against the government*" (ibid., emphasis original).

others is not only an act of love but one of the most noble things we can do? Many Christians believe we should be willing to engage in war for the sake of those in need even if it costs us our life.

At one level, this sounds quite reasonable. We *should* be eager to help others and willing to make sacrifices to do so. But here's the rub. While there is nothing wrong with laying down our life, there is something terribly wrong with taking another's. Moreover, while I agree that doing nothing to help a neighbor in need fails to fulfill the command to love our neighbor as ourselves,[48] showing love to one neighbor while killing another misses the point. We should do all we can to aid the neighbor in need—and we will discuss many nonviolent ways to do this in the following chapters, so I ask for your patience here—but *faithful Christian discipleship does not allow us to help one neighbor while hurting another.* The call of Jesus is to love everyone, enemies included. We need to find a better way.

A Disarming Interrogation at Abu Ghraib

In their book *Soul Repair*, Brock and Lettini tell the story of Joshua Casteel, a young soldier whose convictions against killing were formed through an experience he had interrogating a Muslim prisoner in Iraq.[49] During the war in Iraq, Casteel was assigned to the now infamous Abu Ghraib prison after the scandal there had been exposed. Joshua conducted over a hundred interrogations, concluding that the vast majority of detainees (95 percent) were not terrorists or threats of any sort.

On one occasion, however, he interrogated a Saudi man who admitted to intentionally coming into Iraq to fight against the American-led coalition. When Joshua questioned him about why he had come to Iraq to kill, the Saudi man said it was his religious duty. He did so to defend Muslim territory from foreign invaders. What happened next changed Joshua's life forever.

> The man abruptly turned the tables and asked Joshua the same question. Joshua, who had not had to fire his gun at anyone, denied he entered Iraq to kill and asserted that his duty was to serve his country and to defend Iraq's people. The man rejected this answer and insisted, "If the U.S. military didn't want people to get killed, they would have sent others, not soldiers who are sent when people need to be killed." Finally, the man asked Joshua how he could call himself a Christian—Jesus had

48. Recall the parable of the Good Samaritan (Luke 10:25–37).
49. Brock and Lettini, *Soul Repair*, 36–37.

asked his followers to turn the other cheek, to pray for those who persecute you, and to love your enemies. Joshua found it strange to receive a lesson on the Sermon on the Mount from a jihadist. He began to realize they were both religious men with a strong sense of duty. . . . But Joshua was unsettled by the conversation. . . . This one interrogation with an enemy combatant crystallized Joshua's understanding that to follow Jesus, he had to take off the uniform. When he was sent home, he applied for and received CO [conscientious objector] status.[50]

Like Bob, the veteran/student we met at the beginning of the chapter, Joshua realized that Christians cannot kill, even in context of war. Serving in the military creates many moral dilemmas for those committed to the nonviolent way of Jesus.

Conclusion

Today, the majority of churchgoers around the world believe it is appropriate for Christians to enlist in the military and to go to war under certain circumstances. This is *not* how the early church saw it.[51] Instead, during its first 300 years of existence, the early church thought it was wrong for Christians to take up the sword. They regarded violence and killing as being contrary to Jesus' teachings and discouraged these early Christ-followers from engaging in such acts. And, based upon our own investigation of the teachings of Jesus, it would seem they were right.

If we are serious about following the nonviolent way of Jesus, there are certain things we simply cannot do: killing people is one of them. Killing is incompatible with faithful Christian discipleship.[52] This is true even when it is done with the blessing of the state, and even when it is done to achieve positive ends such as justice, freedom, and security.

Killing violates the most basic teachings of Jesus about how we are to treat others. Killing in war is not an act of service toward our enemies. Rather, it is an act of domination. Nor does war represent an attempt to overcome evil with good. Likewise, the use of lethal force is not an expression of love toward others. In these and many other ways, the violence of war stands diametrically opposed to the teachings of Jesus.

Although many Christians appeal to both the just war theory and the Bible to make their case in support of Christian participation in war, these

50. Ibid., 37.
51. See the end of chapter 5.
52. For a different perspective, see Bell, *Just War as Christian Discipleship*.

efforts are not terribly productive. As we have seen, the just war theory is beset by many problems and the arguments made from the Bible are not particularly compelling. The reason it is so difficult to justify Christian participation in war is quite simple: we are not supposed to do so. Followers of Jesus are to live nonviolently, and living nonviolently rules out the possibility of going to war.[53]

But lest you think living nonviolently is only about what Christians *cannot* do, it is important once again to recall our definition of nonviolence which emphasizes many things Christians *can* do. As defined in chapter 1, Christian nonviolence is *a way of life modeled after Jesus, one that completely rejects violence, actively confronts evil, and unconditionally loves others by practicing gracious hospitality, radical forgiveness, and deep compassion.* To explore some of the positive implications of living nonviolently, and to help us envision what this looks like in the real world, it is beneficial to consider some stories of Christians who have modeled this kind of behavior. These stories, which are both instructive and inspiring, will be the focus of our attention in the following pages.

---

53. There is a long tradition of conscientious objection to military service in the United States and elsewhere around the world. While some conscientious objectors rejected war due to their religious convictions, many others did so for different reasons. For stories and discussion, see Burnham, *Courage of Cowards*; Heisey, *Peace and Persistence*; Kramer, *Conscientious Objectors*.

9

Living Out the Teachings of Jesus in the Real World

Stories of Christians who Loved Enemies, Forgave Offenders, and Made Peace with Adversaries

Stories inspire, enlighten, connect, delight, warn, terrify, admonish, and surprise. We need them with an urgency that resembles hunger. Not merely entertainment, stories can save lives or play a part in turning us into killers.

—JIM FOREST[1]

The stories we tell determine the ethic from which we live and from which we see the world.

—LEE CAMP[2]

SOMETIMES, TO REALLY UNDERSTAND how something works, you need to see it in action. That is where stories come in handy. Stories give concrete form to ideas, beliefs, and convictions. Stories of people actually loving enemies and graciously forgiving others, for example, show us how people put some of Jesus' key teachings into practice. They provide tangible

1. Forest, *Loving Our Enemies*, 21.
2. Camp, *Who Is My Enemy?*, 91.

examples of what it means to live nonviolently in the real world. Hopefully, they also inspire us to go and do likewise. This chapter is devoted to telling stories like these, stories that demonstrate the beauty and power of following the nonviolent way of Jesus.

Most of the stories included here are relatively recent (from the past twenty years or so) and the majority of them take place in North America. While this provides some focus, it should not obscure the fact that stories like these can be found throughout history and around the world.[3] To provide some structure to this chapter, the stories are arranged into four broad categories corresponding to the type of nonviolent action they exemplify. There are stories about loving enemies, forgiving offenders, welcoming strangers, and overcoming evil with good. I realize this arrangement is not entirely satisfactory since these categories are somewhat fluid. A story about overcoming evil with good also tends to be a story about loving enemies, while a story about loving enemies often involves forgiving offenders—and so forth. Still, these categories are useful because they enable us to give focused attention to some of the key attributes of living nonviolently.

In many respects, the stories recounted here speak for themselves. They are powerful just as they stand and could have been included without further comment. Therefore, my remarks will be brief and will primarily serve to provide some context for these stories and to highlight what makes them especially compelling.

Loving Enemies

In one way or another, virtually every story in this chapter is, at its core, a story about loving enemies. The following stories are especially noteworthy in this regard since they explicitly demonstrate how Jesus' command to love enemies played a crucial role in responding to hostility.

Befriending a Bully

At the beginning of his recent memoir *Waging Peace*, longtime activist David Hartsough recounts this formative story from his childhood:

> My first encounter with the power of nonviolence came early. I was seven years old, trudging home from school through a park that I crossed every day on my way to and from the second

3. For a short collection of stories from Africa, see Hostetler, *They Loved Their Enemies*.

grade. A bitter wind was blowing that winter day in Gilman, Iowa. The ice balls that landed on my face and chest stung, some fortified with stones to increase the pain on impact.

My face started to bleed. I was mystified by the glee on the faces of the small gang of older boys who were pelting me. A quick mental review told me that I had never done anything to them to merit this treatment.

On a recent Sunday in church, my father had preached a sermon about love, based on Jesus's command: "You have heard that it was said, 'You shall love your neighbor and hate your enemy.' But I say to you, Love your enemies and pray for those who persecute you" (Matthew 5:43–44). I was certainly feeling persecuted.

I hadn't yet lived long enough for the questioning realism that often overtakes adults to have settled on me. It didn't occur to me to ask: did Jesus really mean these tough words? . . . I just took Jesus's words at face value and asked myself: how *do* I love these guys?

I stood still for a few moments. Then I faced those boys and piped up, "I'd like to be your friend, and I certainly don't have anything against you guys." I wanted them to know that I wasn't afraid of them. They threw a few more ice balls. But eventually the thrill wore off, as I wasn't throwing any back or reacting in any aggressive way to their onslaught.

I walked on home, trying to figure out what else I could do in this challenging situation. The previous summer I had visited several Indian reservations in the Southwest with my family, and my most prized possession at the time was a little copper letter opener inlaid with an Indian precious stone. I decided to give it to the boy who appeared to be the leader of the gang. He received it with surprise and gratitude, and we became good friends after that.[4]

Hartsough's gracious treatment of his tormenters when he was only seven years old is impressive, to say the least. It reminds us that people of all ages can choose to live nonviolently. His actions demonstrate that loving enemies involves more than just refusing to retaliate against them; it involves doing good to those who have harmed us. Hartsough models this by giving his most cherished possession to the ringleader of his juvenile assailants. This generous act had a profoundly positive effect on their relationship and

---

4. Hartsough, *Waging Peace*, 1–2.

converted an enemy into a friend.[5] Hartsough's determination to put into practice what he had learned in church about loving enemies reflects the kind of influence the church should have on people. Hartsough took the words of Jesus seriously and intentionally tried to live them out. It is hard not to be inspired.

Preventing a Riot

During the 1950s and 1960s, African Americans were routinely threatened, harassed, and humiliated during their struggle for racial equality in the United States. But though they suffered greatly due to segregation and racism, few responded violently. Instead, African Americans consistently refused to return evil for evil, choosing to love rather than hate.[6]

One especially poignant example of the power of nonviolence and the importance of loving enemies occurred on January 30, 1956, as Martin Luther King Jr. responded to an act of violence that had been directed against his family. As biographer Stephen Oates tells it:

> King was speaking at a mass meeting when he received dreadful news. His house had been bombed. He sped home in a strange calm. A crowd of Negroes [sympathetic to King] surged about the parsonage, white police trying to hold them back. The bomb had exploded on the porch, breaking it in two and showering the living room with broken glass. The house was full of people; Mayor Gayle and Police Commissioner Sellers had just arrived. King forced his way inside and found [his wife] Coretta and [his daughter] Yoki at the back. He hugged them. "Thank God you and the baby are all right!" . . .
>
> Outside the crowd was getting out of control. A Negro man confronted a policeman: "You got your thirty-eight, and I got mine. Let's shoot it out." Even Negro boys were armed with broken bottles, and there were jeers at the cops. "Let us see Reverend King," a woman cried out. King stepped out onto the shattered porch, which still smelled of dynamite fumes, and surveyed his angry brothers and sisters on the lawn and in the

5. Hartsough's generosity is convicting. We sometimes cherish our "stuff" more than our relationship with others. Would you be willing to give a prized possession to your enemy in hopes of converting him or her to a friend? Thanks are due to Chris Wenger for prompting my thoughts in this direction.

6. For an account of various nonviolent strategies used during the civil rights movement in the United States, see Ackerman and DuVall, *Force More Powerful*, 305–33.

street beyond. "He held up his hand," an observer said, "and they were suddenly silent . . . absolutely still."

"My wife and baby are all right," he said. "I want you to go home and put down your weapons. We cannot solve this problem through retaliatory violence. . . . We must love our white brothers, no matter what they do to us. We must make them know that we love them. Jesus still cries out across the centuries, 'Love your enemies.' This is what we must live by. We must meet hate with love." His voice was quivering. "Remember, if I am stopped, this Movement will not stop, because God is with this Movement."

Slowly his people dispersed, melting away in the night. Afterward a policeman told a reporter, "I'll be honest with you. I was terrified. I owe my life to that . . . Preacher, and so do all the other white people who were there."[7]

It is chilling to consider what might have happened if King had decided to unleash the pent-up anger so palpable that night in Montgomery, Alabama. There would have been a bloodbath. People on both sides would have died, many more would have been injured, and the civil rights movement would have taken a gigantic step in the wrong direction. But King knew retaliation was not the way forward. So instead, he called upon people to live out Jesus' command to love their enemies. This de-escalated the situation, disarmed the crowd, and allowed people to walk away unharmed. Though loving enemies is not easy, it is an essential part of following the nonviolent way of Jesus.

Forgiving Offenders

Part of what it means to love our enemies, or anyone who has harmed us, for that matter, is to forgive them. Forgiveness is crucial to living nonviolently because it disarms us. When we forgive others, we extend grace rather than exact revenge. We choose *not* to harm them for the wrong they did to us. Forgiveness keeps us from evil by preventing us from behaving violently *and* frees us from bondage by delivering us from the corrosive effects of bitterness and resentment.

The following two stories illustrate the power of forgiveness. One story involves a dramatic example of forgiving fellow church members. The other involves forgiving perpetrators of a notorious, and very deadly, terrorist attack.

7. Oates, *Let the Trumpet Sound*, 86–87.

Experiencing the Dramatic Power of Forgiveness

Unfortunately, forgiveness sometimes has been most conspicuously absent where it should be most clearly present, namely, within the walls of the church. Christians often fight and do considerable harm to each other, failing to heed Jesus' words about the importance of forgiving one another. When this happens among members of the same congregation, relationships are strained and the atmosphere can be downright nasty.

Such was the case among members of a small church in Israel in the village of Ibillin in the 1960s until forgiveness broke loose. Elias Chacour, a Palestinian Christian, was very excited when he was appointed as pastor of this church in Galilee. But that excitement soon gave way to dismay when he realized how unwelcome he was and how difficult his first ministry assignment would be. As Father Chacour got to know the people of Ibillin, he became particularly disturbed by the attitudes he encountered. He once described it to a friend this way: "People in some families haven't spoken to each other in years because of divisive feuds. Christians and Muslims, Orthodox and Melkites often hate each other. People with different political ideas are bitterly fighting."[8] Particularly concerning was some bad blood between brothers who attended the church. "One of the most tragic cases," writes Chacour, "was the family where four brothers—one of whom was the village policeman—detested each other so vehemently that people rushed off the streets when they saw two of them walking toward each other. It hurt me deeply to learn that these brothers were believers, once active in the church."[9]

Father Chacour worked tirelessly for many long months, making home visits, trying to repair relationships, and attempting to reunite a very divided congregation. Yet nothing seemed to have any significant effect. So in March of 1967, on Palm Sunday, Father Chacour tried something more daring. At the conclusion of the service, to everyone's surprise, Father Chacour walked to the back of the church, pulled out a chain he had concealed in his pocket, wrapped it around the handles of the doors, and fastened it securely with a padlock. With all eyes on him, he then returned to the front of the church and said:

> "I want you to know how beloved you all are to me and how saddened I am to find you hating and decrying each other. I have tried so often in the six months I have been here to help you reconcile with each other, but I have been unable to do so. . . .

8. Chacour, *We Belong to the Land*, 26–27.
9. Chacour, *Blood Brothers*, 161.

"This morning while I celebrated the liturgy, I found someone who is able to help you. In fact, he is the only one who can
work the miracle of reconciliation in this village. This person
who can reconcile you is Jesus Christ, and he is here with us. . . .

"So on Christ's behalf, I say this to you: The doors of the
church are locked. Either you kill each other right here in your
hatred and then I will celebrate your funerals gratis, or you use
this opportunity to be reconciled together before I open the
doors of the church.[10]

Silence filled the church. Chacour had thrown down the gauntlet, and he
waited with his imprisoned congregation for what seemed like an eternity, agonizing over whether he had made a fatal mistake. Then, at last, the
deathly quiet was broken by a local policeman, one of the four estranged
brothers.

"I am sorry," he faltered. All eyes were on him. "I am the worst
one of all. I've hated my own brothers. Hated them so much I
wanted to kill them. More than any of you I need forgiveness."

And then he turned to me. "Can you forgive me, too,
Abuna?" . . .

"Come here," I replied, motioning him to my side. He came,
and we greeted each other with the kiss of peace. "Of course I
forgive you," I said. "Now go and greet your brothers."

Before he was halfway down the aisle, his three brothers
had rushed to him. They held each other in a long embrace, each
one asking forgiveness of the others.

In an instant the church was a chaos of embracing and repentance. Cousins who had not spoken to each other in years
wept together openly. Women asked forgiveness for malicious
gossip. Men confessed to passing damaging lies about each
other. . . .

The momentum carried us out of the church and into the
streets where true Christianity belongs. For the rest of the day
and far into the evening, I joined groups of believers as they
went from house to house throughout Ibillin. At every door,
someone had to ask forgiveness for a certain wrong. Never was
forgiveness withheld.[11]

This beautiful story demonstrates love in action and reminds us of the
disarming power of forgiveness. What happened at Ibillin can happen anywhere Christians choose to forgive rather than retaliate.

10. Chacour, *We Belong to the Land*, 30–31.
11. Chacour, *Blood Brothers*, 178–9.

Forgiving a Terrorist

Many compelling stories could be told about individuals who found the courage to forgive people who have committed unspeakable atrocities.[12] Lisa Gibson's story is one of these stories. When Lisa was eighteen years old, her brother Ken was in the army. Ken had been stationed in Germany for the past two years and was coming home to Michigan for Christmas. Lisa was very excited to see him again after such a long absence. But Ken never arrived. He was one of the 259 passengers aboard Pan Am flight 103 which exploded over Lockerbie, Scotland in December 1988. There were no survivors. Eventually, it was determined that this bombing was an act of terrorism sponsored by the Libyan government under the leadership of Colonel Muammar Gaddafi.

Lisa was devastated by this tragedy and struggled to make sense of it for nearly a decade. She also struggled to love and forgive those responsible for this brazen act of terror. In time, she realized her attitude needed to change. What follows is an abbreviated adaptation of her fascinating story:

> As a Christian, I knew it was wrong to hate and that I was called to forgive. But as I read the Bible, I was challenged because I learned it was more than not hating my enemy—it was about loving them. . . .
>
> So I made a choice. . . .
>
> I chose to respond in love. With the realization that love is an action, I began to look for opportunities to reach out in love to my enemies.
>
> My first step was to send a letter of forgiveness to the man convicted of the bombing. . . .
>
> Even as I sat down to write the letter, I wasn't completely feeling the forgiveness in my heart. Frankly, it was simply an act of obedience. The Bible said that I was to forgive and love my enemies, and I was attempting to do that in the most concrete way I knew how. . . .
>
> I simply introduced myself and told him my brother was killed on the Lockerbie plane, Pan Am Flight 103.
>
> "Only God really knows if you are responsible for this act," I said. "But as a Christian, I need to forgive you." . . .
>
> I never would have expected my letter would get to him. . . . Not only did he get the letter, but he actually responded to it in early July 2004. . . .

12. To cite just two examples, see Morris, *Forgiving the Dead Man Walking,* and Bishop, *Change of Heart.*

It was a very kind letter that expressed his condolences for my loss and shared verses from both the Koran and the Bible about how God answers prayer. He said he prayed I would be happy in my life and suffer no such sadness in the future.

Reading his letter validated my belief that forgiveness is a powerful instrument of God that does more than hate ever could to bring about change. Following the writing of my letter of forgiveness, I began to build a relationship with the new Libyan ambassador to the United States, and in January 2005, I made a personal reconciliation trip to Libya. I met with individual citizens and government officials, and in each case I simply told them my story: as a Christian I needed to go and get to know them so that I could forgive them and learn to love them.

As I would share my story, time and again, the walls would fall. . . .

As the walls fell, God's grace flowed. I found myself asking questions like "What was it like to live in Libya?" and "What was it like when the U.S. bombed Tripoli in 1986?" The responses I received were honest and heartfelt: "It is so good for you to ask. No one has ever asked me that before." After hearing about their lives I came back to the U.S. inspired to do something to help improve their lives. Out of that experience, the Peace and Prosperity Alliance was birthed to provide humanitarian and education projects to serve the country of Libya.

On September 23, 2009, I engaged in the ultimate act of forgiveness and unconditional love when I met with and forgave Libyan leader Muammar Gaddafi, one of the world's most notorious terrorists and the man many believe was responsible for the Lockerbie bombing. . . .

It was a brief meeting, only about fifteen minutes total. Since I didn't know how much time I would have, I also gave him a card sharing the things I felt led to tell him. . . . What I shared, both in person and in the card, was what Romans 12 calls us to do. I shared with him that I had forgiven, blessed him, told him about my efforts to serve the Libyan people, and even shared about how I had been praying for him daily. In the card I told him that I had bought a "Gaddafi watch" on my first trip to Libya and said, "Every day I look down at the watch, and I say a prayer for you."

Gaddafi's countenance was very stoic throughout the entire meeting until the end, when I gave him a gift. It was a simple gesture of attempting to do something good to him as the scripture says. Since I wanted it to have spiritual meaning but also be something he might actually use, I settled on a Cross pen. When

I gave him the pen, I could tell he was touched. It was the only time he smiled, and he said, "Thank you." As his countenance softened, it was as if for a brief moment I saw his humanity and his heart. . . .

The very next morning, I awoke to my phone ringing off the hook with calls from every major media outlet trying to ascertain if I was the woman who met with Gaddafi. They had gotten my name and contact information from the Libyan ambassador. The other Lockerbie family members who they had called denied the story as a fabrication by Gaddafi. "No Lockerbie family member would meet with Gaddafi," some said.

They were wrong. One woman, on a mission from God, simply trying to love her enemies and overcome evil with good, had chosen to meet with Gaddafi. . . . As such, the story of our meeting went around the world and was covered by nearly every large media outlet. CNN was the first to share my provocative statement that "Love is the most effective weapon in the war on terror." Although there was criticism by some, the positive response far outweighed the negative. My email inbox was flooded with responses from people all over the world who thanked me and asked if there were ways they could help with my work. Many were Muslims and several were Libyans. I believe the response was so positive because when people see unconditional love in action, it is so compelling they are drawn to it. On that day, the message that was communicated to the world was simply this: Daily there is a battle being waged between the forces of good and evil through love and hate, but in the end love always wins.[13]

As Lisa's long journey demonstrates, forgiveness is hard work. It takes time, effort, and intentionality. But it is the way of Jesus. It is what we are called to do—and by God's grace are able to do—when we live out the nonviolent love of Jesus in our broken and hurting world.

Welcoming Strangers

Since the attacks in the United States on September 11, 2001, many Americans have felt—and sometimes expressed—significant hostility toward the followers of Islam. As noted earlier, many *Christians* have a low view of

13. Gibson, "Personal Forgiveness," 71–76. For more background to this story, see Gibson, *Life in Death.*

Muslims,[14] and churchgoers sometimes behave very badly toward the Muslim community. For example, there have been prominent Christian leaders who have said very hurtful things about Muslims, and Christian-Muslim relations have been the worse for it.[15] Truth be told, we have often not been very good neighbors.

But not all Christians have reacted this way. Some have taken concrete steps to practice hospitality and express love for their Muslim brothers and sisters who are routinely condemned and falsely stereotyped *en masse* as dangerous terrorists.

Putting Out a Welcome Mat for Muslims

When Pastor Steve Stone of Heartsong Church in Cordova learned that the Memphis Islamic Center had purchased land adjacent to his church, he did not regard it as a cause for alarm. Instead, he saw it as an opportunity to share the love of God with his soon-to-be neighbors. This story, which first aired on CNN in 2010, illustrates the good that can result when Christians extend hospitality. What follows is Jim Wallis's account of this amazing story.

> Steve Stone, an evangelical pastor, heard that an Islamic cultural center was coming to his neighborhood, so he put up a big sign that said, "Heartsong Church Welcomes Islamic Cultural Center." The local Muslims were astonished. They came the next day and tentatively knocked on the door. They said, "We were hoping to be ignored, but you welcomed us. Why?"
>
> "Because," Steve said, "Jesus tells us to love our neighbors and even our enemies. We don't know much about Islam, but we'd like to learn."
>
> Before long, the barbeques had halal meat, kids were playing together, Muslims and Christians were tutoring and working with the homeless together. When Ramadan came, the Islamic Cultural Center was not finished, so the Muslims asked if they could use the church basement for their Ramadan gatherings. Steve said, "No, you can meet in the sanctuary." This pastor and imam trust and love each other, while still each holding to their own beliefs.

---

14. See chapter 2.

15. One could cite comments by Franklin Graham posted July 17, 2015 on his Facebook page as well as those made by Pat Robertson on *The 700 Club* on December 8, 2015.

Rather than viewing their Muslim neighbors with fear and suspicion, the members of Heartsong built genuine friendships and expressed their love in tangible ways. This is a marvelous example of Christian love in action, one that had ripple effects halfway around the world. Wallis continues:

> After the story had aired on CNN, I called Steve, and he told me that he had received a phone call from a group of men in Pakistan.
>
> "Is this the pastor?" they asked.
>
> "Yes."
>
> "We watched that segment on CNN. We were silent for a long time, and then one of us said, 'I think God may be speaking to us through this man.' Another one said, 'How can we kill these people?'"
>
> After seeing the piece on CNN, one of the men had gone to a little church near their mosque, and with his Muslim hands, he had washed and cleaned the inside and outside of that church. Then the men congregated in a room at 1:30 in the morning to call this pastor that they had seen on television. They said to him, "We want you to tell your congregation, Pastor, that we don't hate them. We love them, and because of what you've done, we're going to look after that little church for the rest of our lives."
>
> So what works in the midst of international conflict and violence? Drones? Or proactive love?[16]

The answer would seem self-evident.

Jesus calls us to extend hospitality rather than hostility, and to welcome others rather than ostracize them, especially those who are different from us. Like the Good Samaritan, we should demonstrate care and compassion for our neighbor, even if that neighbor is perceived as an "enemy." Though neither Pastor Stone nor his congregation could have anticipated the far-reaching impact their actions would have on others, that is the beauty and power of nonviolent love in action. It can disarm those who experience it and can create a desire to reciprocate the love they have received.

Receiving Unexpected Welcome in a War Zone

In his book *The Irresistible Revolution*, Shane Claiborne tells a wonderful story about the hospitality he and other Americans received at the hands of complete strangers in Iraq. What makes the story especially remarkable is

16. Wallis, "Where We Have Been," 103–4. See also Wallis, *On God's Side*, 137–40.

the fact that it happened during the Iraq War, when Iraqis had every reason to hate Americans given the heavy bombing and huge casualties they were suffering.

Claiborne and others had traveled to Iraq in 2003 to stand in solidarity with the Iraqi people during the war. On one occasion, while traveling from Baghdad to Jordan with his companions, Claiborne was involved in a serious automobile accident. One of the tires of the car they were riding in blew out. The car went off the road, flipped over, and crashed, leaving Claiborne and all his travelling companions injured, two very seriously. Here is Claiborne's account of what happened after he emerged from the wreckage:

> The first thing I noticed was a car of Iraqi civilians that had stopped to help us. . . . Without a second thought, they piled all of us into their car and headed to the nearest town, waving a white sheet out the window as the war planes continued to fly overhead. Miraculously, only minutes away, there was a little town called Rutba. . . . As they drove us to the hospital, many thoughts went through my mind, including the worry that we would become hostages. So I handed them a sheet that explained in Arabic who we were, and they nodded with smiles.[17]

Upon their arrival in Rutba, they could not be taken to the hospital since it had been bombed. Nevertheless, a number of doctors greeted them upon their arrival and one said, "But you are our brothers, and we will take care of you. We take care of everyone—Christian, Muslim, Iraqi, American . . . it doesn't matter. We are all human beings. We are sisters and brothers."[18] Claiborne continues:

> And they set up a little clinic with four beds and saved my friend's life, apologizing for the scarcity of supplies due to the sanctions. The townspeople began to bring blankets and water. When we inquired about going back to the car to get our passports and bags, they looked at us like we were crazy, explaining that even their ambulances had been hit by the bombs, but they smiled and invited us to live in Rutba.[19]

The extraordinary hospitality of the doctors and inhabitants of Rutba is at once inspiring and instructive. It helps us envision what welcoming the stranger looks like in the real world.[20]

17. Claiborne, *Irresistible Revolution*, 202.

18. Ibid., 203

19. Ibid.

20. For a longer account of this story and a description of a return trip to Iraq by

Overcoming Evil with Good

Following the nonviolent way of Jesus also involves overcoming evil with good. It means treating others the way we want to be treated, and finding creative ways to use what is good in this world to triumph over what is not. Many Christians struggle with this when it comes to their own personal safety. Conventional wisdom says if you are threatened with harm, you have every right to do whatever is necessary to protect yourself, even if that means harming (or killing) someone else in the process. Many Christians would agree. Creative nonviolent action is rarely considered as a viable option in situations like these. But it should be. There are many true stories of how people got through dangerous situations like these without being harmed or harming others in the process. These are stories of overcoming evil with good, and we will discuss some of these in the next chapter. To whet your appetite, here is one such story told by Daniel Buttry.

From Mugger to Hugger

Daniel Buttry recounts how his wife, Sharon, responded to a man who attempted to rob her at gunpoint.[21]

> Our family had a direct experience with handguns when Sharon was held up at gunpoint going into work one morning. At that time Sharon was the executive director of Friendship House, a Christian neighborhood action center in Hamtramck, a diverse urban municipality completely surrounded by Detroit. She had pulled our van into her parking spot behind Friendship House, and as she was tidying up the inside of the van, a man with a gun came up and pointed it toward her belly. He demanded money. Sharon told him, "You picked the wrong woman to rob today. I only have a dollar. I just gave my kids their lunch money for school." She kept up a stream of conversation that she had credit cards but would cancel them. She suggested that she and the robber go through her purse together to see what they could find. As she talked, she took control of the situation and presented herself as a human being—not an anonymous victim.
>
> When Sharon presented her purse the man put the gun on the seat of the van. She thought for a moment about trying to grab the gun, but that would have changed the whole dynamic of the situation into one in which she was now threatening the

Claiborne and others after the war, see Barrett, *Gospel of Rutba*.

21. Buttry, *Peace Warrior*, 175–77.

robber. The potential for violence would have dramatically escalated. Instead she continued her conversational connection with the man robbing her.

As the man went through Sharon's wallet he discovered that, sure enough, there was only one dollar. He began to cry. "I guess I'm not very good at this," he said. Sharon asked him what was the matter, and he began to unfold the story of his troubles. He had no job. His wife had recently left him and his eleven-year-old daughter. He had to care for his daughter, but with no work, he had no money to feed her. Furthermore, his mother had just died, and his confusion and grief had been bubbling close to the surface. "What would your mother think of you doing this?" Sharon inquired. She asked the man if his mother was a praying woman, which he affirmed. So they prayed, the robber with his eyes closed, Sharon with hers open!

Sharon said, "Maybe you did pick the right woman to rob today." They sat together on the floor of the van by the open side door, and Sharon counseled him for a while. She found out he had taken the gun from his father's house. She told him to return the gun to his father, confess what he had done, and ask forgiveness. He had been drinking to gather the courage to commit his robberies, and since Sharon's policy was never to provide direct assistance when someone was under the influence of alcohol or drugs she asked him to come back sober later in the week so she could help him look for work. They set an appointment and exchanged phone numbers. The man repeatedly sought assurances that Sharon wouldn't call the police.

The robber started to walk away, then turned and came back. "You won't call the police?" he asked. Sharon replied that just as Christ had forgiven her, she had forgiven him. That seemed to reassure him. He started to leave again, then returned and said, "Could I ask for one thing more?" Sharon expected him to ask for a cigarette, the common request she got on the streets of Hamtramck, even as a nonsmoker. Instead he asked for a hug! Sharon hugged the would-be mugger, the man who had held a gun to her half an hour earlier.

When the man failed to show up for his appointment, Sharon called him up saying they had made a deal and reassuring him that she was serious about her offer to help. He came back to Friendship House two days later. Sharon helped him develop a plan and made some contacts. Within a couple of weeks he had landed a job. He would come visit her occasionally, once saying, "Rev. Sharon, I'm so happy now!" He even volunteered for a bit at the food bank that Friendship House operated and joined a men's Bible study at the food bank. Once when Sharon drove him back to his ravaged-looking street, he assured her that she would be safe in his neighborhood. Everyone knew what she had done—the man had been telling the story of the mugging that turned into a hugging in his neighborhood even as Sharon and I were telling the story in our circles.

This is a wonderful story on all sorts of levels. Sharon overcomes evil with good by engaging this man in conversation, treating him with kindness and compassion, and helping him get back on his feet again. If only every thief were so fortunate! Her actions remind us that nonviolence *can* work in situations like these if we are willing to give it a try.

The Neighbors from Hell

Sometimes, overcoming evil with good is a longer, more protracted process, one that may take multiple expressions of love and kindness before hatred and hardness melt away. Philip Gulley tells one such story.

> I have a friend who purchased a home in a Southern city. The house had sat empty for some time and was so reasonably priced that my friend feared something was wrong with it. But he could find no defects, so he bought the house and moved in with his wife. Within a few days, he discovered the neighbors on each side of him had been locked in a vicious fight of long duration. The police had been called many times to settle disputes, their children fought, the men had gone so far as to arm themselves, and each had gotten restraining orders against the other. Each neighbor visited him, trying to enlist my friend on his side. My friend listened carefully, expressed his hope that they would get along, and said that insofar as it depended upon him, he was going to live in peace with all of his neighbors. They each interpreted his refusal to take sides as taking the other's side, and both of them left angry at my friend.
>
> He nevertheless remained kind and took every opportunity to interact with each of them in a positive, loving way. He and his wife invited their children into their home and helped them reconcile their differences. He extended one kindness after another to his neighbors, not taking it personally when they treated him with scorn and disrespect. A year passed with little discernible change, but my friend continued to treat his neighbors with gentle dignity, infusing the area about his home with a spirit, almost an aura, of love. One evening, he looked out his

window to see his two neighbors standing together in the street, looking on as their children played together. A while later, they shook hands and returned to their homes. Within a few weeks, the restraining orders were forgotten and the families were barbecuing together (a Southern sacrament of reconciliation if ever there were one!).

Had my friend repaid their antagonism with further hostility, the ill will would have escalated and spread. Instead, he recognized the power of peace, patiently extended it to others, and witnessed firsthand the fruit it bore. . . . It was the power not of an overwhelming force that bludgeoned others into submission but of a persistent love that, as water erodes stone, wore down the hard hate of others.[22]

Treating others with dignity and respect can work wonders. In the face of suspicion and hostility, acts of love and kindness can overcome evil with good and can even transform enemies into friends.

Conclusion

The Gospel of John ends with these words: "But there are many other things that Jesus did; if every one of them were written down, I suppose that the world itself could not contain the books that would be written" (John 21:25). The same could be said about the kind of stories told in this chapter. Despite the church's spotty past, there have always been Christians who have taken the words of Jesus seriously and tried to live accordingly by loving enemies, forgiving offenders, welcoming strangers, and overcoming evil with good. Stories like these help us see more clearly what it actually looks like to follow the nonviolent way of Jesus. They also remind us that living nonviolently is not just about being *against* violence, it is about being *for* love. Just as God loved us, we are to love others (1 John 4:19). Seeing people live out this kind of love in all kinds of circumstances expands our imagination and encourages us to do likewise.

In the chapters that follow, we will continue to explore how people have used nonviolence to overcome evil with good, sometimes in situations more complicated or dangerous than the ones we have encountered thus far. We will hear stories about people who were able to resolve conflict, correct injustice, and stop oppression *without* resorting to violence. These stories provide us with some additional tools that are very useful for living out our commitment to follow the nonviolent way of Jesus.

22. Gulley, *If the Church Were Christian*, 150–51.

10

Responding to Personal Assault with Hospitality Rather Than Hostility

How to Remain Unharmed without Harming Others

If nonviolence is to have any credibility, it must answer the questions that violence purports to answer, but in a better way. Saying no to violence is good, but having alternatives is better.

—JIM WALLIS[1]

MANY CHRISTIANS WHO STRUGGLE to embrace nonviolence whole-heartedly do so not for biblical or theological reasons, but for pragmatic ones. They may have no quarrel with the idea that Jesus was non-violent and called his disciples to live nonviolently. They just do not think nonviolence is very practical in certain situations. They believe violence is sometimes the only thing that actually works. Whether it's dealing with an unwanted intruder at home, protecting someone being physically assaulted or removing a dictator from power, some people are convinced that violence is not only an appropriate response, but a necessary one. Therefore, despite what Jesus taught, they are hesitant to repudiate all forms of violence.

The purpose of the next three chapters is to look more carefully at some of these "only-violence-will-work" scenarios from a different angle.

---

1. Wallis, *God's Politics*, 160.

We will do so by analyzing a number of true stories that feature people who chose to behave nonviolently in situations where a violent response is often assumed. What you find here might surprise you. We are not often told stories about people using creative nonviolent alternatives even though there are countless examples of people doing just that. Hearing these stories enlarges our imagination and equips us with the tools we need to follow the nonviolent way of Jesus with courage and conviction.

In this chapter, we focus on nonviolent ways people can respond when they themselves are threatened with personal harm. The next chapter considers various nonviolent strategies that a person can use to help someone who is being threatened or harmed. And in chapter 12, the last chapter in this section, we explore how nonviolent struggle can work on a large scale to resolve conflict, correct injustice, and stop oppression.

What Would You Do?

Suppose you were home alone and heard someone breaking into your house. What would you do? Hide? Try to escape? Call 911? Talk to the intruder? Pick up a baseball bat? Many Christians would have no qualms about using violence, if necessary, to protect themselves in a situation like this. Even if that meant seriously injuring, or possibly killing, the intruder, many churchgoers would feel fully justified using violence in self-defense. While that kind of response is certainly understandable—we are hard-wired for self-preservation—such a response is problematic for Christians since it runs counter to the teachings of Jesus.

So how should we respond? Should we just let the intruder do whatever they want to do? Or should we take some kind of *nonviolent* action in an effort to exercise some measure of control over the situation and to keep *us* from harm? If so, what might that look like? To help us process these questions, we turn our attention to some true stories of people who found themselves in very dangerous situations and chose to respond nonviolently.

Responding Nonviolently to Personal Threats: Two True Stories

There are many stories about people who have faced serious personal threats and have gotten through unharmed because of their nonviolent response.[2] We have already encountered one of these in the previous chapter in the

2. See Samuel, *Safe Passages on City Streets*; Yoder, *What Would You Do?*, 91–94, 108–36; Buttry, *Christian Peacemaking*, 152–55.

account of the mugger turned hugger. As we saw, Sharon Buttry's creative and compassionate response when held at gunpoint not only kept her safe, it radically transformed the life of the man who accosted her.

We are now ready to consider two more stories that also illustrate the effectiveness of nonviolence in situations like these. One is a first person account written by Angie O'Gorman, which describes her thoughts and actions when facing an intruder who broke into her room in the middle of the night. The other recounts an encounter Nathan and Louise Degrafinried had with an escaped convict who came to their front door brandishing a shotgun.

My purpose in telling these stories is not to "prove" nonviolence always works or to offer a foolproof way to get out of dangerous situations like these unharmed. Rather, I have included them here to illustrate the kinds of things that *can* be done when threatened in this way and to challenge the commonly held assumption that a violent response is necessary. These stories demonstrate the power of nonviolence to ease tensions, reduce hostility, and prevent harm on all sides.

As you read about Angie O'Gorman and the Degrafinrieds, pay close attention to the way they behave toward their respective intruders. What do they do? How do their actions defuse these potentially life-threatening situations?

Engaging an Intruder: The Story of Angie O'Gorman

In 1982, Angie O'Gorman was spending the night alone in the third floor bedroom of a Catholic Worker House that was temporarily closed for repairs.[3] This is her account of what happened that night:

> I was awakened late one night several years ago by a man kicking open the door to my bedroom. The house was empty. The phone was downstairs. He was somewhat verbally abusive as he walked over to my bed. I could not find his eyes in the darkness but could see the outline of his form. As I lay there, feeling a fear and vulnerability I had never before experienced, several thoughts ran through my head—all in a matter of seconds. The first was the uselessness of screaming. The second was the fallacy of thinking safety depends on having a gun hidden under your pillow. Somehow I could not imagine this man standing patiently while I reached under my pillow for my gun. The third

---

3. This detail is from Angie O'Gorman's telling of the story on the video tape "Nonviolent Response to Personal Assault," Pax Christi USA, 1986.

thought, I believe, saved my life. I realized with a certain clarity that either he and I made it through this situation safely—together—or we would both be damaged. Our safety was connected. If he raped me, I would be hurt both physically and emotionally. If he raped me he would be hurt as well. If he went to prison, the damage would be greater. That thought disarmed *me*. It freed me from my own desire to lash out and at the same time from my own paralysis. It did not free me from feelings of fear but from fear's control over my ability to respond. I found myself acting out of a concern for both our safety which caused me to react with a certain firmness but with surprisingly little hostility in my voice.

I asked him what time it was. He answered. That was a good sign. I commented that his watch and the clock on my night table had different times. His said 2:30, mine said 2:45. I had just set mine. I hoped his watch wasn't broken. When had he last set it? He answered. I answered. The time seemed endless. When the atmosphere began to calm a little I asked him how he had gotten into the house. He'd broken through the glass in the back door. I told him that presented me with a problem as I did not have the money to buy new glass. He talked about some financial difficulties of his own. We talked until we were no longer strangers and I felt it was safe to ask him to leave. He didn't want to; said he had no place to go. Knowing I did not have the physical power to force him out I told him firmly but respectfully, as equal to equal, I would give him a clean set of sheets but he would have to make his own bed downstairs. He went downstairs and I sat up in bed, wide awake and shaking for the rest of the night. The next morning we ate breakfast together and he left.[4]

Put Down Your Gun—The Story of Nathan and Louise Degrafinried

William Willimon tells the story of an unexpected encounter Nathan and Louise Degrafinried had with an escaped convict who came to their home in 1984. He writes:

> It all started early Tuesday morning, February 21, when Louise Degrafinried's husband, Nathan, got up from bed in Mason, Tennessee, to let out the cat. "Cat," as they call him, stood at the

4. O'Gorman, "Defense through Disarmament," 242–43. This story can also be found in Wink, *Engaging the Powers*, 234, and *Powers that Be*, 147–49.

edge of the porch, his hair bristled up on his arched back, and he hissed.

"What you see out there, Cat?" Nathan asked.

A big man stepped from around the corner of the house and pointed a shotgun at Nathan.

"Lord, Honey," Louise heard her husband shout. "Open the door, he's got a gun."

Before she could open the door, the man with the gun had shoved Nathan inside, pushing him and Louise against the wall.

"Don't make me kill you!" he shouted, thrusting the gun in their faces. The couple knew immediately that the intruder was one of the escaped inmates whom they had heard about on the radio. He was Riley Arzeneaux of Memphis, who, with four other inmates, had escaped from Fort Pillow State Prison the previous Saturday.

Louise Degrafinried, a 73-year-old grandmother, stood her ground. "Young man," she said, "I am a Christian lady. I don't believe in no violence. Put that gun down and you sit down. I don't allow no violence here."

The man relaxed his grip on the shotgun. He looked at her for a moment. Then he laid his gun on the couch.

"Lady," he said quietly. "I'm so hungry. I haven't had nothing to eat for three days."

"Young man, you just sit down there and I'll fix you breakfast. Nathan," she said, "go get this young man some dry socks."

With that, Louise went to work. She fixed him bacon, eggs, white bread toast, milk and coffee. Then she got out her best napkins, and set her kitchen table.

"When we sat down, I took that young man by the hand and said, 'Young man, let's give thanks that you came here and that you are safe.' I said a prayer and then asked him if he would like to say something to the Lord. He didn't say anything, so I said, 'Just say, "Jesus wept."' Then we all ate breakfast."

("Why did you tell him to say, 'Jesus wept'?" I asked her later. "Because," she said, "I figured that he didn't have no church background, so I wanted to start him off simple; something short, you know.")

"After breakfast, we sat there and I began to pray. I held his hand and kept patting him on the leg. He trembled all over. I said, 'Young man, I love you and God loves you. God loves us all, every one of us, especially you. Jesus died for you because he loves you so much.'

"'You sound just like my grandmother,' he said. 'She's dead.' Nathan said that he saw one tear fall down the boy's cheek.

"About that time, we heard police cars coming down the road. 'They gonna kill me when they get here,' he said.

"'No, young man, they aren't going to hurt you. You done wrong, but God loves you.' Then me and Nathan took him by the arms, helped him up, and took him out of the kitchen toward the door. 'You let me do all the talking,' I told him. The police got out of their cars.

They had their guns out. I shouted to them, 'Y'all put those guns away. I don't allow no violence here. Put them away. This young man wants to go back. Nathan,' I said, 'you bring the young man on out to the car.' Then they put the handcuffs on him and took him back to the prison."[5]

Responding Nonviolently When Threatened

Obviously, both of these stories could have had very different endings. It is not difficult to imagine any number of tragic outcomes. Angie O'Gorman could have been raped. Nathan and Louise Degrafinried could have been killed. Things could have gone very badly; *but they did not.* Why? What did Angie O'Gorman and Louise Degrafinried do to reduce the tension and emerge from these dangerous encounters intact?

In both accounts, O'Gorman and the Degrafinrieds established a human connection with the intruder at the very beginning of their ordeal by engaging them in conversation. That simple act seemed to make all the difference. What began as an adversarial relationship, at least in the mind of the intruder, was transformed into something quite different and unexpected. O'Gorman started a dialogue by asking questions about the time and how he (the intruder) had gotten into the house. She also told him the broken glass presented a problem for her since she did not have the money to pay for it to be replaced. He then responded by sharing some of his own financial troubles. Louise took a more direct approach, making it unmistakably clear that violence would not be tolerated in her home. Conversation almost always plays an essential role in stories like these. For O'Gorman and the Degrafinrieds, as well as for Sharon Buttry, talking normalized the situation and created space for a more positive outcome.

Second, both O'Gorman and the Degrafinrieds chose to extend hospitality rather than engage in hostility. When O'Gorman's intruder refused

---

5. Willimon, "Bless You, Mrs. Degrafinried." See also Forest, *Loving Our Enemies*, 170–73. He tells the Degrafinried's story in an epilogue titled "Two Old People and a Young Man with a Gun."

to leave, she gave him clean sheets and a place to sleep for the night. Louise Degrafinried made an elaborate breakfast for Riley Arzeneaux, the escaped inmate who had not eaten for days. She also gave him dry socks, prayed for him, spoke of God's love, and calmed his fears when the police came. Acts of human kindness, compassion, and hospitality such as these are powerful. They can change the dynamics of a hostile situation, and they have the potential of converting enemies into friends.

Something else both O'Gorman and Louise Degrafinried did was to introduce an element of surprise or wonder into the situation. This made it difficult for the would-be assailant to carry through with his intentions. As O'Gorman writes,

> While fear, panic, helplessness, and counter-violence can heighten hostility and cruelty, psychologists tell us that wonder tends to diffuse them. *It seems to be nearly impossible for the human psyche to be in a state of wonder and a state of cruelty at the same time.* Thus, introducing an element of wonder into the assault situation tends to be disarming—both to the person initiating the wonder and to the person responding to it.[6]

O'Gorman talks about creating "a context for conversion."[7] She writes, "Creating the context for conversion . . . means doing something wonderful; something nonthreatening and unexpected."[8] O'Gorman created this sense of wonder by expressing curiosity about the different times on her clock and his watch and by engaging the trespasser in an extended conversation, something that was certainly unexpected. Reflecting on this, O'Gorman writes:

> Several things happened that night. I allowed someone who I was afraid of to become human to me and as a result I reacted in a surprisingly human way to him. That caught him off guard. Apparently his scenario had not included a social visit and it took him a few minutes to regain his sense of balance. By that time the vibes were all wrong for violence. Whatever had been motivating him was sidetracked and he changed his mind.[9]

Similarly, Louise's firm declaration that violence had no place in her home allowed Riley Arzeneaux to disarm. He had come prepared to kill but

6. O'Gorman, "Defense through Disarmament," 245, emphasis mine.

7. Ibid., 243–46.

8. Ibid., 245–46.

9. Ibid., 243.

soon realized that was unnecessary. He was in a violence-free zone and was safe.

Fourth, in both situations, O'Gorman and the Degrafinrieds refused to play the victim role. They did not scream, fight back, run away, or show signs of being afraid. In other words, they did not behave the way most victims typically behave. As O'Gorman notes, "Sociologists tell us that most assailants work from a definite set of expectations about how the victim will repond [sic] and they need the victim to act as a victim."[10] When people do not fight back or freak out, when they refuse to act like victims and respond with acts of kindness, it throws off the aggressor. Such unanticipated and magnanimous behavior is wonderfully disorienting, making it much more difficult for would-be assailants to follow through with their original intentions.

Fifth, throughout the entire situation, both O'Gorman and Degrafinried treated their intruders with dignity and respect. In a sense, this summarizes what has already been said. O'Gorman and Degrafinried conversed with these individuals, provided for some of their basic needs, and treated them with compassion. By connecting with them on a human level and by finding tangible ways to offer expressions of care, they were able to neutralize the situation and find a safe way forward.

These stories, and others like them, demonstrate the effectiveness of nonviolent action. They belie the frequent assertion that violence is the only thing that "works" in situations like these. Clearly, it is not. In fact, a strong argument could be made that nonviolence has a *better* chance of succeeding in such cases since it *de*-escalates tensions. Resorting to violence, or just threatening to use violence, has the opposite effect. It ratchets things up, making it much more likely someone will get hurt or killed in the process.

Miraculous Intervention

At this point it might be helpful to say a brief word about the possibility of divine intervention in situations like the ones we have been discussing. God can—and sometimes does—intervene in miraculous ways to rescue people from evil. Numerous stories could be told to illustrate this point. Allow me to share just one.

During the 1950s, Tom Skinner led a violent gang in New York City called the Harlem Lords. Then, one night, listening to a preacher on the radio, he became a Christian.[11] The next night, Skinner met with all 129 gang

10. Ibid., 245.
11. See Skinner, *Black and Free*, 54–64.

members for one simple reason: he needed to tell them he could no longer be their leader because of his recent decision to follow Jesus. For saying this, he was certain they would kill him. Yet inexplicably, after he finished speaking, he walked away unharmed. No one came after him.

He did not know why until a couple days later when he ran into "The Mop," the second most powerful man in the gang. When "The Mop" saw him he said:

> "Tom, I wanna talk to you."
>
> We stopped and he grinned. "You know," he said, "the other night when you got up and walked out of that meeting I was gonna really cut you up. I was all set to put my knife right in your back."
>
> "And why didn't you?"
>
> "I couldn't move," he said, his eyes growing wider. "It was like somebody was holding me back—like I was glued to my seat!"
>
> He licked his lips and continued. "And I talked to some of the other guys, too. I wasn't the only one. They said the same thing—that something, or somebody, actually held them back in their seats."
>
> Now my eyes widened and I felt the hair on the back of my neck rise.
>
> "What d'ya make of it, Tom?" he asked.
>
> "I know that the Christ I've committed myself to isn't just some fictitious character who lived two thousand years ago. . . . I know now that Jesus Christ is alive! He's real!"[12]

This story—and others like it—reminds us that what happens in situations like these does not depend solely on us. God is present with us and is able to deliver us from evil in miraculous ways. We should not lose sight of this fact, even as we respond nonviolently to whatever threat we are facing.

Living Out Prior Commitments

The ability to respond nonviolently in dangerous situations like the ones mentioned above does not come automatically or naturally for most people. On the contrary, when our safety and well-being is threatened in some way, our natural response is either fight, flight, or freeze. We are preoccupied with our own self-preservation. What must I do to stay alive? We do not instinctively think about striking up a conversation or sharing breakfast with

12. Ibid., 66–67.

an uninvited "guest," especially one who seems intent on doing us harm! This is what makes stories like Angie O'Gorman's and Nathan and Louise Degrafinried's so remarkable. What kept them from fighting back or being incapacitated by fear, thereby enabling them to treat these strangers with dignity and respect?

In both cases, their response grew out of the prior decisions and commitments they had made. O'Gorman attributes her ability to respond as she did to "the effects of prayer, mediation, training and the experience of lesser kinds of assault."[13] Her overall way of life conditioned her to react this way. Similarly, Louise Degrafinried's response to Riley Arzeneaux reflected her core convictions. Her actions were consistent with some of her deepest beliefs, namely, that God loves everyone and that violence is always wrong. These beliefs gave her the fortitude to respond courageously and nonviolently in this moment of crisis.

This illustrates the need to embrace a nonviolent lifestyle long before we find ourselves in danger. If we hope to be able to respond compassionately rather than confrontationally in situations like these, we need to prepare ourselves now. As Wink recognizes:

> Our capacity to discover creative nonviolent responses in moments of crisis will depend, to some degree at least, on whether we rehearse them in our everyday lives. If we live in the spirit of Christian nonviolent love in the little things, then in the great things we will be more likely to have something to call upon.[14]

This involves living nonviolently in *all* our relationships—with members of our family and people in our church, with employers and co-workers, with local and national leaders—with everyone! We have multiple opportunities every day to practice living nonviolently. Rather than speaking unkindly, screaming at our children, or sending that nasty email, we can, by the grace of God, choose to respond differently. Later, we will say more about how to develop a greater capacity to love others and how to live nonviolently with those around us. Doing so is crucial if we want to be able to respond similarly to an intruder or assailant.

Another way to prepare ourselves for situations like these is to talk with others about possible ways to respond. Imagine different scenarios and brainstorm nonviolent actions you could take.[15] Or try role-playing hypo-

13. O'Gorman, "Defense through Disarmament," 243.

14. Wink, *Powers that Be*, 154. Wink attributes this insight to Emmanuel Charles McCarthy.

15. Some of the playlets Walter Wink prepared can be useful in this regard. These can be downloaded from http://www.creducation.org/resources/Nonviolence_Playlets.

thetical situations to experiment with different ways of responding. This would work especially well in a small group or church setting where you could debrief after doing the role-play. By living lovingly in our day-to-day relationships, and by thinking carefully beforehand how we might respond nonviolently in situations like these, there is a far greater likelihood our responses will look like Angie O'Gorman's and Louise Degrafinried's—and, thus, more like Jesus.

Does Nonviolence Always Succeed?

While treating other people with dignity and respect, offering hospitality, and engaging in friendly conversation certainly *may* neutralize a potentially life-threatening situation, it would be naïve to think that things always turn out well for people who respond this way. Nonviolence does not always succeed (then again, neither does violence). Every situation is unique, and a host of factors come into play in determining the outcome. If the assailant is drunk, under the influence of drugs, or psychotic, the nonviolent alternatives described in this chapter may be less effective.

Similarly, if someone's *primary* objective is to do violence, dissuading them from their violent intentions will undoubtedly be more challenging. Although the *potential* for violence was present in the two stories discussed in this chapter (as well as the story about Sharon Buttry), it was not the *reason* for the confrontation. The assailants were seeking things such as food, money, and shelter. But what if the sole reason for the attack is to do violence? What if the assailant is a disgruntled employee seeking revenge or a jealous lover out to settle a score? In such cases, when the primary purpose of the attack is to cause bodily harm or death, using the nonviolent alternatives described in this chapter are likely to be less effective. That is *not* to suggest nonviolence would not work in situations like these. It simply recognizes that there is no "one size fits all" approach that can be used with equal effectiveness in every circumstance.

Even though nonviolence does not come with guarantees of success, it is still important for Christians to respond this way because that is what faithfulness to Jesus requires. Jesus calls us to love others, not to behave violently towards them, even if they are threatening us. Self-preservation is not a Christian's highest value. Jesus never commands his followers to save themselves at all costs, or to do whatever is necessary to stay alive. On the contrary, Jesus says, "Those who want to save their life will lose it, and those who lose their life for my sake will save it" (Luke 9:24).

doc.

Our job is to love *all* people, even those who hate us and would do us harm. If our love converts our enemies into friends, we praise God. If we come through the experience unharmed, we give thanks. But if that does not happen, if things turn out very badly, we can take comfort in the fact that we have been faithful to the teachings of Jesus. We have extended grace. We have offered compassion. We have lived in love. That is what we are called to do *regardless* of the consequences. Thus, while a good case can be made that nonviolence has more potential than violence to produce positive results, the primary reason Christians live nonviolently is because that is what faithful Christian discipleship requires. Even when nonviolence does not produce the desired outcome, it is always the right course of action because it is the way of Jesus.

A Brief Postscript to the Degrafinried Story

The Degrafinried's encounter with Riley Arzeneaux did not end with him being taken back to prison in handcuffs. There is more to the story.[16] Jim Forest provides a fuller account based on information gleaned from Memphis newspapers after the death of Louise Degrafinried in 1998 along with an audio recording of a presentation Riley Arzeneaux made at Northwest Elementary School in Mason, Tennessee. Before his escape, Arzeneaux was serving a twenty-five–year prison sentence for murder. After his return— now with an additional twenty years on his record—Louise Degrafinried reached out to him. Although Louise and her husband Nathan had been asked to press charges, they refused. Rather than seeking some form of retribution, Louise decided to develop a relationship. She began writing to Arzeneaux in prison, and he reciprocated. She asked him to send her a picture of himself, and he did. When she received it, she placed it in her family photo album. Over time, "the Degrafinrieds came to regard Riley as a member of the family," says Jim Forest.

In 1988, four years after his brief escape from Fort Pillow State Prison, Riley Arzeneaux became a Christian. "I realized," he explained, "that meeting the Degrafinrieds and other things that happened in my life just couldn't be coincidences. After all that, I realized someone was looking over me." Seven years later, in 1995, Arzeneaux was freed from prison, "partly thanks to her." When Mrs. Degrafinried died, "Riley was given a place of honor at Louise's funeral, was called on to speak, and joined family members in

---

16. See Forest, "Pascal Hospitality." The details and quotes that follow are from this post.

carrying her body to its final resting place." At her funeral, Riley said, "Mrs. Degrafinried was real Christianity. . . . No fear."

Although Louise Degrafinried rejected violence, she embraced a violent offender. By reaching out to Riley Arzeneaux and developing a relationship with this convicted murderer, Louise played an instrumental role in his conversion to Christ and his release from prison.

As Jim Forest asks, "Where does one obtain the kind of fearlessness that makes it possible to receive an escaped murderer as a guest sent by God? All I can guess from the articles and interviews I have read and my contact with family members is that Louise and Nathan had been freed from paralyzing fear by the depth of their conversion to Christ." Due to their Christian faith, the Degrafinrieds were not paralyzed by fear; they were compelled by love. Their actions demonstrate the truth of 1 John 4:18: "Perfect love casts out fear." Indeed, it does.

11

Creative Nonviolent Intervention

Rescuing People under Attack without Resorting to Violence

There is no footnote or proviso [in the Sermon on the Mount] where Jesus says, "You are to live this way except when it comes to the defense of your neighbors, then you must use the violence at your disposal to protect them."

—D. STEPHEN LONG[1]

JESUS SAID LOVING OUR neighbor is the second greatest commandment, and he told his followers that their love for one another would be the way others recognized they were his disciples. But what does it mean to love our neighbor when we see them being harmed? What does love require of us when someone is being attacked? Whatever else it means, this much is certain: it does *not* mean standing idly by and doing nothing. Love gets involved. Loving others means caring about their safety and well-being. It means doing everything possible to protect them with one crucial exception: violence is not allowed. Since Jesus' command to love others includes

---

1. Long, "What about the Protection of Third-Party Innocents?," 21. Long is speaking *against* the idea that pacifism is only applicable in the personal realm and not the political one.

164

everyone, victims *and* perpetrators alike, loving our neighbors does not give us a license to harm some to help others.

So what should we do when we encounter someone being threatened or attacked? How can we help this person without hurting others in the process? As we continue to explore what it means to live nonviolently in situations like these, we can once again look to stories for some answers. The first two stories illustrate the power and effectiveness of using nonviolent alternatives to come to the aid of someone being viciously beaten.

Stopping Abuse on a Commuter Train: John Roth's Story

In his book *Choosing Against War*, Goshen College professor John Roth describes a time when how he intervened in a dangerous situation to protect a man who was being verbally and physically assaulted.

> Late one evening, while attending a conference in the German city of Hamburg, I boarded a commuter train and headed for an outlying suburb where I was planning to spend the night. The train car was completely empty at that late hour, and I dozed sleepily as it rattled past the harbor and then through the industrial district. Some minutes into the trip, however, my reverie was sharply interrupted when an elderly man, dressed in rags and clearly suffering from a mental disability, shuffled into the car, closely followed by four teenagers. The young men, sporting an assortment of chains, tattoos, and body piercings, entered the car amid raucous laughter and loud talk. Almost immediately their attention focused on the old man who had seated himself near the center doors.
>
> As I watched uneasily, the four began to taunt him, shouting obscenities and making humiliating references to his mental condition. Then one of the teens shook up a half-filled can of beer and aimed the foamy spray directly into the old man's face. Without warning, their verbal abuse suddenly escalated into a physical attack as they began kicking his legs with their heavy boots and punching him in the arms and face.
>
> Seated toward the back of the car, I looked on with a mixture of horror and fear as the terrible scene unfolded before me. I am not a big person; I am not trained in any of the martial arts; I have never considered myself particularly brave. Even more crucially, I have been a professing Christian for most of my adult

life, and I have always understood pacifism to be at the very core of the good news of the gospel. Yet I knew with absolute certainty that I could not simply sit back and watch this helpless old man be mercilessly beaten. . . .

Despite my long-standing commitment to peacemaking, nothing in my years of Sunday school classes in a pacifist denomination had prepared me to respond to such a situation. If I jumped in, what would keep them from attacking me? If they did assault me, would I try to defend myself? Did they have weapons? Were they drunk enough to kill us? There was no one else in the car to turn to for help, and the next stop was still several miles away. . . .

This is what I remember from the next few minutes of that drama. As the teenagers began to kick and pummel the old man, I whispered a deep prayer: "God, calm my fear. Show me the right thing to do." And then, without really giving my next actions any careful thought, I got out of my seat and walked purposefully toward the old man and his attackers. "Hans!" I called out in my best German, "Hans, how are you? It's been such a long time since we've seen each other!" And then, slipping between two of the surprised young men, I embraced him, helped him to his feet and said, "Come sit with me, Hans. We have so much to catch up on."

In the sudden silence that ensued, the old man followed me toward the rear of the car, slid into the window seat, and slowly, haltingly, began to respond to my onslaught of questions about his health and his family. The teens looked on, not sure how they should respond. For a time they talked among themselves. But when the train pulled into the next stop, they got out. And at the following stop, "Hans" left as well, mumbling a word of thanks.[2]

Many aspects of this story are helpful for thinking about various options Christians have in situations like these. First, it is instructive to note that before John Roth acted, he prayed, albeit briefly. Prayer is *always* an appropriate response, and we should not underestimate its importance. Prayer reminds us that we are not alone and that what happens next is not solely dependent on what we do. As we ask God for wisdom and courage to respond effectively, we can trust God's Spirit to direct us and work through us, sometimes in ways we never would have imagined.

2. Roth, *Choosing against War*, 3–4, 9. For a story about a pastor intervening to stop an act of violence, see Troyer, "A Stranger Hugged Me."

Prayer is also helpful from a neurological perspective. It can calm us and break us free from the typical fight, flight, or freeze responses that come naturally in situations like these. Praying opens up new possibilities, and this enables us to react more creatively and compassionately to those around us.[3]

Second, Roth's story illustrates the power of responding to violence in creative and unexpected ways. Roth pretended to know the old man being assaulted. His decisive action introduced an element of surprise into the situation and this took the four young men completely off guard. They were not expecting one of Han's "friends" to be on the train. Roth's conversation with "Hans" created the necessary space to move him out of danger and to change the dynamics of the situation. The assailants were uncertain about how to respond and ultimately gave up their attack.

Third, this story illustrates the value of focusing on the victim rather than the violent perpetrators. We sometimes falsely assume that the only way to rescue someone under attack is by incapacitating the attackers. That simply is not true. Roth completely ignored the four young men and never engaged them. He did not need to. Instead, his entire focus was on "Hans." In this case, that was the only thing necessary.

Obviously, Roth's actions were risky. He could have become the target of their attack and could have been harmed or even killed. Still, his behavior was consistent with the nonviolent way of Jesus. John Roth fulfilled Jesus' command to love his neighbor, "Hans," without harming anyone else in the process.

"Kill Me First": Bruxy Cavey's Story

Bruxy Cavey is teaching pastor at The Meeting House, a large church in Ontario, Canada. More importantly, Bruxy is a person deeply committed to Jesus' way of peace. In a sermon series titled "Inglorious Pastors," Bruxy talks about the way he intervened to protect someone's life in an incident of racially motivated violence.

> I was on the streets of Ottawa doing street evangelism, talking to people about Jesus, when I saw someone run by super fast. It was a young black woman—and her color is important for the story. She was running, not with the kind of velocity that says "I'm late for a bus." But she was running with the "I'm running for my life" kind of pace. I took note of it but kept talking. Then, a few moments later, a whole gang of white skinheads in army

3. My thanks to Dr. Elisa Joy Seibert for help with the material in this paragraph.

fatigues went running after her. And you don't have to think to
know something bad is happening.

I stopped the conversation, and my feet started running. I
had no idea where they were taking me or what their plan was.
It is as though they were running instinctively, saying to my
brain, "You've got time to think of something; we run slow. But
in the meantime, we're getting you closer to the action." When I
got there, I came around the corner, and she was in an alleyway
curled up on the ground with multiple skinheads around her
kicking the life out of her.

I moved closer and . . . pushed my way through. . . . I got
to the front, and I turned around. I remember leaning over her
body looking up at the rest of them, and out of my mouth came:
"I follow Jesus. And that means that there are two things I cannot do."

They all kind of stopped and were like, "What the heck?"

"Two things I cannot do: One, is fight you. And two, is sit
by and do nothing. So all I can say is, 'Kill me first.'" (And my
brain said, "Tongue, that was not the plan!")

They tried to talk me out of it. "You're a whitey like me
(you're a hippie but we'll give you a haircut!). What are you doing?" I knew that this was not the time for rational discussion. I
couldn't talk them out of their prejudice. They were in the heat
of anger which puts blinders on. So all I could say is, "Kill me
first." And I kept repeating that, "Just kill me."

They started talking amongst themselves for a moment.
"Well, I don't know, should we kill the whitey?" "I don't know
if we should kill him." "This is just crazy." And they got increasingly confused. They were probably afraid it was taking too
long, that the police would come, so they just walked away. My
friends came . . . we called for an ambulance, and she was taken
to the hospital.[4]

Bruxy's commitment to follow the nonviolent way of Jesus led him to
intervene in a courageous and creative way. He literally put his life on the
line, placing his body between the skinheads and the young woman they
were assaulting. For Bruxy, neither fighting back nor doing nothing was a
viable option. Rather, his understanding of Christian discipleship involved
active engagement in this situation. He did what he could to protect this
young woman and to prevent her from experiencing any further harm.

In this instance, nonviolence worked, just as it had when John Roth
befriended "Hans." But even if nonviolence had not succeeded, it still would

4. Cavey, *Inglorious Pastors*, disc 3, part 5.

have been a faithful example of what it means to follow the nonviolent way of Jesus. As Bruxy puts it:

> May I say this would be a story of following Christ if it was told differently? If instead it was told by Tim Day [a fellow pastor at The Meeting House] saying, "You know years ago when my friend Bruxy Cavey died [trying to protect a black women being beaten by skinheads], he died in the way of Christ." That would have been okay too. In this case it had a happier ending.[5]

This reminds us of an important point discussed in the previous chapter. As Christians, the primary reason we live nonviolently is not because it succeeds (though it often does), but because it is what faithfulness to Jesus requires.

Distinguishing between Force and Violence

Before we look at a couple more stories, this is a good place to comment on a rather different way to help someone under attack than what we have discussed thus far. Depending on the situation, one might feel the best course of action is to physically *restrain* the attacker so the victim has a chance to escape. For instance, suppose you come upon a man assaulting an elderly woman. You could intervene by trying to forcibly restrain the assailant, possibly wrestling him to the ground and holding him there until help arrives or the woman gets to safety. Although some might regard this kind of physical restraint an act of violence, a crucial distinction needs to be made here between force and violence.

Earlier, we defined violence as *physical, emotional, or psychological harm done to a person by an individual(s), institution, or structure that results in serious injury, oppression, or death*. Force, on the other hand, involves the use of power "to compel through pressure or necessity."[6] As it relates to people, using force often involves exercising some form of power over them to get them to do what you want. Obviously, if the type of force used is oppressive or unjust, it is violent. But there are various ways to use force that do not cause harm to others and, consequently, are not violent.

In the summer of 2003, my wife, Elisa, worked at a state hospital as part of an internship that was one of the requirements in her doctoral program in counseling psychology. While there, she received training in how to physically restrain someone who was a danger to themselves or others. This

5. Ibid.
6. *American Heritage Dictionary*, 2nd college ed., s.v. "force."

was done through de-escalating techniques such as talking respectfully and using a bear hug from behind, always trying *not* to hurt the person being restrained. Although staff members needed to use force in these situations, they were not allowed to be—and did not need to be—violent to successfully restrain the individual in question.

When people conflate force with violence, suggesting these are one and the same, they give the impression that any kind of physical intervention constitutes an act of violence. This is surely not the case. It is possible to intervene forcefully but not violently. Consider again the example of a man assaulting an elderly woman. Physically restraining the attacker would involve the use of force, but it would not require the use of violence. In your attempt to restrain him, you would not be trying to break bones, inflict severe pain, or cause irreversible damage. Rather, you would be trying to stop the assault without harming the assailant in the process.

Admittedly, getting involved physically carries significant risk. If you are unable to restrain attacker, your efforts are very likely to escalate the situation. You yourself could get hurt or killed in the process. Therefore, it seems best to try other options first whenever that is possible. Still, this it is a viable option for Christians. Restraining someone is consistent with the nonviolent way of Jesus and does not violate the law of love.

Thwarting a Kidnapping in Progress: Marcia Poole's Story

Sometimes, one of the best things we can do when we see people being harmed is to enlist the help of others. In November 1999 two sisters, Chanti (age seventeen) and Lalitha (age fifteen), were found unconscious from carbon monoxide poisoning in a Berkeley, California apartment. They were discovered there by their eighteen-year-old roommate Laxmi. The apartment belonged to a man named Lakireddy Bali Reddy, a wealthy slumlord and human trafficker who controlled many rental properties in Berkeley. Reddy had trafficked these three young women from India and was using them as his own personal sex slaves.

When Laxmi found her roommates unconscious, she contacted some of Reddy's family members who worked at a local Indian restaurant he owned. They contacted Reddy and he came to the apartment. Diana Russell describes what happened next.

> When Reddy arrived at the Bancroft Way apartment, he failed to call either the police or an ambulance. Instead, he had his company van brought to the front of the apartment house where he, some of his employees and members of his family proceeded

to remove the girls down a dark, enclosed stairwell that was adjacent to an open, clearly visible staircase. They carried Lalitha, who was unconscious, out of the building to Reddy's awaiting van, attempting to conceal her body by wrapping her in a carpet or cloth. . . . They also tried to drag Laxmi into the van despite the fact that she was screaming and resisting their attempts in great agitation.

Berkeley resident Marcia Poole happened to be driving down Bancroft Way when this suspicious-looking scene unfolded before her. She watched as three or four men proceeded to the van carrying a large bundle with a discernible sag in the middle. She was horrified when she saw a leg dangle from the bundle before it was deposited in the van. She slowed her car to a crawl as she watched the men run back to a larger group of Indian men and women who had surrounded Laxmi. They attempted to push and pull her toward the van. Laxmi was crying and resisting their efforts with all her might.

Poole hastily jumped out of her car and attempted to thwart the efforts of Laxmi's would-be kidnappers by demanding that they stop trying to force her into Reddy's van. They ignored Poole's plea and a man whom she later identified as Lakireddy Bali Reddy told her, "Mind your own business! Go away! This is a family affair." Poole refused to oblige him. Instead, she hailed two passing motorists and begged them to call 911 as she continued her efforts to prevent the attempted kidnapping from succeeding. Although the two male motorists would not get out of their cars to assist Poole with her solitary intervention of the kidnapping, one of them called the police. When sirens were heard approaching, the group that had been trying to force Laxmi into the van melted away into the surrounding area, leaving only Poole and the young girls at the scene.[7]

Soon after, the police and paramedics arrived. The two sisters suffering from carbon monoxide poisoning were taken to the hospital. Chanti died at the hospital, but her younger sister Lalitha survived and was released the following day. It is frightening to think what would have happened to Lalitha and Laxmi had it not been for Marcia Poole's heroic and persistent efforts. Poole's decision to get involved not only stopped a kidnapping in progress, it insured Lalitha got the medical care she needed.

Poole's actions illustrate two additional nonviolent alternatives we can use. First, we can tell people who are harming others to stop what they are

7. Russell, "Death of Lakireddy Bali Reddy's Sex Slave." For a brief version of this account, see Batstone, *Not for Sale*, 1–3.

doing. If they know they are being watched, and realize their violent behavior has not gone unnoticed, sometimes they actually will stop for no other reason than fear of getting into trouble. In this instance, Poole was unable to convince the men and women trying to force Laxmi into the van to leave her alone. Rather than giving up when her own efforts failed, Poole elicited help from passing motorists. Although neither of the people she stopped was willing to get personally involved in this situation, she was able to persuade one of them to call 911. That simple act possibly saved Lalitha's life.

Sometimes calling the police may be the best way to help someone being harmed. It was the sound of police sirens that caused the would-be kidnappers to stop their efforts. Even just telling those doing harm that you have called the police and that they are on their way (regardless of whether you actually have called the police or whether they actually are on their way) might be enough to cause them to stop their assault. The threat of police officers arriving on the scene is a strong deterrent.[8]

Pink Alert: The Saskatchewan Nurses' Story

In addition to the stories examined thus far in which one individual is primarily responsible for rescuing someone from harm, other stories demonstrate the way a group of people can work together to protect someone. The following story, told by Walter Wink, illustrates this well and confirms the old adage "there is strength in numbers."

> The nurses in a hospital in Saskatchewan were tired of being browbeaten, corrected in front of patients, and generally made to feel inferior by the doctors on staff. The nurses put their heads together and came up with a plan. They went to a sympathetic administration and set up a "pink alert," which would be transmitted over the intercom the next time a doctor started abusing a nurse. From all over the hospital, nurses who were free converged on the scene, surrounded the doctor, holding hands, and waited for him to make the first move. He located the smallest

8. Most Christians would have no qualms about calling the police in a situation like the one just described or in many others like it. Yet some believe calling the police is inconsistent with a commitment to nonviolence since police officers are authorized to use lethal violence. For a helpful introduction to the issues, see Schlabach, "Must Christian Pacifists Reject Police Force?" For an argument against Christian involvement in policing, see Alexis-Baker, "The Gospel or a Glock?," and for a critique of Alexis-Baker's position, see Ewert, "Law and Its Enforcement." For a range of opinions on the question of Christians serving as police officers, see Winright, "From Police Officers to Peace Officers."

nurse and plunged toward her. But the circle merely gave with his charge. He tried another nurse; same result. It became like the childhood game Red Rover. The circle was like an amoeba that simply gave with his every move. Finally he dropped his hands, acquiescing in their lesson. That pretty much took care of that problem from then on out, for their circle . . . was ready at a moment's notice.[9]

Collectively, people have much more power than they often realize. These nurses were able to support one another by using a simple nonviolent strategy to stop workplace bullying. As we will discover in the next chapter, the positive effects of nonviolent action are multiplied exponentially when utilized by large numbers of people working together.

A Brief Word about Christians and Guns

This chapter has highlighted a number of different *nonviolent* actions a person could take in a hostile situation to come to the aid of someone being harmed. None of these involved using a gun. The reason for this omission is obvious: shooting someone with a lethal weapon is an act of *violence*. That notwithstanding, many Christians carry handguns because they believe they have a right to use lethal force, if necessary, to defend themselves or to protect others. They also carry to be able to respond to any number of violent situations they might encounter: an active shooter on school grounds, a hostile gunman at church, or a vengeful employee in the workplace, to name a few. Some pastors even take a concealed weapon into the pulpit on Sunday mornings, prepared to protect the congregation by any means necessary. They believe it is right to take *one* life to save many others. But is it? Is taking another human life, even when doing so has the potential to save other lives, an act of Christian faithfulness? Or, to put it more succinctly: Are Christians ever called to kill? The answer we have been giving throughout this book is a resounding "No."

Since gun ownership and second amendment rights are very sensitive—and highly politicized—issues in the United States, it is important to be clear here.[10] The issue is *not* whether it is right for Christians to own

9. Wink, *Jesus and Nonviolence*, 32–33.

10. Christians should support sensible gun legislation and close loopholes that make it far too easy to purchase deadly weapons. This would include stopping straw purchases, *always* requiring background checks (even at gun shows), and passing an assault weapons ban. The United States desperately needs to respond to this crisis and the church can be a constructive voice in this critical conversation. Thankfully, there are good resources available to churches. The booklet "Preventing Gun Violence," produced

firearms for hunting or recreation (e.g., skeet shooting or trapshooting). Responsible gun ownership for purposes like these is not the problem.[11] Rather, the issue here is whether it is right for Christians to carry concealed weapons or to purchase guns to defend themselves or others. Is this consistent with faithful Christian discipleship? Evangelical pastor Rob Schenck thinks not. As Schenck explains it, the problem with carrying a gun is that you need to be prepared to use it:

> Whenever someone intentionally carries a deadly weapon, he or she must be ready to kill. A military-trained firearms instructor explained it to me this way. "If you are not ready to kill, you are more dangerous with the weapon than without it, because it will likely be taken from you and used to kill you and others."[12]

Carrying a deadly weapon inevitably alters the way we see people. "Readiness to kill," writes Schenck, "changes our disposition toward others. We must view the people around us through a lethal lens, asking, Whom will I kill? When will I kill? For what will I kill?" Schenck finds this disposition particularly problematic since it "seems . . . contradictory to three paramount New Testament principles: Love of neighbor, love of enemy, and fear of God only."[13]

This really gets to the heart of the problem. Being "ready" to kill someone is at odds with loving them. Moreover, relying upon a concealed weapon to protect ourselves, or others, suggests that our faith is misplaced. As Christians, we are to place our faith in God, not guns. We do not arm ourselves and rely upon weapons to keep us safe. Rather, we take reasonable precautions and trust God to care for us. Likewise, when others are threatened with harm, God does not command us to respond with lethal force, taking one life to save another. Instead, our love for both victim *and* perpetrator should compel us to do everything possible to help one without

---

by Mennonite Central Committee, can be easily accessed online and contains a brief overview of the issues involved in the current debate along with action steps to take. Also helpful is the recent collection of essays in Pearson, ed., *Reclaiming the Gospel of Peace*, which includes liturgical resources, suggested readings, names of organizations addressing gun violence, actions to take, and much more. Concerned individuals can also partner with groups like Heeding God's Call (http://heedinggodscall.org/), which describes itself as "a faith-based movement to prevent gun violence." For a recent analysis of the issues in the American context, see Atwood, *Gundamentalism*.

11. Some pacifists would disagree since they object to killing animals for food, by guns or any other means.

12. Schenck, "Should Christians Own Guns?," 16

13. Ibid. For more on this point, see Schenck's recent film, *The Armor of Light*.

harming the other. This is precisely why the nonviolent strategies we have been discussing are so very important since they allow us to do just that.

In addition, it bears repeating that resorting to violence has the potential to make the situation worse, not better. Carrying a concealed weapon, and believing it somehow makes you and those around you safer, rests on some rather big assumptions. It assumes you will be able to use your weapon to accomplish what you desire in a hostile situation. Specifically, it assumes that you will hit the "target" (rather than innocent bystanders) and that this will neutralize the "threat" (rather than escalate the situation). These are *very* big assumptions—and extremely risky ones at that. Pulling out a gun *might* make the situation better—at least for some people involved—but it could also make things far worse. Recall what happened to the man who came out of his house with a gun to confront two of the inmates who had escaped from Fort Pillow Prison. He was shot and killed, and his wife was taken hostage.[14]

Also, as noted earlier, what happens if you decide to shoot, but miss? What if that provokes the gunman, causing him to kill many more people than he ever intended—if he ever intended to kill anyone at all? Or suppose you shoot and unintentionally kill an innocent bystander: an elderly man, a pregnant women, a small child. *You* are now the one guilty of destroying innocent life. There are just too many variables to know exactly how things will transpire. Maybe the shooter will be killed, maybe not. Maybe lives will be saved, or maybe the number of casualties will be greater. It is hard to say. There is no way to guarantee the outcome will be what you desire, and there is a real probability that your violent actions will make things worse. Nonviolent strategies have the benefit of allowing *all* parties to get through the situation unharmed. Most importantly, nonviolent strategies are consistent with faithful Christian discipleship.

But What If Someone Threatens My Family?

The stories in this chapter have been about people using nonviolent means to help *strangers* under attack. But what if the person being threatened is someone we know and love, like our spouse or one of our children? Do the "rules" change? Should we do whatever is necessary to protect our family *even if* that means resorting to violence? Many people think so. That is why they carry a concealed weapon and/or have a handgun under their pillow or in the nightstand beside their bed. But is this the way of Jesus? Does Jesus call us to protect our family at all costs?

14. Chapter 4.

The desire we feel to protect family members is not only normal, it is admirable. In fact, it would be strange *not* to feel protective of the people closest to us. I love my family more than words can express, and it is agonizing to imagine life without them. If someone tried to hurt or kill *my* wife or children, I would do everything I possibly could to protect them—*except* resort to violence. I could not live with myself otherwise.

My reasons for not using violence are both practical and theological. As just discussed, there is a high likelihood that pulling out a gun or using some other form of violence might actually aggravate the situation. Rather than making things better, there is a good chance it could make things worse. I do not want to do anything that might put my family at even greater risk. I would also be unwilling to resort to violence, even to try to protect those most dear to me, because I have made a commitment to follow Jesus. Jesus commanded his followers to love their enemies and to treat others the way we want to be treated. We do neither when we behave violently. Resorting to violence is inconsistent with the nonviolent nature of Christian discipleship, and it directly violates the teachings of Jesus.[15]

Obviously, the stakes are much higher for us personally when it comes to protecting a family member than when it comes to protecting a stranger. These are our loved ones, after all! Still, the rules do not change. Jesus provides no exception clauses or provisos that say, "Love your enemies except when they attempt to harm your family. Then you can use violence to incapacitate or kill them." No. The call to love others, even our enemies, is comprehensive and unequivocal. We do not show our love for others by killing them. The two are mutually exclusive.

So how can we protect our family if violence is out of the question? What can we do? As we have seen in the stories we examined in this chapter and the preceding one, creative acts of nonviolence have the potential to disarm hostility and de-escalate dangerous situations. There are nonviolent alternatives that have proven to be effective in situations like this and can be used with great skill, ingenuity, and creativity. They have the potential to protect our loved ones from those who would do them harm. In fact, some would argue they have a greater likelihood of being successful than violent options. Therefore, if we hope to respond to threats against family members in ways that are consistent with our Christian faith, we need to be familiar with the broad range of nonviolent options at our disposal. Then, if we find ourselves in a situation where those we love are being threatened, we will have good options at hand, options that will enable us to do everything

15. See chapters 5 and 7.

possible to try to protect our family in a manner that is fully faithful to the nonviolent way of Jesus.

Trusting God to "Deliver Us From Evil"

As important as it is to do everything possible to protect our family, we need to be careful not to presume that our family's safety is ultimately dependent on us. Rather, we need to trust God for their well-being. Trusting God is a major theme in the Bible and is central to the life of faith, but it is a concept often misunderstood. Some people equate trusting God with doing nothing. Just "let go and let God," is the old cliché. But trust is not antithetical to faithful, responsible action. It does *not* mean doing nothing when harm comes and letting God figure it all out. Engaging in creative nonviolent action and trusting in God are *not* mutually exclusive. On the contrary, we can trust God to give us wisdom about how to respond and about what to say and not say. And, as we take certain actions, we can trust God to use those in the most effective way possible.

On the other hand, as important as our efforts are, we need to remember they are only part of the equation. If we think it is up to us, and us alone, to protect our family, we have ceased trusting God. Perhaps God will intervene in ways we do not expect and would not have predicted. Maybe God will do something truly wonderful and miraculous. So while we should do all we can to keep our family safe, we must never forget that God can protect them and care for them in ways that far exceed even our best efforts.

To illustrate this, consider the following story from Africa told by Kathy Stuebing. Kathy and Rich Stuebing attend my home church and were missionaries in Africa for over forty years. Listen to how God protected both of them and their two young children one night many years ago.

> A sudden crash woke us with a start, as broken glass from our bedroom window sprayed over the bed. Strong hands reached through the window, yanking the curtains and shaking the steel bars we had installed to deter burglars. Rich and I knew immediately what was happening: our house was being attacked, just as we had heard of other houses being attacked by bands of thieves with no fear of the authorities. We were living outside of Ndola, Zambia, because we answered God's call to teach at the Theological College of Central Africa, preparing pastors and Christian workers for service to the growing churches in Zambia.

The thieves had cut the telephone lines to our area, so even as we turned on our alarm siren, we knew our neighbors could not call for help. We checked the kitchen, and just as we had relocked the kitchen door behind us we heard a loud bang, and men began ramming the door we had just locked. We then heard our children, Beth age 4, and David almost 2, calling us and we brought them with us to the living room while the melee continued in the kitchen and the siren blared on the roof.

I had been praying that the Lord would prevent an attack like this so our children would not be traumatized, but here we were sitting with the children while the unthinkable happened around us. I began praying aloud, having them very much in mind. My prayer made no sense humanly speaking, since I was asking for impossible things: that Jesus would take care of us and no one would be hurt (the thieves had already shot at us from behind the kitchen door); that Jesus would make the thieves run away (they were clearly unafraid of our siren and considered us helpless); and that Jesus would send our friends to help us (our neighbors lived at a distance, and people don't generally enter situations like this).

But the Lord answered each part of my prayer. A Christian neighbor came to the noisy attack with a squeezy bottle of ammonia that he kept as a burglar deterrent. He waited until the group of ten or more men gathered around him (after shooting at him but missing), and then he sprayed them with his ammonia. They all fled into the night! Even more amazing to me, our children went back to sleep that night and never had a bad dream or sleep problem over this attack. The Lord preserved them from the trauma I had feared for them, and in later years they would point to this night as evidence of God's love and care for them.[16]

God delivers people in all sorts of different ways and seems to delight in doing so. We should never lose sight of this. It should give us hope and confidence. As a brief postscript to this story, Kathy writes:

In the days after our house attack, other missionaries were among those who insisted that we must get a gun if we were going to continue living in our house outside town. When the house next door had been attacked a month before our attack, that man never slept in his house again! He moved immediately into town. We stayed where we were and assured people that since God took care of us without a gun this time, we felt we

16. Stuebing, "Whom Shall I Fear?," 3.

should not compromise our understanding of our Christian faith by getting a gun for the future.[17]

Conclusion: Violence is Never the Only Viable Option

The stories included in this chapter have demonstrated many nonviolent ways to help people who are being harmed. Many more stories like these could be told—and *should* be told—far more often than they usually are.[18] They are inspiring, encouraging, and instructive. Each story, in its own way, illustrates the power and effectiveness of nonviolence. Each one reminds us that violence is never the only viable option. Our choices are not limited to doing nothing or using violence. Instead, an endless number of creative nonviolent possibilities are at our disposal between these extremes in addition to the possibility of divine intervention in ways we can only begin to imagine.

We encountered a sampling of these nonviolent options in the stories we have heard. These included things such as praying, using a rouse to get someone out of harm's way, interposing oneself between a person being harmed and her attackers, persuading someone to call the police, and joining together with others to surround an abuser, putting him on notice that his behavior would not be tolerated. In addition, we discussed the possibility of physically restraining an individual who was harming someone to allow that person to get away. Many other nonviolent options could be added to this list, including the ones described in the previous chapter such as engaging in conversation, extending hospitality, or introducing an element of surprise or wonder.

The effectiveness of these approaches in the stories above demonstrates that creative nonviolent intervention is neither wildly idealistic nor hopelessly naïve. On the contrary, it is actually quite possible to help someone being harmed without harming others in the process. Nonviolence works and is often a very effective way to respond to those who threaten others.

Obviously, nonviolent intervention does not always work. Nor is there any guarantee that the person using it will remain unharmed. John Roth could have gotten beaten up on the subway, and Bruxy Cavey could have

17. Personal email correspondence from Kathy Stuebing, October 28, 2016.

18. For a wonderful story about some friends in Washington, DC who respond with hospitality rather than hostility when threatened by a robber, listen to the first part of National Public Radio's (NPR's) *Invisibilia* podcast "Flip the Script." As described on the website, "The episode starts with a story about a dinner party in DC, when an attempted robbery was foiled by . . . a glass of wine and some cheese."

gotten killed on the street. Getting involved entails genuine risk. But that is true regardless of whether you decide to intervene violently *or* nonviolently. Ultimately, what is important for followers of Jesus is not avoiding all risk, but helping those in need in ways that are congruent with faithful Christian discipleship. This chapter has illustrated some of the ways that is possible.

We have been considering what living nonviolently looks like in situations involving just a handful of individuals. Now we are ready to consider how it might work on a much larger scale. If Christians are not supposed to go to war, assassinate heads of state, or torture terrorists, how can they respond effectively to some of the world's most pressing problems: brutal dictatorships, terrorism, genocide, and the like? We will take up that question in the next chapter as we consider the principles of nonviolent struggle and witness some of the amazing ways nonviolent action has been used to help large groups of people suffering from oppression, injustice, and warfare.

12

Nonviolent Struggle 101

Confronting Injustice, Stopping Wars, and Bringing Down Dictators without Firing a Shot

Christians are called to nonviolence, unequivocally. They are to engage evil nonviolently, in every circumstance, without exception.

—WALTER WINK[1]

The concrete victories of modern nonviolent campaigns, the spiraling dangers of lethal weapons, and the moral demands of Christian faith bring into focus a clear imperative. It is time for the Christian church—indeed, all people of faith—to explore, in a more sustained and sophisticated way than ever before in human history, what can be done nonviolently.

—RONALD J. SIDER[2]

IN THE PREVIOUS CHAPTER, we explored a number of stories about people who used creative nonviolent responses to de-escalate tensions and neutralize dangerous situations in which someone was being threatened or harmed. The benefit of stories like these is that they demonstrate there *are*

---

1. Wink, *Engaging the Powers*, 237.
2. Sider, *Nonviolent Action*, xv.

nonviolent alternatives that can be used in such cases. They also remind us that violence is not the *only*—or even the best—way to defend ourselves and others. This is particularly important for Christians to realize, especially those who are serious about following the nonviolent way of Jesus.

While these stories are certainly inspiring, they inevitably leaves certain questions unanswered since they only address situations dealing with a handful of people. How well does nonviolence work on a much larger scale? Is it as effective in dealing with despots, terrorists, and oppressive regimes? Can it really bring about sweeping social, political, and economic change? These are important questions, especially for Christians determined to do justice without doing violence.

When it comes to addressing conflict on a national or international level, many people are convinced that violence is sometimes necessary, even if regrettable. The purpose of this chapter is to suggest otherwise, to demonstrate that nonviolent action *is* a viable option, one that often has a greater chance of success than violence. To make this case, we will consider what makes nonviolent struggle work and will discover how effective it has been in dealing with situations of large-scale conflict, injustice, oppression, and war. Along the way, we will reference some of the amazing success stories of nonviolent action in the twentieth century, particularly those occurring in the last few decades. To begin, let's consider one of the most arresting stories from the turn of the century.

The Nonviolent Overthrow of Slobodan Milosevic

Dubbed the "Butcher of the Balkans," Slobodan Milosevic was one of the most brutal dictators of the late twentieth century.[3] For thirteen years (1987–2000) he ruled the Yugoslav federation with an iron fist. During that time, Milosevic led Yugoslavia into catastrophic economic disaster. Many lived in desperate poverty on salaries averaging under $70/month. People suffered crippling inflation, and unemployment rates were extremely high.

Like most dictators, Milosevic was rich, powerful, and ruthless. Life under Milosevic was harsh and repressive. Critique was dangerous and freedom of expression limited. Milosevic was politically well-connected, had the support of both the police and military, and controlled the state-run media. Those who openly opposed the Serbian president could expect to be harassed, arrested, and detained—sometimes even killed.

---

3. The following information about Milosevic and the effect he had on Yugoslavia come from Paulson, "Removing the Dictator," 315–16.

While president, Milosevic led Serbia into four wars. Most chillingly, he authorized and encouraged genocide in Croatia, Bosnia-Herzegovina, and Kosovo. All told, approximately 210,000 people died and another three million became refugees. Clearly, Milosevic needed to be removed. Unfortunately, he was determined to do whatever was necessary to stay.[4]

How could the people of Serbia remove such a powerful dictator from office? Opposition candidates had run against Milosevic previously, but none ever gained enough of the vote to defeat him. They could attempt a violent overthrow, but such a move would be very risky with no guarantee of "success." Besides, whatever the outcome, this much was certain: using violence against Milosevic was certain to result in a great deal of death and destruction on all sides. Wisely, the Serbians tried a different approach.

Through the efforts of a student-led group called Otpor!, the people of Serbia defeated the Butcher of the Balkans without firing a shot. How? By engaging in nonviolent struggle.[5] The members of Otpor! used a variety of nonviolent tactics that eventually eroded support for Milosevic. These tactics included mass protests, clever slogans, street theater, and television commercials, to name just a few. They also worked to unite all the opposition parties around a single candidate, Vojislav Kostunica. This was crucial. Without this unity, the vote would get divided up among too many different opposition candidates, ensuring yet another win for Milosevic.

In the end, Otpor's hard fought efforts paid off. Kostunica won the election. Yet just as predicted, Milosevic falsely said neither candidate had received the required 50 percent of the vote needed to win the election in the first round and announced a run-off election would be needed. The opposition expected this and was prepared. With significant help from Otpor! leaders, the people of Serbia organized a general strike that slowly shut down the capital, bringing everyday life to a halt. Businesses closed, public transportation stopped operating, roads were impassible. This general strike culminated in a massive demonstration at the Serbian capital in Belgrade on October 5, 2000 in which hundreds of thousands of people converged on the city from all directions, making it clear that Milosevic was finished. Milosevic finally conceded, and on October 7, 2000, Kostunica, Yugoslavia's democratically elected leader, took office. The people of Serbia had

---

4. At one point, Milosevic even rewrote part of the constitution, allowing him to govern beyond the standard two-term limit.

5. The inspiring story of how these young, unarmed, politically inexperienced students were able to topple such a powerful politician is brilliantly told in Steve York's award-winning documentary *Bringing Down a Dictator*. For a narrative description of these events, see Paulson, "Removing the Dictator in Serbia."

succeeded in removing a dictator from power without bloodshed or killing, and with virtually no casualties.[6]

The nonviolent overthrow of Slobodan Milosevic challenges many of the assumptions people have about violence and power. As Ackerman and DuVall astutely observe:

> The greatest misconception about conflict is that violence is always the ultimate form of power, that no other method of advancing a just cause or defeating injustice can surpass it. But Russians, Indians, Poles, Danes, Salvadorans, African Americans, Chileans, South Africans, and many others have proven . . . that other, *nonviolent measures can be a force more powerful.*"[7]

This is precisely what the people of Serbia demonstrated by removing Milosevic from office *without* resorting to violence.

The Success of Nonviolent Action in the Twentieth Century

What happened in Serbia is just one of many stories that could be told. In fact, what is especially striking about nonviolent struggle in the twentieth century (and beyond) is not just how frequently it has been used, but how successful it has been. As Walter Wink writes:

> In the past two decades [1980s and 1990s] the world has seen nonviolence used in an escalating number of situations. In 1989–90 alone, thirteen nations underwent nonviolent revolutions, all of them successful but one (China), and all of them nonviolent on the part of the revolutionaries except one (Romania, and there it was largely the secret police fighting the army, with the public maintaining nonviolent demonstrations throughout). Those nonviolent struggles affected 1.7 billion people—one-third of the population of the world. If we add all the nonviolent efforts of this century [twentieth century], we get the astonishing figure of 3.3. billion—over half of the human race! No one can ever again say that nonviolence doesn't work.[8]

Similarly, Ron Sider claims that "at no time in history, perhaps, has the concrete evidence of the tangible success of nonviolent action been clearer."[9]

6. Only two people died in the takeover of parliament on October 5, 2000, one in a traffic accident and one from a heart attack (*Bringing Down a Dictator*).

7. Ackerman and DuVall, *Force More Powerful*, 9, emphasis mine.

8. Wink, ed., *Peace is the Way*, 1. Cf. Wink, *Powers that Be*, 116–17.

9. Sider, *Nonviolent Action*, 176.

Although it is difficult to quantify precisely how successful nonviolence has been in bringing about social and political change, an attempt has been made by Erica Chenoweth and Maria Stephan in a comprehensive study of 323 violent and nonviolent resistance campaigns between 1900 and 2006.[10] One of the most significant findings of this study is the *effectiveness* of non-violent resistance in contrast to the relative ineffectiveness of violence when used to achieve similar goals. What makes this particularly noteworthy is that it flies in the face of conventional wisdom. People generally assume that violence is the most effective way—indeed, the *only* way—to resolve certain kinds of conflict. Nonviolence, on the other hand, is regarded as idealistic and utopian, a nice idea but one that does not actually work in the rough and tumble of the real world. This study powerfully refutes that assumption, demonstrating that nonviolent efforts often prove far more effective than violent ones. Chenoweth and Stephan regard this to be their "most strik-ing finding," namely, "that between 1900 and 2006, nonviolent resistance campaigns were *nearly twice as likely to achieve full or partial success* as their violent counterparts."[11] These findings lead Chenoweth and Stephan to draw the following conclusion: "Nonviolent civil resistance works, both in terms of achieving campaigns' strategic objectives and in terms of promot-ing the long-term well-being of the societies in which the campaigns have been waged. Violent insurgency, on the other hand, has a dismal record on both counts."[12]

The importance of a study like this is *not* to suggest that nonviolence *always* works—it does not[13]—but to demonstrate that nonviolence *often* works, and does so even more frequently than violence. Thus, using non-violence to confront even the harshest and most repressive regimes is not suicidal. On the contrary, using nonviolent tactics strategically to achieve social, political, or economic change is really quite sensible. It may actually provide activists with the greatest chances of survival and the best hope that real and lasting change will occur.

10. Chenoweth and Stephan, *Why Civil Resistance Works*.

11. Ibid., 7, emphasis mine.

12. Ibid., 222.

13. Chenoweth and Stephan acknowledge this and contend "that nonviolent cam-paigns fail to achieve their objectives when they are unable to overcome the challenge of participation, when they fail to recruit a robust, diverse, and broad-based member-ship that can erode the power base of the adversary and maintain resilience in the face of repression" (*Why Civil Resistance Works*, 11).

What Has Nonviolence Wrought?

The diverse range of contexts in which nonviolent struggle has been used over the past one hundred years to achieve substantial social, political, and economic change is truly remarkable. As Gene Sharp summarizes these achievements:

> Higher wages and improved working conditions were won. Oppressive traditions and practices were abolished. Both men and women won the right to vote in several countries in part by using this technique. Government policies were changed, laws repealed, new legislation enacted, and governmental reforms instituted. Invaders were frustrated and armies defeated. An empire was paralyzed, coups d'état thwarted, and dictatorships disintegrated.[14]

To illustrate this further, I have identified just a few of many historical examples that could be given to demonstrate how nonviolent action was used successfully to effect change. What follows is a *very* brief sampling of what nonviolent struggle has wrought in the twentieth century.

One of the most dramatic and well-known examples of nonviolent struggle being used to free people from oppressive rule is Gandhi's nonviolent campaign against the British. His efforts, and the efforts of those who joined with him, culminated in India's independence from Britain in 1947. More recently, nonviolent action has been instrumental in liberating countries from Communist rule. The "Velvet Revolution" in Czechoslovakia (1989) and the Solidarity movement in Poland (1980–1989) are two noteworthy examples.

Nonviolent action was successfully used on numerous occasions to topple tyrants such as the Filipino dictator Ferdinand Marcos (1986), the Yugoslavian president and indicted war criminal Slobodan Milosevic, noted above (2000), and more recently, the Egyptian dictator Hosni Mubarak (2011). Each of these efforts involved masses of people engaging in collective acts of nonviolent protest and resistance. These efforts, sometimes referred to as "people power" movements, brought widespread change and encouraged democracy and reform.[15]

In a number of instances, nonviolent struggle in the twentieth century played a prominent role in achieving economic justice by confronting unjust labor practices and challenging unfair wages. Examples include the boycott

14. Sharp, *Waging Nonviolent Struggle*, 16.

15. Of course, these impulses are not always sustained. In Egypt, for example, things have not developed so positively. The current Sisi regime is very authoritarian and functions like a dictatorship.

of grapes and the grape workers strike in California, led by Cesar Chavez (1965–1970),[16] and the African workers strike in Namibia (1971–1972).[17]

Nonviolent struggle has also been used to end warfare. One of the most dramatic examples in recent years comes from Liberia. After decades of warfare and violence, Liberian women, both Muslim and Christian, joined together to bring an end to decades of bloodshed and killing. Their dramatic story is told by Leymah Gbowee in her memoir, *Mighty Be Our Powers: How Sisterhood, Prayer, and Sex Changed a Nation at War*, and in the documentary film "Pray the Devil Back to Hell." Through prayer, nonviolent action, and determination, the women of Liberia succeed in securing a peace agreement and ousting their ruthless president, Charles Taylor.

Sometimes, nonviolent actions have been used to assist a particular *group* of people being oppressed. For example, during World War II, many people engaged in nonviolent acts to rescue Jews who were being systematically rounded up, imprisoned, and killed.[18] The entire Jewish population of Bulgaria, some 50,000 individuals, was saved by the nonviolent actions of the people living there.[19] Similarly, virtually all the Jews in Finland, and most Jews in Denmark, were protected and kept from concentration camps.[20] Pastor Andrew Trocme and the citizens of Le Chambon, a small village in southern France, sheltered and saved thousands of Jews in their city.[21] And, in one of the most astonishing, but seldom heard stories from that era, German wives protesting in Berlin secured the release of their Jewish husbands from Auschwitz.[22]

The civil rights movement (1950s–1960s) also demonstrates how nonviolent struggle can help those being oppressed. Through a series of nonviolent tactics—letters, speeches, sit-ins, boycotts, marches—this movement, under the leadership of Rev. Martin Luther King Jr., ended segregation in the American South. It changed legislation and brought a measure of racial justice to African Americans. Across the Atlantic, nonviolent efforts were also crucial in freeing blacks in South Africa from the grip of Apartheid (1990s).

16. Merriman, "California Grape Workers' Strike," 173–87.

17. Sharp, *Waging Nonviolent Struggle*, 205–16.

18. Sider, *Nonviolent Action*, 10–11.

19. Ibid., 11.

20. Wink, *Powers that Be*, 152.

21. For this story, see Hallie, *Lest Innocent Blood Be Shed*.

22. For a full account, see Stoltzfus, *Resistance of the Heart*, 209–57. Contrary to popular opinion, nonviolence was used effectively against Hitler and the Nazi regime. The problem is that "it was used too seldom" (Wink, *Powers that Be*, 153). For an excellent discussion of nonviolent efforts in Nazi Germany, see Ackerman and DuVall, *Force More Powerful*, 207–39.

Although these represent just a handful of the many historical examples that could be cited, they provide a general sense of what nonviolent struggle has achieved in the past one hundred years.[23] In many cases, Christians were very involved in these nonviolent actions and played a significant role in confronting injustice and stopping oppression.[24]

What is Nonviolent Struggle and How Does it Work?

To this point, we have talked about nonviolent struggle without defining it or discussing how it works. For help with this, we turn to Dr. Gene Sharp, Professor Emeritus of Political Science at the University of Massachusetts Dartmouth. Although Gene Sharp is not a household name in the Christian community, perhaps it should be. Sharp is an expert on all aspects of nonviolent struggle. For over half a century he has researched and written about nonviolence and has provided practical support and advice to people engaged in nonviolent struggle around the world. His numerous books, pamphlets, and articles have been translated into more than thirty languages, and many of his writings can be accessed for free online.[25] Currently, Sharp is a senior scholar at the Albert Einstein Institution (AEI) in Boston, a nonprofit organization he founded in 1983 that "works to advance the worldwide study and strategic use of nonviolent action."[26]

Nonviolent struggle is fundamentally about power. Sharp defines nonviolent struggle (or nonviolent action) as "a technique of action by which the population can restrict and sever the sources of power of their rulers or other oppressors and mobilize their own power potential into effective power."[27] The "sources of power" to which Sharp refers include powerful political alliances, profitable business partnerships, tribal loyalties, revenue

23. To read more about these stories and other fascinating accounts of nonviolent struggle and the great success they have had, see especially Ackerman and DuVall, *Force More Powerful*; Sharp, *Waging Nonviolent Struggle*; and Sider, *Nonviolent Action*. Ackerman and DuVall describe the use of nonviolence around the world in places like Russia, India, Poland, Denmark, El Salvador, Argentina and Chile, the southern United States, and the Philippines, among others. Sharp's book explores twenty-three cases where nonviolent struggle was used in a variety of different situations around the world. Sider retells many of the most inspiring stories of successful nonviolent campaigns from 1900 to the present including the women's movement in Liberia (2003) and the Arab Spring (2011) that felled numerous dictators.

24. For specific examples of nonviolent action in which *Christians* were prominently involved, see Duffey, *Peacemaking Christians*, 113–42.

25. Sharp's writings can be accessed at www.aeinstein.org/free-resources/.

26. www.aeinstein.org.

27. Sharp, *Waging Nonviolent Struggle*, 39.

from natural resources, obedient soldiers, compliant police officers, and so forth. These sources of power, or "pillars of support" as they are sometimes called, are what enable an oppressor, or an oppressive regime, to stay in power.[28] If these pillars are weakened or taken away altogether, it becomes exceedingly difficult for those in power to remain in control. Removing, or seriously degrading, these sources of power has the same effect as taking a battery out of a car or unplugging an oven. Tyrants cannot operate without a power supply any more than an unplugged oven or a car without a battery.

Therefore, one of the first objectives of those who wage nonviolent struggle is to identify the sources of power that enable the leader in question to remain in power. Once these have been identified, the opposition needs to decide its strategy for severing these sources of power from the oppressor. This could involve such things as cutting off revenue streams, persuading soldiers and police officers to shift their loyalty to the opposition, and encouraging people to stop cooperating with the oppressive regime (e.g., stop broadcasting state-run media, start publically demonstrating against the regime, create economic hardship and societal paralysis through work stoppages, strikes, boycotts, etc.).

For this to be effective, lots of people need to work together. As Eric Stoner observes, "Power ultimately rests not in the grip of presidents, generals and billionaires, but in the hands of millions of ordinary people who keep society running smoothly on a day-to-day basis, and who can shut it down should they so choose."[29] Most people do not realize how much power they have collectively. "The strength of even dictatorships," writes Sharp, "is dependent on sources of power in the society, which in turn depend on the cooperation of a multitude of institutions and people."[30] In other words, the reason dictators, oppressive regimes, and corrupt governments can exercise power over others is because people make it possible for them to do so. But here is the catch. If people are the ones who make it *possible* for a government to function, they are also the ones who can make it *impossible*. If people refuse to obey the government's wishes, if they refuse to cooperate and comply, either by their action or inaction, it becomes very difficult for those in power to stay in power.[31]

It is important to note that the success of nonviolent struggle does *not* depend upon the "reasonableness" of the oppressor, or upon his or her

28. Stoner, "Pillars of Support," 248–49.

29. Ibid., 249.

30. Sharp, *There Are Realistic Alternatives*, 3.

31. There is nothing inherently "unchristian" about resisting the government, despite the way passages like Rom 13:1–7 and 1 Pet 2:13–14 are sometimes understood. See the discussion in chapter 8.

willingness to sit down and negotiate. Obviously, mediation, negotiation, and diplomacy are always desirable and should be used whenever possible to resolve conflicts and address injustice. But as we know all too well, there are some people who cannot be persuaded this way, our finest diplomatic and persuasive skills notwithstanding.

Nonviolent struggle works because it restricts or altogether eliminates the sources of power these individuals depend upon to dominate others. As Ackerman and DuVall put it, "Strategic nonviolent action is not about being nice to your oppressor, much less having to rely on his niceness. It's about dissolving the foundations of his power and forcing him out."[32] This is why nonviolent struggle can be so effective against even the most radical individuals and the most oppressive regimes. Dictators, terrorists, and religious extremists are only as effective as the sources of power they control and use to their advantage. When their pillars of support are stripped away, they lose their ability to retain their hold on power.

With this in mind, consider what might have happened if the people of Iraq had mounted a nonviolent campaign to oust Saddam Hussein. Saddam had many sources of power, one of the greatest being the revenue he received from Iraq's oil reserves. What would have happened had this pillar of support been shaken? How long would Saddam been able to stay in power if deprived of this vital resource? This question was actually posed in the run-up to the war in Iraq.

> Earlier this year [2002], a leading nonviolent Iraqi oppositionist expressed exasperation that the Bush administration appeared to be considering every possible military strategy for regime change without realizing "that 22 million Iraqis detest Saddam Hussein" and that they represent an enormous potential resource in ungluing critical levers of his control. At a recent conference on the future of democracy, another Iraqi oppositionist stood up and reminded other, more skeptical Iraqis in the room that Saddam's regime cannot function without oil revenues, and there is a limited number of civilian oil workers who, if they were to abandon their jobs, could create a crisis by themselves. If Saddam starts shooting oil workers or workers at electrical utility installations, how would that keep the oil fields running or the power flowing to his palaces and prisons?[33]

An uprising by Iraqi oil workers would have put Saddam Hussein in a real bind, and would have represented a significant step toward *nonviolently*

---

32. Ackerman and DuVall, "With Weapons of the Will," 23.

33. Ibid.

forcing him out of power. As we will discuss later, it was precisely this kind of action (taken by coal miners) that was part of a coordinated nonviolent struggle that brought down Milosevic, a dictator every bit as brutal and ruthless as Saddam Hussein.

The Methods of Nonviolent Struggle

When people engage in nonviolent struggle, there are many tactics they can use to achieve their objectives. Some of these are well known; others are less familiar. Some are perfectly legal; others involve breaking laws and risking arrest. Since the particulars of every nonviolent struggle differ, there is no "one-size-fits-all" approach. Instead, activists need to consider carefully which tactics have the greatest chance for success in their particular situation.

In his now classic book, *The Politics of Nonviolent Action*, Gene Sharp identified no less than 198 different methods that can be used to bring about change which he organized into three main categories: 1) "nonviolent protest and persuasion," 2) "noncooperation," and 3) "nonviolent intervention."[34] The methods of nonviolent protest and persuasion are designed as "actions to send a message" and include things such as making public speeches, writing letters of opposition or support, circulating petitions, and expressing opinions in newspapers and journals.[35] The second category, noncooperation, includes "actions to suspend cooperation and assistance" such as boycotting elections, severing diplomatic relations, and participating in a general strike.[36] The final category, nonviolent intervention, includes "methods of disruption" such as participating in a sit-in, defying blockades, and overloading administrative systems.[37] As you move from one category to the next, the actions become more confrontational and carry more risks. It is one thing to write letters to members of Congress, urging them to stop funding drone warfare (category 1). It is quite another to physically try to block workers from entering a building where drones are assembled (category 3). Both are nonviolent actions, but one is inherently much more risky than the other.

A more recent discussion of nonviolent tactics is found in *Beautiful Trouble*, a handbook on the practice and theory of nonviolence edited by Andrew Boyd and Oswald Mitchell. This book examines thirty different

---

34. Sharp, *Politics of Nonviolent Action*, 109–445.

35. Sharp, *Waging Nonviolent Struggle*, 51–54.

36. Ibid., 54–61.

37. Ibid., 62–64.

tactics used in nonviolent struggle: advanced leafleting, artistic vigil, banner hang, blockade, creative disruption, creative petition delivery, debt strike, détournement/culture jamming, direct action, distributed action, electoral guerrilla theater, eviction blockade, flash mob, forum theater, general strike, guerrilla projection, hoax, human banner, identity correction, image theater, infiltration, invisible theater, mass street action, media-jacking, nonviolent search and seizure, occupation, prefigurative intervention, public filibuster, strategic nonviolence, and trek.[38] Typically, two or three pages of the book are devoted to each tactic—describing what it is, identifying key principles undergirding it, and noting pitfalls to avoid when using it. Sometimes, there is also some discussion of how the tactic has been used in specific situations. Books like these are helpful because they remind us of the many nonviolent options we have at our disposal. Activists need to develop a strategy and then select the tactics they think will be most effective for achieving their objectives.[39]

When discussing individual tactics, we should not lose sight of the fact that these are often used in combination with one another. Although one particular tactic may be especially prominent in a given struggle—such as the use of sit-ins to desegregate lunch counters in Nashville, Tennessee during the civil rights movement (1960), or the boycott of Taco Bell restaurants to raise wages for Florida's tomato growers (2001–2005)—most rely on multiple tactics for success. This was clearly the case with the overthrow of Milosevic discussed at the beginning of the chapter. Many different nonviolent tactics were used to topple the dictator.

Four Essential Elements of Successful Nonviolent Struggles

Although many things go into making a nonviolent campaign successful, there are several key components common to them all: people, preparation, perseverance, and personal sacrifice. For nonviolent struggle to succeed, you need people—often lots of them—who are deeply committed to the cause.[40] This is especially true when the goal is to make sweeping changes, such as stopping a war or toppling a dictator. In such instances, the sheer number of people participating is crucial to the success of the movement since they are facing a much greater opponent. As Nobel Peace Prize winner

38. Boyd and Mitchell, eds., *Beautiful Trouble*, 8–91.

39. For a practical handbook on how to wage nonviolent struggle, see Popovic et al., *CANVAS Core Curriculum*.

40. Of course, smaller groups of people can also achieve significant results. Sider cites the work of Witness for Peace and Peace Brigades International as two examples (*Nonviolent Action*, 172). For a discussion of their activities, see ibid., 52–66, 144–46.

Adolfo Pérez Esquivel observed, "True the elephant is stronger. But the ants
. . . well, there are more of us."[41]

The people power movements that changed the political landscape
over the past few decades involved tens of thousands of participants. These
participants were people from all walks of life. This is one of the great ad-
vantages of nonviolent struggle. *Everyone* can participate regardless of age,
sexual orientation, ethnicity, nationality, religious affiliation, socioeconomic
status, level of education, or any other potentially limiting factor.[42] This is
significant since it opens the door for large numbers of people to get involved. People can participate regardless of whether they have a religious or
philosophical commitment to absolute nonviolence. As Gene Sharp points
out, "In order to use nonviolent action effectively, people do not have to be
pacifists or saints. Nonviolent action has been predominantly and successfully practiced by 'ordinary' people."[43] All that is needed is a commitment to
use nonviolent methods in the struggle at hand.[44]

Nonviolent struggle brings people from all walks of life together to
rally against a common enemy or injustice. Part of what made the nonviolent effort to end years of warfare in Liberia so successful was the simple fact
that both Muslim *and* Christian women decided to join hands and work
together. They realized they had a common enemy that did not discriminate
based on religious preferences. As they put it: "Does the bullet know Christian from Muslim? Does the bullet pick and choose?"[45]

In addition to involving lots of people, nonviolent action is most effective when accompanied by significant planning and preparation. Careful
thought and attention must be given to a whole range of issues. Organizers
need to articulate their objectives, develop a strategy, and select which tactics they will use. They also need to develop good systems of communication and make decisions about when to actualize their plans.

Nonviolent movements do *not* just happen. People do not wake up
in the morning and decide to stage a sit-in that afternoon. Things like this
require serious coordination and planning. The tactics used by Liberian
women to gain an audience with President Charles Taylor, for example,
were strategic and intentional. "There was nothing spontaneous about it,"
writes Gbowee, a leader of the movement, "managing a huge daily public
protest was a complicated task and we planned every move we made."[46]

41. Esquivel, *Christ in a Poncho*, 32. Quoted in Sider, *Nonviolent Action*, 159.
42. See Wink, *Powers that Be*, 118.
43. Sharp, *Waging Nonviolent Struggle*, 21, emphasis original.
44. Ibid., 19.
45. Gbowee, *Mighty Be Our Powers*, 129.
46. Ibid., 138–39.

In addition to planning the logistics of various actions, the participants themselves should be well-trained in nonviolent tactics and discipline. They need to know what to do and what *not* to do, especially in situations where the potential for violence is likely. The young African American women and men who helped desegregate lunch counters in Nashville, Tennessee in 1960 were carefully trained by Jim Lawson, a Methodist minister who had spent time in India studying the nonviolent methods of Gandhi. Lawson used realistic role plays to help these young activists learn how to remain nonviolent in the face of the insulting and demeaning behavior they anticipated experiencing at the lunch counters.

It comes as no surprise that extensive training in nonviolent theory and practice stands behind many successful nonviolent movements. For example, the dramatic four day uprising in 1988 that toppled Filipino dictator Ferdinand Marcos, the "Hitler of Asia," was preceded by a year and half of careful preparation. As Wink tells it:

> Hildegard and Jean Goss-Mayr and Richard Deats were brought in to train trainers in nonviolence. In little more than a year, these trainers and others taught *a half million* poll watchers nonviolent means to protect the ballots from theft by the henchmen of the dictator Marcos. These poll watchers then formed the nucleus of the street demonstrators that stopped tank columns with their own bodies. The fall of the Marcos regime didn't just "happen." It had been prepared.[47]

Careful planning and preparation is essential to maximize the effectiveness of nonviolent movements. They help ensure that resources are used wisely and that sacrifices are not made in vain.[48]

Successful nonviolent movements also tend to require a great deal of patience and perseverance. Waging nonviolent struggle is more like running a marathon than sprinting the 100 meter dash. Victories are hard won and do not come easily. Those engaged in the struggle need to remember

47. Wink, *Powers that Be*, 121–22, emphasis original.

48. It is true that a number of nonviolent movements of the twentieth century were not characterized by this kind of careful planning and preparation. Some of these movements happened before much had been written about nonviolent struggle and people did not always have easy access to the literature that was available or to experts who might guide them. In fact, Sharp claims that, "Almost always in the 23 cases [included in *Waging Nonviolent Struggle*] there was . . . little or no prior consideration of strategy, advance planning, preparations or training, or even review of the range of available methods and selection of the most suitable ones for that particular conflict" (*Waging Nonviolent Struggle*, 349). This does not suggest planning and preparation are unimportant. Rather, it highlights how much *more* effective and successful nonviolent movements can be when it does happen.

that the problems they are confronting did not arise overnight and will not vanish overnight. They need to stick with it and see things through to completion regardless of how long it takes.

This is precisely what the workers at the Kolubara mine in Serbia were prepared to do to pressure Slobodan Milosevic to leave office. This particular mine was responsible for providing coal to a power station that supplied about 50 percent of the country's electricity. Aware of the mine's strategic importance to the regime, these miners not only went on strike, they removed key pieces of equipment that rendered the mine inoperable. After the strike began, Milosevic's Chief of Staff, Nebojsa Pavkovic, was sent to try to force the miners back to work. He failed. The miners were not budging. As one of the workers said, "We can either stay here four more days or four more years. It's really a very simple choice."[49] These workers were determined to stay the course. They were not going to end the strike until Milosevic stepped down and recognized Kostunica as his duly elected successor.

The women of Liberia demonstrated that same kind of perseverance in their struggle against President Charles Taylor. Day after day, they gathered at a field that became the focal point of their protest. They stood outside in the rain and in temperatures that rose above 100 degrees to demand an audience with the Liberian president in hopes of bringing the violence and killing to an end. "We will continue to sit in the sun and in the rain until we hear from the president!" they proclaimed.[50] Eventually, their request was granted and a meeting was arranged. Unfortunately, this did not bring the war to an end. So, the women continued meeting at the field to plan and to protest. Gbowee writes, "Every day we were on that field. *Every day*. We refused to go away. Refused to let our suffering remain invisible. If people didn't take us seriously at first, it was our persistence that wore them down."[51] It is that kind of determination and grit which makes for a successful nonviolent movement.

Another essential aspect of nonviolent struggle, and one very closely related to persistence and perseverance, is personal sacrifice. For nonviolent struggle to succeed, people need to be prepared to make sacrifices. They must be ready to devote *considerable* time and energy to the movement and should expect to be inconvenienced. Depending upon the kind of nonviolent action taken, there is the possibility of being fined, arrested, or imprisoned. Those who dare to challenge the status quo, who stand up for what

49. Paulson, "Removing the Dictator in Serbia," 333.
50. Gbowee, *Mighty Be Our Powers*, 138.
51. Ibid., 148, emphasis original.

is right and courageously cry out for justice, may be harassed, tortured, or even executed. As Walter Wink reminds us, "If we are to make nonviolence effective, we will have to be as willing to suffer and be killed as soldiers in battle. *Nonviolence is not a way of avoiding personal sacrifice.*"[52] Engaging in nonviolent struggle when the stakes are high will cost us something, and we should be prepared for that.

This may be difficult to accept since most of us spend our lives doing everything we can to avoid pain, suffering, and death. Still, it is consistent with the message of the gospel. Jesus himself was persecuted for doing what was right. He suffered and died for no fault of his own. Therefore, followers of Jesus should not be surprised if the path of discipleship leads them down a similar road.[53]

While many other components of successful nonviolent movements could be discussed, these four highlight some of the most important ones.[54] When you have a significant number of people committed to bringing about change nonviolently, people who are well-prepared and plan carefully, who are willing to persevere regardless of how long it takes or what it costs them, you have the building blocks of a successful nonviolent movement.

Why Don't Brutal Regimes Simply Crush the Opposition?

At this point, it may be helpful to address an important question that might cast doubt on the wisdom of engaging in nonviolent struggle in certain contexts, particularly in situations where those in power have clearly demonstrated their willingness to use fear, intimidation, violence, and killing to get what they want. How can nonviolence even have a chance to work in situations like these? Won't the Powers that Be simply order the police and military to use whatever means necessary to eliminate all dissent and to stop all protest? After all, what do soldiers and police officers have to fear from *non*violent activists? Why not just use force, even violent force, to disperse, detain, and even destroy the opposition? Sometimes, that *is* precisely what happens. Dictators, tyrants, and other oppressors often do arrest, imprison, torture, beat, and kill their opponents. Sometimes this is done in secret; other times it is very public. The Chinese government's massacre of protesters in Tiananmen Square in 1989 is one particularly deadly example of the kind of response that sometimes takes place.

52. Wink, *Powers that Be*, 118, emphasis mine.

53. As discussed earlier, followers of Jesus are people who are prepared to suffer harm, not inflict it. See chapter 7.

54. For other key elements, see especially Popovic, *Blueprint for Revolution*.

Still, the question remains. Why don't repressive regimes *always* deal with dissidents this way? Why don't they always respond with all the firepower at their command? For one simple reason: using violence is a political gamble. It can backfire. Oppressors resort to violence because they believe it will sow fear in the hearts and minds of the opposition and will cause them to stop protesting. Yet ironically, it may have precisely the opposite effect. Rather than *eliminating* dissent, repression can *embolden* it. Gene Sharp refers to this as "political ju-jitsu."[55]

When a government uses overwhelming force and violence against its own people, it exposes the government's ugly underbelly. The unintended effect is that the government's harsh repression often creates sympathy for those who have been harmed, turning public opinion against the regime. Some citizens, even some who have not yet taken a side in the conflict, may be so infuriated by what their leaders have done that they decide to join the resistance. Others, who had previously been loyal to the government, might switch sides after witnessing the brutality of their leaders. Even some soldiers and police officers may refuse to obey orders after witnessing the government's brutality against unarmed civilians.

There are other dangers as well. Countries that use violence to counter the *non*violent protests and actions of their citizens run the risk of being ostracized by the global community. Violent repression creates an image problem and generates a lot of bad press. It strains diplomatic relations and may result in various sanctions, economic and otherwise. Since responding violently is a calculated risk, one that potentially may have some very negative consequences, not every leader is prepared to use it, or at least not to the extent they could. Instead, they will often look for other ways to undermine the opposition that are less costly and less risky.

Using Nonviolence to Fight Terrorism

Before drawing this chapter to a close, it seems important to say a few words about what a nonviolent response to terrorism might entail. Simply defined, terrorism is "the practice of using violence against civilians"[56] in order "*to spread fear as a means to a political goal.*"[57] Though terrorism obviously predates September 11, 2001, it has become a much more significant part of our conversation since then. We are no longer surprised when we hear of yet

55. Sharp, *Waging Nonviolent Struggle*, 47. For an extended discussion of political jujitsu, see ibid., 397–413.

56. Hastings, *Nonviolent Response to Terrorism*, 6.

57. Mock, *Loving without Giving In*, 36, emphasis original.

another terrorist attack somewhere in the world. They occur too frequently, and we are all too familiar with the death, destruction, and fear that such attacks leave in their wake.

Many people are convinced that violence is the only effective way to fight terrorism. And, given terrorists' penchant for killing, it might seem they have a point. What good are nonviolent efforts against terrorist groups such as al-Qaeda and ISIS? Isn't it foolish, and more than a little naïve, to believe nonviolence has any real chance of stopping terrorists, especially those who are prepared to kill themselves in order to kill others? It would seem violence is the only viable solution.

But here is the problem: using violence to fight terrorism simply does not work. True, it might eliminate key leaders and "degrade" a terrorist organization's ability to coordinate its efforts, making it more difficult to carry out attacks, but in the end, terrorism always survives. One terrorist group morphs into another, and people continue to join their ranks daily.

In fact, rather than deterring terrorists, using violence against them strengthens their resolve to fight. It also serves as an ideal tool to persuade new recruits to join with them. "If we believe that using violence ends terrorism, or deters terrorists," writes Tom Hastings, director of peace and nonviolence studies at Portland State University, "we have only to check the historical record at countless decision-making junctures."[58] What we find is just the opposite. Consider, for example, how the United States' military efforts in the Middle East have helped, rather than hindered, ISIS. According to David Cortright, director of policy studies at Notre Dame's Kroc Institute for International Peace Studies:

> U.S. military involvement in Iraq and Syria is having unintended effects that could make matters worse. Battling the United States gives ISIS a transcendent objective beyond its political agenda in Iraq and Syria. . . . It allows ISIS to portray itself as the victim and to claim that it is defending Islam from Western attack. After the start of airstrikes in August [2014], support for the group increased.[59]

"Violence has not worked to eliminate terrorism," says Hastings. "It is time to try the nonviolent approach."[60]

What might this look like? What kind of "nonviolent approach" can one use to confront the threat of global terrorism? In many respects, a nonviolent approach to terrorism is not all that different from what we have

58. Hastings, *Nonviolent Response to Terrorism*, 12.
59. Cortright, "Power of Peacebuilding," 18.
60. Hastings, *Nonviolent Response to Terrorism*, 2.

already discussed in this chapter. Fundamentally, it still boils down to issues of power and control. What are the sources of power that enable terrorists to do what they do, and how can these be compromised and eroded? As Maria Stephan, senior policy fellow at the US Institute of Peace wrote about ISIS, "As ruthless as ISIS' circa 30,000 fighters might be, the organization still relies on the active and passive obedience of large numbers of people. The challenge is to use collective action to weaken these dependency relationships."[61] The specific nature that such "collective action" will take differs from one geopolitical context to the next, but it would be consistent with the nonviolent strategies set forth in this chapter.

Of course, one of the greatest obstacles that keeps people from taking this kind of action is fear. As Hastings recognizes, "Overcoming fear is the first battle against terror."[62] People who are fearful of what might happen to them or their family members if they challenge terrorists often do nothing. To be sure, some of these fears are justified. Terrorists do terrible things to people. They kidnap, rape, torture, and kill. Fearful of such reprisals, many who live among terrorists and disapprove of their behavior decide to remain silent and compliant. This is precisely what terrorists want since it allows them to continue their reign of terror unhindered.

But this picture does not tell the whole story. For example, what do you think would happen if a Middle Eastern woman went to ISIS's headquarters in Syria and stood outside with a placard criticizing the organization for recent kidnappings? You would expect armed men to rush out, drag her inside, torture her, and possibly rape or even kill her. You can't stand up to terrorists—right? Wrong. Just ask Sooad Nofal. Day after day, this Muslim schoolteacher went to ISIS headquarters in Raqqa, Syria carrying a large cardboard sign protesting ISIS's kidnapping of nonviolent activists. Not only was she unharmed, her protest inspired others to join her and eventually resulted in the release of some of the activists held by ISIS.[63] Terrorists can be challenged. Protest is possible.

Stephan highlights numerous ways people in Syria and Iraq have successfully resisted ISIS. She speaks of a prominent imam who refused to pledge his allegiance to ISIS and was not killed. She also recounts an incident in which Muslims formed a human chain around a mosque to prevent ISIS fighters from destroying it. More generally, Stephan notes that "satire has become a particularly powerful weapon of nonviolent resistance that

61. Stephan, "Resisting ISIS," 16. For an extensive discussion of this point, see Stephan, "Civil Resistance vs. ISIS."

62. Hastings, *Nonviolent Response to Terrorism*, 11.

63. Stephan, "Resisting ISIS," 15.

Syrians, Iraqis, and others in the Arab world are using to delegitimize ISIS. Videos dramatizing the absurdity and illegitimacy of ISIS' tyranny have gone viral on social media and have been shown on satellite television stations."[64] Humor is effective because it "breaks fear and builds confidence."[65] It lets people know criticism is possible. This weakens the control oppressors have over others.

The examples just cited illustrate some of the ways people can protest the actions of terrorists living in their midst. But what about those of us who live a great distance from ISIS headquarters? What can we do? What does a nonviolent response to terrorism look like for us? First, we can urge our government to stop using violence against terrorists. As noted above, fighting terrorism with violence is not only ineffective, it is counterproductive. We can make the case that violence only exacerbates the problem and can implore those in power to find more creative and constructive ways to respond.

Second, we can encourage our elected officials to do everything within their power to cut off all sources of funding and material support to terrorist organizations. It takes an enormous amount of money to fund terrorist activities, and terrorists cannot operate effectively without it. That is why one of Erin Niemela's three "strategies for nonviolent counterterrorism" is to "immediately stop sending funds and weapons to all involved parties."[66]

In an opinion piece in the *New York Times* titled, "To Hurt ISIS, Squeeze the Cash Flow," the writers argue that "stopping the revenue flow must be central to any serious effort to defeat ISIS."[67] By their calculations, it costs approximately 10 million dollars a month just to pay the salaries of an estimated 30,000 ISIS fighters. Where does ISIS get that kind of money? Much of it comes from oil extracted in areas under ISIS control, possibly to the tune of one million dollars a day. Stopping ISIS means impeding the flow of that oil money and drying up other revenue streams as well.

Third, we should do all we can to support nonviolent efforts in countries where terrorists live and operate.[68] There are often many such efforts

---

64. Ibid., 17.

65. Popovic, *Blueprint for Revolution*, 110.

66. Niemela, "Before the Next ISIS." Niemela's other two proposals are to "fully invest in social and economic development initiatives in any region in which terrorist groups are engaged" and to "fully support any and all nonviolent civil society resistance movements."

67. Editorial Board, "To Hurt ISIS."

68. DuVall and Merriman propose the following efforts that both governments and NGOs could use to support civil resistance on the ground: "1. Underwriting independent efforts to furnish tools, equipment and training in strategic nonviolent action

underway in troubled regions around the world. Yet, we tend to be unaware of them because they get very little media attention. As Stephan writes about efforts to oppose ISIS, "Though typically out of the headlines, there is much nonviolent activism in Syria and Iraq that could be bolstered through international efforts."[69] She explains:

> An interactive map developed by the Syrian Nonviolence Movement shows where civil resistance is still happening inside Syria via noncooperation, civil disobedience, and the building of parallel structures and institutions. A major challenge for Syrian activists . . . is finding ways to link these various initiatives.
>
> This is where international support could come in. External actors could support these groups with grants and help to connect Syria activists to each other and to nonviolent leaders from other protracted conflicts . . . to share lessons and best practices. The most dynamic and creative media projects advocating nonviolent approaches to transforming the conflict should be given the financial and technical means to vastly expand their reach inside Syria and regionally via FM and satellite broadcasting.[70]

Providing financial, technological, and logistical support to nonviolent activists living and working among terrorists and terrorist organizations is an excellent way to engage in nonviolent counterterrorism.

As Christians, one way we can learn about efforts like these is by reaching out to our partners around the world (e.g., our missionaries, parachurch organizations, non-profits) who live where terrorists organize and operate. Our friends on the ground will have a better sense of who is engaged in nonviolent resistance and how we might most effectively support their efforts.

Fourth, we should attempt to address the primary issues and concerns that give rise to terrorism in the first place. This is critical. As Cortright observes, "Overcoming the threat posed by ISIS cannot be achieved by military means. What's needed is a comprehensive strategy that addresses the underlying conditions that have led to the rise of ISIS and related extremist groups."[71] In other words, we need to get to root causes. Wardah Khalid, a peace fellow in Middle East policy at the Friends Committee on National Legislation, agrees. She proposes five *nonviolent* ways to stop ISIS, one of

---

to civic groups resisting oppression; 2. Defending the rights of nonviolent resisters; 3. Promoting accurate media coverage of nonviolent struggles; and 4. Promoting the new underlying discourse through educational and public information programs" ("Dissolving Terrorism at its Roots," 230).

69. Stephan, "Resisting ISIS," 16.

70. Ibid.

71. Cortright, "Power of Peacebuilding," 18.

which is to "address the political and economic grievances in the area that are causing civilians to join the Islamic State group."[72] According to Khalid, "Job creation, education, financial support and an open political process to create long-term stability should be prioritized—not bombs."[73] We should not underestimate the importance of identifying and responding to these root causes.[74] As Tom Hastings asks, "*What if the terrorists—or the population base from which they draw—had enough of life's necessities? What if they had secure jobs, decent living standards, drinkable water and healthy food for their children? Do we seriously think they would provide a recruiting base for terrorism?*"[75] In addition, we (in the United States) should make a special effort to address the grievances others have against us due to our foreign policy, military presence, and warmaking in the Middle East.[76] Doing these things would go a long way toward stopping terrorism before it starts.

Given the complexities involved in making any kind of meaningful response to global terrorism, I am keenly aware that what I have written here only begins to scratch the surface. Much, much more needs to be said. Still, I hope enough has been said to demonstrate that there are viable nonviolent responses to terrorism. Those interested in reading more could consult Tom Hastings' book *Nonviolent Response to Terrorism*, which considers both immediate and long-term responses to the problem.[77]

"It Can Never Happen Here"

Even after reading a chapter like this one, which emphasizes the power and success of nonviolent struggle in various contexts, I suspect there are some who still doubt nonviolence can work in certain situations. This skepticism is not uncommon.

72. Khalid, "Bombs Are Not the Answer."

73. Ibid.

74. For an interesting program being carried out in Denmark that attempts to reintegrate radicalized youth into society, listen to the second part of NPR's *Invisibilia* podcast "Flip the Script." As described on the website, "Then [after a beautiful story about a potentially deadly incident in Washington DC that ends with hugs all around] we travel across the pond, to Denmark, where police officers are attempting to combat the growing problem of Islamic radicalization with . . . love."

75. Hastings, *Nonviolent Response to Terrorism*, 130–31, emphasis original.

76. For deeper analysis, see Pearse, *Why the Rest Hates the West*.

77. Also of help is the collection of essays edited by Ram and Summy in *Nonviolence: An Alternative for Defeating Global Terror(ism)*, particularly the essays in Parts IV and V. For a distinctly Christians response, see Mock, *Loving without Giving In*.

In June 2009, a little over a year and a half before the Arab Spring, a group of fifteen Egyptian activists met with Srdja Popovic, one of the student leaders of Otpor!. Weary of living under the oppressive and corrupt rule of Egyptian president Hosni Mubarak, they were eager to see this dictator removed from power. The first thing Popovic shared with this Egyptian contingent was his experience with Otpor! and the way the people of Serbia had used nonviolence to remove Milosevic from power. After several hours, a young Egyptian man raised his hand. "Srdja, . . . we are all impressed with what happened in Serbia. But Egypt is very different. It can never happen there."[78] Popovic has heard this before.

> The nonviolent activists in Georgia, I told him, had said the same thing . . . just before they brought down their own dictatorship in 2003's Rose Revolution, using Otpor!'s methods. And I had heard the same concerns raised in the Ukraine before Leonid Kuchma was toppled in the Orange Revolution in 2004, a year later in Lebanon on the eve of the Cedar Revolution, and three years after that in the Maldives, where pro-democracy activists ultimately deposed the country's strongman. *All of these revolutions were wildly successful, and all of them started with their organizers arguing that whatever happened in Serbia could never happen in their home countries.*[79]

Obviously, every situation is unique and one cannot simplistically expect the exact same set of tactics that worked in one situation to be equally successful in another. Tactics need to be selected based on what activists think will work most effectively in their own particular context. That notwithstanding, the general principles undergirding nonviolent struggle remain constant and "are universal," as Popovic recognizes.[80] "They can work in anyone's country, town, community, or even college."[81] If nonviolence is ever going to have a chance to succeed, people need to get beyond the paralyzing—and false—belief that "it can't work here." It can work—and it *does* work.

---

78. Popovic, *Blueprint for Revolution*, 16.

79. Ibid., emphasis mine.

80. Ibid., 19.

81. Ibid.

Conclusion

One of the reasons the church continues to be so accommodating toward violence is because many Christians, like the activists Popovic consulted, continue to doubt that nonviolence will work in certain situations. Instead, they continue to believe violence is the only viable solution. We examined a number of these difficult situations here and in the previous two chapters and have found this to be unfounded. Not only does nonviolence "work" in a wide range of settings and diverse contexts, there is evidence to suggest it works even better than violence.

If we are to disarm the church, Christians need to stop dismissing nonviolence as utopian and idealist and start embracing it as doable and practical. The church needs to become more informed about the theory and practice of nonviolence and how successful it has been. We need to invest more time learning about nonviolence and nonviolent struggle, and should be ready to put these principles into practice whenever possible. This is why it is terribly important for Christians to learn about nonviolent principles, strategies, and tactics.

Ron Sider has proposed that the church be instrumental in developing "study centers" and "training centers" for this purpose. "If the Christian church is serious about exploring nonviolence," writes Sider, "then we must develop financial resources and the scholars needed to make possible large numbers of new and expanded study centers on nonviolence around the world."[82] Sider also believes "we need hundreds of action-oriented training centers to produce thousands of trained nonviolent activists . . . who are ready to lead nonviolent campaigns."[83] Facilities and programs like these would be enormously beneficial.

In the meantime, Christians can avail themselves of the growing literature on this subject, attend nonviolent trainings, and partner with organizations actively working to do justice without violence. We can take steps to expand our imagination by learning more stories of nonviolent struggle and witnessing the great success people have had in resolving conflict and bringing about change over the years. This will encourage us and inspire us to find creative ways to engage the problems of our world through nonviolent efforts that are consistent with the nonviolent way of Jesus.

82. Sider, *Nonviolent Action*, 169.
83. Ibid., 170.

13

Developing a Nonviolent Mind-Set
Seeing Others through the Eyes of God

The first step is to remember we are all God's children, all equal brothers and sisters, all sons and daughters of God. From this worldview and understanding, all our acts of peace and justice follow.

—JOHN DEAR[1]

Whether the person confronting me is an enemy or a friend, they confront me as loved and valued by God, and I need to be careful with what God values.

—ANGIE O' GORMAN[2]

THE STORIES DISCUSSED IN the previous chapters have demonstrated the effectiveness of using nonviolent strategies to respond to situations as diverse as dealing with an unwanted intruder at home to removing a dictator from power. They remind us that nonviolence works, and they encourage us to think more creatively about how to act in similar circumstances.

Still, I suspect some people may feel that many of these scenarios are rather far removed from their own lives. Thankfully, most of us have probably never experienced an unwanted intruder in our home or come upon

1. Dear, *Disarming the Heart*, 45.
2. O'Gorman, "Defense through Disarmament," 245, emphasis mine.

someone being physically assaulted in a subway (or elsewhere). Likewise, most North American Christians have little—if any—experience with organized efforts to topple dictators or overthrow oppressive regimes. Thus, for many of us, the struggle to live nonviolently happens elsewhere, in our day-to-day relationships, not in a chance encounter with a stranger or in international affairs. This sometimes proves the more difficult challenge.

I once saw a cartoon that illustrates this well. As I recall, the cartoon had a single frame showing two individuals standing near a field. One of them, clearly a farmer, turned to the other and said, "Sometimes it's easier to work for world peace than to make peace with a neighbor who plows a furrow into your field." Isn't that the truth! We sometimes have the hardest time getting along with those closest to us, people we see day in and day out: the nasty co-worker, the overbearing boss, the obnoxious neighbor, the disrespectful child, the unreasonable parent. These are the people we sometimes really struggle to love, the ones who test our commitment to nonviolence and expose the violence within our heart. So while the previous section of the book discussed how we could *use* nonviolence to help those being threatened, harmed, or oppressed, this section explores what it means for us to *live* nonviolently with people we interact with on a regular basis.

Earlier, we defined Christian nonviolence as *a way of life modeled after Jesus, one that completely rejects violence, actively confronts evil, and unconditionally loves others by practicing gracious hospitality, radical forgiveness, and deep compassion.* But how do we develop the capacity to live this out in our day-to-day lives? How do we learn to live nonviolently with neighbors, co-workers, family members, and church friends, especially during moments when conflict erupts and tensions run high?

Unfortunately, there is no quick three-step process that enables us to cast aside our violent tendencies and instantly become perfect examples of nonviolent love. Still, there are things we can do that move us in this direction. One of the most important, and the focus of this chapter, is to cultivate what I call a "nonviolent mind-set."

Cultivating a Nonviolent Mind-Set

A mind-set can be defined as "a mental attitude or disposition that predetermines a person's responses to and interpretation of situations."[3] We all know people who have a negative mind-set, for example. They constantly see the downside of everything. For them, the glass is *always* half empty, never half

3. *American Heritage Dictionary*, 2nd college ed., s.v. "mindset."

full. Someone with a positive mind-set, on the other hand, is much more optimistic. They are able to see good even in the most trying circumstances.

Since our mind-set profoundly impacts both the way we interpret events and the way respond to those around us, it is critical to cultivate a *nonviolent* mind-set if we want to live nonviolently. A nonviolent mind-set enables us to approach all people peacefully, with love in our hearts, prepared to help them any way we can and determined never to harm them regardless of how they treat us. It is this mind-set that enabled people like Sharon Buttry, Angie O'Gorman, and Louise Degrafinried to respond to their assailants with hospitality rather than hostility (see chapters 8–9). It is also what prompted people like John Roth and Bruxy Cavey to put their lives at risk to protect others (see chapter 10). And it is what has inspired Christians around the world to engage in *nonviolent* struggle against dictators, oppressive regimes, and systems of injustice (see chapter 11).

So how do we cultivate a nonviolent mind-set? What can we do to train ourselves to see people through God's eyes of love and grace? Several things are especially helpful in this regard. As we consider these, we should remember we are not alone in this important work. God is with us and is eager to help us. A nonviolent mind-set cannot be developed by our willpower alone. Rather, we rely on God's assistance. Thus, as we take steps to cultivate a nonviolent mind-set, we recognize God is at work within us, helping us along the way.

See Each Person as Created in God's Image

One of the most important things we can do to cultivate a nonviolent mind-set is to remember and embrace the crucial theological claim made in the first chapter of the Bible, that each person is created in the image of God.

> Then God said, "Let us make humankind in our image, according to our likeness; and let them have dominion over the fish of the sea, and over the birds of the air, and over the cattle, and over all the wild animals of the earth, and over every creeping thing that creeps upon the earth." So God created humankind in his image, in the image of God he created them; male and female he created them (Gen 1:26–27).

Precisely what it means to be created in God's image has been a matter of considerable debate, but surely it says something marvelous about the value and significance of human beings. It suggests we have the capacity to reflect God-likeness more than anything else in the world, and it reminds us that we are of great worth to God. This insight alone encourages us to treat others with great care and respect, lest we harm that which is precious to God.

Since each of us bears the image of God, we get a glimpse of God when we see another person. Quakers have a special way of talking about this. They speak about "seeing that of God in everyone." The "everyone" is all-inclusive, reminding us that *each* person has value and worth. One of the core values of my own theological tradition, the Brethren in Christ Church, states: "*We value all human life* and promote forgiveness, understanding, reconciliation, and nonviolent resolution of conflict."[4] As Harriet Bicksler insightfully comments:

> The "all" word is the challenge. Do we really mean all human life—the murderer on death row; the ruthless dictator who massacres his own citizens while amassing great personal wealth; the unborn baby conceived by a rape; the homeless alcoholic who won't accept help; the nasty coworker who is always criticizing? Surely there are limits![5]

But there are not. As Bicksler points out, "We [the Brethren in Christ] haven't allowed ourselves any escape clauses."[6] We are to value *all* human life, regardless of who the person is or what they have done. We do this because every person bears the image of God. Regardless of how broken they are, or how tarnished God's image in them may appear to be, each person is of infinite worth to God and must be treated with dignity and respect.

As the nineteenth-century Russian Christian, St. John of Kronstadt, reportedly said:

> Never confuse the person, formed in the image of God, with the evil that is in him; because evil is but a chance misfortune, an illness, a devilish reverie. But the very essence of the person is the image of God, and this remains in him despite every disfigurement.

Saint John warns against defining people by the evil they have done, thereby forgetting their *primary* identity as someone created in God's image. What we see when we look at others, especially those whose wrongs are well known, is critically important. Do we see a criminal, terrorist, cheat, loser, or offender? Or do we see a person created in God's image, one who is loved unconditionally by their Creator? How we see people really matters.

4. Bicksler, "Pursuing Peace," 129, emphasis mine.
5. Ibid., 133–34.
6. Ibid., 134.

Fred Rogers, the beloved and genial host of *Mister Rogers' Neighborhood*, understood this better than most. He constantly affirmed the value, worth, and specialness of each and every person. What motivated Mr. Rogers to emphasize this on his show and embody it in his life? Amy Hollingsworth explains it this way in her wonderful book about the friendship she had with Fred Rogers:

> At the center of Fred's theology of loving your neighbor was this: Every person is made in the image of God, and *for that reason alone*, he or she is to be valued—"appreciated," he liked to say. He believed there is sacredness in all creation—including fallen man.[7]

Seeing each person as someone created in God's image reminds us of their preciousness to God. Remembering this is extremely helpful when dealing with difficult people. I am especially fond of the way Richard Mouw articulates this in his book *Uncommon Decency: Christian Civility in an Uncivil World*.

> Every human being is a work of divine art. God has crafted each of us; we are all "special creations." Even when we have rebelled against God and distorted his handiwork in our lives, he continues to love us—much as an artist loves something which she has worked on lovingly, even when it has been severely damaged. *I can learn a lot about how to treat an unlikable person with reverence if I keep reminding myself of the value the person has in the eyes of God.*[8]

Seeing people as valuable in God's eyes, and remembering that they have been created in God's image, can help restrain our violent inclinations. It prompts us to treat others graciously, hospitably, and reverently (a beautiful notion!) regardless of how they treat us.

One simple practice that can help us see people this way is prayer. When we meet someone, we can silently prayer something as basic as "Thank you God for Janette, a person created in your image." Praying this way takes only a few seconds and reminds us that the person before us bears God's image and deserves to be treated with care and respect.

Another way to put this into practice—especially when dealing with people we find difficult to like—is to focus on the person's strengths rather than their weaknesses. Richard Mouw tells a story about a judge who tried

---

7. Hollingsworth, *Simple Faith of Mister Rogers*, 78, emphasis mine.
8. Mouw, *Uncommon Decency*, 24–25, emphasis mine.

this after hearing a homily in church one Sunday about trying to see situations through the eyes of Jesus.

> A few days later a young man from the inner city appeared before the judge's bench. He had been there several times before. "I was ready to give him a rather harsh sentence," the judge said. "Then suddenly I remembered the priest's words. I stopped and asked myself, What would Jesus see if he were sitting in my place.
>
> "I decided that he would see a young person with much street-savvy, who is using his considerable intelligence and skill to get the most he can from a social system that he feels is stacked against him. I looked this young man in the eye and told him that I thought he was a bright and talented human being. And then I said to him, 'Let's talk together about how we can get you living in more creative and constructive ways.'
>
> "We had a surprisingly good conversation. . . ."
>
> What the judge had done was to reflect upon this young man's *value and potential.* And this same attitude is what I owe to the person whom I find it impossible to like. I can choose to concentrate, not on his disagreeable characteristics, but on the value and potential he has in the sight of God.[9]

Humanize, Rather than Demonize, Others (Especially Your Adversaries)

As the judge's actions demonstrate, part of what it means to see people as created in God's image involves making an effort to humanize rather than demonize them. This is especially important with regard to those who are significantly different from us or whom we perceive as our enemies. Our natural tendency is to demonize those we dislike. This is evident in the way we think about them, talk about them, and behave toward them. In fact, we are often unable to see (or say) anything good about them. We focus on—and often magnify—their *undesirable* qualities. We are so intensely fixated on their negative characteristics that we are virtually blind to other qualities they possess that are much more commendable.[10] We often do this unthinkingly, without realizing it. But if we are not careful, we end up vilify-

9. Ibid., 23–24, emphasis original.

10. Jim Forest raised my awareness of this in his excellent book *Loving Our Enemies.* Forest invites readers to make a list of their enemies and to pray for them. He then asks, "Have you allowed yourself to be aware of qualities that are admirable in those you have listed or have you preferred to see only what, from your perspective, is flawed in them?" (*Loving Our Enemies,* 90).

ing others, viewing them as monsters who are inherently evil and barely human. This tremendously complicates our efforts to love them and live nonviolently toward them.

To counter this tendency to demonize others, we might experiment with what Jon Huckins and Jer Swigert call "*virtuous gossip*." It is an exercise they describe this way:

> Refuse to speak ill of others. Instead, speak only of the virtue of others. Start with one day at a time and see if this doesn't become a habit. Pay attention to how God shifts your perspective and adjusts your "truth" about the other through this practice.[11]

This is a great idea, one that would certainly help us see others more accurately. Of course, this is not to suggest we should never talk about the bad things someone has done to us. We should speak honestly with trusted mentors and close friends who can keep confidences and can help us process these experiences. We need safe spaces like that. But it does invite us to be very careful about how we speak about others in casual conversation. Part of what it means to love our enemies is to be able to see the good in them—and to say so.

At this point it is helpful to add an important caveat. While humanizing our enemies invites us to see the good in them, it does *not* mean whitewashing their behavior—that would be dishonest. Nor does it mean refraining from any kind of critique—that would be irresponsible. This is especially true when it comes to talking about people who wield considerable power in our world today. For example, what would you say about a politician who stands against virtually everything you stand for and whose behavior and beliefs you find repulsive? You surely would not say, "He is a nice person who has done a lot of good for our people." Rather, you would critique offensive remarks that have been made and troubling positions that have been taken—and you would be fully within your rights to do so. There is nothing wrong, or "unchristian," about speaking out against bad policy decisions or holding politicians accountable for their actions. In fact, in democratic societies, this is part of our civic duty. Yet as Christians, we must take care to avoid engaging in personal attacks when we launch our critique. One thing that may help in this regard is simply remembering who the real enemy is.[12] As the writer of Ephesians puts it:

> For our struggle is not against enemies of blood and flesh, but against the rulers, against the authorities, against the cosmic

11. Huckins and Swigart, "Invitations to Action," 182.
12. To quote Haymitch Abernathy.

> powers of this present darkness, against the spiritual forces of
> evil in the heavenly places (Eph 6:12).

We need to mindful that there are other forces at work in the world.

We never prevail over evil by attacking "evil" people.[13] That simply reproduces the very evil we are seeking to eliminate. Moreover, while we do have a responsibility to confront individuals who behave violently and oppressively, it is not for the purpose of denigrating or humiliating them. Rather, we do so to challenge—and ideally change—their poor choices and harmful practices. There are many persuasive ways to engage in that kind of critique without resorting to character assassination. So while humanizing *does not* mean idealizing, it *does* mean speaking the truth in ways that are honest, fair, and respectful. Admittedly, all this is easier said than done. Still, it is important for Christians to grapple with this and to find ways to criticize—and not demonize—those with whom they disagree and often intensely dislike.[14]

Another way to humanize others is to avoid labeling or stereotyping since that kind of behavior can be very harmful and reductionistic. When we label someone, we often lose sight of that person as a unique individual. Their individuality gets lost and they become just one more representative of an undesirable group. When we label someone a "terrorist," for example, that one word comes to define them. It dominates our perception, making it very hard to see them as anything else. Even if the label is accurate, it does not tell the whole story. There is more to the person than being a terrorist. They have family and friends, joys and grievances just like each of us. When someone is defined by a label or stereotype, it becomes much easier to disregard them and, in extreme cases, to justify harming or even killing them. This is especially true when the labels carry pejorative connotations: "fundamentalists," "religious extremists," "illegal aliens," and so on. Such labels make it far too easy to demonize others, causing us to lose sight of their humanity in the process.

As Christians, we are called to see others, first and foremost, as people—unique individuals created in God's image. This helps us remember that the other person is just that: a person. Like us, they too have hopes and dreams, strengths and weaknesses, fears and failures—this is our shared

---

13. As it says in Article VI of the Schleitheim Confession of 1527, an early statement of Anabaptist beliefs and convictions: "The worldlings are armed with steel and iron, but the Christians are armed with the armor of God, with truth, righteousness, peace, faith, salvation and the Word of God." My thanks to Michelle Curtis for bringing this to my attention.

14. For an excellent reflection on the difficulty of maintaining this balance, see Bicksler, "My Internal Political Struggle."

human experience. And, like us, they have similar needs: to have adequate food, shelter, and medical care, to have meaningful work to do, to be loved and accepted, to feel safe and secure. By focusing on our common humanity, and by avoiding harmful labels and stereotypes, we can push back against the tendency to see only the worst in certain people.

In many respects, our ability to humanize others is connected to our ability to develop compassion toward them. One way to do this, especially with individuals we find very difficult to love, is to try to imagine what might be causing them to behave the way they do. A pastor once told me he creates a backstory for people he finds difficult. He tries to imagine what might be causing them to act the way they are. Is their marriage on the verge of collapse? Are they struggling financially to make ends meet? Has their family disconnected from them? Is their boss overbearing? Do they hate their job? Did they recently receive devastating medical news? Have they just been laid off from work? Has a trusted friend just revealed a secret told in strict confidence? The list goes on.

People who are short-tempered, nasty, or just generally unpleasant to be around have often experienced a significant amount of pain themselves. As the adage goes: "hurt people," hurt people. In many cases, we may never know the specifics. Still, being able to imagine what *might* underlie their abrasive behavior can help us begin to feel some measure of compassion for them. Being cognizant that they have a backstory, a history—whatever that may be—helps us move beyond seeing them as nothing more than "that really annoying person who makes my life miserable." When we remember they too have experienced grief and loss, we start to see them through different eyes.

While none of this excuses their behavior, it goes a long way toward helping us view them more compassionately. As Henry Wadsworth Longfellow once wrote, "If we could read the secret history of our enemies, we should find in each man's life sorrow and suffering enough to disarm all hostility."[15] Humanizing others and developing compassion toward them keeps our violent tendencies in check and enables to extend grace to others, even when they are our enemies.

Get to Know the "Other"

Another important aspect of cultivating a nonviolent mind-set involves getting to know people who are very different from us in some way—religiously, culturally, ethnically, ideologically, economically, racially, nationally, or

15. Longfellow, "Drift-Wood," 405.

otherwise. Most of us tend to have very little meaningful contact—let alone deep friendships—with people who differ from us in fundamental ways. For example, how many people in your church regularly hang out with atheists? Or how many upper-class Christians become good friends with those who are extremely poor? As Shane Claiborne writes, "The great tragedy in the church is not that rich Christians do not care about the poor but that rich Christians do not know the poor."[16] People we perceive to be very unlike us—the "Other," as they are sometimes called—are not often part of our inner circle. Instead, they tend to be the people we understand least and fear the most. Since we do not know them personally, we sometimes form strong opinions about them based largely on stories we have heard from secondhand sources about "them and their kind." Unfortunately, many of these stories are uncomplimentary and serve only to reinforce negative stereotypes and misconceptions. Consequently, the "Other" becomes a victim of our ignorance, prejudice, and violence.

In order to cultivate a nonviolent mind-set toward those who are most unlike us—those who do not look like us, dress like us, talk like us, think like us, or behave like us—we need to take time to get to know them.[17] There is no substitute for this, especially in a world that seems increasingly polarized and divided. As Lee Camp expresses it:

> We desperately need to learn to talk to people who are different from us, who have profound convictions that stand at deep odds with our own, to sit down at the table with them, to share coffee with them, to drink tea with them, to listen to their stories and their experiences, to extend hospitality rather than mere tolerance.[18]

Engaging in these kinds of face-to-face conversations can work wonders. They can alleviate our fears and shatter false stereotypes we have adopted.

This is exactly what happened to Jim Forest when he went to the Soviet Union in the 1980s. Before traveling to Russia, Forest was strongly influenced by a lot of "Cold War imagery" that caused him to view Russians with great suspicion and mistrust.[19] This is reflected in the way he describes his first day in Russia. "Once inside my hotel room," he writes, "I could all

16. Claiborne, *Irresistible Revolution*, 99.

17. For a brief article describing a scientific study conducted at Ohio State University demonstrating "that living with someone of a different race can help to reduce anxiety and other negative feelings towards minorities," see Shook, "Interracial Roommate Relationships."

18. Lee Camp, *Who Is My Enemy?*, 153.

19. Forest, *Loving Our Enemies*, 129.

but see a KGB agent in an adjacent room listening to my rustling noises as I unpacked my suitcase. In my mind's eye the walls might as well have been made of glass. I looked around the room, curious where the microphone was hidden."[20] Yet, after spending time in Russia, Forest's paranoia evaporated as his fears were disconfirmed. He found Russians to be both approachable and hospitable and noticed how strikingly similar Russians were to people back home. All this had a dramatic effect on his life. His positive experiences led to future visits and ultimately to the publication of two books about religion in Russia.

Forest reflects on the impact of those two trips in his most recent book, *Loving Our Enemies*. "Looking back," writes Forest, "it occurs to me that this book had its beginnings in Moscow. It was in the course of conversations with strangers that I began to think afresh about Jesus' remarkable stress on love of enemies. If that's to happen, surely it happens best by meeting the people at whom our weapons are aimed."[21] Forest understood the value and importance of getting to know the "Other." Through the process of talking to Russians and developing relationships with them, Forest found these people quite different from the stereotypes propagated by the West.

Getting to know others allows us to see friends where previously we only saw enemies. As Forest puts it:

> Beginning to know personally those who are the targets of war, praying for them daily, listening to their music, reading their literature, bringing their food to the table—*these are truly disarming experiences*. It becomes unthinkable to do anything that might result in their being shot or burned alive, for truly they are our sisters and brothers. We discover that their lives are in our care, and ours in theirs.[22]

Getting to know the "Other" takes time, intentionality, and courage, but it is an invaluable part of cultivating a nonviolent mind-set.

But how does this happen, practically speaking? What can you do to get to know the "Other"? One thing you might do is travel internationally, like Jim Forest, and make friends with people whose lives are very different from your own. Or, staying closer to home, you might consider inviting a colleague or co-worker who sees the world radically differently than you out to lunch. Take time to ask about their family, their hobbies, their hopes and dreams, their fears. Try to discover things about them you actually appreciate. If you find it difficult to love people whose skin color, sexual orientation,

20. Ibid.
21. Forest, *Loving Our Enemies*, 131.
22. Ibid., 135, emphasis mine.

or ethnicity differs from your own, actively look for opportunities to interact with them. Listen to their stories. Learn about their lives. See them for the beautifully complex people they really are—not the shallow stereotype we often construct. Christians who are particularly daring should try Randal Rauser's suggestion:

> If you're really courageous, you might want to visit the local chapter of an atheist, humanist, and/or skeptic club. That would be a great way to get to know people. And talk about really stepping out of your comfort zone! Of course, it'd be up to you whether you want to advertise that you're a Christian or whether you'd prefer to go incognito. . . . One more thing: if you do visit an atheist meeting, be ready to follow the group out afterwards to a coffee shop or pub. I've found that the best (and most honest) conversations tend to happen after the formal agenda is concluded.[23]

Doing things like these can have a powerful impact on the way we see others. They can reduce prejudice, break down stereotypes, diminish hostility, and generate genuine love and compassion for those who differ from us in significant ways.

To illustrate one way this happened for me, allow me to share a personal story. After my book, *Disturbing Divine Behavior*, was published, I was curious to know how people were reacting to it and therefore spent time online to see what I could find. As expected, the reactions were mixed. Some liked it; others clearly did not.

In the process of searching online, I encountered one particular blogger who made some less than complimentary comments about the book. That was fine. I knew there would be critique. What bothered me was that his comments kept popping up on multiple sites. I would find some discussion about my book online, and he would make a critical comment in the discussion thread. I would then visit another site, where different people were discussing the book, and once again he would appear and register his disagreement with my approach. This really started to bother me, and I began to develop some very negative feelings toward this person even though we had never met. He was quickly becoming my enemy. I knew I needed to do something—fast.

So, in the fall of 2010, I took bold and decisive action—I sent him an email! I knew we would both be attending a large conference in Georgia the following month, and I wanted to meet him. In the email, I told him that I was aware he was "not enthusiastic about my book" and communicated my

willingness to listen to more of his "thoughts and concerns in that regard."
I offered to buy him lunch or coffee or just to talk together in one of the
conference hotels if he preferred. Then I hit the send button.

Less than two hours later, I had my reply—and a very gracious one
at that. He was willing to meet! On the first day of the conference in late
November, I met this "enemy" blogger for the first time and treated him to
lunch. Though we did not resolve all our biblical/theological differences—I
did not expect we would—something far more wonderful happened: I made
a new friend. By spending face-to-face time getting to know him, I came to
see him as more than some "anonymous" blogger in cyberspace who was
critical of my book (and actually only certain aspects of the book). He became a real person. He was someone with a family, a home, a job. We had
lots to discuss and had a great time being together.

For a number of years thereafter, we always had lunch together whenever we both attended this annual conference. To this day, we continue to
keep in touch and I look forward to opportunities to see him in the future.
Had I not reached out to him, I would probably still regard him as an "enemy" of sorts. What's worse, I would have missed an opportunity to get to
know a really great person and would have deprived myself of a wonderful
friendship.

Meet the Needs of Your Adversaries

As just illustrated, sometimes one of the best ways for our attitudes to change
is through the actions we take. That is why cultivating a nonviolent mind-set
involves more than just thinking differently. It involves behaving differently
as well. Paul instructs Christians in Rome to behave differently toward their
enemies by treating them with kindness and compassion: "If your enemies
are hungry, feed them; if they are thirsty, give them something to drink"
(Rom 12:20). Notice that in this instance, providing food and drink is not
regarded as just some *random* act of kindness (not that there would be anything wrong with that). Rather, it is a specific act of kindness in response to
a particular need. Whenever possible, Christians should take concrete steps
to meet the real needs of their enemies. Doing so enhances our ability to
cultivate a nonviolent mind-set.

The following story from Terry Brensinger's sermon "Converting Enemies into Friends" nicely illustrates this point.

> On an especially dark, cold, wintery night in Kalandia [a refugee
> camp north of Jerusalem] two Israeli soldiers stood shivering
> beside one of the entrances to the camp. Approximately fifty to

sixty feet away sat an old Palestinian woman with a fire built at her feet. Before long, she summoned a few Palestinian youths and held a brief conversation with them. Suddenly, the youths picked up a couple pieces of wood and started walking to the soldiers. The soldiers' immediate reaction, of course, was one of fear and anticipated violence. "The enemy is coming to fight with sticks and boards," they surely thought to themselves. How surprised they were when the youths stopped just in front of them, put down the wood, and built a fire.[24]

Gestures like these are powerful and have the potential to transform both parties. On the one hand, they create a context for converting enemies into friends. These soldiers experienced unexpected kindness at the hands of their "enemies." This could reshape the way they viewed Palestinians. At the very least, it would challenge certain stereotypes they may have had about young Palestinians males. On the other hand, I imagine this act enhanced the Palestinian youths' capacity to feel compassion towards Israeli soldiers. It is, after all, much harder to hate someone you have chosen to help.

Since feelings often follow actions, our capacity to cultivate a nonviolent mind-set is enhanced when we take practical steps to meet the needs of those we consider to be our enemies—people who oppose us, offend us, and wrong us. Do these individuals need financial help, medical aid, a job, or some other kind of assistance? Are there concrete ways we could meet these needs? If so, we should seize the opportunity by reaching out to them and doing what we can to help. This not only demonstrates our love for them, it changes *us* in the process. It deepens our ability to feel compassion for those who stand against us, and it strengthens our commitment to live nonviolently.

Pray for God's Help and Pray for Your Enemies

Ultimately, if we are going to be able to love all people unconditionally, to see them as God sees them, we will need divine assistance. We need God's help to keep us from being fearful and suspicious of people who are different from us. And we need God's help to overcome our natural inclination to retaliate, seek revenge, and hate those who wrong us. Prayer is one of the most powerful tools we have in this regard. Therefore, we should pray—fervently—for God to exchange the violent inclinations we have toward others

24. Brensinger, "Converting Enemies into Friends," 30–31.

with genuine love and compassion, and to help us see each and every individual as a person created in God's image and beloved by God. I am quite
certain God is ready and eager to answer prayers like this.

In addition to asking for God's help, we are commanded to pray *for*
our persecutors (Matt 5:44). Jesus says, "Bless those who curse you, pray
for those who abuse you" (Luke 6:28). There are many ways we can pray
for our enemies. We can ask God to heal their wounds, soften their hearts,
and transform their minds so they stop behaving violently toward us (and
others). We can pray that they would know of God's great love for them
and would experience God's grace in very real and tangible ways. We can
pray that they would be open to the work of God's Spirit in their lives and
that they would come to repentance and faith in Christ. We can also ask
God to radically reorient their priorities so that working for peace and justice become some of their top concerns. We can pray for all this, and much
more, believing God desires the same things *and* is able to bring them to
pass. God loves the whole world and longs to redeem all creation. When
we pray for our enemies along these lines, we are praying in harmony with
the will of God. Therefore, we can pray with great confidence, knowing not
only that God hears our prayers, but that God is pleased by them and is
actively working to answer them. Of course, even our most fervent prayers
will not override human freedom, and we cannot be sure how our enemies
will ultimately respond to the promptings of God's Spirit.

Whatever effect our prayers will have upon our enemies, we can be
certain they will have a profound effect upon us. As Forest puts it, "In prayer
for an enemy, at the very least there is a change in you—the creation of a
bond of care for the other."[25] Praying for our enemies establishes a connection between us that ultimately alters the way we think about them. It helps
us see our enemies as people loved by God just as much as we are: no more,
no less.[26]

Praying for our enemies also keeps us from plotting evil against them.
It is difficult to ask God to bless someone one day, then plan to harm them
the next. Moreover, if we happen to meet our enemy after praying for them,
chances are we will respond more positively and graciously to them than we
would have otherwise.

Admittedly, it is sometimes very difficult to pray for our enemies, especially those who have hurt us deeply. In those cases, we might simply start
by asking for God's assistance:

25. Forest, *Loving Our Enemies*, 97.

26. As Wink reminds us, "We are to regard the enemy as beloved of God every bit
as much as we" (*Engaging the Powers*, 269).

> Please help me love this person I find so unlovable and disagree-
> able. Please keep me from treating her the way she has treated
> me. Please help me see her through your eyes of love and grace.

I am convinced God honors prayers like this and transforms us as we seek
to live nonviolently toward others.

Conclusion

Developing a nonviolent mind-set is crucial to living nonviolently. We can
do this by seeing each person as created in God's image, by humanizing
people rather than demonizing them, by getting to know the "Other," by
meeting the needs of our adversaries, and by praying, both for God's help
and for our enemies. As we do these things, we can be assured that God
will transform us and enable us to see others through eyes of love and
compassion.

In many respects, cultivating a nonviolent mind-set is foundational to
what follows in the remainder of this book. It provides the basis for a wide
variety of actions and responses. In the next few chapters, we will discuss
how to live nonviolently in everyday life: at home with family, at work with
colleagues, at school with students and teachers, in church with other Christians. The degree to which we succeed or fail in this endeavor is likely to
depend upon our basic mind-set. The attitudes we have toward others, and
the assumptions we hold about them, often dictate the way we treat them.
As we have emphasized, how we see others really matters. By cultivating a
nonviolent mind-set, we are much more likely to respond compassionately
to both friends *and* enemies, to those who are like us and those who are
not. Therefore, as we turn our attention to some of the more practical ways
we can live out our commitment to follow the nonviolent way of Jesus, we
should keep these things in mind.

14

How to Handle Conflict without Becoming Violent

Living Nonviolently with the People Around You

Live in harmony with one another. . . . If it is possible,
so far as it depends on you, live peaceably with all.

—THE APOSTLE PAUL[1]

There are many circumstances in which it is easier to love one's enemies
than it is to love those with whom one lives, works, and worships day
after day.

—GAIL O'DAY[2]

IN THEIR BOOK, *SAVING Your Marriage Before It Starts*, Drs. Les and Leslie Parrott describe a fight they had some years ago.

> We were late for a weekend marriage retreat—and *we* were the speakers. Leslie was still in her office pulling together some last-minute materials, and I was waiting impatiently in the car.

---

1. Rom 12:16, 18.

2. O'Day, "Gospel of John," 525. Quoted with slight variations in Gench, *Encountering God*, 34.

"Okay, Parrott, don't lose it," I murmured to myself. "She will be out any minute now, just relax and don't get angry at her." Five minutes turned into fifteen. "Here she comes now, just bite your tongue."

It was raining lightly as Leslie climbed into the car. But as she reached to close the car door, her armful of notes and hundreds of handouts slipped away, some into a curbside puddle, most scattering across the wet street.

I couldn't contain myself. "That's it," I said sternly. "I can't believe this! What are we going to do now? Couldn't you see that—"

"You're the one that wanted to do this retreat," Leslie interrupted.

"Oh, don't give me that. You—" My raised voice suddenly stopped as I tried to swallow my sentence. With the car door swung open wide and papers flying everywhere, I suddenly realized our derogatory remarks were being heard by several colleagues who were passing by. Keeping their eyes straight ahead, they pretended not to notice the "marriage experts" having their tiff, but there was no denying that the Parrotts were having a blowup.[3]

Everyone experiences conflict—even the experts. We experience conflict at work and at home, in our churches, schools, and communities. Since people have different personalities, perspectives, and priorities, conflict is to be expected. Some conflicts are relatively insignificant in the grand scheme of things (two toddlers fighting over the same toy). Other conflicts are far more serious (two adults contemplating divorce). Some are quickly resolved (settling a dispute over whose night it is to do the dishes), others seem intractable (the Israeli-Palestinian conflict). Although conflict is not necessarily bad, it is often handled quite badly. When that happens, the potential for violence is great.

Unfortunately, many people do not deal with conflict very constructively. We allow our anger and frustration to get the best of us and become relationally violently with our friends, family members, and co-workers. We treat others with hostility and sometimes can be downright mean. We blame, shame, and speak unkindly in an effort to get our way or prove our point. This kind of behavior is problematic, to say the least, *especially* for those of us who call ourselves Christians. If we want to follow Jesus faithfully, we need to manage our emotions and develop better ways of responding when we get into a confrontation.

3. Parrott, *Saving Your Marriage*, 118, emphasis original.

Few of us have seen this modeled well, and fewer still have received much guidance—let alone formal training—in conflict resolution. Thus, when conflict arises we often experience intense frustration, engage in heated verbal exchanges, and sometimes even resort to physical violence. That's the bad news. The good news is there are some rather simple things we can do to rectify this undesirable state of affairs. There *are* alternative ways to handle conflict that do not depend on violence. We can learn how to "fight" fairly in order to minimize the possibility of a violent confrontation.

How to Handle Conflict without Becoming Violent

Like many topics we have addressed, this one deserves a book all its own.[4] Since I don't have that luxury, I will focus on a number of very practical suggestions that are helpful for dealing with conflict nonviolently. As we'll see, having good communication skills and a basic understanding of conflict negotiation go a long way toward navigating challenging conversations without becoming physically, emotionally, or verbally violent. Though much of what follows is geared toward *interpersonal* conflict, many of the same principles apply to conflicts involving larger groups of people, like labor disputes and church conflicts.

Cultivate a Nonviolent Mind-Set

One of the most important things we can do to prepare ourselves to handle conflict well is to cultivate a nonviolent mind-set, a point stressed in the previous chapter. Possessing a nonviolent mind-set is immensely helpful when we are engaged in conflict with a friend, neighbor, relative, co-worker, politician, landlord, store clerk—or anyone else for that matter—since it governs the way we treat them. It reminds us that regardless of our differences, our "opponent" is also a child of God. Rather than seeing that person as an adversary, we see them as a fellow human being created in God's image. This cautions us against demonizing them or focusing only on their undesirable qualities.

Entering into difficult conversations with a nonviolent mind-set orients us and grounds us. It does not magically solve the problem or resolve the issue, but it encourages us to engage the other person with care and respect. When we do, we create a positive environment that reduces the

4. For accessible, book-length treatments of this topic, see Lederach, *Reconcile*, and Rosenberg, *Nonviolent Communication*.

risk of violent confrontation and offers the best chance for differences to be resolved peaceably.

Speak Graciously to Others

Beyond this, there are a number of things we can do when we are actively engaged in conflict. Many of these are related to how we speak to others. A lot of damage can be done with the words we say, especially when emotions run high. When we are upset with someone, it is very easy to say things we later regret. Therefore, we need to be especially careful about *how* we speak. We would do well to heed the exhortation in Colossians to "Let your speech always be gracious" (Col 4:6). Gracious speech is courteous, respectful, and humble. It does not ridicule, demean, or demonize. Gracious speech avoids accusations and innuendoes, and it refuses to engage in the kind of inflammatory and incendiary rhetoric all too common on talk radio, in political campaigns, and even from certain well-known Christian leaders. Gracious speech is characterized by compassion and grounded in love. Once again, the Golden Rule can be our guide. We should speak to others the same way we want others to speak to us.

This point also extends to the way we communicate electronically, through texts, email, and social media accounts. An enormous amount of interpersonal conflict is generated through these modes of communication. Some of us type things we would never say to someone in person and send texts and tweets that are disrespectful and mean-spirited. Speaking graciously means being very vigilant about the way we communicate digitally. We should never type, text, or tweet anything we would be uncomfortable saying directly to someone. Our words are powerful, and we should be very careful how we use them.[5]

Use "I" Statements

One very simple and practical way to speak graciously is to use "I" statements rather than blaming statements. "I" statements enable us to share our feelings and perspective in a non-defensive way. These statements allow us to speak the truth in a way that communicates respect and increases the chance of our words being received positively.

To illustrate how these work, consider the following scenario. Suppose you and a friend spend time together regularly: eating out, going to the

---

5. See Jas 3:1–12.

movies, exercising, and so on. While you enjoy these times together, you are annoyed that your friend is habitually late. You plan to meet at 7:00 PM but he doesn't arrive until 7:25 PM. This happens repeatedly and you become increasingly frustrated by his behavior. If you don't deal with this you realize you are going to snap and say things that will undoubtedly hurt your friend and harm your relationship: "What's wrong with you? Why are you always late? Can't you get your act together?" Rather than exploding, you decide to find a way to tell your friend how his behavior is impacting you. You might say, "I really like spending time together, and I feel disrespected when we agree to do something at a certain time and you arrive late." Or, "When you don't come on time, it makes me feel like I'm not all that important to you." Chances are, your friend will be much more receptive to statements like these than to a barrage of accusations and put-downs.

Avoid blaming

Whenever we are engaged in conflict, we want to de-escalate the situation and speak in ways that lower defenses. This is why it is so important to avoid blaming others. Nothing raises people's defenses faster than blaming statements, especially when they are expressed with superlatives like "always" or "never." "You *never* respond to my text messages!" "You're *always* saying negative things about me in public!" Although these statements may be *generally* true, they are usually an exaggeration when stated in such absolute terms. In any case, statements like these tend to make people *really* defensive.

An alternative approach would be to state your concern in way that genuinely expresses how you feel *without* attacking the other person in the process: "I'm confused about not getting a response to my text messages yesterday." Or, "I was really embarrassed when you made that comment about me in public. It makes me feel like you don't really care about me when you talk that way in front of others." Statements like these may still be hard for some people to hear, but they are respectful and they avoid blaming and shaming. Again, the key is to find a nonthreatening way to share how their behavior is negatively impacting you. This gives you the best chance of being heard and moving toward a positive outcome. While training ourselves to talk this way takes time and intentionality, it is well worth the effort. It keeps us from becoming verbally violent and de-escalates situations in which it is all too easy to say hurtful things.

Marshall Rosenberg has pioneered a way of interacting with others called "nonviolent communication," in which he emphasizes and elaborates on the points we have been making here, among others.[6] In a chapter titled "Taking Responsibility for Our Feelings" Rosenberg writes, "It has been my experience over and over again that from the moment people begin talking about what they need rather than what's wrong with one another, the possibility of finding ways to meet everybody's needs is greatly increased."[7]

To illustrate briefly, consider the following two statements. Rosenberg believes both are good examples of this kind of speech.

> I'm sad that you won't be coming for dinner because I was hoping we could spend the evening together.
> When you said you'd do it and then didn't, I felt disappointed because I want to be able to rely upon your words.[8]

In each instance, notice how the speaker avoids blaming, reveals his/her feelings, and identifies a need. Statements like these can serve as models for us as we strive to talk with others in ways that do not unnecessarily raise defenses.

Stay Focused on the Issue

When we are in the midst of conflict, it is important to identify key issues and to stay focused on them. People often have a very hard time doing this. What may begin as a simple disagreement between neighbors about their property line may end as a heated argument covering a laundry list of unresolved grievances from the past ten years. When this happens, it becomes nearly impossible to make any real progress. As the tension and frustration escalates, verbal violence—and sometimes even physical violence—is not far behind. Keeping the main issue the main issue avoids this and increases the chances of resolving conflict nonviolently.

So what can you do if you find yourself in a situation like this, with lots of issues swirling around? Gently try to redirect the conversation back to the main issue. You might say something like this: "It sounds like you have a number of important concerns we could address. I'm having a difficult time focusing on all of these at once and am wondering if we could just deal with the issue of our property line now and maybe come back to some of these other issues later." Maintaining that kind of focus gives you a much better chance of dealing with conflict constructively.

6. As Rosenberg, *Nonviolent Communication*, 25–89, describes it, there are four parts of nonviolent communication: observing, feeling, needing, and requesting.

7. Ibid., 54.

8. Ibid., 65 and 66, respectively.

Listen Well

Listening well is another very important part of constructive conflict resolution. When people disagree, they do a lot of talking—often over and past
each other. Yet, sometimes they do remarkably little listening.[9] If you have
ever been in a confrontation with someone who keeps repeating the same
thing over and over again, chances are you may not be listening well. They
probably don't think you have heard their concern, and they are determined
to repeat it until you do. One way to help them know you have heard what
they have said is to paraphrase it back to them. "So, if I understand you cor-
rectly, it sounds like you're saying I should spend more time with the kids
in the evenings." Or, "Let me be sure I'm hearing you right. You don't think
I'm doing my fair share of chores around the house?" If questions like those
are met with a resounding "Yes!," you have hit the nail on the head. You have
little hope of resolving a conflict until a person feels like their concerns are
heard and respected. Listening well is often the first step toward having a
productive conversation about the issue at hand.

Move Beyond Positions and Get to Interests

Perhaps one of the most important guidelines for resolving conflict nonviolently is to move beyond positions to interests.[10] A position is *what* someone wants; an interest is *why* they want it. Put differently, *interests* represent
the underlying reasons people hold the *positions* they do. If you never get
beyond positions to interests, some conflicts are simply unresolvable.

For example, imagine two neighbors, Frank and Joe, who live side-by-
side. Frank wants to put up a fence along their property line. Joe is adamant-
ly opposed to the idea. He does *not* want a fence put up along their property
line. These are their *positions*, and they seem incompatible. You can't *have* a
fence and *not have* a fence at the same time. As long as Frank and Joe stay at
the level of positions, this conflict is unresolvable. There is no way around
this. It is no-win situation. One neighbor will be happy; the other will not.

But let's dig a little deeper. Let's figure out why Frank wants this fence
and why Joe is so opposed to it. In other words, let's get to their interests.
Frank wants a fence because he wants to keep his dog Fido on his property.
Lately, Fido has been running around the neighborhood leaving "deposits."
Frank can't bear the thought of chaining Fido, since that seems inhumane,

9. As a society on the whole, we are not very good listeners. For a wonderful book
exploring ways we can develop this lost art, see McHugh, *Listening Life*.

10. Schrock-Shenk, ed., *Mediation and Facilitation Training Manual*, 183–86.

but he doesn't want to ruin his relationships with the neighbors. Since getting rid of Fido is simply out of the question, Frank has decided that he is going to put up a fence. What he has not yet decided is what kind of fence to get and whether he will try to put it up himself. Frank is not particularly handy with projects like these so he is contemplating hiring a professional to install it.

When Frank sees Joe outside the next day, he tells him about his plans. Joe is less than enthusiastic and immediately tells Frank he does not want a fence along their property line. He is concerned that a fence will block the beautiful view he now has and will crowd out some of his shrubbery. He also is concerned about the additional time it will take to trim around the fence on his side of the property. Joe tells Frank all this, and he even diplomatically intimates that he is concerned that if Frank tries to put up a fence, it might not come out looking all that great.

With their interests on the table, Frank and Joe are now able to work toward a mutually satisfactory solution. Joe might be open to Frank putting up a chain-link fence (especially if a professional installs it) since this would not block his view the same way a wooden fence would. An even better solution would be for Frank to have an *invisible* fence installed underground. This would give Fido freedom while keeping him on Frank's property. Moreover, since the fence is underground, *all* of Joe's concerns would be satisfactorily addressed. Both of these are good solutions, but they only came to light *after* Frank and Joe moved beyond their respective positions to the interests beneath them.

If you find yourself in a conflict and it seems there is no way forward, try to get beneath the positions being expressed to the interests driving them. Sometimes, this opens up new possibilities. One way to get at interests is to ask questions. Let's suppose Frank and Joe both stated their positions and did not say anything about why they did, or did not, want a fence. In that case, Joe could have asked Frank: "Could you help me understand your reasons for wanting to put up this fence?" And Frank could have asked Joe: "What concerns do you have about me installing a fence?" Asking (and answering) these questions can help the conversation move beyond positions to interests.

Get the Facts and Allow Different Perceptions to Coexist

When dealing with conflict, it is important to be as clear as possible about the "facts." The reason for this is simple. Some conflicts are the direct result of misinformation and misunderstanding. Once people get the facts straight, some conflicts basically resolve themselves. There is an interesting story in the Bible about how getting the facts straight not only resolved a conflict—it prevented a war! In Joshua 22, we are told that the Israelites living on the west side of the Jordan River were preparing to go to war with the Israelites living on the east side of the Jordan because they had erected an altar. The Israelites on the West side regarded this as an act of religious faithlessness since they believed the only proper place to offer sacrifices was at the tabernacle (located on the west side of the Jordan). What they did *not* know is that the Israelites on the east side had set up this altar to be a "witness," symbolizing the unity and connectedness of the tribes on both sides of the Jordan. It was intended to be symbolic and was never meant to be a functioning altar. Once this became known, the conflict was resolved, and war was averted.

Unfortunately, most conflicts are not resolved this easily. Sometimes, the facts themselves are in dispute. People often have a hard time agreeing on what happened, why it happened, or who's at fault. I may interpret a situation one way, while those around me may interpret it very differently. The presence of these different perceptions about the same event make it challenging to move forward. If you think you need to make others see things from your perspective in situations like these, you are probably setting yourself up for failure. It is not always possible or even desirable. Sometimes you simply need to say, "I understand we interpret what happened quite differently, and I realize we may never see things the same way. Can we agree to disagree about the past and try to find a way to move forward together?" Rather than getting stuck in an endless debate about the past, you can talk about how you will relate to each other if something like this happens again. Allowing different perceptions to coexist, rather than trying to force someone to see things your way, is often vital to restoring a healthy relationship.

Always Communicate Respect

Finally, we should engage in conflict in a way that respects the other person. We have already discussed the importance of speaking graciously to others. In addition, if we are going to raise an issue that we expect to be confrontational, we should plan the timing of our conversation carefully. We should schedule the conversation when it is convenient for them and when they have sufficient time to devote to it. This communicates respect for them and provides the best chance for a constructive conversation.

The Value of Mediation

If you find yourself entangled in a particularly difficult or complicated conflict, you might consider utilizing a trained mediator to help you work through the issues at hand. The role of the mediator is to facilitate a process that can help both parties work through their differences in a way that is respectful and constructive. Ultimately, it is not the mediator's job to "solve" the problem. That remains the responsibility of those who are in conflict. The mediator serves as a neutral presence and creates a safe space for conversation.

The advantage of mediation over using the legal system is that it keeps power in hands of those who are in dispute. The legal process tends to produce winners and losers. Mediation—which is not legally binding—keeps all parties at the table and gives everyone a voice in the decisions that are made. This has the greatest potential to produce an outcome everyone can feel good about, even if some concessions are made along the way. Mediation often results in some type of agreement that is acceptable to everyone at the table. Even if an agreement is not reached, disputants often leave this process with greater insight about the issues at hand and the other parties' concerns.

Many communities have mediation centers that offer these services for little or no cost. For a time, I volunteered as a mediator with an organization in Harrisburg, Pennsylvania, that asked for a ten-dollar donation from each party in the dispute. Having been a mediator myself, I can testify firsthand to its power and effectiveness. It is truly amazing to see what can happen when people who are at odds—and who sometimes clearly hate each other—sit down and talk. Grievances can be aired, differences can be reconciled, and a new way forward can be forged. I have seen this happen time and again, and it has made a believer out of me. I have seen neighbors, who did not even know one another's phone numbers, agree to call each other before they call the police the next time they have a dispute. I have witnessed college professors, who worked in the same department and refused to talk to each other, find a way to resolve their differences and more forward after a series of mediation sessions. Mediation really works.

Obviously, not every issue can be resolved through mediation. Like anything, mediation has its limits. Still, mediation has the potential to help people beyond an impasse and to do so in ways that enables everyone involved to feel heard, respected, and empowered.[11]

11. Many community mediation centers offer twenty-four–hour trainings you can take if you would like to become a volunteer mediator. These trainings are extremely valuable and well worth the investment of time and energy. Regardless of whether you

A Very Important Word about Self-Care

Before concluding this chapter, I want to say a word about good self-care since it is directly linked to our ability to deal with conflict constructively and nonviolently. It is much more difficult to follow the suggestions discussed in this chapter when our physical and emotional resources are depleted. If we are maxed out, stressed out, and exhausted, we are far less likely to respond well when conflict arises. That is why practicing good self-care is so vital.

Good self-care involves getting enough rest, eating right, and exercising regularly. It means balancing competing demands for our time, developing margins, and not overcommitting. Living this way reduces our stress and provides us with the necessary resources to respond patiently, graciously, and compassionately to difficult people and tense situations.

One of the most important components of good self-care involves finding ways to renew. What is renewing differs from person to person. For some people it is taking an early morning walk. For others, it is playing a musical instrument. Still others are renewed by doing artwork such as sketching, woodworking, or painting. Doing something truly renewing is more than just doing something "fun" (though obviously it is something enjoyable). Instead, that which renews us fills our tank, reorients our perspective, and gives us the internal fortitude we need to face another day with courage and grace. Renewal is absolutely essential for our physical, emotional, and spiritual well-being. Without it, living nonviolently is very difficult indeed.

Another part of good self-care is learning to love ourselves. This is difficult for many of us. Lots of people—even Christians—suffer from a poor self-image, low self-esteem, and self-loathing. Some people find it difficult to *like* themselves, let alone *love* themselves. But we *must* do this, not only to find peace within, but to live peaceably with other people. As John Dear puts it, "Peace begins within each of us. It is a process of repeatedly showing mercy to ourselves, forgiving ourselves, befriending ourselves, accepting ourselves, and loving ourselves. As we learn to appreciate ourselves and accept God's gift of peace, we begin to radiate peace and love to others."[12] It is very hard to be kind to others when we are at war with ourselves. If we see ourselves as unlovely and unlovable, chances are we will see others similarly and will find it difficult to love them unconditionally.

---

decide to volunteer as a mediator after completing such a training, the skills you learn will enhance your ability to deal with conflict more constructively and nonviolently.

12. Dear, *Living Peace*, 10.

Learning to love ourselves can take time, especially if we have developed unhealthy patterns of negative self-talk over an extended period of time. Sometimes, it is very beneficial to turn to a trusted pastor, spiritual director, or good counselor for help in this regard. They can help us break free of destructive patterns that inhibit our ability to love ourselves for who we are. This too is an essential part of good self-care.

While good self-care alone cannot prevent us from behaving violently, it goes a long way toward keeping our violent tendencies at bay. When we take care of our basic needs, find ways to renew, and learn to love ourselves, we are much less likely to lash out at others and behave in ways we later regret.

Conclusion

Following the nonviolent way of Jesus requires us to deal with conflict in ways that communicate love and respect for those with whom we disagree. We need to develop strategies for handling difficult conversations and tense situations that are not verbally, emotionally, or physically violent. Hopefully, the suggestions offered in this chapter have better equipped you to do that and have piqued your interest to learn more about dealing with interpersonal conflict nonviolently.[13]

13. For helpful resources written from a secular perspective, see Stone, Patton, and Heen, *Difficult Conversations*, and Patterson et al., *Crucial Conversations*. For a popular Christian approach, see Sande, *Peacemaker*, and also Sande and Johnson, *Resolving Everyday Conflict*. For an interesting examination of selected biblical texts used to reflect on issues of conflict and peacemaking, see Dempsey and Shapiro, *Reading the Bible, Transforming Conflict*.

15

Nonviolent Parenting

Treating Children with Respect and Talking about Violence

Children grow toward peace as they live with persons who practice and interpret the spirit of Christ.

—KATHRYN ASCHLIMAN[1]

IN HER INSIGHTFUL ARTICLE, "One Mean Mennonite Mama," Valerie Weaver-Zercher describes a bad parenting moment many parents understand all too well:

> I did something not long ago that I've always claimed I'd never do: I spanked my child. Not only did I spank him, but I did it in a moment of complete unfettered rage. Even if you think spanking is effective discipline, everyone knows you're not supposed to do it out of anger.
>
> My 5-year old was disappointed that he couldn't go to a picnic and was slamming doors, kicking and yelling, "Bad Mama!" (Considering what happened next, this was probably a fitting moniker.) The 3-year old and the 1-year old were also throwing minor fits, and I was facing several more hours with these

1. Aschliman, ed., *Growing toward Peace*, 15. Quoted in Byler, *How to Teach Peace to Children*, 17.

tykes. I was depleted, and after almost six years of parenting, I should have been able to read the handwriting on the wall: You are tired. You are angry. You will hurt your child if you do not shut yourself in the bathroom and repeat the Christ Prayer 20 times while breathing deeply.

But I couldn't read the warning signs because my vision was blurred with fury—or maybe I chose not to read the signs, because rage has such a strangely delicious taste. So instead of walking away or praying or calling a friend, I grabbed by eldest with my left hand and delivered several robust whacks to his bottom with my right.

Fortunately my arms are puny, and fortunately I woke up from my fuming stupor after about five whacks. I held him close and apologized profusely, and somehow we both straightened up enough to make it through the evening with a semblance of normalcy.

Let me be clear: I know better. I've taken conflict transformation classes, and I've led trainings on anger management. Yet I have talked to enough other parents to know that I'm not the only one who should know better—and doesn't.[2]

In moments like these, many parents struggle to treat their children with love and respect and are tempted to resort to violence. Yet this is precisely when it is most important to follow the nonviolent way of Jesus.

The purpose of this chapter is to help parents think about what it means to parent nonviolently and to explore various strategies for doing so. We'll begin with a discussion of nonviolent discipline since this is where the temptation to behave violently can be very great. Even though we love our children dearly, their behavior sometimes brings out the worst in us. After we have repeatedly told them to do something to no avail, or when our efforts to correct bad habits seem to fall on deaf ears, we grow increasingly frustrated and annoyed. In those moments, we sometimes behave in ways we are later ashamed to admit. We might scream and yell. We might become physically aggressive. We may even be abusive. Surely there must be a better way, especially for those of us committed to living nonviolently.

To provide some context here, it might help to know I have three children of my own (ages eleven, nine, and four). They are creative, talented, inquisitive, beautiful, and bright—and they are not easy to parent. Sure, there are times when things run smoothly and parenting is a breeze. But there are other times, *many* other times, when parenting is exceedingly difficult. For example, after one especially horrific ordeal with our children during

2. Weaver-Zercher, "One Mean Mennonite Mama," 11.

story time, just before putting them to bed, my wife Elisa quietly said to me, "That's why some animals eat their young!" My children have sorely tested my commitment to nonviolence on more than one occasion. This is not because they are bad kids—they are not. It is simply because parenting is one of the most challenging tasks on the planet. It takes great skill, wisdom, and patience to parent well and to resist the urge to lash out when things are going badly.

Nonviolent Parenting

So what can be done? How can we shape, guide, and correct our children without being physically, verbally, or relationally violent?[3] As with many topics we have addressed, adequately responding to this one would also take a book in itself—and books have been written.[4] What I can offer here are some simple suggestions that point to an alternative way of parenting, one that does not require any violence.

One way to frame this discussion is to consider two very different aspects of parenting, what I call "preemptive parenting" and "redemptive parenting." "Preemptive parenting" refers to everything we can do to help our children from misbehaving, or having a meltdown, in the first place. It involves taking preventative measures to reduce the likelihood that they will be disobedient and behave badly. While nothing can guarantee that our children will be compliant and well-behaved, there are things we can do that make this more likely. For example, we can ensure our kids get enough food, rest, creative stimulation, one-on-one time with us, and so forth. These things provide children with the internal resources they need to make good choices. We can also provide positive incentives for good behavior. Offering things such as stickers, money, small gifts, additional screen time, or special outings motivate children to do what they are supposed to do.

In addition, we should be very intentional about letting our kids know how much we *like* them. While it is important to tell our children we love them, they need to sense that we genuinely like them. Let them know you are glad they are part of the family. When they come home from school, tell them how happy you are to see them and how nice it is to have them back. Communicate your desire to spend time with them—one-on-one—and

3. For a brief, but very helpful, answer to that question, see the list of ten ideas proposed by Dr. Sears at http://www.askdrsears.com/topics/parenting/discipline-behavior/discipline-for-children.

4. See, e.g., Markham, *Peaceful Parent*; Flower, *Adventures in Gentle Discipline*; Cecil, *Raising Peaceful Children*.

then do it. It is important to find time that is as free from distractions as possible so you can give your full and undivided attention. This is not the time for multi-tasking. Rather, each child needs to have time when they feel you are fully present to them and not preoccupied with all sorts of other "really important things" that need to be done.

There simply is no substitute for carving out this kind of focused time with your kids on a regular basis. Spending quality time together not only strengthens your relationship, it directly impacts how your children behave. All this is part of preemptive parenting, parenting that tries to stop bad behavior before it starts by being attuned to our children's needs and doing what we can to meet them.

"Redemptive parenting," on the other hand, refers to the way we deal with our children after they have done something wrong. When our children misbehave and are disobedient, when they treat us disrespectfully and are unkind to other family members, we need to respond. And, as followers of Jesus, we need to do so nonviolently. One thing that will help to insure we respond this way is to practice the kind of good self-care we discussed at the end of the previous chapter. That will provide us with sufficient reserves to respond in measured, constructive, and ultimately redemptive ways. It's really difficult to respond well to our children when we are tired, hungry, and stressed.

Fortunately, there are many ways to respond to our children's misbehavior that are not physically or relationally violent.[5] We can ask them to write a letter that expresses their understanding of why their behavior was so harmful and that describes what they might do differently next time. The benefit of doing something like this is that it is not just punitive but actually provides our children with an opportunity to reflect on their poor behavior in a way that may help them do better in the future.

Depending upon what has been done and the age of the child, we can also institute a loss of privileges, such as the loss of "screen time" (TV, computer, iPad, etc.) or the loss of time going out with friends. This is most effective when these losses are natural consequences.[6] For example, if your teenager was supposed to bring the car back by 8 PM with a full tank of gas, and returns at 10 PM with the car running on empty, it makes sense to lose the privilege of using the car for a period of time. Or if you discover your child visiting Internet sites you have explicitly forbidden or using social media in destructive ways, it makes sense to impose a loss of screen time as a natural consequence. Consequences like these make a whole lot more sense

5. For a helpful discussion of ten ideas, see Sears, "Healthy Discipline."
6. See Markham, *Peaceful Parent*, 176–79.

than imposing random, unrelated punishments. If the consequence does not seem connected to the behavior, our children may see *us* as the problem for imposing it. The goal is to keep the focus on the child and to help them realize that the issue here is their own inappropriate behavior, not whatever consequences might follow.

Whenever possible, we should encourage our children make things right when they have done something wrong. If they steal something, they should return the item to its rightful owner. If that is no longer possible, they should pay whatever it costs to replace it. If they have damaged someone's reputation, they should apologize to that person and take concrete steps to try to undo as much of the damage as possible. Having our children respond like this is much more likely to help them understand the seriousness of what they have done and how their behavior negatively impacts others. Hopefully, this will encourage them to think twice before they act that way again in the future.

While we have a responsibility to guide and correct our children, there is nothing Christian or "biblical" about using violence to do so. Finding nonviolent ways of parenting is important because it keeps us from harming our children and because it is consistent with our commitment to follow the nonviolent way of Jesus. Whether we like it or not, our children are watching us—closely. And, though they typically do not say this in so many words, they are looking to us for guidance. They watch how we behave and react, and they listen to what we say and leave unsaid. This provides them with important information about how to behave in the world, and they use this information to form their own thoughts and opinions. If we tell our children we are opposed to violence and then behave violently toward them, what kind of messages are we sending? If we want our children to be nonviolent, we need to practice what we preach by modeling nonviolent living in all areas of our life, *especially* in the way we parent.

What about Spanking?

As the story at the beginning of this chapter illustrates, it is all too easy to react violently to our children in moments of extreme parental frustration and anger. This is especially true when our children are very young. We are bigger, stronger, and more powerful, and we can dominate them by our size, strength, words, and deeds. Still, regardless of how irritated we may be with our child's attitude or behavior, our children deserve to be treated with dignity and respect. However we decide to respond, we must take care not to harm them in any way. I suspect most Christians agree with this. We condemn child abuse and neglect, and we applaud organizations that work for the prevention of violence against children.

In light of this, it strikes me as ironic that so many Christians have no qualms about using violence to discipline their children. They regard spanking, and other forms of corporal punishment, as entirely appropriate.[7] But spanking is hitting. Moreover, it is hitting done with the intention of causing some degree of pain and discomfort (otherwise, what's the point?). Regardless of how "lovingly" it is done, or how controlled the parent may be while doing it, spanking *is* a form of violence. One might even argue it is a form of abuse. If hitting an animal is considered inhumane and unacceptable, why do so many parents, even *Christian* parents, believe that hitting their child is permissible?

Part of the answer has to do with the way we were raised. For better or worse, we often tend to parent the way we were parented. If we were spanked as children, we are likely to spank our children without giving it much thought. We do what we know because it feels "normal." Other parents spank because they believe it is absolutely necessary to stop bad behavior in certain situations. It is not uncommon to hear parents say, "I spank to get their attention. One good swat lets them know I really mean business." That may be true—as far as it goes. Spanking may get their attention. It may teach them you mean business. Unfortunately, that's not all it will teach them. It will also teach them there are circumstances in which hitting is permissible and violence is acceptable. They will learn that it is okay to cause someone pain when they do something wrong. These are powerful messages that become deeply engrained and are not easily dislodged.

Given the potential damage spanking can do, it would be irresponsible not to inquire about its effectiveness. Setting aside questions of morality for a moment, we need to ask a more basic question: Does it work? The research here is conclusive. In what is considered the state of the art study on corporal punishment, Dr. Elizabeth Gershoff examined *sixty* years of research and concluded the *only* thing corporal punishment is good for is "immediate compliance."[8] In other words, spanking is only effective as a short-term "solution." It momentarily stops a child from misbehaving. The downside is that this "immediate compliance" comes at a high cost, namely, harmful long-term consequences. Spanking causes emotional harm and relational trauma. As Dr. Laura Markham observes, "Spanking has repeatedly been shown to lower intelligence, while it increases tantrums, defiance, bullying,

---

7. For an extensive treatment of this topic, see Webb, *Corporal Punishment in the Bible.*

8. Cited in Markham, *Peaceful Parent*, 171. The study itself was published in 2002.

sibling violence, adult mental health problems, and later spousal abuse."[9] Markham notes that "*every* study of this issue that is considered scientifically credible (meaning it is peer-reviewed and meets scientific standards for publication) shows that spanking damages kids' psyches and worsens behavior."[10] In short, rather than correcting bad behavior, spanking makes it worse and harms the child in the process. Sadly, these negative effects are rarely known, let alone considered, by parents (and others) who spank their children.

While this research alone should be enough to persuade parents to stop spanking their children, *Christian* parents should also be dissuaded from spanking their children since spanking is violent and violence is inconsistent with the life and teachings of Jesus. Yet studies show that Christians are actually *more likely* to spank their children than the general population. According to an annual poll conducted by the University of Chicago, "Born-again Christians are, on average, 15 percentage points more likely than the rest of the population to agree that spanking is an acceptable form of punishment."[11] Why?

This can be explained, at least in part, by the fact that some Christians believe they have a biblical mandate to discipline their children this way. These parents spank because they believe God requires it. In their minds, failing to spank would be an act of disobedience. They take their cues from a handful of verses in the book of Proverbs like this one: "Those who spare the rod hate their children, but those who love them are diligent to discipline them" (Prov 13:24).[12] This "spank because the Bible tells you to" view is championed in popular books like Tedd Tripp's *Shepherding a Child's Heart*[13] as well as by Christian organizations such as Focus on the Family.[14]

The problem is that this approach to the Bible generally, and to Proverbs particularly, is fundamentally flawed. Proverbs are not divine directives. Instead, the book of Proverbs is a collection of wisdom sayings written by sages who were intent on offering practical advice for living based on what they observed in the world around them. The enormous historical and cultural distance between their world and ours means that the specifics of

9. Ibid., 171.

10. Ibid., emphasis original.

11. Enten, "Americans' Opinions on Spanking Vary."

12. Other verses commonly appealed to include Prov 22:6, 15; 23:13–14; 29:15

13. Tripp, *Shepherding a Child's Heart*, 103–17.

14. For example, Focus on the Family has a webpage with an article titled "The Biblical Approach to Spanking" (http://www.focusonthefamily.com/parenting/effective-biblical-discipline/effective-child-discipline/biblical-approach-to-spanking). It contains material from Ingram, *Effective Parenting*, 110–18.

many of these Proverbs no longer apply to us today even though the general principles still do. What is true about Prov 13:24, for example, is that parents who truly love their children will not allow their bad behavior to go unchecked. Instead, they will find appropriate ways to discipline them. That is what good parents do. But our understanding of child psychology and effective parenting has advanced considerably in the 2,500-plus years since these Proverbs were written. Therefore, it is a huge mistake for parents to uncritically adopt ancient forms of discipline as modern prescriptions for parenting. We need to remember the historical and cultural context in which verses like these emerged and then do the important work of figuring out in what ways they do—and do not—apply to parents living in the twenty-first century.

Obviously, spanking is just one way of being physically violent with children. Even parents who have decided not to spank will sometimes respond violently to their children in other ways: pinching, pushing, squeezing, shaking, slapping, yelling, blaming, shaming, name-calling, and so forth. Treating our children like this is not loving or respectful and does not communicate God's care for them.

Early on in the child-rearing process, my wife and I ruled out spanking as an appropriate form of discipline. In our home, we established a "no hitting" policy that applies to everyone. Hitting is an unacceptable way to treat anyone in the family (or outside the family for that matter). We tell our children that hitting is never okay. Mommy doesn't hit Daddy. Daddy doesn't hit Mommy. Mommy and Daddy don't hit Nathan. Nathan doesn't hit Mommy and Daddy. Nathan doesn't hit Rebecca. Rebecca doesn't hit Nathan. And so on. We have a consistent message that matches our behavior. It would be more than a little hypocritical to prohibit our children from hitting and then turn around and hit (spank) them as a form of punishment. And it would be completely absurd to do this if they were being punished for hitting one another! My wife and I have also chosen not to spank because we decided we wanted our hands to be associated with tenderness and care, not with violence. Keeping spanking off limits is a decision that has served us well and kept us from treating our kids in ways we would have regretted later.

Similarly, all forms of child-shaming are inconsistent with the nonviolent way of Jesus. Whether the shaming happens in public or through some form of social media, this way of parenting is terribly destructive and violent. "Shaming and humiliating children," writes Dr. Karyl McBride, "is emotionally abusive. It is not ok to smack children physically or with words."[15] McBride goes on to say that "solid parenting shows children respect and empathy." We should seek ways to *honor* our children, to let them

15. McBride, "Shaming Children."

know they are valued and loved unconditionally, regardless of what they do. Even when they test the limits of our patience, our children deserve to be treated with care and compassion. They are a gift to us, and we should communicate our love for them even in the most difficult parenting moments.

Talk about Violence with Your Kids (and Subvert It)

Thankfully, dealing with a child's misbehavior is just one part of parenting (though, depending on the child, there may be times when it feels like the *only* part!). In addition to how we treat our children in these moments, there are many other ways we can shape their views about violence. One of the most important things we can do is to talk with our children about violence and our opposition to it. These conversations can take many different forms and can be spontaneous or planned.

A very natural way to begin conversations like these is to discuss the violent images and ideas our children find in what they read and what they see. Talking with kids about this is especially important when the violence they encounter is portrayed positively and regarded as necessary. We can help them evaluate the violence they encounter in the books they read, the games they play, and the programs they watch by raising questions about the necessity and efficacy of violence. We can challenge "virtuous" views of violence and can expand our children's imagination by helping them envision other ways of dealing with danger, threats, and conflict.

This is nicely illustrated in the comic strip *Pearls Before Swine*. Rat and Zebra are sitting side-by-side on a couch in front of a screen.[16] Rat turns to Zebra and asks, "Want to play 'Halo' with me? The guys in red are our enemy." "Okay," says Zebra. But curiously, Zebra sits there without pushing any buttons on his control panel. Puzzled, Rat says, "Dude, what are you doing? Why aren't you shooting at the enemy?" Zebra replies, "I'm looking for a button that lets us talk it out." Unimpressed, Rat remarks dryly, "Perhaps you don't understand gaming." Zebra's final query only serves to confirm Rat's suspicions: "Is there a way to send flowers?"

In this brief interchange, Zebra not only raises questions about the rules of the game, he challenges the very premise upon which the game operates. Why *must* this conflict be settled violently? Why *must* players on one side kill those on the other? Why can't they find some way to work out their differences so they can peacefully coexist? These are precisely the kind

---

16. Stephen Pastis, 2013. The copy I have appeared in a daily calendar on November 19, 2015. My thanks to Meg Ramey for giving me this calendar page.

of questions we should raise with our children when they play video games that require them to use violence to win.

Another way to challenge the ubiquitous violence in so many video games is to make statements like these: "Wouldn't it be really cool if there was a way to make friends with the ogre rather than destroying him?" Or, "Wouldn't it be neat if you could win the game by talking out your differences rather than shooting at each other?"

For a time, my two oldest children were captivated by (okay, addicted to) Minecraft, the hugely successful video game based on blocks. As video games go, Minecraft has much to commend it since the game allows for an enormous amount of creativity (think Legos on a computer). Still, the game is not without danger and violence (unless you play in peaceful or creative mode). You must learn to survive in a world populated by a variety of hostile mobs—spiders, zombies, creepers, endermen, and the like—that attempt to kill you. There are also villagers in Minecraft that are harmless unless they are touched by a zombie, which then turns them into one. The good news for these zombified villagers is that they can be cured. Give them a special potion and a golden apple and soon they are de-zombified and become normal villagers once again. Unfortunately, the vast majority of zombies in Minecraft are not the villager-turned-zombie type and thus, cannot be cured. Native-born zombies are a constant threat and must be avoided or killed. Because of that, I once told my son, "I wish all zombies could be cured." It was a simple comment, but one that said, "I don't like the fact that this game provides no other option for dealing with zombies than destroying them. I wish there was another way. I wish you could cure zombies rather than kill them." Although our children may get annoyed if we say things like this too often, it sends an important message. It lets them know how we feel about violence and encourages them, at least for a moment, to see things differently. It challenges them to resist assumptions about the inevitability of violence and invites them to imagine another way.

We can do the same kind of thing with movies, television shows, and books. Why can't Harry Potter and Voldemort find some way to forgive and reconcile so both can live? Why can't orcs and humans share Middle Earth in peace and harmony rather than constantly warring with one another? After watching a movie with our kids that contains violence, we should process what we have just seen. We can tell our kids we enjoyed the movie even though we wish the two sides had resolved their differences in some other way. "What do you think would have happened if they sat down and tried to talk through their differences? How would the story have been different if one side chose to forgive—rather than fight—the other? Think of all the pain and suffering that could have been avoided!" Questions like these are subversive in the best sense of the world. They undermine violence and point to a better way. Hopefully, over time, our kids will internalize this critique of violence and make it their own.

Christian parents should also give careful consideration to the way they talk with their children about violence in the Bible. It sends very confusing messages to a child to condemn violence in the modern world while simultaneously praising it in the ancient world. We should be especially cautious about how we handle violent Old Testament texts that celebrate acts of warfare and killing. For example, when retelling the story of David and Goliath, we should avoid giving the impression that we approve of David's bloody deed. Instead, as I've written elsewhere, we might ask our children questions like these:

> How do you feel about the way Goliath treated David, and about what David did to Goliath? How do you think God felt about the way David and Goliath behaved? What are some other ways they might have tried to work out their differences? What would you have done if you were David? How do you think God would have liked this story to end? Rather than engaging in simplistic moralizing that tends to reinforce "virtuous" violence, exploring questions like these is much more likely to develop an ethical sensitivity in children and to help them come to their own realization that violence is harmful and displeasing to God.[17]

As parents, we have the ability to limit how much violence and the kind of violence our children are exposed to at home (though the easy access to so much technology makes this increasingly more difficult to monitor). Christians have different opinions about where the boundaries should be in this regard. Some forbid all video games, movies, television programs, or books that contain violence (except the Bible). While I respect this parental desire to "protect" their children, I am not convinced an all-out ban on violent content is the best way forward. Since children are inevitably going to encounter violent entertainment at some point, it seems important to find ways to help them process this under our guidance.

Obviously, some forms of violent entertainment are inappropriate for children. Video games like Grand Theft Auto, and first-person shooter games like the wildly popular Halo series, come to mind. Likewise, horror movies and slasher films like *Halloween*, or *Nightmare on Elm Street*, should be strictly off limits for children. It is irresponsible to allow children to play violent video games like these or to watch movies containing such graphic scenes of gratuitous violence. Violent entertainment like this can traumatize

17. Seibert, *Violence of Scripture*, 154. For further discussion, see ibid., 152–54.

children. Still, rather than instituting a comprehensive ban on any form of entertainment containing violence—which would effectively rule out many of the most popular books, movies, and video games today—parents can develop reasonable restrictions that eliminate the worst forms of violent entertainment without eliminating everything.

Parents should also be cautious about the kind of toys they purchase for their children since many popular toys are inherently violent. Action figures come fully armed, and weaponized vehicles and aircraft overflow store shelves. But what kind of play do toys like these inspire? Do we want our children to act out violent scenarios that involve domination, destruction, and death? Wouldn't it be better to encourage play in ways that involve creativity and cooperation, that teach the value of working together for the common good?

As with violent video games and movies, Christian parents have different opinions about whether or not to allow their children to play with violent toys and which ones might be acceptable. As Harriet Bicksler observes in her excellent article about war toys, "There is a long continuum between total prohibition of all war toys and acceptance of anything."[18] The trick is knowing where to draw the line. "In our family," writes Bicksler, "we allowed such fantasy toy systems as Masters of the Universe, Star Wars, and the Transformers, but we refused to buy G. I. Joe and Rambo toys because the latter were more closely connected to the American military system and the line between fantasy and reality became much less clear."[19] That strikes me as a helpful parameter and represents a balanced approach.

I do think we should discourage children from pointing toy weapons at each other (with the possible exception of colorful, non-realistic looking squirt guns). It is one thing for a child to make one Star Wars action figure battle another. It is something altogether different when a child chases someone with a toy gun pretending to shoot and kill them.

Whatever guidelines we decide to set in place—and, as much as possible, we should do this in cooperation with our children—the key is conversation. Rather than just setting limits, we should explain our reasons for those limits. This provides us with an opportunity to explain our concerns about violent toys and to emphasize our commitment to nonviolence. Hopefully, as our children grow up and become adults they will embrace these commitments as their own.

Another way to help our children develop a Christian perspective on violence is by talking with them about the violence they encounter—and

18. Bicksler, "Teaching Peace to Children Who Play War," 137.
19. Ibid., 138.

sometimes experience—at school, online, or elsewhere. Take bullying, for example. We should discuss some nonviolent ways to respond if they experience this form of violence. What kind of things might they say or do in an effort to stop the bullying without striking back? And how should they respond if they see someone else being bullied? It is very helpful to talk through questions like these with our children.[20]

Likewise, when our children hear about a school shooting, terrorist attack, or "successful" drone strike, it is important to discuss this with them. We should find out what they think and feel about these events and should help them process feelings of fear, confusion, sadness, anger, or anxiety that may result. We should also share how *we* feel about the violence in our world. This gives us an opportunity to express our grief over the loss of life and to discuss nonviolent alternatives that might have been used.

What we should *not* do—yet this is so common among Christians—is express a sense of joy and gladness that a shooter has been killed or a terrorist assassinated. Saying things like "It's about time" or "This is a good day for America" reinforces the myth of redemptive violence. It also sends the wrong message to our children. Comments like these suggest that violence is acceptable in certain situations, that it's okay to shoot and kill people who shoot and kill people. While many people think this way, Christians should not. Instead, we believe *every* person is valuable, and we reject acts of violence against others as inconsistent with the teachings of Jesus and the will of God.

Since our children are constantly being taught that it is necessary to use violence to deal with evil in the world, we need to be intentional about offering nonviolent alternatives. We need to teach our children that followers of Jesus do not return violence for violence. Rather, we try to treat people the same way we want to be treated. We love enemies, pray for persecutors, and forgive offenders. Because we value all life, we grieve all death. Therefore, we view every violent death as a tragedy, whether it's a terrorist who was assassinated or an innocent victim struck by a stray bullet.

The attitudes we, as parents, hold and the way we talk about others can have a powerful influence upon a child's impressionable young mind. Although our children will ultimately need to develop their own decisions about the appropriateness of violence, we should provide them with a moral imagination that enables them to conceive of alternate ways of being in the world. This too is a crucial part of disarming the church.

---

20. For lots of very practical suggestions for having this conversation with your child, complete with questions and brief hypothetical scenarios, see Cappello, *Ten Talks*, 140–70.

Conclusion

I realize that parenting is an intensely personal endeavor. In fact, even the most peaceful among us may find ourselves fiercely defending a certain style of parenting—namely *ours*! We are not eager to hear that the way we have been disciplining our children may be less effective than we think, and perhaps even harmful in certain respects. But the sad reality is that many children *are* harmed by parents who hit, beat, or otherwise physically hurt them. Others suffer at the hands of those who are verbally, emotionally, and relationally violent. None of this is consistent with the nonviolent way of Jesus.

How we treat our children really matters. If we are committed to following Jesus, we need to find ways to guide and correct our children that are loving, respectful, and free of violence. We also need to talk with our kids about the violent entertainment they consume and about the violence they encounter in the real world. Conversations like these can have a profound effect on our children as they make their way in the world and form their own opinions about violence, nonviolence, and Christian faithfulness.

16

Stopping Violence at Home
Addressing the Problem of Domestic Violence in Christian Families

The most dangerous place for a woman in this country [the United States] is her own home, and she's most likely to be beaten or killed by a man she knows.

—GLORIA STEINEM[1]

Domestic abuse doesn't just happen "out there" somewhere—it happens in our town, in our neighborhood, on our street. It happens to people we see at the supermarket, the movie theater, the ballet, the bowling alley, and the PTA board meeting. It happens to our friends, our co-workers, and our family members. Women who have experienced domestic abuse look just like everyone else.

—ELAINE WEISS[2]

HOME SHOULD BE THE safest place on earth, a sanctuary from the evils of the world, a place where you can let down your guard and know

---

1. Jeltsen, "Biggest Issue." See also Gingrich, "Home Is the Most Dangerous Place for Women," and the video embedded in it.

2. Weiss, *Surviving Domestic Violence*, 6.

you are unconditionally loved and accepted. Unfortunately, many people do not experience "home" like that. For them, home is a dangerous and often violent place. Far too often, it is where they experience physical, emotional, and sexual abuse. Sadly, Christian families are not immune from this. Violence manifests itself with alarming frequency in many Christian homes. Therefore, if the church is serious about disarming its members, it must take decisive action to address violence at home.

In this chapter, we take a closer look at domestic violence and what the church can do about it. Although domestic violence takes many forms, our particular focus will be on the abuse many women experience at the hands of their husbands. This should not obscure the troubling fact that men and boys are sometimes victims of violence at home as well. Likewise, while our focus is on domestic violence in *traditional* marriages, same-sex couples sometimes also experience violence at the hands of their partners. This too should be of great concern to the church, regardless of its position on same-sex marriage. Finally, our choice to focus special attention on spousal abuse is not meant to imply that other forms of domestic violence such as child abuse, elder abuse, or various types of sexual abuse, are somehow less important or insignificant. It is all bad. If the church is to be fully disarmed, it cannot overlook any form of violence a Christian might perpetrate against a member of his (or her) own family.[3]

Domestic Violence

Domestic violence, or intimate partner violence (IPV), is an epidemic that affects people from all walks of life regardless of race, gender, religion, nationality, or socioeconomic status. The National Coalition against Domestic Violence defines domestic violence as "the willful intimidation, physical assault, battery, sexual assault, and/or other abusive behavior as part of a systematic pattern of power and control perpetrated by one intimate partner against another. It includes physical violence, sexual violence, psychological violence, and emotional abuse."[4] Although domestic violence typically happens over a period of time, it can also express itself in a single violent

---

3. For an excellent resource for churches related to preventing child abuse, see Harder, *Let the Children Come*.

4. National Coalition against Domestic Violence, "What Is Domestic Violence?" Cf. Miles, who defines domestic violence as "a pattern of abusive behavior in which a person uses coercion, deception, harassment, humiliation, manipulation, and/or force in order to establish and maintain power and control over that person's intimate partner or former intimate partner" (*Violence in Families*, 27).

episode. And while domestic violence does not *only* take place at home, 60 percent of incidents occur there.[5]

A few statistics will suffice to demonstrate the prevalence of domestic violence in our society. Each year, over 12 million men and women "are victims of rape, physical violence, or stalking by an intimate partner in the United States."[6] This means that each minute of every day an average of twenty-four people are victimized.[7] To look at it another way, "more than 1 in 3 women (35.6%) and more than 1 in 4 men (28.5%) in the United States have experienced rape, physical violence, and/or stalking by an intimate partner in their lifetime."[8] Another way to assess the scope of the problem is to consider how frequently calls are made to domestic violence hotlines. A survey conducted in 2013 revealed that over 20,000 calls were made to these hotlines in a single day.[9] While this number is sobering, it only represents a small fraction of the total number of people suffering at the hands of an abuser on any given day. Clearly, we have a serious problem on our hands.

Though many in the church might be hesitant to admit it, this type of violence and abuse is all too common among Christians.[10] As Rev. Al Miles observes, "Many Christians deny the sad reality that some men and boys who 'praise Jesus' on Sunday mornings abuse their wives and girlfriends the rest of the week."[11] Truth be told, domestic violence is just as problematic among churchgoers as it is among people in the general population.[12]

Three Stories of Domestic Violence

In keeping with the focus of this book, my interest here is to address the problem of domestic violence as it relates to Christians and the church. I am especially troubled by the way some Christians use the Bible and their religious beliefs to justify battering and abuse. I am equally disturbed by the church's inattention to this problem, even though most congregations

---

5. domesticshelters.org, "Domestic Violence Statistics." Intimate partner violence also occurs in various other settings like college campuses, the workplace, dating relationships, and so forth.

6. Centers for Disease Control and Prevention, "Understanding Intimate Partner Violence."

7. Ibid.

8. Black et al., *National Intimate Partner and Sexual Violence Survey*, 2.

9. National Coalition against Domestic Violence, "Statistics."

10. See Alsdurf and Alsdurf, *Battered into Submission*.

11. Miles, *Violence in Families*, 24.

12. See chapter 2 for further discussion.

likely have both abusers and survivors sitting in the pews. And I am appalled when I read stories about clergy and other church leaders who blame survivors of domestic violence for the abuse they experienced, suggesting it was somehow their fault.

To set the stage, it is beneficial to hear stories from victims of domestic violence, especially from those who have experienced abuse at the hands of a *Christian* spouse. Real life examples like these personalize the issue and help us put a face on it. They also demonstrate some of the unique dynamics of domestic violence when it occurs in a "Christian" context.

The following three stories illustrate various ways abusers use religious beliefs to exercise power and control over their partners. They also reveal how spectacularly *un*helpful the church has often been when confronted by abuse within its ranks.

Since most victims of domestic violence are women,[13] I have chosen to include stories that describe the kind of abuse some women experience at the hands of their "Christian" husbands. These stories are taken from Al Miles's excellent book, *Violence in Families: What Every Christian Needs to Know*. All three stories are true, though Miles notes that some names and other information have been changed to protect the women involved.[14]

Arlene's Story

Arlene was married to Robert, an ordained deacon, for thirteen years. He would often make demands of her and throw a fit if she did not immediately comply. Robert would "call her vile names and would also accuse her of not being a 'loving Christian wife' because she wasn't willing to 'please' him."[15] These tactics were very effective. Arlene would often acquiesce to her husband's demands and give him what he wanted. But sometimes she would refuse. When that happened, Robert would react violently.

> Arlene says that, initially, her husband focused his physical outbursts on objects. "He'd punch walls, kick doors, and occasionally break a few dishes." But, over time, Robert started battering Arlene as well. "My husband broke many of the bones in my body, gave me several concussions and punctured eardrums, and he left more black and blue marks on me than I care to remember," Arlene says. "This self-proclaimed 'man of God'

13. According to Catalano, "From 1994 to 2010, about 4 in 5 victims of intimate partner violence were female" ("Intimate Partner Violence," 1).

14. Miles, *Violence in Families*, 30.

15. Ibid., 37.

never once took responsibility for the violence he perpetrated. Instead, he'd tell me I was to blame for the abuse. 'If you'd only submit to my will,' he'd shout, 'then I wouldn't have to discipline you.' What real man of God would actually discipline his wife or treat her in such cruel ways?" Depressed and demoralized, Arlene finally turned to her priest for help. But the priest's response made matters worse.

"Father Michael had always been loving to both my husband and me," Arlene says. "However, when I told him about all the degrading ways Robert had treated me over the years, the first phrase out of the priest's mouth was, 'You must be mistaken.' He then proceeded to tell me that no Christian man, especially one with Robert's moral character, would ever treat his wife in the terrible ways I described. So, in my minister's eyes, I guess I was a liar."[16]

Helen's Story

Helen and William were university professors who had been married for eighteen years. They were committed Christians, active in the church for over a quarter century.

"My husband first revealed a side of himself I'd not previously seen a week into our marriage," says Helen. "During our wedding night he told me that he 'requires' sex every night. I thought he was joking, but soon discovered he was dead serious."

The first time Helen declined her husband's lovemaking demand, a week into their marriage, he unraveled. Abruptly getting up out of their bed, William stormed out of the room and went downstairs to the kitchen. "I thought he was making himself a cup of tea because I heard water running into the kettle," Helen recalls.

William returned to the bedroom five minutes later, lifted the blanket off of his wife, who was starting to fall asleep, and poured scalding water all over her body. "I was so shocked and frightened by what he did that I didn't even feel the pain of my second-degree burns until later," Helen says. "As I lay in bed crying uncontrollably over what this man, my husband, had done to me, William put his face very close to mine and said in an angry but even tone, 'Never, ever refuse to have sex with me again.

16. Ibid., 38.

I am your master, you are my servant just as the Bible says. I'll be damned if I let my wife tell me what she will and will not do.'"

The abuse . . . against his wife became even more imprisoning and tortuous after their two children were born. Always accusing Helen of having an extramarital affair with any male—a checkout boy at the grocery store, service station attendants, and most of her male students—William misjudged his wife's maternal love for their children as a "further sign of marital infidelity." He told Helen that the Bible commanded him to "punish" her for being unfaithful. "William not only increased his physical and sexual abuse," Helen says, "but he also made me give away my beloved cat and birds. He then ordered me to cut off all outside relationships, even with my two sisters, and forced me to make up some lie about how I thought they'd stolen something from our home one Christmas. He also stripped me of all financial independence." . . .

While Helen lives in a perpetual hell on earth, William flourishes. Last year he was honored in his town as both professor and community person of the year.

Even though William has constantly told his wife (and children) she would suffer the consequences should she ever leave him or tell anyone about his abuse, Helen says she's thought a lot lately about exposing her husband as "the fraud he's always been." But, the battered wife quickly adds, "William is loved by everyone at the university, in the community, and at church. Our pastors and the entire congregation view him as the perfect husband, father, and man of God. Who would even want to believe that he's an evil monster at home?"[17]

Lani's story

Lani was married to a Christian man named Mark for nine years. Throughout their marriage, she repeatedly experienced verbal, emotional, and psychological abuse from her "godly" husband.

"My husband constantly called me inappropriate names: 'dumb,' 'stupid,' and 'slut,'" Lani says. When we'd have members of the congregation over to our home for dinner, he'd often say and do cruel things to me. For example, one day I tried to bring lunch to Mark at his job site. But, having a terrible sense of direction, I got lost and never located him. That evening Mark read me

17. Ibid., 55–56.

the riot act, calling me all sorts of terrible names in front of his family and our neighbors, all of them people from our church. At some point he threw a whole bunch of stuff in my arms and yelled, 'Now, woman, go to the kitchen and cook dinner!' He thought this was funny but I felt totally humiliated."

Seeking distance from her husband after suffering for years under his emotional and psychological battering, Lani made plans to divorce Mark. But she found herself rebuked by both her family and members of her church. They all told Lani she needed to forgive her husband and then everything would be okay. "There was a major double standard going on in my church," Lani says. "Mark would call me all these terrible names—and many people from our church witnessed this inappropriate behavior firsthand—but no one ever turned their back on him. Although my husband never hit me, his verbal and emotional abuse was certainly contrary to the teachings of the Bible. But the congregation did nothing to address Mark's behavior. Instead, the church kept reminding me about the sinful nature of divorce and the importance of my being a forgiving Christian wife."[18]

How Should the Church Address the Problem of Domestic Violence in Its Midst?

Tragically, stories like these are all too common. Abusers use faith as a weapon to manipulate and control their intimate partners. And, as we will see, the church sometimes enables this kind of abuse—albeit unintentionally—by the way it handles certain biblical passages and by the way it talks about things like marriage and divorce. Yet, domestic violence is clearly at odds with the life and teachings of Jesus and the nature of Christian discipleship. So what can the church do to address this problem?

In the pages to follow, we will offer a number of suggestions designed to help pastors and church leaders confront domestic violence from various angles. While some focus more on prevention, finding ways to reduce the likelihood that church members will engage in acts of domestic violence, others focus on response, helping clergy know what to do when they become aware of situations of violence and abuse.

18. Ibid., 75.

Educate Churchgoers about Domestic Violence
in Order to Raise Awareness

An important first step pastors, youth ministers, Sunday school teachers, and other caregivers can take is to educate people in their congregation about domestic violence.[19] Churchgoers need to know basic facts about domestic violence and about how it manifests itself in intimate relationships. For example, church leaders can help congregants recognize some of the key indicators of abuse. These include things such as "put-downs, name-calling, threatening gestures, driving dangerously, throwing things, yelling, screaming, swearing, verbal threats, damaging property or pets, [the] 'silent treatment,' jealousy, preventing friendships, controlling activities and money, unwanted physical or sexual contact, pushing, spitting, grabbing, choking, [and] public or private humiliation."[20] Pastors could also tell stories about abusive situations, like the ones we just heard, making it clear that this kind of abuse is contrary to the way of Jesus. Obviously, maintaining anonymity is paramount here. No real names or identifying information should be used unless you are discussing a case of public record that is well known and puts no one at risk. This will give people a more concrete picture of what domestic violence looks like in particular situations. It will also raise awareness and help people understand what kind of behavior constitutes domestic violence. The importance of educating the congregation in this way cannot be emphasized enough. People who are unable to recognize domestic violence when they see it, or experience it, will be unable to respond very effectively to it. But once people know what it looks like, they are in a much better position of helping those in need—or seeking help themselves.

Part of raising awareness also involves helping churchgoers know what to do if they themselves are in an abusive relationship or if they suspect someone they know is being abused. People need to know where to turn for help and how to help others.[21] Churches can make this kind of information available in a variety of ways: displaying it on bulletin boards, placing pamphlets in the lobby, posting domestic violence hotline phone numbers and

19. Clergy who themselves are ignorant about these matters should make it a priority to become more informed by reading books on the topic, exploring web-based resources, and attending domestic violence training workshops. An excellent place to begin is with a free online resource designed for church leaders titled "Abuse: Response and Prevention." This booklet addresses domestic violence as well as other forms of abuse. It can be downloaded at https://mcc.org/media/resources/1134.

20. This list is taken from a brochure produced by Mennonite Central Committee titled "Home Shouldn't Be a Place that Hurts."

21. For very practical guidelines, see Weiss, *Family and Friends' Guide*, especially 61–103.

internet addresses in women's restrooms and Sunday school classrooms, mentioning available resources in the bulletin, and so forth.

Denounce Domestic Violence Openly

In addition to raising awareness, the church should be unmistakably clear about how it views domestic violence. It is important to emphasize that domestic violence is abuse, and that abuse is always wrong regardless of who does it or why it is done. "No one deserves to be abused, and no one has the right to abuse another."[22] *No one!* By openly declaring its opposition to domestic violence, the church sends a powerful message to abusers and would-be abusers. It puts them on notice, alerting them to the fact that their behavior is wrong and unacceptable. It will not be condoned or protected.

The church's position on domestic violence can be communicated through doctrinal statements and sermons on the topic,[23] as well as through liturgy and prayer, Christian education programs, special events, and various other means. As Kroeger and Nason-Clark remind us, *"the home is no place for abuse"* and *"the church is no place for silence."*[24] It is crucial for the church to speak clearly on this issue. Parishioners should have no doubt about where it stands.

Speak Responsibly about Forgiveness, Marriage, and Divorce

The church must also be very careful about how it discusses topics that might cause victims of domestic violence to believe their Christian faith requires them to remain in abusive relationships. Forgiveness is one of these topics. If the church is not careful, it can easily send the wrong message. Women in the congregation who are being abused may interpret "you need to forgive" as "you need to continue to let your husband abuse you and remain silent about it." Since they believe telling others about the abuse would be a clear sign they have not forgiven their husband, they often say nothing and allow the abuse to continue. After all, aren't we supposed to forgive seventy times seven?

This is precisely the message Lani was getting from members of her church. They kept telling her that divorce was sinful and forgiveness was

22. Miles, *Domestic Violence*, 1.

23. For an excellent resource on how to preach about domestic violence *and* sexual violence, see McClure and Ramsay, eds., *Telling the Truth*. This volume provides ministers with biblical and theological reflections on the topic along with many practical preaching tips and sample sermons.

24. Kroeger, Clark, and Nason-Clark, *No Place for Abuse*, 20, emphasis original.

necessary. From their perspective, Lani's only option was to stay in the marriage, endure the abuse, and forgive her husband—repeatedly. That is a distorted and perverted understanding of forgiveness. Forgiveness does *not* mean remaining in an abusive relationship. Nor does forgiveness mean ignoring that a wrong has been done. While it is true that forgiving others means deciding not to harm them, we are under no obligation to protect wrongdoers from the consequences of their actions. We need not—and, in fact, *should* not—remain silent if we experience domestic violence. Rather, we should talk to a trusted friend, pastor, family member, or co-worker and should get the help and support we need. The church is helpful to victims of violence when it is clear about what forgiveness does and does not entail.

The church also needs to take care in how it speaks about marriage and divorce. Sermons and homilies that extol the virtues of married life, while denouncing separation and divorce, send subtle but powerful messages to both victims and perpetrators of domestic violence. Victims feel trapped, and perpetrators feel emboldened. While marriage is sacred, and should be preserved whenever possible, not every marriage can be saved. Even though God's ideal is for couples to stay married for life, there are times when getting a divorce is the right thing to do.[25] Through its teaching and preaching, the church should never give the impression that Christian wives—*especially* those who are victims of domestic violence—must "save the marriage at all costs." Nor should the church make blanket condemnations of divorce. When it does these things, battered women in the church feel their only acceptable option is to remain with their abusers.

Provide Alternate Interpretations of Biblical Passages Used to Support Abuse

Many "Christian" men who abuse often misuse Scripture to control their wives and to justify their behavior. They appeal to verses like 1 Cor 7:4, which says a husband has "authority over" his wife's body,[26] or Eph 5:22, which instructs wives to "be subject to your husbands." "Christian" men have committed all kinds of physical and sexual abuse using verses like these.

---

25. Christians have different opinions about whether it is permissible to divorce and, if so, under what conditions. Diversity of opinion also surrounds the question of getting remarried after being divorced. For an overview of various perspectives, see House, ed., *Divorce and Remarriage*, and Wenham et al., *Remarriage After Divorce*.

26. I'm quite certain abusers never mention the rest of the verse: "likewise, the husband does not have authority over his own body, but the wife does."

Ephesians 5 has been particularly troublesome in this regard. In addition to instructing wives to submit to their husbands, it refers to the husband as "the head of the wife" (Eph 5:23). Misguided interpretations of this passage have been enormously harmful to women. As Frances Gench observes:

> Ephesians 5, perhaps more than any other text in the Bible, has proved to be hazardous to women's health. . . . This text in particular has been widely interpreted in ways that have made many Christian women more susceptible to violence, and it has heightened the likelihood that battered women will remain in abusive relationships longer than they should. In addition, the text has wreaked cross-cultural havoc, for Christian women around the globe attest how often it has been used to reinforce existing patterns of subjection and domination.[27]

Obviously, texts like these must be handled with *extreme* caution. The church should not ignore these texts, since that provides people with no guidance about how to interpret them, but should preach and teach from them responsibly. Ministers can address the way these texts are often misinterpreted, and they can offer alternate ways of understanding these problem passages that are more accurate and leave no room for violence.[28]

In the case of Ephesians 5, one might emphasize that the passage speaking about wives submitting to husbands actually begins at verse 21 which reads, "Be subject to one another out of reverence for Christ." Although the verses that follow focus on the wife submitting to the husband, the context here is one of *mutual* submission. Wives are to submit to husbands, *and husbands are to submit to wives.* As Gench comments, this verse "is a stunning ideal, an audacious claim, for the whole community of faith, but one that is not applied to its full potential."[29] One could also point out that the command for the husband to love his wife, "just as Christ loved the church and gave himself up for her" (v. 25), emphasizes the need for the husband to embody qualities like humility and self-sacrifice, not domination and control—and certainly not violence.

Another set of passages that require special attention are those we often regard as "peace passages." Ironically, verses that promote peace and nonviolence are sometimes the very ones used to justify abuse. Take for example Jesus' well-known teaching about turning the other cheek:

---

27. Gench, *Encountering God*, 31

28. For some helpful guidance in this regard, see ibid., 19–36, especially 32–35.

29. Ibid., 32.

But if anyone strikes you on the right cheek, turn the other also (Matt 5:39).

As previously discussed, this verse emphasizes active nonviolent resistance. Jesus is instructing his followers to respond to violence in a way that maintains their dignity and makes it difficult for their oppressors to continue mistreating them. Jesus is *not* commanding them to submit themselves to more abuse. Yet, this is exactly how this verse is sometimes interpreted. To illustrate, consider the following story told by Cyndi Anderson, Director of Lakes Crises Center in Minnesota:

> A Christian woman came into our office with one side of her face very bruised. The victim's husband had broken her jaw. The abused woman said she was shocked over what her husband had done, but was even more stunned by the response of her male pastor. The minister first told his battered parishioner that she needed to be a better wife. As awful as this response was, the woman said she could tolerate it—until the pastor told her that the Bible "required" her to "turn the other cheek." It was simply awful advice to give to anyone—especially to a woman whose husband had just broken her jaw.[30]

This is certainly *not* what Jesus meant by turning the other cheek. It is not an invitation for abuse. On the contrary, as discussed earlier, this command can be understood as a summons to *resist* further abuse by asserting your dignity.[31] Those who preach and teach have a responsibility to alert people to the way texts like these have been misused. Then, after exposing misguided interpretations, ministers and lay leaders can help congregants read verses like these more responsibly, in ways that do not put women, children, and others at risk of violence.

Confront the Problem of Patriarchy

In their recent book on domestic violence, Justin and Lindsey Holcomb claim that "most incidents of domestic abuse can be traced back to a single, toxic assumption: that women are inherently inferior to men."[32] In a nutshell, that is the problem of patriarchy. Patriarchy can be defined as "a social system and . . . an ideology in which women [and children] are subordinated

---

30. Miles, *Violence in Families*, 144.

31. See chapter 5.

32. Holcomb and Holcomb, *Is It My Fault?*, 93.

to men."[33] The problem with patriarchy is that it is inherently violent. As Carolyn Heggen puts it, "The inherent logic of patriarchy says that if men have the right to power and control over women and children, they also have the right to enforce that control. It is this *control-over* component of patriarchy which makes it vulnerable to violence and abuse."[34] Since patriarchy creates a climate in which violence against women (and children)[35] is seen as justifiable, it puts these individuals at much greater risk.[36]

Given this danger, the church should be intentional about challenging patriarchy at every turn. Unfortunately, it often does just the opposite. Rather than critiquing patriarchy, many church traditions routinely reinforce it. This happens, for example, when church leaders prevent women from serving in certain roles in the church—usher, deacon, pastor—solely because of their gender. It also happens when the church expects women to conform to gender stereotypes, particularly when it suggests that a woman's *primary* role is in the home where she is expected to submit to her husband and his authority. Whenever the church behaves in these ways, it devalues women and promotes patriarchy.

To combat this, the church should encourage egalitarian relationships between men and women and should make a special effort to treat women in ways that recognize their full humanity and equality with men. Churches could highlight the extraordinary way Jesus treated women (and children) when he ministered.[37] Jesus did not disparage women or treat them as second-class citizens even though that is how they were viewed in first century Palestine. For example, Jesus engages a Samaritan woman in a lengthy theological conversation (John 4:6–30), demonstrates compassion toward a woman caught in adultery (John 8:1–11), and declares that a woman known to be a sinner showed him greater love than his very respectable male host (Luke 7:36–50). Women traveled freely with Jesus while he was preaching and teaching, and they contributed financially to the needs of Jesus and his disciples (Luke 8:1–3). Perhaps most strikingly, Jesus chose women to be first witnesses to his resurrection (Matt 28:1–10). In these and other ways,

33. Exum, "Feminist Criticism," 66.

34. Heggen, *Sexual Abuse*, 85, emphasis original.

35. Rather than seeing children as a nuisance, Jesus welcomed them, blessed them, and said it is necessary to become like them in order to enter the kingdom of heaven (Matt 18:1–5; 19:13–15).

36. According to Heggen, "As long as a patriarchy is supported and male dominance is considered the appropriate model for human relationships, sexual abuse of children will continue" (*Sexual Abuse*, 87).

37. For more on this, see Witherington, *Women in the Ministry of Jesus*.

Jesus treated women with unusual respect given his historical context. As Alvin Schmidt observes:

> The extremely low status that the Greek, Roman, and Jewish woman had for centuries was radically affected by the appearance of Jesus Christ. His actions and teachings raised the status of women to new heights, often to the consternation and dismay of his friends and enemies. By word and deed, he went against the ancient, taken-for-granted beliefs and practices that defined woman as socially, intellectually, and spiritually inferior.[38]

We should follow Jesus' lead. As Christians, we have an ethical obligation to ensure that women are treated with the same dignity and respect as men, and that they have access to the same opportunities for education, employment, and self-determination as men.

The church should also do everything in its power to encourage women who feel called to ministry to pursue that calling. Women should have the blessing and support of church leaders to serve God in whatever way the Spirit leads them.[39] Elevating the status of women in this way is one of the best avenues the church has of confronting the problem of patriarchy. When the church clearly and consistently communicates a strong message of equality, stressing that women and men are of the same value, domestic violence is less likely to manifest itself.

Believe the Stories Told by Battered Women (and Others)

The single most important thing a pastor or caregiver can do when someone reveals they have been abused is to believe them. One of the reasons many women stay in abusive relationships so long is because they are afraid nobody will believe the hell they have been experiencing at home, especially if the perpetrator is highly respected by others. As Helen expressed it in the story above, "William is loved by everyone at the university, in the community, and at church. Our pastors and the entire congregation view him as the

---

38. Schmidt, *How Christianity Changed the World*, 102–3. Partially quoted in Holcomb and Holcomb, *Is It My Fault?*, 104.

39. Many Christians believe—mistakenly, in my opinion—that women *cannot* exercise spiritual authority over men and should therefore be restricted from certain leadership roles in the church. For two perspectives on this question, the restrictive view (complementarian) and the one advocated here (egalitarian), see Beck, ed., *Two Views on Women in Ministry*.

perfect husband, father, and man of God. Who would even want to believe that he's an evil monster at home?"[40]

Since victims of domestic violence often turn first to a trusted pastor or priest when seeking help, it is absolutely essential to respond appropriately. If a minister bungles this initial encounter, either by refusing to believe the victim or by telling the victim the abuse is her fault, as we observed in the story of the woman with the broken jaw whose pastor suggested "she needed to be a better wife," the consequences can be devastating. As Al Miles puts it, "How we respond and do not respond to these situations could increase the potential for freedom and safety for a victim-survivor—or cause that person greater suffering and even death."[41] There is a lot at stake! In addition to believing the victim, ministers should emphasize that the church's top priority is her safety (and the safety of her children if she has any), and should offer to help the victim take whatever steps are necessary to ensure she is no longer in danger.

When pastors or other caregivers begin working with someone who has been abused, they should never try to help that individual all by themselves. Rather, they should reach out to other agencies and organizations that can come alongside and offer additional assistance. As Miles observes, "To be most effective, we need to partner with and make referrals to community service providers: advocates, batterers' intervention specialists, child protective services providers, crises intervention counselors, law enforcement officers, legal professionals, shelter workers, and victim and witness assistance personnel, to name just a few."[42] Involving a number of different people who can offer a wide range of specialized services greatly increases the likelihood that the person who has experienced abuse will get the help they need and will stay safe in the process.

Hold Abusers Accountable

Just as victims of domestic violence should never be blamed for the abuse they have experienced, victimizers should never be protected from the consequences of their abusive actions. Instead, the church needs to hold perpetrators accountable. If perpetrators feel "protected" by the clergy and have no fear of being punished, they will have little incentive to change their ways. Therefore, the church needs to be very careful to avoid doing or saying

40. Miles, *Violence in Families*, 55–56.

41. Miles, *Domestic Violence*, 77.

42. Ibid., 44.

things that might give them the impression that their violent behavior will be excused or overlooked.

One of the main reasons abusers engage in patterns of violence over an extended period of time is because they do not believe they will ever get in trouble for their behavior. They frequently abuse in secret and are very skilled at coercing their victims to remain silent. Abusive husbands manipulate their wives to keep quiet by threatening to harm their pets, to destroy their prized possessions, to withhold food and other basic necessities, and even to kill them or their children if they ever tell a soul. These threats make it very difficult for abused women to break free and get the help they need, and they give perpetrators a sense of confidence that they can continue abusing without fear of being exposed.

When abusers are confronted, they often place the blame for their behavior elsewhere. "They blame alcohol, drugs, children, job stresses, mood swings, Satan, and, most often, the women they violate."[43] If the church is going to help them stop the abuse, it needs to hold the line here and ensure these individuals take full responsibility for their actions. The person who abuses, and that person alone, is responsible for the abuse.

Just as pastors and others in the church should not "go it alone" when helping someone who has been abused, neither should they "go it alone" when working with an abuser. Instead, they should enlist the help of trained professionals, such as psychologists and social workers, and should partner with other agencies to be sure things are handled appropriately.[44] Perpetrators of domestic violence can be directed to treatment programs specifically tailored to work with them, and the church can support them in getting this kind of treatment.

When working with abusers, the church should make it clear that there is no quick fix. Working through these issues takes time, *lots* of time. Abusers are masters of the art of deception, and church leaders should not by duped by those who claim to have "turned their life around" even if they outwardly exhibit signs of transformation (e.g., leading Bible studies, talking about how much God has changed them, etc.). The only way to know whether they have really changed, is to observe them very closely over an extended period of time, one not measured in months. The church must proceed very cautiously here and must assiduously avoid offering any kind

43. Ibid., 105–6.

44. If children are victims of abuse, many states have mandated reporting laws. In such cases, ministers have a legal obligation to report abuse to the appropriate authorities. In Pennsylvania, for example, this can be reported through the Pennsylvania Family Support Alliance which maintains a website and a 24/7 toll-free number for reporting (800-932-0313).

of "easy" forgiveness and reconciliation. Instead, pastors should partner with local organizations and other agencies to ensure these individuals get the help they need, and they should develop clear structures of accountability to ensure that genuine change has really happened.[45]

But What Can I Do?

This chapter has been written largely with church leaders in mind, and we have been talking about various ways pastors, teachers, and caregivers in the church can address the problem of domestic violence. Before bringing this discussion to a close, it might be helpful to say a few words about how other Christians—those who are not professional ministers and do not have designated caregiving roles within the church—can respond effectively to this form of abuse. What can regular church folks do?

One of the most important things to do is simply become more informed. If this chapter has awakened you to the ugly reality of domestic violence and has prompted you to do something about it, perhaps the best place to begin is to learn more about domestic violence: why it happens, who is affected by it, how to respond to those who experience it, where to find additional resources dealing with it, and so forth. I would strongly recommend taking time to read a good book on the topic, such as Elaine Weiss's excellent work *Family and Friend' Guide to Domestic Violence: How to Listen, Talk, and Take Action When Someone You Care about Is Being Abused*. Or, if you want something from a distinctly Christian perspective, you will not go wrong with either Al Miles's *Violence in Families: What Every Christian Needs to Know* or Catherine Clark Kroeger and Nancy Nason-Clark's *No Place for Abuse: Biblical and Practical Resources to Counteract Domestic Violence*. All these books are very readable and provide lots of helpful information and practical ideas. They also point you to other organizations and online resources devoted to these issues.[46]

Second, part of what it means to become more informed involves being able to recognize the warning signs of domestic violence. It is difficult to help people if we are unaware they are suffering. Elaine Weiss identifies and describes "five warning signs of domestic abuse" of women: 1) her social

---

45. For additional suggestions for holding abusers accountable, see Miles, *Domestic Violence*, 140–41.

46. For numerous online resources, see the National Resource Center on Domestic Violence (http://www.nrcdv.org/) and the National Coalition against Domestic Violence (http://www.ncadv.org/). See also http://www.cdc.gov/violenceprevention/pdf/ipv-factsheet.pdf; http://www.cdc.gov/violenceprevention/pdf/nisvs_report2010-a.pdf; http://www.thehotline.org/resources/statistics/.

264   DISARMING THE CHURCH isarmi ng the church

relationships have narrowed, 2) he makes all the rules, 3) he puts her down, 4) she is afraid, and 5) she has been injured.[47] As the stories earlier in this chapter illustrated, abusers are very controlling. They will try to restrict who their victims can and cannot see and will often have an elaborate set of rules about what the victim can and cannot do. If you see this happening, it is reasonable to suspect an abusive relationship. Also, if someone experiences injuries that are difficult to explain, this too could be evidence of abuse. "Your normally graceful relative or friend has suddenly become 'accident-prone.' She has bruises or injuries that do not match her explanations. She has taken to wearing shirts with long sleeves and high collars."[48] Weiss regards these as warning signs. Being able to recognize these signs enables us to identify and come alongside people who are suffering from domestic violence.

It is important to bear in mind that anyone can be a victim. Victims of domestic abuse do not fit into any one stereotype. As Elaine Weiss reminds us, "She may be a librarian with a daughter in college and a son who teaches high school physics. She may be your running partner or the woman next door. She may be your sorority sister. She may be your mother. . . . A woman's financial status, ethnicity, educational level, and religion do not immunize her against the possibility of being abused."[49] Anyone can be a victim—*anyone*.

Third, to reiterate a point discussed earlier, if someone confides in you and shares her story with you (or more likely, *part* of her story), the most important thing you can do in that moment is to believe her and empathize with her. You want to avoid being critical of her abuser even if she is. She may be planning to stay in this relationship, and you may jeopardize your friendship with her if you speak negatively about her spouse. You also want to avoid asking her questions about why she put up with this abuse for so long. Doing so places blame on her which is the last thing she needs in that very vulnerable moment. Your job is to listen, believe, and promise to journey with her and alongside her as she moves forward.

Fourth, you can support the work your church is doing to confront the issue of domestic violence. Perhaps there is a particular committee or group within the church that gives sustained attention to issues of violence, particularly domestic violence. If so, you might consider joining with them. On the other hand, you might discover that your church is doing nothing to address this issue directly. If that is the case, set up a meeting with the pastor and/or other staff members to discuss your concerns and to determine if

47. Weiss, *Family and Friends' Guide*, 3.
48. Ibid., 3.
49. Ibid., 4.

they would be willing to begin thinking intentionally about ways the church could address the issue of domestic violence.

Fifth, you could link up with local organizations addressing this issue to see what kinds of volunteer opportunities they might have and to find out how else you could get involved. Additionally, you could connect with the broader online community that is actively engaged in issues of family violence and abuse. There are lots of ways to get involved, and there are many groups to partner with in this important work.

Conclusion

As followers of Jesus, we are called to live nonviolently in all of our relationships. This includes the way we treat our spouse, our children, and all those who live under our roof. The stories told at the beginning of the chapter make it clear that Christians have significant work to do in this regard. Tragically, some of the worst acts of violence take place within Christian homes.

The good news is that there are many ways the church can address family violence and encourage Christians to live more faithfully with one another as they strive to follow Jesus. Hopefully, the suggestions offered in this chapter will be helpful to the church as it seeks to confront domestic violence and to encourage its members to live in loving, violence-free relationships with one another, especially with members of their own family.

17

Practical Suggestions for the Church

Helping Christians Live Less Violently and More Faithfully

The church's own witness should be understandable by the smallest child: we oppose violence in all its forms.

—WALTER WINK[1]

WHEN PEOPLE LOOK AT the church, I want them to see a community that rejects violence and is committed to peace, justice, and reconciliation. Christians should be part of the solution to what ails the world, not part of the problem. In order for that to happen, the church needs to prepare its members to follow the nonviolent way of Jesus.[2] Thankfully, there are many practical things the church can do in this regard. Some are quite simple and take little time and effort. Others are much more involved and require significant planning and intentionality. We will explore several of these in the pages that follow.

Since the focus of this chapter is on what the church *as an institution* can do to help Christians live nonviolently, it is specifically addressed to church leaders—pastors, priests, Sunday school teachers, church administrators,

1. Wink, *Engaging the Powers*, 229.

2. Portions of what follows here are adapted from Seibert, "Pacifism and Nonviolence."

lay leaders, and ministers of all stripes. These individuals are uniquely positioned to prioritize nonviolent discipleship and to implement policies and programming that contribute to this essential part of the church's mission.

How the Church Can Promote Living Nonviolently: Some Practical Suggestions

What follows are numerous suggestions designed to help you, as church leaders, encourage and equip your congregants to live nonviolently. Some suggestions are aimed at persuading people to recognize the importance of living nonviolently in all walks of life; others provide practical tools for doing so. Depending upon the nature and constitution of your particular congregation, some parts of this chapter will undoubtedly be more useful than others. Still, I am hopeful the broad range of options offered here will expand your imagination and assist you in the important work of calling people to ever deeper levels of obedience to the nonviolent way of Jesus.

Emphasize that Following Jesus Faithfully Involves Living Nonviolently

One of the most important things the church can do in this regard is to send a clear and consistent message that following Jesus involves living nonviolently. Churchgoers need to be aware of the *nonviolent* nature of Christian discipleship. Church leaders can help them recognize that extending hospitality, offering forgiveness, working for reconciliation, and making peace are characteristic of nonviolent living and are, therefore, essential practices for followers of Jesus. Jesus himself embodied these practices as he rejected violence and embraced a life of service.

All this suggests nonviolence is not an "add-on" or "extra" some Christians can accept and others can ignore. Rather, it is an integral part of what it means to follow God faithfully. As Henri Nouwen so forcefully expresses it:

> Nobody can be a Christian without being a peacemaker. . . .
> What we are called to is a *life* of peacemaking in which all that
> we do, say, think, or dream is part of our concern to bring peace
> to this world. Just as Jesus' command to love one another cannot be seen as a part-time obligation, but requires our total
> dedication, so too Jesus' call to peacemaking is unconditional,
> unlimited, and uncompromising. None of us is excused! . . .
> Peacemaking is a full-time vocation that includes each member
> of God's people.[3]

3. Nouwen, *Road to Peace*, 6–7, emphasis original.

The church should prioritize this message so Christians understand that living nonviolently is essential to faithful Christian discipleship. When you commit to follow Jesus, you commit to live nonviolently.

Describe Nonviolence Holistically

The church can also help Christians live more faithfully by emphasizing that living nonviolently is a way of life. It impacts everything about us and influences how we make decisions, spend our money, exercise authority, deal with conflict, treat the environment, raise our children, relate to co-workers, interact with other religions, and so forth. No area of life is unaffected. Envisioning nonviolence holistically reminds us that a commitment to peace involves much more than a rejection of war. While that is a crucial part of it, living nonviolently cannot be reduced to this one issue alone.

The church has countless opportunities to demonstrate how following the nonviolent way of Jesus influences everything we think, say, and do. For example, the church could discuss how a commitment to nonviolence should inform our response to contemporary social issues like capital punishment, mass incarceration, and the epidemic of gun violence in the United States. The church could also discuss how living nonviolently impacts our behavior toward people who are often marginalized, misunderstood, and mistreated, such as undocumented workers or members of the LGBTQ community. In addition, ministers can raise important questions designed to help people think more holistically about nonviolence. How might a commitment to nonviolence affect our financial investments? For instance, should we invest in companies that manufacture weapons? Or, how does a commitment to nonviolence relate to the kind of entertainment we enjoy? Is it appropriate to watch violent sporting events like mixed-martial arts? Questions like these encourage us to think more broadly about what it means to live nonviolently. By helping people view nonviolence holistically, the church demonstrates how living nonviolently impacts all aspects of our lives and relationships.

Inform the Congregation of Your Church's Official Position on Peace and Nonviolence

Many churches have official statements describing their position on warfare, militarism, capital punishment, peacemaking, nonviolence, and related matters. These statements are often very helpful and provide natural ways to begin conversations around these important topics. For example, consider this paragraph from the Articles of Faith and Doctrine of the Brethren in Christ Church (my tradition):

> Christ loved His enemies and He calls us as His disciples to love our enemies. We follow our Lord in being people of peace and reconciliation, called to suffer and not to fight. While respecting those who hold other interpretations, we believe that preparation for or participation in war is inconsistent with the teachings of Christ. Similarly, we reject all other acts of violence which devalue human life. Rather, we affirm active peacemaking, sacrificial service to others, as well as the pursuit of justice for the poor and the oppressed in the name of Christ.[4]

Also, as noted earlier, one of the ten core values of the Brethren in Christ Church states: "We value all human life and promote forgiveness, understanding, reconciliation, and nonviolent resolution of conflict."[5] These two statements are succinct summaries of some of the church's key convictions. Ministers can use statements like these to talk about what nonviolent living entails. They can also use these statements to demonstrate that living nonviolently is consistent with the theological teachings and behavioral expectations of the church.

If you are unaware of your denomination's stance on issues of violence, war, and peacemaking, I would encourage you to do some investigating. If you find your church has no official statement on matters like these, consult other church leaders and consider drafting one. Or if you regard your church's stated position on these matters to be inadequate or problematic in certain respects, advocate for revisions that would bring the church's position in line with the life and teachings of Jesus.

Declare the Church's Opposition to Violence

It is helpful for the church to find ways to state clearly and unequivocally its opposition to all forms of violence. This could be verbalized in worship services and other contexts. People need to hear church leaders say: "The church opposes all forms of violence."[6] This rather simple declaration should be made with sufficient frequency that regular attenders will have

4. Under the heading "Mission of the Church: In Relation to the World" at http://www.bic-church.org/about/beliefs/holyspirit_church.asp.

5. All ten core values are discussed in Brensinger, ed., *Focusing Our Faith*.

6. See the epigraph for this chapter.

no doubt about the church's position. For this to happen, churches need to avoid sending mixed messages about the acceptability of violence. Instead, they need to declare that it is all bad. In the words of Miguel D'Escoto, "Violence is simply not Christian."[7]

In addition to making general declarations like these, the church should address various types of violence such as warfare, capital punishment, gun violence, elder abuse, physician-assisted suicide, rape, racism, domestic violence, workplace violence, sexual assault, discrimination, human trafficking—the list goes on. *Any* type of violent behavior—behavior that harms people physically or psychologically—is at odds with the church's cherished values and core commitments. The church needs to speak up and speak out against all forms of violence. This is especially important given the church's terribly violent history. This history has tarnished the church's witness and led to confusion about what the church believes about violence. The church has the opportunity to clear up this misunderstanding by clearly stating its opposition to all forms of violence even as it repents of past failings in this regard.

When the church declares its opposition to violence, it has a golden opportunity to explain its rationale for this position. Church leaders can make people aware of the biblical and theological reasons behind why the church rejects violence. They can also help churchgoers understand the negative ramifications of resorting to violence *even when* it is used with the best of intentions (e.g., to protect the innocent, for the sake of justice, etc.). Our previous discussion of these matters provides some resources that should be helpful in this regard.[8]

Train Christians How to Live Nonviolently by Providing Practical Alternatives to Violence

For most people, living nonviolently does not come naturally. It is something that must be learned. Therefore, if the church is really serious about helping people follow the nonviolent way of Jesus, those in leadership will need to invest time and energy training people to live this way. Sadly, this is precisely where the church frequently fails. Christians often know *what* they are supposed to do—love enemies, forgive offenders, make peace, reconcile relationships, resolve conflict—without knowing *how* they are to do it. This is precisely where the church can help by equipping people with the skills they need to live nonviolently.

7. Quoted in Wink, *Engaging the Powers*, 239.
8. See chapters 4, 5, and 7.

There are many ways to go about doing this. For example, the church can discuss nonviolent strategies that can be used to confront oppression and injustice.[9] The church can also teach basic conflict mediation skills, introduce congregants to nonviolent ways of parenting, and discuss creative ways to respond when they—or someone they love—are threatened with harm.[10] Sunday school classes and small groups are ideal settings for this since they allow time for role plays, short instructional videos, and *lots* of discussion.[11] A church might even decide to host a basic conflict mediation training event or a nonviolent training workshop in its facility. People need to have the opportunity to try things out (even if only in hypothetical scenarios), and they need to have the space to raise questions and objections. The church can provide this space and can equip Christians with the tools they need to live out their commitment to follow the nonviolent way of Jesus in all walks of life. Doing this is vitally important. Before many people are ready and willing to disarm, they need to have viable alternatives to violence.

Tell Stories of Christians (and Others) Who Model Nonviolent Living

In addition to providing practical training for living nonviolently, pastors and other church leaders can tell stories of Christians who exemplify this way of life. Earlier generations of believers in my own church tradition were inspired by the witness and testimony of E. J. Swalm, a Canadian bishop who refused military service and served time in jail for standing up for his beliefs.[12] This generation also needs to hear stories of people who, in big ways and small, engage in the practice of peacemaking and reconciliation. Telling these stories is one of the best ways to encourage others to join in.

The church can introduce people to nonviolent peacemakers past and present such as Daniel Berrigan, Bono, Shane Claiborne, Dorothy Day, John

9. For a twelve-week guide designed for groups that explores living nonviolently in everyday life *and* waging nonviolent struggle on a larger scale, see Slattery et al., *Engage*. This book includes readings, homework, instructions for the facilitator, and much more.

10. I am hopeful churches will find *Disarming the Church* helpful in this regard. Other books that address many important issues related to violence and nonviolence include Roth, *Choosing against War*, and Wink, *Powers that Be*.

11. The DVD *Thermostat* (with study guide), produced by Mennonite Central Committee (2005), is ideal for use with youth in church settings and is available in both English and Spanish (mcc.org). Also very useful is *Peace DVD* produced by MennoMedia (mennomedia.org).

12. Swalm, *Nonresistance Under Test*, 27–57. See also Swalm, ed., *"My Beloved Brethren . . . ,"* 23–33.

Dear, Leymah Gbowee, Hildegard Goss-Mayr, Martin Luther King Jr., Jim Wallis, and countless others. Pastors can highlight their heroic efforts and can recount the way these individuals have worked nonviolently for peace and justice around the world. Churchgoers will be inspired by their stories. They excite the imagination and remind us of how much good can be accomplished without violence. The church can also tell stories about the role Christians played in many successful nonviolent struggles of the twentieth and twenty-first centuries. From desegregating the American South to toppling the Filipino dictator Ferdinand Marcos, Christians were instrumental in using nonviolent means to bring about significant social and political change.

In addition, churches might consider providing opportunities for their own members to share publically how they are pursuing peace and living nonviolently in their daily lives. This could be part of a Sunday morning worship service or could be a special event held at the church. Having the opportunity to hear personal stories like these from people you know can be particularly powerful and persuasive.

For some individuals, a commitment to peace and nonviolence is something more "caught" than taught. Hearing stories that illustrate what nonviolence looks like in real life may be precisely what it takes to convince them that living nonviolently is not only possible, but desirable. Storytelling like this goes a long way toward beating swords into plowshares.

Encourage (and Model) Reconciliation within the Church

Another way the church can help its members learn to live nonviolently is by emphasizing the importance of forgiveness and reconciliation. Although one might assume that Christians who attend the same church get along well with each other, this is not always the case. Even when things *look* "peaceful" and "nice," all sorts of tensions are sometimes simmering just below the surface. Sometimes these are well hidden; sometimes they boil to the surface. Sometimes they are between two individuals; sometimes they involve most of the congregation.

In light of this, the church should encourage its members to work at being in right relationships with one another. There is something tragically ironic about a Christian who works for world peace but won't speak to the person sitting two rows ahead of him on Sunday morning because of some altercation that has poisoned their relationship. Those who wish to follow the nonviolent way of Jesus must eradicate hatred from their heart and let go of hostility in order to mend fences and make peace with others. Jesus emphasized the importance of this point in the Sermon on the Mount. He said, "So when you are offering your gift at the altar, if you remember that your brother or sister has something against you, leave your gift there before the altar and go; first be reconciled to your brother or sister, and then come and offer your gift" (Matt 5:23–24). Being reconciled with others is that important.

One way the church could prioritize relational reconciliation is by embedding it in the requirements for church membership. When people desire to become members of a church, they typically go through a period of training and instruction before being presented to the congregation as candidates for membership. When that day comes, the candidates are typically asked certain questions in the presence of the entire congregation before being received into membership. Those questions often have to do with their faith in Christ, their commitment to live godly lives, and their promise to serve the church and support its ministries. While these are all important questions, they do not deal directly with being in right relationships with others in the congregation. For a period of time, a minister in the church I attend asked new members two very simple, but extremely significant, questions: 1) Do you promise to go directly to a brother or a sister who has offended you?, and 2) Do you promise to graciously receive a brother or sister who you have offended who comes to you? These questions underscore the crucial importance of being in right relationship with others. They emphasize that confession, forgiveness, and reconciliation are things that should be happening all the time within the life of the church.

Another way church leaders could emphasize the importance of relational reconciliation is by offering to mediate conflicts that arise in the church. When my home church went through a period of significant and painful conflict a number of years ago, we facilitated numerous conversations between disaffected members of the congregation and both the pastor and church board chair in an effort to work at increasing understanding and restoring relationships. Churches should have some mechanism in place to help people address their grievances in safe and respectful ways. If the pastor is not equipped to do this, or is viewed as being partial to one party in the dispute, then arrangements could be made to use a local mediation center.

Churches could also develop rituals or hold events that provide natural opportunities for people to work at relational reconciliation. Some churches observe a love feast, a communal meal that culminates in celebrating communion. Historically, this was an important practice in my own church tradition. People from various churches would gather before the meal and would take time to examine their hearts to determine if they needed to be reconciled with anyone who was there. If they did, they would approach these individuals in an effort to make things right prior to the meal. Having an event like this as a regular part of the life of the church sends a powerful message about the importance of being in right relationships. It helps us live nonviolently and models the kinds of relationships we should strive to have with all people.

Design a Comprehensive Peace Education Program

To ensure good coverage of a broad range of topics related to peace and nonviolence, churches may wish to develop a comprehensive peace education program.[13] There are many ways to conceive of this, and the particulars would undoubtedly look different from church to church. Still, the goal would be to create a "master plan" that would identify various places in the life of the church where specific kinds of peace education would be sure to happen.

For example, churches might decide to introduce certain topics at particular age levels: children in elementary school could be taught about bullying and how to respond to it; middle schoolers could be taught basic skills in handling interpersonal conflict to help them deal with peer pressure; high schoolers could discuss healthy dating relationships and how to recognize signs of abusive behavior; and so forth. Developing a plan like this would ensure that key topics are systematically addressed at particular junctures over the lifespan of our children and youth.

Churches could use membership classes to discuss the basic biblical and theological foundations for peace and nonviolence and to introduce newcomers to the church's position on these topics. Class members could be encouraged to do some reading about these issues, including whatever official statements the church has produced. Even if perspective members do not fully align with the church's position, it is important for them to have a clear understanding of what the church believes about peacemaking, violence, and war before joining.

Another part of a comprehensive peace education program might involve setting aside one Sunday a year to give special focus to peacemaking and nonviolence. At the church I attend, we celebrate "Peace Sunday" each year. We typically focus on one aspect of peacemaking for this day (e.g., restorative justice, racism in the church), and we attempt to connect the

---

13. For an extensive collection of practical suggestions in this regard, including a chapter specifically addressing things that could be done for "children and youth," see Buttry, *Peace Ministry*.

many things that happen on Peace Sunday to this issue. We have a special speaker (or speakers) with expertise on the topic who facilitates an adult Sunday school class and preaches the morning sermon.

Churches could also decide to make various peace and justice resources available. For example, the church could purchase books and DVDs for the church library that focus on these issues. From time to time, church leaders could feature one of these books in the bulletin or church newsletter inviting members of the congregation to read it. The church could also periodically encourage small groups to read and discuss a book about Christian peacemaking or about a Christian peacemaker.

Obviously, there is no single blueprint for developing a comprehensive peace education program. There are many ways to do this, and churches will need to decide how to accomplish this most effectively in their unique context. Church leaders should assess what they are currently doing, determine where the gaps are, and consider ways to address peace education more systematically.

Churches may find it helpful to appoint a particular group, or committee, within the church to give special oversight to peace-related concerns. I serve on the Missions, Peace and Service Commission at the church I attend. Among other things, this group is responsible for raising awareness and facilitating programming related to peace. Committees, or commissions, like these can be very useful in helping the church give sustained attention to peace over the long haul. They take some of the burden off the pastor, and they connect like-minded individuals who are willing to invest time and energy to keep these important issues before the church.

Infuse Worship Services with Nonviolent Emphases

Regardless of whether or not a church develops a comprehensive peace education program, it is important for all churches to find ways to emphasize peace and nonviolence in their weekly worship services. This gathering is one of the most important moments in the life of the church since it represents the one time a week when the entire community comes together to worship God, receive instruction, and encourage one another. Careful planning should be done to ensure that various elements of the worship service reflect the church's commitment to peace and nonviolence. Songs, prayers, and liturgies all provide opportunities to emphasize this commitment in subtle—and not so subtle—ways.[14]

14. See Nelson-Pallmeyer and Hesla, *Worship in the Spirit of Jesus*, and Bender, *Just Prayer*.

One way to help congregants hear the message of peace in fresh, new ways is to take familiar hymns and rewrite the lyrics. This is precisely what Jane Parker Huber has done in her book *A Singing Faith*. She has ten hymns related to "Peacemaking and Justice" that can easily be used in worship services. The lyrics to "God, Teach us Peacemaking" set to a traditional Irish melody ("Be Thou My Vision") are especially useful.

God, teach us peacemaking, justice, and love.
Blessed by Christ's teaching, we're lifted above
All thought of vengeance or envy or hate.
Help us, your children, shalom to create.

God, teach us peacemaking in church and home,
In school and hall, beneath Capitol dome,
In shop and industry, city and farm:
Show us the pathways that cause no one harm.

God, teach us peacemaking in every role.
In each relationship make peace our goal.
Yet give us insight that keeps us aware
Justice and mercy in balance to share.

God, teach us peacemaking unto the end—
Parent or child, or as stranger or friend—
Fill all our hearts with the power of shalom,
Living together, the whole world our home.[15]

Prayers are also a powerful way to communicate our desire for peace within the world and the church's commitment to work for it. The book *Just Prayer: A Book of Hours for Peacemakers and Justice Seekers* has many wonderful prayers that could be used in public worship. Consider this example:

God of Mercy, your son Jesus Christ taught us the way of peace and compassion, which you ordained from the foundation of the world. Still, the daily conflicts and the unending wars in our world expose our failure to follow his example. And so we pray today for peace in our hearts and in our world: *Lord, may peace reign in our hearts and in our lives.*

15. Huber, *Singing Faith*, hymn 64.

Heal the bodies and spirits of victims of war, aggression, and violence of any kind. We pray to the Lord.

Bless and multiply the efforts of peacekeepers, mediators, intercessors, and healers to end violence and restore security. We pray to the Lord.

Teach all people of goodwill to resolve their differences peacefully. We pray to the Lord.

For what else shall we pray this morning? [Pause for participants to add their own intentions.] We pray to the Lord.[16]

Responsive readings also provide good opportunities to emphasize themes related to peace and justice. Carefully selected readings can be used with great power and effectiveness.

At various times throughout the year, ministers can also craft sermons that offer a clear, consistent, and compelling rationale for following the nonviolent way of Jesus. This is one of the most direct—and potentially one of the most persuasive—ways to encourage people to live nonviolently. However church leaders choose to emphasize the church's commitment to peace and nonviolence, whether through songs, prayers, liturgies, sermons, or in countless other ways, the weekly worship service provides a golden opportunity to highlight these key concerns.

Emphasize Loving Acceptance of All People by Confronting Prejudice, Bigotry, Discrimination, and Exclusion

Any honest reckoning of church history must grapple with the fact that Christians have often behaved very badly toward certain groups of people over the years. It is all too easy to demonstrate how Jews, Muslims, members of the LGBTQ community, atheists, and many others have suffered greatly at the hands of the church.[17] Yet, this is not just a thing of the past. People today still experience prejudice and bigotry at the hands of Christians far too often. In order to disarm its members, the church needs to challenge these unchristlike attitudes toward others.

Changing these attitudes can be difficult. Our attitudes toward others, particularly toward other *groups* of people, are often firmly entrenched in us.

16. Bender, *Just Prayer*, 11.

17. See chapter 2.

Typically, these attitudes have been formed over a long period of time and *informed* by a host of factors: what we were taught in school, how we were raised, our family of origins, our friends, the news media, popular culture, and so forth. All these "forces" shape our views about others, sometimes in ways we don't even realize. Our biases, prejudices, and presuppositions about people grow deep roots and are often very difficult to change.

Helping people become more understanding and compassionate toward others whom they intensely dislike, or even disdain, does not happen easily or automatically. It takes hard work and intentionality. If the church is going to persuade people to change these harmful views, it will need to employ various strategies for doing so.

For example, the church should be diligently about helping people cultivate a nonviolent mind-set, a point discussed at some length earlier.[18] People need to be reminded that every person—*every single one*—has been created in God's image and is beloved by God. This should utterly transform the way we see others. In addition, the church should constantly be pointing people to the life and teachings of Jesus, reminding them of the many ways in which Jesus reached out to the marginalized, misunderstood, and mistreated of his day. As Gushee puts it, "*We must cling to Jesus' example and the way he conducted his ministry. We must spend a lot of time in the gospels.*"[19] It is sadly ironic that the people the church often condemns are the very ones Jesus seems most interested in comforting.

The church will also need to read certain biblical texts more carefully and critically. As Dale Martin observes, "Any interpretation of Scripture that hurts people, oppresses people, or destroys people cannot be the right interpretation, no matter how traditional, historical, or exegetically respectable."[20] I wholeheartedly agree.[21] Passages that historically have been used to oppress non-heterosexuals and non-gender-conforming individuals, for instance, should be reexamined in light of the life and teachings of Jesus and the good news of the gospel, particularly as it relates to those who are disenfranchised. This is precisely the kind of important work currently being done by Christians who are troubled by the enormous harm the church's traditional teaching about gender norms and same-sex attraction have had on countless people who identify as LGBTQ.[22]

18. See chapter 13.
19. Gushee, *Changing Our Mind*, 141, emphasis original.
20. Martin, *Sex and the Single Savior*, 50.
21. This is the major premise of my book, *Violence of Scripture*.
22. See Vines, *God and the Gay Christian*.

If the church hopes to change harmful attitudes some Christians harbor toward ethnic minorities, women, undocumented workers, and others, it will need to address these matters directly. One of the real gifts the church can offer is to create a safe space where people can talk about these things honestly and openly, recognizing there will be a wide range of diverse opinions.[23] The church should make a concerted effort to facilitate important conversations among its members about race, gender, and sexual orientation.[24] This could happen in many ways: sponsoring workshops, encouraging people to attend conferences and other events devoted to these concerns, offering a variety of Christian education programming surrounding these issues, and so forth.

While the church obviously needs to address overt forms of racism, sexism, and discrimination, it should also be attuned to the more subtle ways these harmful attitudes and practices express themselves in words and deeds. These less explicit forms of oppression are sometimes referred to as "microaggressions."[25] Cody Sanders and Angela Yarber regard them as a major problem in the church.

> While blatant discrimination is often condemned, underhanded slights that assault the souls of oppressed groups still rage from the pulpit, the pew, the Sunday school class, the hymnal, the seminary curriculum, the ordination process, and in pastoral counseling. These everyday slights, insults, and invalidations are called microaggressions, and they accost the spirits of women, persons of color, and LGBTQs on a regular basis in our churches, seminaries, and denominations.[26]

Sanders and Yarber speak of microaggressions as "the hidden violence of everyday church" and urge us to put a stop to them.[27]

The church should also encourage its members to get to know "Others" whenever possible. This, perhaps more than anything else, has the power to

23. For an innovative example of an organization committed to this task, consider the work being done by The Colossian Forum (http://www.colossianforum.org/).

24. For a recent treatment addressing the problem of racism in American churches, see Hart, *Trouble I've Seen*, especially 167–80. See also Wallis, *America's Original Sin*, 97–126, and Perkins and Rice, *More Than Equals*.

25. For further discussion, see Sue and Capodilupo, "Racial, Gender, and Sexual Orientation Microaggressions," 105–30.

26. Sanders and Yarber, *Microaggressions in Ministry*, 1–2.

27. Ibid., 2. Church leaders who are unaware of what constitutes a "microaggression" should learn more about this (reading the book by Sanders and Yarber would be an excellent place to start) and should commit themselves to raising awareness and overcoming this very hurtful type of behavior.

change our most fundamental beliefs and assumptions. Evangelical ethicist David Gushee talks about the way in which "transformative encounters with real human beings" can result not just in a paradigm shift, but in what he calls a "paradigm leap."[28] When you get to know people who have been hurt by the church simply because they are African American, or lesbian, or undocumented, or poor, or Muslim, or—you fill in the blank—it is hard to respond with anything but compassion. It no longer is an "issue" out there; it is a person right here. Getting to know people who are different from us is one of the best ways to change the way we see them.

If the church is to be disarmed, harmful attitudes toward others which poison the church and hurt people need to confronted and challenged—rigorously. We should do all in our power to root these out of our own hearts and minds and to encourage our sisters and brothers in Christ to do likewise.

Two Pitfalls to Avoid

In addition to the many positive and constructive things the church can do to inspire people to live nonviolently, there are also things the church should avoid doing since they undermine efforts to convince people to fully embrace the nonviolent way of Jesus.

Avoid Approving of "Virtuous" Violence in the Bible

Numerous passages in the Bible, particularly in the Old Testament, sanction and sometimes even celebrate the use of violence. Phinehas is commended for thrusting a spear through an Israelite man and a Midianite woman (Num 25:6–13), and Jael is praised for hammering a tent peg through Sisera's skull (Judg 5:24–27). The Israelites are commanded to kill Canaanites without mercy (Deut 7:1–2), and later they are divinely directed to slaughter every last Amalekite (1 Sam 15:1–3). Texts like these that contain "virtuous" violence can be extremely dangerous if not handled with great care.[29]

Throughout the centuries, Christians have appealed to violent biblical texts to justify acts of violence and war. Countless people have been harmed and killed as a result. Since the church should not condone acts of violence, ministers and other Christian educators need to be very careful how they use Bible verses that do.

---

28. Gushee, *Changing Our Mind*, 106–11, first quote from 109.

29. This is illustrated in various ways in Jenkins, *Laying Down the Sword*.

When we preach and teach from these texts—and we *should* preach and teach from them—we need to do so in a way that does not reinforce positive portrayals of violence. Otherwise, we will find ourselves working at cross-purposes. It makes little sense to tell people to love their enemies one week, only to turn around and praise those who kill their enemies the next.[30] If we want people to live nonviolently, we should not celebrate those who don't—regardless of how the Bible portrays them. This means we need to be very cautious how we talk about stories like David and Goliath, stories that sanction killing and suggest violence can be virtuous.[31] If we accept the assumptions embedded in these stories, we undermine the values we are trying to instill in others.

Thankfully, there *are* ways to use stories like these that do not perpetuate the problematic assumptions about violence they contain.[32] While an adequate discussion of *how* to use violent biblical texts this way lies outside the scope of our present study, a few suggestions may be helpful at this point. For example, reading these texts from the perspective of the victims helpfully problematizes the positive portrayals of violence they contain. Reading with the victims exposes the destructive and dehumanizing nature of violence and challenges the notion that violence can ever be good or "virtuous." Once you read the flood narrative (Gen 6–8) from the perspective of those *outside* the ark, or the conquest narrative (Josh 6–11) from the perspective of those *inside* the city, it is far more difficult to justify the violence these narratives contain. Another way to mitigate some of the problems these texts raise is by bringing them into conversation with other Old Testament passages that portray alternative ways of handling conflict. As briefly discussed earlier, the Old Testament contains a significant emphasis on peace and peacemaking.[33] Passages that exemplify this emphasis can be used to critique others that condone acts of violence, bloodshed, and killing. It is also helpful to keep in mind that not every text that seems to approve of violence actually does. Some violent biblical texts, like the story of Elijah's slaughter of the prophets of Baal (1 Kgs 18), actually appear to be critiquing the violence they contain.[34] When this "internal critique" is perceived and brought to light, it mitigates some of the more problematic applications that

30. Cf. Seibert, *Violence of Scripture*, 154.

31. Recall the previous discussion of how to use this story with children (chapter 15).

32. For my approach to this problem, see Seibert, *Disturbing Divine Behavior* and *Violence of Scripture*. For an alternate perspective from a fellow Anabaptist, see Martens, "Toward Shalom." For an evangelical approach, see Sprinkle, *Fight*, 37–91.

33. See chapter 5.

34. For this argument, see Flannery, "'Go Back the Way You Came.'"

might otherwise result. Employing strategies like these—and others—can help pastors, professors, and religious educators of all stripes use these texts more responsibly.[35]

Religious leaders have a significant role to play in shaping how people read and understand troublesome texts. If they are not careful about how they use texts that sanction violence, they may unwittingly promote the very same attitudes and actions they wish to prevent. In the words of Rabbi Jonathan Sacks, "Hard texts need interpreting; without it, they lead to violence."[36]

Avoid Mixing God and Country

The church should also take deliberate steps to avoid mixing God and country or doing anything that would suggest the church approves of state-sponsored violence, killing, and warfare. As discussed in the first part of this book, one of the reasons so many Christians approve of violence is because the church sends mixed messages about violence, particularly when it behaves in ways that encourage nationalism and militarism.[37] When churches sing patriotic hymns, give special recognition to veterans (or those currently serving in the military) for their service, say the pledge of allegiance, and pray for victory for "our troops," they blur the crucial distinction between the church and the state. This, in turn, encourages nationalism and gives people the impression that the church supports Christian participation in the military. And, truth be told, many churches that behave this way *do* support Christians going into the armed forces. But rather than supporting Christian participation in the military through its songs, prayers, and programming, the church should be doing precisely the opposite. As noted earlier, the church should infuse its worship services with an emphasis on living nonviolently.

Since being in the armed forces and *fully* following the nonviolent way of Jesus appear to be mutually exclusive, the church should take great pains to avoid saying or doing anything that would suggest otherwise. Instead, the church should encourage young people to develop strong convictions against war and military service as they grow in their understanding of what it means to follow the nonviolent way of Jesus. To this end, the church should provide opportunities for teenagers to think through their personal beliefs about these matters. Church leaders could encourage their young people to

35. For more on these strategies, see Seibert, *Violence of Scripture*, 76-87.

36. Sacks, *Not in God's Name*, 208.

37. See chapter 3. For a discussion of nationalism and Christian faith, see Roth, *Choosing against War*, 126–157, and Camp, *Mere Discipleship*, 15–54.

read first person accounts from soldiers who decided they could no longer serve in the armed forces because of their religious beliefs. Helpful is this regard is Logan Mehl-Laituri's book, *Reborn on the Fourth of July*, which chronicles his journey from soldier to conscientious objector and explores a number of important issues and questions related to war, nationalism, and patriotism. Also helpful is a series of short videos featuring Benjamin Peters, a veteran of the Iraq War.[38] This six-part series, available free online, recounts Peters's own journey and considers some of the problems that accompany acts of violence and war.

Churches could also encourage young people to take steps to declare their opposition to warfare and killing. Currently, when young men reach the age of eighteen in the United States, they are required to register with the Selective Service so the government has their information on file in the event of a draft. Unfortunately, there is no place on the registration form for them to indicate they are a conscientious objector. As a way to address this, some religious groups have designed a process that allows them to document their opposition to war on religious and moral grounds.[39] Mennonite Central Committee, for example, encourages Christians to fill out and file a "Peacemaker Registration Form."[40] Going through this process is beneficial for young people not only because it provides a formal record of their religious convictions, but also because it challenges them to think deeply about what they believe about participating in war and why.

If the church is serious about discouraging young men and women from joining the military, it will need to address root causes that lead some to enlist in the first place. For many young people, joining the military is largely a pragmatic decision, not an ideological one. The military offers a good-paying job, housing, healthcare benefits, and financial assistance to attend college. These financial incentives are extremely attractive to people whose economic options are otherwise limited. For people who lack specialized vocational training and cannot pay for higher education, what the military offers may look quite appealing. This makes them easy targets for recruiters. The church must recognize this and redouble its efforts to seek financially viable alternatives for young people who are economically disadvantaged.

But what about Christians who do enlist? What might we say of them? Please hear me carefully. I am *not* suggesting that Christians who decide to

38. http://mcc.org/learn/more/bens-story.

39. The Church of the Brethren, for example, has developed the website "Call of Conscience," for this purpose (http://www.brethren.org/CO/).

40. This can be found at http://mcc.org/media/resources/1130.

serve in the military are therefore automatically "bad" Christians. There are many Christians in the armed forces who live godly lives and embody many of the virtues we expect of Christian men and women. There is no question about that. What I *am* saying is that it is impossible for these individuals to *fully* follow the nonviolent way of Jesus given their decision to join the military. Individuals who enlist must swear an oath in which they promise to "support and defend the Constitution of the United States against all enemies, foreign and domestic" and to "obey the orders of the President of the United States" as well as the orders of their superior officers. Unfortunately, supporting and defending the United States often involves the use of violent and lethal force, behavior that is inconsistent with the nonviolent nature of discipleship. Even servicemen and women who are not involved in combat, and who never actually pull the trigger, are still complicit in the actions taken by those they support. Actively participating in an organization that uses violent force to impose its will on others is not the way of Jesus.

Finally, before leaving this point, a brief—but *very* important—pastoral word is in order. Churches that take a strong stance against war should be extremely careful not to communicate disrespect or disdain toward those who serve in the military. Instead, the church should always be respectful to servicemen and women and should be intentional about finding ways to express genuine care and concern. One way to do this would be to pray for them from time to time during the worship service. Although it is inappropriate to pray that they be victorious in battle, since that mixes God and country and sanctions killing,[41] it is always appropriate to pray for their safety, security, and speedy return home. Prayers could also be offered asking God to keep them from engaging in behaviors that would violate their conscience or cause moral injury to themselves (or others). The church can also express its care to servicemen and women by reaching out to family members left behind when soldiers are deployed to see if there are tangible ways they can be of assistance with meals, transportation, emotional support, or other needs.

In addition, the church can be instrumental in helping military personnel transition back to civilian life when they return home.[42] Ministers can advocate for quality health care and for good psychological services to help them process what they have experienced while on duty. There is a lot

41. For a powerful expose of what is really involved in praying for victory in war, see Mark Twain's posthumously published "War Prayer," conveniently located in Sider and Keefer, eds., *Peace Reader*, 195–97.

42. See, e.g., the six-week Sunday school curriculum titled, "Returning Veterans, Returning Hope: Seeking Peace Together" that is designed to help soldiers heal after war. The curriculum can be downloaded at https://mcc.org/media/resources/1719.

of healing that often needs to take place when soldiers return home, and the church can have a vital ministry among veterans in this regard. In these ways and others, the church can take intentional steps to demonstrate its love for people in the military, just as the church should demonstrate its love for all people, regardless of their profession or their beliefs about the morality of Christian participation in war.

Conclusion: Promoting Nonviolence Nonviolently

If the church is to be successful in helping people disarm and live nonviolently, it must use means consistent with those ends. The church cannot beat peace into people—nor should it want to. Rather, church leaders need to embody the virtues they wish to instill in others. People will have little inclination to consider nonviolence—let alone embrace it—if they do not see God's love reflected in the people calling them to this way of life. As Henri Nouwen once observed:

> One of the reasons why so many people have developed strong reservations about the peace movement is precisely that they do not see the peace they seek in the peacemakers themselves. Often what they see are fearful and angry people trying to convince others of the urgency of their protest.[43]

That kind of behavior is neither attractive nor persuasive. The church's efforts to form people of peace should be characterized by love, patience, compassion, and *lots* of grace.

I especially appreciate the way John Roth talks about this in his excellent book, *Choosing Against War*. Roth discusses how people who are opposed to war should speak with those who hold different views.

> For the pacifist . . . the lingering questions should always be: did I present my case in a way that consistently reflected Christ's love and compassion, even in the midst of profound disagreements? Have I come to a deeper understanding of the worldview of my conversation partner? Can we leave the exchange with a sense of mutual trust and respect despite . . . significant differences?[44]

Roth's questions are excellent and their applicability to conversations about peace and nonviolence more generally are easily apparent. *How* we dialogue with others about sensitive issues is extremely important. If we are

---

43. Nouwen, *Road to Peace*, 41.
44. Roth, *Choosing Against War*, 117.

aggressive or combative, or if people feel nonviolence is being forced upon them, they are likely to become very defensive and resistant. This is exactly what the church does *not* want to happen. If we hope to persuade people to follow the nonviolent way of Jesus, our appeal should be inviting, not confrontational.

While it is important for the church to be absolutely clear about its rejection of all forms of violence, it must be equally clear that those who disagree with this stance—or have significant questions about it—are just as welcome as anyone else. Their voice is important and needs to be heard. People need to be given space to consider various options and to raise their questions and objections without fear of being judged or ostracized. When this happens, the church becomes a safe space. People are able to disagree with one another *and still remain friends*. When the church facilitates this sort of healthy dialog, people feel loved and respected as they wrestle with important issues—regardless of where they come out at the end of the day. Churches that are able to create this kind of environment have the greatest chance of helping people disarm.

Thus, while it is important for the church to engage in various efforts to encourage people to live nonviolently, it is also important that the church takes great care in *how* it goes about doing so. If the goal is to persuade people to follow the nonviolent way of Jesus, and if people are only likely to be persuaded if the means are consistent with the ends, then it becomes imperative for the church to take great care to be nonviolent in its efforts to encourage people to live nonviolently.

Postscript

The Church as the World's Imagination

Violence is for those who have lost their imagination.

—AN IRAQI HOSPITAL MANAGER[1]

One of the most underestimated forces for good at our disposal is our own imagination.

—LOGAN MEHL-LAITURI[2]

WHEN THE CHURCH EMBRACES violence, it abandons Jesus.[3] Therefore, I have argued throughout this book that violence is *not* an option for followers of Jesus. Jesus did not allow it, the New Testament never endorses it, and the early Church refused to participate in it.[4] No matter how noble the cause, Christians are never to resort to violence to administer justice. Rather, Christians are to put away the sword, love enemies, pray for persecutors, and resolve conflict nonviolently. In short, they are to follow the nonviolent way of Jesus.

We spent a considerable amount of time in the preceding pages exploring what it means to live nonviolently. Along the way, we discovered that living nonviolently involves much more than being *against* certain things (warfare, killing, and bloodshed); it means being *for* certain things

1. Quoted in Claiborne, *Irresistible Revolution*, 265–66.

2. Mehl-Laituri, *Reborn on the Fourth of July*, 193.

3. I am indebted to Terry Brensinger for the idea of the church as the world's imagination expressed in the title of this postscript. See further below.

4. On this last point, see Driver, *How Christians Made Peace with War*, and Sider, *Early Church on Killing*.

(life, peace, and well-being). In addition, we learned that living nonviolently is about more than just the positions we hold on issues such as capital punishment, gun rights, or the use of torture—as important as these are. Living nonviolently is a way of life, one that impacts *all* our relationships and *everything* we think, say, and do.

While I would like to think that every reader who picks up this book will be persuaded to follow the nonviolent way of Jesus fully, I realize that is overly optimistic. So, if you happen to be one of those readers who are not (yet!) fully persuaded, I hope this book has made you less accepting of violence than you were before and more willing to pursue nonviolent means of confronting evil and resolving conflict. At the very least, you now have more options at your disposal. All of us can find ways to reduce violence and make peace, even if we are not absolutely committed to complete nonviolence in every situation.

Being the World's Imagination

In a world often trapped in destructive patterns of violence, warfare, and killing, Christians are uniquely positioned to demonstrate a better way. As Terry Brensinger observes:

> The abnormalities of violence and war, so drastically opposed to life as God intended it, have become so normal that the world cannot imagine anything else. The world cries out for alternatives. The world needs an imagination. Therein lies a portion of our task.[5]

The church can be the world's imagination.[6] It can help people imagine nonviolent ways of responding to a broad range of threats ranging from an unwanted intruder at home to a brutal dictator in power. The church can also introduce people to *nonviolent* ways of parenting, handling interpersonal conflict, and dealing with difficult neighbors and co-workers. It can help people realize that forgiveness is much better than retaliation, and that hospitality is more powerful than hostility. And it can demonstrate how love triumphs over hate time and time again.

The importance of this imaginative task should not be underestimated since imagination is often the catalyst for real change. As the Catholic monk and psychologist Thomas Moore puts it, "Slight shifts in imagination have

---

5. Brensinger, "War in the Old Testament," 31.
6. See Brensinger, "Church as an Imaginative Community."

more impact on living than major efforts at change. . . . Deep changes in life follow movements in imagination."[7]

Of course, if the church is to be the world's imagination it will need to cultivate its own. One of the best ways the church can encourage "slight shifts in imagination," particularly among Christians who approve of—and even participate in—various forms of violence, is by telling stories. Stories, particularly stories of Christians living out a commitment to nonviolence, ignite our imagination. They help us see what nonviolence looks like in real life and can persuade us of its effectiveness. When we hear stories of people loving their enemies, forgiving offenders, offering hospitality to would-be assailants, removing dictators without firing a shot, and so forth, we not only become aware of alternatives to violence, we are challenged to go and do likewise. In fact, I am convinced that once people hear these stories, and realize there are many, many practical tools for living nonviolently and confronting evil, this becomes the "slight shift" in imagination needed to send them further down the path of following the nonviolent way of Jesus.

There are many great books that tell the stories of Christians (and others) who have worked tirelessly for peace and justice.[8] Consider putting some of these on your Christmas and birthday lists and then make time to read them. You will be challenged and inspired as you hear stories of women and men who used nonviolent techniques to topple oppressive regimes, change unjust legislation, and advocate on behalf of those most at risk.

The Bible is also a marvelous resource for expanding our imagination. If you want to witness a woman single-handedly preventing a bloody massacre by using words rather than weapons, read the story of Abigail in 1 Sam 25. Or treat yourself to 2 Kgs 6 and observe what happens when Elisha decides to *feed* rather than *fight* his enemies. If you really want to fire up your imagination, take a stroll through the prophets. Some of the most wild and wonderful peaceful imaginings come from this part of the Bible. Consider Isaiah's amazing vision of a time when nations will "beat their swords into plowshares, and their spears into pruning hooks," when "nation shall not lift up sword against nation, neither shall they learn war any more" (Isa 2:4). Or sit at the feet of Jesus for a while, and listen again to the Sermon on the Mount (Matt 5–7). Hear anew his call to love enemies and watch how he demonstrates love in action everywhere he turns. And don't forget about the Apostle Paul, whose peaceful imaginings invite us to overcome evil with

7. Moore, *Soul Mates*, viii. Partially quoted in ibid., 10.

8. For brief vignettes of over sixty peacemakers, see Buttry, *Blessed Are the Peacemakers*. For fifty more stories, see True, *People Power*.

good (Rom 12:21). If we soak in these texts and reflect deeply upon them, our capacity to imagine peace is bound to increase dramatically.

It is also helpful to cultivate our peaceful imagination in community with others, especially with other Christians who are committed to following the nonviolent way of Jesus. We can encourage each other and spur one another on as we try to imagine new ways, nonviolent ways, to respond to the seemingly intractable problems of our world.

The good news is that God is already at work, healing the broken places, bringing peace where there is strife, and doing justice in the midst of oppression. God invites us to participate by joining in this good work being done all around the world. We are to be co-laborers, advancing God's kingdom of peace and justice over all creation.

Conclusion

Given the broad range of topics we have covered throughout this book, I would be surprised if you have come to the end of it with all your questions answered. Thus, let me encourage you to continue exploring the issues raised here. Hopefully, the footnotes and extensive bibliography in this book provide you with many helpful directions to go as you reflect further on questions related to Christian faith and nonviolence.[9]

When the church courageously confronts injustice, resolves conflict, and stops oppression *without* resorting to violence, it shows the world a better way. By living nonviolently and loving unconditionally—even as it engages the most pressing problems of our day—the church can be the world's imagination. When people see Christians committed to ending violence, extending hospitality, promoting peace, and reconciling all creation, they see the church as it should be—disarmed and beautiful. As we work toward this vision, let us live ever more daring lives of faithful obedience to God so that the world may see Jesus in us and may come to know the God of peace who works to make all things new.

9. For helpful responses to objections raised about Christian nonviolence, see York and Barringer, eds., *Faith Not Worth Fighting For.* For an excellent and wide-ranging treatment of issues that need to be addressed when grappling with the problem of violence in Scripture, see Flood, *Disarming Scripture.*

Discussion Guide

Part 1: Understanding the Church's Problematic Relationship to Violence

Chapter 1: Introduction: Getting Beyond an Eye for an Eye

1. Discuss your personal beliefs about violence and nonviolence. Specifically, can you envision yourself using violence in certain situations or are you committed to living nonviolently in every circumstance?

2. Which would be more surprising to you: to see Christians behaving violently or to see Christians behaving nonviolently?

3. What prompted you to read this book, and what do you hope to gain from doing so?

Chapter 2: A Violent Church: Believers Behaving Badly

1. This chapter discusses a number of ways the church has sanctioned and participated in violence (e.g., supporting warfare and torture, using violence for self-defense, mistreating Jews and Muslims, perpetrating domestic violence, etc.). Which of these do you find most distressing? Why?

2. What other forms of violence are sometimes endorsed by the church that might be added to those discussed in this chapter?

3. Do you think Christians' acceptance of—and involvement in—violence is as problematic and pervasive as this chapter suggests, or do you feel this point has been overstated?

Chapter 3: Why Do Christians Condone So Much Violence?

1. Eight reasons are given in this chapter for why so many Christians condone so much violence. Discuss two or three of these you believe can best explain why the church is so accommodating in this regard.

2. To what extent do you agree that the reasons given in this chapter are key factors that explain why the church condones various forms of violence?

3. Who or what has been most influential in shaping your own beliefs around the question of Christians endorsing—or even engaging in—acts of violence?

Chapter 4: The Truth about Violence: It's All Bad

1. Do you believe Christians are ever justified in using violence? If not, explain why. If so, under what circumstances do you believe this to be the case?

2. To what extent do you agree that using violence to fight violence will likely make things worse?

3. Which of the "truths" about violence discussed in this chapter do you find most striking? Which do you believe might be the greatest deterrent for Christians who condone certain forms of violence?

Part 2: Making a Case for Nonviolence from the New Testament

Chapter 5: The Nonviolent Way of Jesus: Providing a Model for Christians to Follow

1. Indicate your agreement with the following statement on a scale of one to ten (one indicating the lowest amount of agreement and ten the highest): Jesus was nonviolent and commanded his followers to be nonviolent. Explain your position.

2. Many Christians regard Jesus' teaching about loving enemies as one of the strongest arguments *against* behaving violently toward others. Do you agree? Is it possible to love your enemies and treat them violently at the same time?

3. In addition to the verses discussed in this chapter, what other passages from the Gospels might you cite in support of the view that Jesus lived nonviolently?

Chapter 6: A Violent Jesus? Responding to Objections to Viewing Jesus as Nonviolent

1. In your opinion, which New Testament passage seems most persuasive for the argument that Jesus was not entirely nonviolent? How might someone refute this?

2. Do you think there is sufficient evidence to support the claim made by Hector Avalos (*Bad Jesus*, 90) that in the New Testament "Jesus is sometimes portrayed as endorsing violence and as actually committing violence"? Why or why not?

3. If Jesus actually did behave violently, as some believe the Gospels suggest, what impact does that have on the question of whether or not Christians can engage in the use of violent force?

Chapter 7: Why Followers of Jesus Must Forsake Violence: The Nonviolent Nature of Christian Discipleship

1. Near the beginning of the chapter, the author claims the following: "Being a disciple means following Jesus, and *following Jesus means living like Jesus lived and obeying what he taught*." To what extent do you think this accurately reflects what it means to be a Christian?

2. This chapter maintains that followers of Jesus are to serve rather than dominate, forgive rather than retaliate, suffer harm rather than inflict it, repay evil with good rather than with more evil, and love rather than hate. What other key aspects of Christian discipleship would you add to this list?

3. Do you believe using violence against others is compatible with serving, forgiving, suffering harm, repaying evil with good, and loving others? If so, how? If not, why not?

Chapter 8: Can Christians Go to War? Some Implications of Living Nonviolently

1. To what extent do you believe the just war tradition is a viable option for Christians today?

2. How persuasive do you find the biblical evidence used to support Christian participation in warfare?

3. Regardless of your view on the just war theory, do you believe Christian participation in the military is compatible with faithful Christian discipleship? Are there times when Christians can go to war, or is warfare completely forbidden?

Chapter 9: Living Out the Teachings of Jesus in the Real World: Stories of Christians who Loved Enemies, Forgave Offenders, and Made Peace with Adversaries

1. What impact did reading these stories have on you? How did they affect your thinking about nonviolence?

2. Which of the stories did you find most powerful and compelling? Explain why.

3. To what extent can you envision yourself behaving like the people in these stories?

4. Share other stories have you heard like the ones included here.

Part 3: Exploring Practical Alternatives to Violence

Chapter 10: Responding to Personal Assault with Hospitality Rather Than Hostility: How to Remain Unharmed without Harming Others

1. What would you do if you were home alone and you heard someone breaking into your house or apartment? In what way, if any, would your response be different if you were home with your five-year-old niece when this happened?

2. How well do you think the type of responses offered by Angie O'Gorman and Nathan and Louise Degrafinried would work in similar situations?

3. Walter Wink says, "Our capacity to discover creative nonviolent responses in moments of crisis will depend, to some degree at least, on whether we rehearse them in our everyday lives." (*Powers That Be*, 154). To what degree do you "rehearse" such "creative nonviolent responses" in your day-to-day life? What more could you do in this regard?

Chapter 11: Creative Nonviolent Intervention: Rescuing People under Attack without Resorting to Violence

1. Make a list of the creative nonviolent alternatives discussed in this chapter. What others might you add to the list?

2. After reading this chapter, how convinced are you that nonviolence often is a very effective way to help individuals being harmed like "Hans," the young black woman assaulted by skinheads, or Laxmi?

3. Share additional stories you have heard about people who have been rescued from danger through creative nonviolent intervention.

4. Why does the author argue that Christians should *not* carry concealed weapons? Do you agree? What are your views on Christians and gun ownership?

Chapter 12: Nonviolent Struggle 101: Confronting Injustice, Stopping Wars, and Removing Dictators without Firing a Shot

1. What is meant by the following statement: "Nonviolent struggle is fundamentally about power"?

2. What historical evidence is there that nonviolent struggle actually works?

3. Do you believe violence or nonviolence would be more effective in combating terrorism and religious extremism? Why?

4. Toward the end of the chapter, the author states: "The church needs to become more informed about the theory and practice of nonviolence and how successful it has been." What steps could your church take to make this happen?

Part 4: Living Nonviolently in Everyday Life

Chapter 13: Developing a Nonviolent Mind-Set: Seeing Others through the Eyes of God

1. What does it mean to cultivate a nonviolent mind-set and why is doing this so important for Christians?

2. Who do you find most difficult to love? How do you think your attitude toward these people would change if you focused on seeing them as being created in God's image and worked at humanizing rather than demonizing them?

3. What kinds of people do you perceive as being most unlike you, as being the "Other"? What tangible steps are you willing to take to get to know the "Other"?

Chapter 14: How to Handle Conflict without Becoming Violent: Living Nonviolently with the People around You

1. What are some of the most effective conflict resolution techniques you have learned from this chapter and from your own personal experience?

2. Describe a time when you were able to resolve a conflict with someone else peacefully. What made this possible?

3. What kind of self-care do you practice on a regular basis? Is it sufficient? If not, what will you do to make the necessary changes?

Chapter 15: Nonviolent Parenting: Treating Children with Respect and Talking about Violence

1. Generally speaking, how committed are you to nonviolent discipline and nonviolent parenting? What, if anything, keeps you from being fully committed?

2. What are your views about spanking children?

3. This chapter provides numerous suggestions about how to shape your children's views about violence. Which of these have you tried? Which do you believe might be most successful?

Chapter 16: Stopping Violence at Home: Addressing the Problem of Domestic Violence in Christian Families

1. This chapter includes three stories from wives who were victims of domestic violence. Did these stories surprise you in any way? Why or why not?

2. What experience have you had with domestic violence?

3. Based on the advice given in this chapter about how the church should address the problem of domestic violence, what is your church doing that may be helpful—or harmful—to victims of domestic violence?

4. What steps will you take to help your church address the problem of domestic violence more effectively in Christian homes and beyond?

Chapter 17: Practical Suggestions for the Church: Helping Christians Live Less Violently and More Faithfully

1. Which of the suggestions offered here would people in your church welcome with open arms and which would encounter the most resistance?

2. If you had to prioritize the practical suggestions offered in this chapter, which two or three do you believe would be most important for your particular congregation to put into practice?

3. What else can the church do, beyond the suggestions offered here, to encourage members to disarm and live nonviolently?

Postscript: The Church as the World's Imagination

1. In what ways have your views about violence changed and/or been confirmed as a result of reading this book?

2. How has reading this book expanded your imagination about living nonviolently and using nonviolence to respond to conflict, injustice, and oppression?

Bibliography

Achtemeier, Paul. *Romans*. Interpretation. Atlanta: John Knox, 1985.

Ackerman, Peter, and Jack DuVall. *A Force More Powerful: A Century of Nonviolent Conflict*. New York: St. Martin's, 2000.

———. "With Weapons of the Will." *Sojourners* 31, no. 5 (September–October 2002) 20–23.

Aichele, George. "Jesus' Violence." In *Violence, Utopia and the Kingdom of God: Fantasy and Ideology in the Bible*, edited by George Aichele and Tina Pippin, 72–91. New York: Routledge, 1998.

Alexis-Baker, Andy. "The Gospel or a Glock? Mennonites and the Police." *Conrad Grebel Review* 25 (Spring 2007) 23–49.

———. "Violence, Nonviolence and the Temple Incident in John 2:13–15." *Biblical Interpretation* 20 (2012) 73–96.

———. "What about the Centurion? A Roman Soldier's Faith and Christian Pacifism." In *A Faith Not Worth Fighting For: Addressing Commonly Asked Questions about Christian Nonviolence*, edited by Tripp York and Justin Bronson Barringer, 170–83. Eugene, OR: Cascade, 2012.

Alsdurf, James, and Phyllis Alsdurf. *Battered into Submission: The Tragedy of Wife Abuse in the Christian Home*. Downers Grove, IL: InterVarsity, 1989.

Arner, Rob. *Consistently Pro-Life: The Ethics of Bloodshed in Ancient Christianity*. Eugene, OR: Pickwick, 2010.

Aschliman, Kathryn, ed. *Growing toward Peace: Stories from Teachers and Parents about Real Children Learning to Live Peacefully*. Scottdale, PA: Herald, 1993.

Aslan, Reza. *Zealot: The Life and Times of Jesus of Nazareth*. New York: Random, 2013.

Atwood, James E. *Gundamentalism and Where It Is Taking America*. Eugene, OR: Cascade, 2017.

Augsburger, David. *Dissident Discipleship: A Spirituality of Self-Surrender, Love of God, and Love of Neighbor*. Grand Rapids: Brazos, 2006.

Avalos, Hector. *The Bad Jesus: The Ethics of New Testament Ethics*. The Bible in the Modern World, 68. Sheffield: Sheffield Phoenix, 2015.

Bailey, Sarah Pulliam. "Jerry Falwell Jr.: 'If more good people had concealed-carry permits, then we could end those' Islamist terrorists." *The Washington Post*. December 5, 2015. https://www.washingtonpost.com/news/acts-of-faith/wp/2015/12/05/liberty-university-president-if-more-good-people-had-concealed-guns-we-could-end-those-muslims/.

Bailey, Wilma Ann. *"You Shall Not Kill" Or "You Shall Not Murder"? The Assault on a Biblical Text*. Collegeville, MN: Liturgical, 2005.

Bainton, Roland H. *Christian Attitudes Toward War and Peace: A Historical Survey and Critical Re-evaluation*. Nashville: Abingdon, 1960.

Baker, Sharon L. *Razing Hell: Rethinking Everything You've Been Taught about God's Wrath and Judgment*. Louisville: Westminster John Knox, 2010.

Barak, Gregg. *Violence and Nonviolence: Pathways to Understanding*. Thousand Oaks, CA: Sage, 2003.

Barnett, Victoria. "Beyond Complicity: The Challenges for Christianity after the Holocaust." In *Must Christianity Be Violent? Reflections on History, Practice, and Theology*, edited by Kenneth R. Chase and Alan Jacobs, 97–106. Grand Rapids: Brazos, 2003.

Barrett, Greg. *The Gospel of Rutba: War, Peace, and the Good Samaritan Story in Iraq*. Maryknoll, NY: Orbis, 2012.

Barringer, Justin Bronson. "What about Those Men and Women Who Gave Up Their Lives so that You and I Could Be Free? On Killing for Freedom." In *A Faith Not Worth Fighting For: Addressing Commonly Asked Questions about Christian Nonviolence*, edited by Tripp York and Justin Bronson Barringer, 85–106. Eugene, OR: Cascade, 2012.

Barthel, Tara Klena, and David V. Edling. *Redeeming Church Conflicts: Turning Crisis into Compassion and Care*. Grand Rapids: Baker, 2012.

Batstone, David. *Not for Sale: The Return of the Global Slave Trade—and How We Can Fight It*. San Francisco: HarperSanFrancisco, 2007.

Beck, James R., ed. *Two Views on Women in Ministry*. Rev. ed. Grand Rapids: Zondervan, 2005.

Bell, Daniel M. *Just War as Christian Discipleship: Recentering the Tradition in the Church Rather Than the State*. Grand Rapids: Brazos, 2009.

Bender, Alison M. *Just Prayer: A Book of Hours for Peacemakers and Justice Seekers*. Collegeville, MN: Liturgical, 2015.

Berger, Rose Marie. "Game Changer?" *Sojourners* 45, no. 11 (December 2016) 16–23.

Bicksler, Harriet Sider. "My Internal Political Struggle." WordPress.com. July 20, 2016. https://harrietbicksler.wordpress.com/2016/07/20/my-internal-political-struggle/.

———. "Pursuing Peace." In *Focusing Our Faith: Brethren in Christ Core Values*, edited by Terry L. Brensinger, 129–44. Nappanee, IN: Evangel, 2000.

———. "Teaching Peace to Children Who Play War." In *A Peace Reader*, edited by E. Morris Sider and Luke Keefer, Jr., 130–39. Nappanee, IN: Evangel, 2002.

Bishop, Jeanne. *Change of Heart: Justice, Mercy, and Making Peace with My Sister's Killer*. Louisville: Westminster John Knox, 2015.

Black, Michele C., et al. *The National Intimate Partner and Sexual Violence Survey: 2010 Summary Report*. Atlanta: National Center for Injury Prevention and Control and Control, Centers for Disease Control and Prevention, 2011. http://www.cdc.gov/ViolencePrevention/pdf/NISVS_Report2010-a.pdf.

Blitzer, Wolf, et al. "CNN Late Edition with Wolf Blitzer." *CNN*. Aired October 24, 2004. cnn.com. http://www.cnnstudentnews.cnn.com/TRANSCRIPTS/0410/24/le.01.html.

Bonhoeffer, Dietrich. *The Cost of Discipleship*. Rev. ed. New York: Collier, 1963.

Boyd, Andrew, and Dave Oswald Mitchell, eds. *Beautiful Trouble: A Toolbox for Revolution*. New York: OR, 2012.

Boyd, Gregory A. "Does God Expect Nations to Turn the Other Cheek?" In *A Faith Not Worth Fighting For: Addressing Commonly Asked Questions about Christian Nonviolence*, edited by Tripp York and Justin Bronson Barringer, 107–24. Eugene, OR: Cascade, 2012.

———. *The Myth of a Christian Nation: How the Quest for Political Power is Destroying the Church*. Grand Rapids: Zondervan, 2005.

Brandon, S. G. F. *Jesus and the Zealots: A Study of the Political Factor in Primitive Christianity*. New York: Scribner, 1967.

Bredin, Mark R. "John's Account of Jesus' Demonstration in the Temple: Violent or Nonviolent?" *Biblical Theology Bulletin* 33 (2003) 44–50.

Brensinger, Terry L. "The Church as an Imaginative Community: Reclaiming the Liberating Power of Imagination." *Seek* 118, no. 1 (Summer 2005) 10–13.

———. "Converting Enemies into Friends (2 Kings 6:8–23)." In *Preaching the Word: Sermons by Brethren in Christ Ministers*, edited by E. Morris Sider, 23–31. Grantham, PA: Brethren in Christ Historical Society, 1994.

———. "War in the Old Testament: A Journey Toward Nonparticipation." In *A Peace Reader*, edited by E. Morris Sider and Luke Keefer Jr., 22–31. Nappanee, IN: Evangel, 2002.

Brensinger, Terry L., ed. *Focusing Our Faith: Brethren in Christ Core Values*. Nappanee, IN: Evangel, 2000.

Brethren in Christ Member Profile 2006. http://www.bic-church.org/momentum/april2007/CMP_US.pdf.

Bringing Down a Dictator. Directed by Steve York. Washington, DC: York Zimmerman, 2001. DVD.

Brock, Rita Nakashima, and Gabriella Lettini. *Soul Repair: Recovering from Moral Injury after War*. Boston: Beacon, 2012.

Brubaker, David. *Promise and Peril: Understanding and Managing Change and Conflict in Congregations*. Herndon, VA: Alban Institute, 2009.

Burnham, Karyn. *The Courage of Cowards: The Untold Stories of First World War Conscientious Objectors*. Barnsley, England: Pen and Sword, 2014.

Burwell, Ronald. "Results of the 2014 Global Anabaptist Profile: Brethren in Christ Church in the U.S." *Brethren in Christ History and Life* 38 (2015) 335–76.

Buttry, Daniel L. *Blessed Are the Peacemakers*. Canton, MI: Read the Spirit, 2011.

———. *Christian Peacemaking: From Heritage to Hope*. Valley Forge, PA: Judson, 1994.

———. *Peace Ministry: A Handbook for Local Churches*. Valley Forge, PA: Judson, 1995.

———. *Peace Warrior: A Memoir from the Front*. Macon, GA: Mercer University Press, 2012.

Byler, Anne Meyer. *How to Teach Peace to Children*. 2nd ed. Scottdale, PA: Herald, 2003.

Camp, Lee C. *Mere Discipleship: Radical Christianity in a Rebellious World*. Grand Rapids: Brazos, 2003.

———. "Theological Ground for Peaceful Co-existence." *Restoration Quarterly* 49 (2007) 241–46.

———. *Who Is My Enemy? Questions American Christians Must Face about Islam—and Themselves*. Grand Rapids: Brazos, 2011.

Cappello, Dominic. *Ten Talks Parents Must Have with Their Children about Violence*. New York: Hyperion, 2000.

Catalano, Shannan. "Intimate Partner Violence, 1993–2010." U.S. Department of Justice. November 2012 (revised September 29, 2015). http://www.bjs.gov/content/pub/pdf/ipv9310.pdf.

Cavey, Bruxy. *Inglorious Pastors: Waging Peace in a World of War.* The Meeting House. Oakville, Canada, 2010. DVD set.

Cecil, Nancy Lee. *Raising Peaceful Children in a Violent World.* With Patricia L. Roberts. San Diego: LuraMedia, 1995.

Centers for Disease Control and Prevention. "Understanding Intimate Partner Violence: Fact Sheet, 2014." http://www.cdc.gov/violenceprevention/pdf/ipv-factsheet.pdf.

Chacour, Elias. *Blood Brothers.* Grand Rapids: Chosen, 2003.

———. *We Belong to the Land: The Story of a Palestinian Israeli Who Lives for Peace and Reconciliation.* With Mary E. Jensen. New York: HarperCollins, 1990.

Charles, J. Daryl. *Between Pacifism and Jihad: Just War and Christian Tradition.* Downers Grove, IL: InterVarsity, 2005.

Chase, Kenneth R. "Introduction: The Ethical Challenge." In *Must Christianity Be Violent? Reflections on History, Practice, and Theology,* edited by Kenneth R. Chase and Alan Jacobs, 9–19. Grand Rapids: Brazos, 2003.

Cheney, Dick. Graduation Speech. United States Military Academy. West Point, New York, 2003. http://www.westpoint.edu/classes2/sitepages/gradspeech03.aspx.

Chenoweth, Erica, and Maria J. Stephen. *Why Civil Resistance Works: The Strategic Logic of Nonviolent Conflict.* New York: Columbia University Press, 2011.

Claiborne, Shane. *Executing Grace: How the Death Penalty Killed Jesus and Why It's Killing Us.* San Francisco: HarperOne, 2016.

———. *The Irresistible Revolution: Living as an Ordinary Radical.* Upd. and exp. Grand Rapids: Zondervan, 2016.

Claiborne, Shane, and Ben Cohen. *Jesus, Bombs, and Ice Cream: Building a More Peaceful World, Six Sessions Study Guide.* Grand Rapids: Zondervan, 2012.

Clough, David L., and Brian Stiltner. *Faith and Force: A Christian Debate about War.* Washington, DC: Georgetown University Press, 2007.

Clouse, Robert G., ed. *War: Four Christian Views.* Rev. ed. Downers Grove, IL: InterVarsity, 1991.

Cole, Darrell. *When God Says War Is Right: The Christian's Perspective on When and How to Fight.* Colorado Springs: Waterbrook, 2002.

Cortright, David. "The Power of Peacebuilding." *Sojourners* 44, no. 4 (April 2015) 18–19.

Cowles, C. S. "A Response to Tremper Longman III." In *Show Them No Mercy: Four Views on God and Canaanite Genocide,* C. S. Cowles et al., 191–5. Grand Rapids: Zondervan, 2003.

Croy, N. Clayton. "The Messianic Whippersnapper: Did Jesus Use a Whip on People in the Temple (John 2:15)?" *Journal of Biblical Literature* 128 (2009) 555–68.

Davies, Eryl W. *The Immoral Bible: Approaches to Biblical Ethics.* London: T & T Clark, 2010.

Dear, John. *Disarming the Heart: Toward a Vow of Nonviolence.* Scottdale, PA: Herald, 1993.

———. *Living Peace: A Spirituality of Contemplation and Action.* New York: Doubleday, 2001.

Dempsey, Carol J., and Elayne J. Shapiro. *Reading the Bible, Transforming Conflict.* Maryknoll, NY: Orbis, 2011.

Desjardins, Michel. *Peace, Violence and the New Testament.* Sheffield: Sheffield Academic, 1997.

domesticshelters.org. "Domestic Violence Statistics: The Hard Truth about Domestic Violence." May 01, 2014. https://www.domesticshelters.org/domestic-violence-articles-information/faq/domestic-violence-statistics#ftn3.

Doyle, Thomas P., A.W. Richard Sipe, and Patrick J. Wall. *Sex, Priests, and Secret Codes: The Catholic Church's 2,000 Year Paper Trail of Sexual Abuse.* Los Angeles: Volt, 2006.

Driscoll, Mark. "Is God a Pacifist?" markdriscoll.org. October 21, 2013. http://markdriscoll.org/is-god-a-pacifist/.

Driver, John. *How Christians Made Peace with War: Early Christian Understandings of War.* Scottdale, PA: Herald, 1988.

Duffey, Michael K. *Peacemaking Christians: The Future of Just Wars, Pacifism, and Nonviolent Resistance.* Kansas City: Sheed & Ward, 1995.

Dunn, James D. G. *Romans 9–16.* Word Biblical Commentary 38B. Dallas: Word, 1988.

DuVall, Jack, and Hardy Merriman. "Dissolving Terrorism at Its Roots." In *Nonviolence: An Alternative for Defeating Global Terror(ism),* edited by Senthil Ram and Ralph Summy, 221–34. New York: Nova Science, 2008.

Editorial Board, The. "To Hurt ISIS, Squeeze the Cash Flow." *New York Times.* March 3, 2015. http://www.nytimes.com/2015/03/03/opinion/to-hurt-isis-squeeze-the-cash-flow.html?_r=0.

Ellerbe, Helen. *The Dark Side of Christian History.* Windermere, FL: Morningstar and Lark, 1995.

Emerson, Michael O., and Christian Smith. *Divided by Faith: Evangelical Religion and the Problem of Race in America.* New York: Oxford University Press, 2000.

Enns, Elaine, and Ched Myers. *Ambassadors of Reconciliation: Diverse Christian Practices of Restorative Justice and Peacemaking.* Vol. 2. Maryknoll, NY: Orbis, 2009.

Enten, Harry. "Americans' Opinions on Spanking Vary By Party, Race, Region And Religion." *FiveThirtyEight,* September 15, 2014. http://fivethirtyeight.com/datalab/americans-opinions-on-spanking-vary-by-party-race-region-and-religion/.

Esquivel, Adolfo Pérez. *Christ in a Poncho: Testimonials of the Nonviolent Struggles in Latin America.* Edited by Charles Antoine. Translated by Robert R. Barr. Maryknoll, NY: Orbis, 1983.

Ewert, Lowell. "Law and Its Enforcement: A Substitute for Violence: A Response to 'The Gospel or a Glock.'" *Conrad Grebel Review* 26 (Spring 2008) 72–79.

Exum, J. Cheryl. "Feminist Criticism: Whose Interests Are Being Served?" In *Judges and Method: New Approaches in Biblical Studies,* 2nd ed., edited by Gale A. Yee, 65–89. Minneapolis: Fortress, 2007.

Fitzmyer, Joseph A. *The Gospel According to Luke (X–XXIV): Introduction, Translation, and Notes.* Anchor Bible 28A. Garden City, NY: Doubleday, 1985.

Flannery, Frances. "'Go Back the Way You Came': An Internal Textual Critique of Elijah's Violence in 1 Kings 18–19." In *Writing and Reading War: Rhetoric, Gender, and Ethics in Biblical and Modern Contexts,* edited by Brad E. Kelle and Frank Ritchel Ames, 161–73. SBLSymS 42. Atlanta: Society of Biblical Literature, 2008.

Flood, Derek. *Disarming Scripture: Cherry-Picking Liberals, Violence-Loving Conservatives, and Why We All Need to Learn to Read the Bible Like Jesus Did.* San Francisco: Metanoia, 2014.

Flower, Hilary. *Adventures in Gentle Discipline: A Parent-to-Parent Guide.* Schaumburg, IL: La Leche League, 2005.

Forest, Jim. *Loving Our Enemies: Reflections on the Hardest Commandment.* Maryknoll, NY: Orbis, 2014.

———. "Pascal Hospitality." jimandnancyforest.com. April 9, 2011. http://www.jimandnancyforest.com/2011/04/09/paschal-hospitality/.

Foster, Richard J. *Celebration of Discipline: The Path to Spiritual Growth.* Rev. ed. San Francisco: Harper & Row, 1988.

Foxe, John. *Foxe's Book of Martyrs: A History of the Lives, Sufferings and Triumphant Deaths of the Early Christian and the Protestant Martyrs.* Edited by William Byron Forbush. Philadelphia: John C. Winston, 1926.

Friesen, Philip E. *The Old Testament Roots of Nonviolence: Abraham's Personal Faith, Moses' Social Vision, Jesus' Fulfillment, and God's Work Today.* Eugene, OR: Wipf and Stock, 2010.

Gbowee, Leymah. *Mighty Be Our Powers: How Sisterhood, Prayer, and Sex Changed a Nation at War.* New York: Beast, 2011.

Gench, Frances Taylor. *Encountering God in Tyrannical Texts: Reflections on Paul, Women, and the Authority of Scripture.* Louisville: Westminster John Knox, 2015.

———. *Faithful Disagreement: Wrestling with Scripture in the Midst of Church Conflict.* Louisville: Westminster John Knox, 2009.

Germanos, Andrea. "CIA Chief Just Confirmed 'War on Terror' Has Created a Lot More Terrorists." *CommonDreams.* June 16, 2016. http://www.commondreams.org/news/2016/06/16/cia-chief-just-confirmed-war-terror-has-created-lot-more-terrorists.

Ghosh, Palash. "How Many People Did Joseph Stalin Kill?" *International Business Times.* March 5, 2013. http://www.ibtimes.com/how-many-people-did-joseph-stalin-kill-1111789.

Gibson, Lisa R. *Life in Death: A Journey from Terrorism to Triumph.* Maitland, FL: Xulon, 2008.

———. "How Personal Forgiveness Created a Platform for Global Peacemaking." In *Evangelical Peacemakers: Gospel Engagement in a War-Torn World,* edited by David P. Gushee, 68–78. Eugene, OR: Cascade, 2013.

Gingrich, Janeen. "Home Is the Most Dangerous Place for Women." *Women AdvaNCe.* October 15, 2015. http://www.womenadvancenc.org/2015/10/15/home-is-the-most-dangerous-place-for-women/.

Green, Joel B. *The Gospel of Luke.* The New International Commentary on the New Testament. Grand Rapids: Eerdmans, 1997.

Grossman, David A. *On Killing: The Psychological Cost of Learning to Kill in War and Society.* Rev. ed. New York: Back Bay, 2009.

Gulley, Philip. *If the Church Were Christian: Rediscovering the Values of Jesus.* San Francisco: HarperCollins, 2010.

Gushee, David P. *Changing Our Mind: A Call from America's Leading Evangelical Ethics Scholar for Full Acceptance of LGBT Christians in the Church.* 2nd ed. Canton, MI: Read the Spirit, 2015.

Hallie, Philip. *Lest Innocent Blood Be Shed: The Story of the Village of Le Chambon and How Goodness Happened There.* New York: HarperPerennial, 1994.

Harder, Jeanette. *Let the Children Come: Preparing Faith Communities to End Child Abuse and Neglect.* Scottdale, PA: Herald, 2010.

Harstad, Adolph L. *Joshua.* Concordia Commentary. St. Louis: Concordia, 2004.

Hart, Drew G. I. *Trouble I've Seen: Changing the Way the Church Views Racism.* Harrisonburg, VA: Herald, 2016

Hart, Michael H. *The 100: A Ranking of the Most Influential Persons in History.* Rev. ed. Secausus, NJ: Citadel, 1994.

Hartsough, David. *Waging Peace: Global Adventures of a Lifelong Activist.* With Joyce Hollyday. Oakland, CA: PM, 2014.

Haruf, Kent. *Benediction.* New York: Alfred A. Knopf, 2013.

Hassan, Carma and Steve Almasy. "During Sermon on Violence, N.C. Pastor Confronts Man with Rifle." *CNN,* January 4, 2016. http://www.cnn.com/2016/01/02/us/north-carolina-pastor-man-with-gun/index.html.

Hastings, Tom H. *Nonviolent Response to Terrorism.* Jefferson, NC: McFarland, 2004.

Haugen, Gary A., and Victor Boutros. *The Locust Effect: Why the End of Poverty Requires the End of Violence.* New York: Oxford University Press, 2014.

Hays, Richard B. *The Moral Vision of the New Testament: Community, Cross, New Creation: A Contemporary Introduction to New Testament Ethics.* San Francisco: HarperSanFrancisco, 1996.

Heggen, Carolyn Holderread. *Sexual Abuse in Christian Homes and Churches.* Scottdale, PA: Herald, 1993.

Heisey, M. J. *Peace and Persistence: Tracing the Brethren in Christ Peace Witness through Three Generations.* Kent, OH: Kent State University Press, 2003.

Hill, Jim, and Rand Cheadle. *The Bible Tells Me So: Uses and Abuses of Holy Scripture.* New York: Doubleday, 1996.

Hill, Wesley. *Washed and Waiting: Reflections on Christian Faithfulness and Homosexuality.* Upd. and exp. Grand Rapids: Zondervan, 2016.

Holcomb, Justin S., and Lindsey A. Holcomb. *Is It My Fault? Hope and Healing for Those Suffering Domestic Violence.* Chicago: Moody, 2014.

Hollingsworth, Amy. *The Simple Faith of Mister Rogers: Spiritual Insights from the World's Most Beloved Neighbor.* Nashville: Integrity, 2005.

Hostetler, Marian. *They Loved Their Enemies.* Scottdale, PA: Herald, 1988.

House, H. Wayne, ed. *Divorce and Remarriage: Four Christian Views.* Downers Grove, IL: InterVarsity, 1990.

Huber, Jane Parker. *A Singing Faith.* Philadelphia: Westminster, 1987.

Huckins, Jon, and Jer Swigart. "Invitations to Action." In *Reconcile: Conflict Transformation for Ordinary Christians,* edited by John Paul Lederach, 181–90. Harrisonburg, VA: Herald, 2014.

Hughes, Richard T. *Christian America and the Kingdom of God.* Urbana, IL: University of Illinois Press, 2009.

———. "A Vision for Christian Leaders of the Future: Christianity Was Never Designed as a Tool for War." *Vital Speeches of the Day* 73 (2007) 536–40.

Hussain, Amir. "Building Faith Neighbors: Church Colleges and Muslim Communities." *Cresset* 73, no. 4 (Easter 2010) 31–38.

Hybels, Bill, and Lynne Hybels. "Foreword." In *Reconcile: Conflict Transformation for Ordinary Christians,* edited by John Paul Lederach, 9–11. Harrisonburg, VA: Herald, 2014.

Ingram, Chip. *Effective Parenting in a Defective World: How to Raise Kids Who Stand Out from the Crowd.* Carol Stream, IL: Tyndale, 2006.

Invisibilia. "Flip the Script." NPR.org. July 15, 2016. http://www.npr.org/programs/invisibilia/485603559/flip-the-script.

Isaak, Jon. "The Christian Community and Political Responsibility: Romans 13:1–7." *Direction* 32 (2003) 32–46.

Jacobsen, Douglas, and Rodney J. Sawatsky. *Gracious Christology: Living the Love We Profess.* Grand Rapids: Baker, 2006.

Jeltsen, Melissa. "The Biggest Issue Women Face Today, According to Gloria Steinem." *The Huffington Post.* October 27, 2015 (updated November 10, 2015). http://www.huffingtonpost.com/entry/gloria-steinem-biggest-issue-women-face_us_562fa575e4b06317990f884a.

Jenkins, Philip. *Laying Down the Sword: Why We Can't Ignore the Bible's Violent Verses.* New York: HarperOne, 2011.

Johnson, Luke Timothy. *Reading Romans: A Literary and Theological Commentary.* New York: Crossroad, 1997.

Joseph, Simon J. *The Nonviolent Messiah: Jesus, Q, and the Enochic Tradition.* Minneapolis: Fortress, 2014.

Juhnke, James C., and Carol M. Hunter. *The Missing Peace: The Search for Nonviolent Alternatives in United States History.* 2nd exp. ed. Kitchener, ON: Pandora, 2004.

Kang, Sa-Moon. *Divine War in the Old Testament and in the Ancient Near East.* BZAW 177. Berlin: de Gruyter, 1989.

Khalid, Wardah. "Bombs Are Not the Answer: 5 Non-Military Ways to Stop the Islamic State Group." *U.S. News & World Report.* February 18, 2015. http://www.usnews.com/opinion/blogs/world-report/2015/02/18/stopping-the-islamic-state-group-without-the-bombs.

Kinnaman, David, and Gabe Lyons. *Unchristian: What a New Generation Really Thinks about Christianity . . . and Why It Matters.* Grand Rapids: Baker, 2007.

Knight, George W., III. "Can a Christian Go to War?" *Christianity Today* 20, no. 4 (November 21, 1975) 4–7.

Kramer, Ann. *Conscientious Objectors of the Second World War: Refusing to Fight.* Barnsley, England: Pen and Sword, 2013.

Kraybill, Donald B. *The Upside-Down Kingdom.* 2nd ed. Scottdale, PA: Herald, 1990.

Kraybill, Donald B., Steven M. Nolt, and David L. Weaver-Zercher. *Amish Grace: How Forgiveness Transcended Tragedy.* San Francisco: Jossey-Bass, 2007.

Kroeger, Catherine Clark, and Nancy Nason-Clark. *No Place for Abuse: Biblical and Practical Resources to Counteract Domestic Violence.* 2nd ed. Downers Grove, IL: InterVarsity, 2010.

Larson, Jeanne, and Madge Micheels-Cyrus, eds. *Seeds of Peace: A Catalogue of Quotations.* Philadelphia: New Society, 1987.

Lederach, John Paul. *Reconcile: Conflict Transformation for Ordinary Christians.* Harrisonburg, VA: Herald, 2014.

Lee, Justin. *Torn: Rescuing the Gospel from the Gays-vs.-Christians Debate.* New York: Jericho, 2012.

Leiter, David A. *Neglected Voices: Peace in the Old Testament.* Scottdale, PA: Herald, 2007.

Lilly, Ingrid E. "What about War and Violence in the Old Testament?" In *A Faith Not Worth Fighting For: Addressing Commonly Asked Questions about Christian Nonviolence,* edited by Tripp York and Justin Bronson Barringer, 125–39. Eugene, OR: Cascade, 2012.

Long, D. Stephen. "What about the Protection of Third-Party Innocents? On Letting Your Neighbors Die." In *A Faith Not Worth Fighting For: Addressing Commonly Asked Questions about Christian Nonviolence*, edited by Tripp York and Justin Bronson Barringer, 18–30. Eugene, OR: Cascade, 2012.

Longfellow, Henry Wadsworth. "Drift-Wood: Table-Talk." In *The Prose Works of Henry Wadsworth Longfellow, with Bibliographical and Critical Notes*, vol. 1, 403–8. Cambridge: Riverside, 1895.

Longman III, Tremper. "A Response to C. S. Cowles." In *Show Them No Mercy: Four Views on God and Canaanite Genocide*, C. S. Cowles et al., 57–60. Grand Rapids: Zondervan, 2003.

Luther, Martin. "The Jews and Their Lies" (1543). Jewish Virtual Library. https://www.jewishvirtuallibrary.org/jsource/anti-semitism/Luther_on_Jews.html.

Mann, Monroe. *To Benning and Back: Volume I, The Making of a Citizen Soldier*. 2nd ed. Bloomington, IN: AuthorHouse, 2007.

Markham, Laura. *Peaceful Parent, Happy Kids: How to Stop Yelling and Start Connecting*. New York: Perigee, 2012.

Marshall, I. Howard. *The Gospel of Luke*. The New International Greek Testament Commentary. Grand Rapids: Eerdmans, 1978.

Martens, Elmer A. "Toward Shalom: Absorbing the Violence." In *War in the Bible and Terrorism in the Twenty-First Century*, edited by Richard S. Hess and Elmer A. Martens, 33–57. Bulletin for Biblical Research Supplements 2. Winona Lake, IN: Eisenbrauns, 2008.

Martin, Dale B. *Sex and the Single Savior: Gender and Sexuality in Biblical Interpretation*. Louisville: Westminster John Knox, 2006.

McBride, Karyl. "Shaming Children is Emotionally Abusive." *The Legacy of Distorted Love* (blog). *Psychology Today*, September 10, 2012. https://www.psychologytoday.com/blog/the-legacy-distorted-love/201209/shaming-children-is-emotionally-abusive.

McClure, John S., and Nancy J. Ramsay, eds. *Telling the Truth: Preaching about Sexual and Domestic Violence*. Cleveland: United Church Press, 1998.

McDonald, Patricia M. *God and Violence: Biblical Resources for Living in a Small World*. Scottdale, PA: Herald, 2004.

McHugh, Adam S. *The Listening Life: Embracing Attentiveness in a World of Distraction*. Downers Grove, IL: InterVarsity, 2015.

McKnight, Chuck. "How One Church Reacted to the Threat of Violence—and the Questions It Forces Us to Ask." *Hippie Heretic* (blog). January 4, 2016. http://www.patheos.com/blogs/hippieheretic/2016/01/how-one-church-reacted-to-threat-of.html.

McKnight, Scot. "Foreword: Following the Prince of Peace." In *A Farewell to Mars: An Evangelical Pastor's Journey Toward the Biblical Gospel of Peace*, Brian Zahnd, 19–21. Colorado Springs: David C Cook, 2014.

McLaren, Brian D. *A New Kind of Christianity: Ten Questions That Are Transforming the Faith*. New York: HarperOne, 2010.

Meagher, Robert Emmet. *Killing from the Inside Out: Moral Injury and Just War*. Eugene, OR: Cascade, 2014.

Mehl-Laituri, Logan. *Reborn on the Fourth of July: The Challenge of Faith, Patriotism and Conscience*. Downers Grove, IL: InterVarsity, 2012.

Mennonite Central Committee. "Preventing Gun Violence." https://mcc.org/sites/mcc. org/files/media/common/documents/mccu.s.gunviolencepreventionguide.pdf.

———. "Home Shouldn't Be a Place that Hurts." https://mcccanada.ca/sites/mcccanada. ca/files/media/common/documents/homeshouldnthurtweb.pdf.

Merrill, Eugene H. "The Case for Moderate Discontinuity." In *Show Them No Mercy: Four Views on God and Canaanite Genocide*, C. S. Cowles et al., 63–94. Grand Rapids: Zondervan, 2003.

Merriman, Hardy. "California Grape Workers' Strike and Boycott—1965–1970." In *Waging Nonviolent Struggle: 20th Century Practice and 21st Century Potential*, Gene Sharp, in collaboration with Joshua Paulson, 173–87. Boston: Extending Horizons, 2005.

Merritt, Carol Howard, and Tyler Wigg-Stevenson. *Fighting for Peace: Your Role in a Culture Too Comfortable with Violence*. Grand Rapids: Zondervan, 2013.

Middleton, J. Richard. *The Liberating Image: The Imago Dei in Genesis 1*. Grand Rapids: Brazos, 2005.

Miles, Al. *Domestic Violence: What Every Pastor Needs to Know*. 2nd ed. Minneapolis: Fortress, 2011.

———. *Violence in Families: What Every Christian Needs to Know*. Minneapolis: Augsburg, 2002.

Mock, Ron. *Loving without Giving In: Christian Responses to Terrorism and Tyranny*. Telford, PA: Cascadia, 2004.

Mommsen, Peter. "Building the Jesus Movement: An Interview with Shane Claiborne." *Plough Quarterly* 10 (Autumn 2016) 26–33.

Moore, Thomas. *Soul Mates: Honoring the Mysteries of Love and Relationship*. New York: HarperPerennial, 1994.

Morris, Debbie. *Forgiving the Dead Man Walking: Only One Woman Can Tell the Entire Story*. With Gregg Lewis. Grand Rapids: Zondervan, 1998.

Mouw, Richard J. *Uncommon Decency: Christian Civility in an Uncivil World*. Downers Grove, IL: InterVarsity, 1992.

Murray, Stuart. *The Naked Anabaptist: The Bare Essentials of a Radical Faith*. Scottdale, PA: Herald, 2010.

National Coalition against Domestic Violence. "What Is Domestic Violence?" http://www.ncadv.org/need-help/what-is-domestic-violence.

———. "Statistics." http://www.ncadv.org/learn/statistics.

National Priorities Project. "Discretionary Spending 2015: $1.15 Trillion." nationalpriorities.org. April 2, 2014. http://savvyroo.com/chart-705907769336-discretionary-spending-2015-1-15-trillion.

Nelson-Pallmeyer, Jack, and Bret Hesla. *Worship in the Spirit of Jesus: Theology, Liturgy, and Songs without Violence*. Cleveland: Pilgrim, 2005.

Neufeld, Thomas R. Yoder. *Killing Enmity: Violence and the New Testament*. Grand Rapids: Baker Academic, 2011.

Neville, David J. *A Peaceable Hope: Contesting Violent Eschatology in New Testament Narratives*. Grand Rapids: Baker Academic, 2013.

Niemela, Erin. "Before the Next ISIS, We Need Nonviolent Counterterrorism Strategies." Peace Voice, July 6, 2014. http://www.peacevoice.info/2014/07/06/before-the-next-isis-we-need-nonviolent-counterterrorism-strategies/.

Noll, Mark A. "Have Christians Done More Harm Than Good?" In *Must Christianity Be Violent? Reflections on History, Practice, and Theology*, edited by Kenneth R. Chase and Alan Jacobs, 79–93. Grand Rapids: Brazos, 2003.

———. *The Scandal of the Evangelical Mind*. Grand Rapids: Eerdmans, 1994.

Nouwen, Henri. *The Road to Peace: Writings on Peace and Justice*. Edited by John Dear. Maryknoll, NY: Orbis, 1998.

Oates, Stephen B. *Let the Trumpet Sound: The Life of Martin Luther King, Jr.* New York: New American Library, 1982.

O'Day, Gail R. "Gospel of John." In *Women's Bible Commentary*, edited by Carol A. Newsom, et al., 517–30. 3rd ed. Louisville: Westminster John Knox, 2012.

O'Gorman, Angie. "Defense through Disarmament: Nonviolence and Personal Assault (1983)." In *The Universe Bends Toward Justice: A Reader on Christian Nonviolence in the U.S.*, edited by Angie O'Gorman, 241–47. Philadelphia: New Society, 1990.

Parrott, Les, and Leslie Parrott. *Saving Your Marriage Before It Starts: Seven Questions to Ask Before—and After—You Marry*. Exp. and upd. Grand Rapids: Zondervan, 2006.

Patterson, Kerry, et al. *Crucial Conversations: Tools for Talking When Stakes Are High*. 2nd ed. New York: McGraw-Hill, 2012.

Patterson, Linda J. *Hate Thy Neighbor: How the Bible is Misused to Condemn Homosexuality*. West Conshohocken, PA: Infinity, 2009.

Paulson, Joshua. "Removing the Dictator in Serbia—1996–2000." In *Waging Nonviolent Struggle: 20th Century Practice and 21st Century Potential*, Gene Sharp, in collaboration with Joshua Paulson, 315–39. Boston: Extending Horizons, 2005.

Pearson, Sharon Ely, ed. *Reclaiming the Gospel of Peace: Challenging the Epidemic of Gun Violence*. New York: Morehouse, 2015.

Pearse, Meic. *Why the Rest Hates the West: Understanding the Roots of Global Rage*. Downers Grove, IL: InterVarsity, 2004.

Perkins, Spencer, and Chris Rice. *More Than Equals: Racial Healing for the Sake of the Gospel*. Rev. and exp. Downers Grove, IL: InterVarsity, 2000.

Pew Research Center. "How Americans Feel About Religious Groups." July 16, 2014. http://www.pewforum.org/2014/07/16/how-americans-feel-about-religious-groups/.

———. "The Religious Dimensions of the Torture Debate." April 29, 2009 (updated May 7, 2009). http://www.pewforum.org/2009/04/29/the-religious-dimensions-of-the-torture-debate/.

———. "Shrinking Majority of Americans Support Death Penalty." March 28, 2014. http://www.pewforum.org/2014/03/28/shrinking-majority-of-americans-support-death-penalty/.

Popovic, Srdja. *Blueprint for Revolution: How to Use Rice Pudding, Lego Men, and Other Nonviolent Techniques to Galvanize Communities, Overthrow Dictators, or Simply Change the World*. New York: Spiegel and Grau, 2015.

Popovic, Srdja, et al. *CANVAS Core Curriculum: A Guide to Effective Nonviolent Struggle*. Serbia: CANVAS, 2007. http://canvas3.cervinistrategies.com/wp-content/uploads/2015/08/CANVAS-Core-Curriculum_EN.pdf.

Ram, Senthil, and Ralph Summy. *Nonviolence: An Alternative for Defeating Global Terror(ism)*. New York: Nova Science, 2008.

Rauser, Randal. *Is the Atheist My Neighbor? Rethinking Christian Attitudes toward Atheism*. Eugene, OR: Cascade, 2015.

Relevant Magazine. "7 Big Questions." Originally appeared in *Relevant Magazine* 24 (January/February 2007). http://web.archive.org/web/20071013102203/http://relevantmagazine.com/god_article.php?id=7418.

Rosenberg, Marshall B. *Nonviolent Communication: A Language of Life.* 3rd ed. Encinitas, CA: PuddlerDancer, 2015.

Roth, John D. *Choosing against War: A Christian View: A Love Stronger Than Our Fears.* Intercourse, PA: Good Books, 2002.

Russell, Diana E. H. "The Death of Lakireddy Bali Reddy's Sex Slave." dianarussell.com. http://www.dianarussell.com/reddy_sex_slavery_case.html.

Sacks, Jonathan. *Not in God's Name: Confronting Religious Violence.* New York: Schocken, 2015.

Samuel, Dorothy T. *Safe Passages on City Streets.* Exp. ed. Providence, RI: Liberty Literary Works, 1991.

Sande, Ken. *The Peacemaker: A Biblical Guide to Resolving Personal Conflict.* 3rd ed. Grand Rapids: Baker, 2004.

Sande, Ken, and Kevin Johnson. *Resolving Everyday Conflict.* Grand Rapids: Baker, 2011.

Sanders, Cody J., and Angela Yarber. *Microaggressions in Ministry: Confronting the Hidden Violence of Everyday Church.* Louisville: Westminster John Knox, 2015.

Schenck, Rob. *The Armor of Light.* Directed by Abigail Disney. Culver City, CA: Samuel Goldwyn Films, 2016. DVD.

———. "Should Christians Own Guns?" *Sojourners* 45, no. 5 (May 2016) 14–18.

Schlabach, Gerald W. "Must Christian Pacifists Reject Police Force?" In *A Faith Not Worth Fighting For: Addressing Commonly Asked Questions about Christian Nonviolence,* edited by Tripp York and Justin Bronson Barringer, 60–84. Eugene, OR: Cascade, 2012.

Schmidt, Alvin J. *How Christianity Changed the World.* Grand Rapids: Zondervan, 2004.

Schrock-Shenk, Carolyn, ed. *Mediation and Facilitation Training Manual: Foundations and Skills for Constructive Conflict Transformation.* 4th ed. Akron, PA: Mennonite Conciliation Service, 2000.

Schwager, Raymund. *Must There Be Scapegoats: Violence and Redemption in the Bible.* Translated by Maria L. Assad. New York: Crossroad, 2000.

Scovell, Rhett. "Church Member Profile 2006: The Brethren in Christ Church." Slide presentation prepared by Ronald Burwell. http://slideplayer.com/slide/3529781/.

Sears, Dr. "Healthy Disciple for Children." AskDrSears.com. http://www.askdrsears.com/topics/parenting/discipline-behavior/discipline-for-children.

Seibert, Eric A. *Disturbing Divine Behavior: Troubling Old Testament Images of God.* Minneapolis: Fortress, 2009.

———. "The Old Testament as a Problem for Pacifists (and What to Do about It)." In *Exploring the Gospel of Peace: Essays on Christian Pacifism,* edited by Shawn M. Graves and Marlena Graves. Downers Grove, IL: InterVarsity, forthcoming.

———. "Pacifism and Nonviolence." In *Celebrations and Convictions: Honoring the Life and Legacy of Dr. Luke L. Keefer, Jr.,* edited by J. Robert Douglass and Wyndy Corbin Reuschling, 195–212. Mechanicsburg, PA: Brethren in Christ Historical Society, 2015.

———. *The Violence of Scripture: Overcoming the Old Testament's Troubling Legacy.* Minneapolis: Fortress, 2012.

Senior, Donald. *Matthew*. Abingdon New Testament Commentaries. Nashville: Abingdon, 1998.

Sharp, Gene. *The Politics of Nonviolent Action*. Boston: Porter Sargent, 1973.

———. *There Are Realistic Alternatives*. Boston: Albert Einstein Institution, 2003.

———. *Waging Nonviolent Struggle: 20th Century Practice and 21st Century Potential*. In collaboration with Joshua Paulson. Boston: Extending Horizons, 2005.

Shook, Natalie J. "Interracial Roommate Relationships: An Experimental Field Test of the Contact Hypothesis." Association for Psychological Science, July 1, 2008. http://www.psychologicalscience.org/news/releases/interracial-roommate-relationships-an-experimental-field-test-of-the-contact-hypothesis.html#.WKcKabk5P2Z.

Sider, E. Morris and Luke Keefer, Jr., eds. *A Peace Reader*. Nappanee, IN: Evangel, 2002.

Sider, Ronald J. *The Early Church on Killing: A Comprehensive Sourcebook on War, Abortion, and Capital Punishment*. Grand Rapids: Baker, 2012.

———. *Nonviolent Action: What Christian Ethics Demands but Most Christians Have Never Really Tried*. Grand Rapids: Brazos, 2015.

———. *The Scandal of the Evangelical Conscience: Why are Christians Living Just Like the Rest of the World?* Grand Rapids: Baker, 2005.

Skinner, Tom. *Black and Free*. Grand Rapids: Zondervan, 1968.

Slattery, Laura, et al. *Engage: Exploring Nonviolent Living: A Study Program for Learning, Practicing, and Experimenting with the Power of Creative Nonviolence to Transform Our Lives and Our World*. Oakland, CA: Pace e Bene, 2005.

Solzhenitsyn, Aleksandr I. *The Gulag Archipelago: 1918–1956*. New York: Perennial, 2002.

Spong, John Shelby. *The Sins of Scripture: Exposing the Bible's Texts of Hate to Reveal the God of Love*. San Francisco: HarperSanFrancisco, 2005.

Sprinkle, Preston M. *Fight: A Christian Case for Nonviolence*. Colorado Springs: David C Cook, 2013.

Sprinkle, Preston M., ed. *Four Views on Hell*. 2nd ed. Grand Rapids: Zondervan, 2016.

———. *Two Views on Homosexuality, the Bible, and the Church*. Grand Rapids, Zondervan, 2016.

Stassen, Glen H., and David P. Gushee. *Kingdom Ethics: Following Jesus in Contemporary Context*. Downers Grove, IL: InterVarsity, 2003.

Stephan, Maria J. "Civil Resistance vs. ISIS." *Journal of Resistance Studies* 1, no. 2 (2015) 127–50.

———. "Resisting ISIS." *Sojourners* 44, no. 4 (April 2015) 14–17.

Stoltzfus, Nathan. *Resistance of the Heart: Intermarriage and the Rosenstrasse Protest in Nazi Germany*. New Brunswick, NJ: Rutgers University Press, 2001.

Stone, Douglas, Bruce Patton, and Sheila Heen. *Difficult Conversations: How to Discuss What Matters Most*. New York: Penguin, 2000.

Stoner, Eric. "Pillars of Support." In *Beautiful Trouble: A Toolbox for Revolution*, edited by Andrew Boyd and Dave Oswald Mitchell, 248–49. New York: OR, 2012.

Stuebing, Kathy, "Whom Shall I Fear?" *Shalom! A Journal for the Practice of Reconciliation* 36, no. 2 (Spring 2016) 3–4.

Sue, Derald Wing, and Christina M. Capodilupo. "Racial, Gender, and Sexual Orientation Microaggressions: Implications for Counseling and Psychotherapy." In *Counseling the Culturally Diverse: Theory and Practice*, 5th ed., Derald Wing Sue and David Sue, 105–30. Hoboken, NJ: Wiley, 2008.

Swalm, E. J. *"My Beloved Brethren . . .": Personal Memoirs and Recollections of the Canadian Brethren in Christ Church*. Nappanee, IN: Evangel, 1969.

Swalm, E. J., ed. *Nonresistance Under Test: A Compilation of Experiences of Conscientious Objectors as Encountered in Two World Wars*. Nappanee, IN: E. V., 1949.

Swartley, Willard M. *Covenant of Peace: The Missing Peace in New Testament Theology and Ethics*. Grand Rapids: Eerdmans, 2006.

———. *John*. Harrisonburg, VA: Herald, 2013.

———. *Slavery, Sabbath, War, and Women*. Scottdale, PA: Herald, 1983.

Thatcher, Adrian. *The Savage Text: The Use and Abuse of the Bible*. Malden, MA: Wiley-Blackwell, 2008.

Tripp, Tedd. *Shepherding a Child's Heart*. 2nd ed. Wapsallopen, PA: Shepherd, 2005.

Trotta, Daniel. "Iraq War Costs U.S. More Than $2 Trillion: Study." *Reuters*. March 14, 2013. http://www.reuters.com/article/us-iraq-war-anniversary-idUSBRE92ndoPG20130314.

Troyer, Marty. "A Stranger Hugged Me." *The Mennonite*, April 7, 2009. https://themennonite.org/feature/web-exclusive-stranger-hugged/.

True, Michael. *People Power: Fifty Peacemakers and Their Communities*. Jaipur, India: Rawat, 2007.

van Braght, Thieleman J. *The Bloody Theater: Or, Martyrs Mirror of the Defenseless Christians Who Baptized Only Upon Confession of Faith, and Who Suffered and Died for the Testimony of Jesus, Their Saviour, from the Time of Christ to the Year A.D. 1660*. 2nd Eng. ed. Scottdale, PA: Herald, 2005.

Vines, Matthew. *God and the Gay Christian: The Biblical Case in Support of Same-Sex Relationships*. New York: Convergent, 2014.

Volf, Miroslav. *Exclusion and Embrace: A Theological Exploration of Identity, Otherness, and Reconciliation*. Nashville: Abingdon: 1996.

Wallis, Jim. *America's Original Sin: Racism, While Privilege, and the Bridge to a New America*. Grand Rapids: Brazos, 2016.

———. *God's Politics: Why the Right Gets It Wrong and the Left Doesn't Get It*. San Francisco: HarperSanFrancisco, 2005.

———. *On God's Side: What Religion Forgets and Politics Hasn't Learned about Serving the Common Good*. Grand Rapids: Brazos, 2013.

———. "Where We Have Been—and Where We Go from Here." In *Evangelical Peacemakers: Gospel Engagement in a War-Torn World*, edited by David P. Gushee, 99–105. Eugene, OR: Cascade, 2013.

Warren, Rick. *The Purpose Driven Life: What on Earth Am I Here For?* Grand Rapids: Zondervan, 2002.

Washington Post, The. "Majority Says CIA Harsh Interrogations Justified." Washington Post—ABC News Poll December 11–14, 2014. *The Washington Post*. January 4, 2015. https://www.washingtonpost.com/page/2010-2019/WashingtonPost/2014/12/16/National-Politics/Polling/release_376.xml?tid=a_inl.

Weaver-Zercher, Valerie. "One Mean Mennonite Mama: A Pacifist Parent Faces Her Anger." *The Mennonite* 9, no. 19 (October 3, 2006) 11–13.

Webb, William J. *Corporal Punishment in the Bible: A Redemptive-Movement Hermeneutic for Troubling Texts*. Downers Grove, IL: InterVarsity, 2011.

Weiss, Elaine. *Family and Friends' Guide to Domestic Violence: How to Listen, Talk, and Take Action When Someone You Care about Is Being Abused*. Volcano, CA: Volcano, 2003.

————. *Surviving Domestic Violence: Voices of Women Who Broke Free.* Volcano, CA: Volcano, 2000.

Wenham, Gordon J., et al. *Remarriage after Divorce in Today's Church: 3 Views.* Grand Rapids: Zondervan, 2006.

————. *Story as Torah: Reading Old Testament Narrative Ethically.* Grand Rapids: Baker, 2004.

Willard, Dallas. *The Great Omission: Reclaiming Jesus's Essential Teachings on Discipleship.* New York: HarperOne, 2006.

Willimon, William H. "Bless You, Mrs. Degrafinried." *The Christian Century* 101 (March 14, 1984) 269–70.

Wink, Walter. *Engaging the Powers: Discernment and Resistance in a World of Domination.* Minneapolis: Fortress, 1992.

————. *Jesus and Nonviolence: A Third Way.* Minneapolis: Fortress, 2003.

————. *The Powers that Be: Theology for a New Millennium.* New York: Doubleday, 1998.

Wink, Walter, ed. *Peace is the Way: Writings on Nonviolence from the Fellowship of Reconciliation.* Maryknoll, NY: Orbis, 2000.

Winright, Tobias. "From Police Officers to Peace Officers." In *The Wisdom of the Cross: Essays in Honor of John Howard Yoder,* edited by Stanley Hauerwas, et al., 84–114. Grand Rapids : Eerdmans, 1999.

Witherington III, Ben. *Women in the Ministry of Jesus: A Study of Jesus' Attitudes to Women and Their Roles as Reflected in His Earthly Life.* Cambridge: Cambridge University Press, 1984.

Wright, N. T. *Jesus and the Victory of God.* Minneapolis: Fortress, 1996.

————. "The Letter to the Romans: Introduction, Commentary, and Reflections." In *The New Interpreter's Bible,* edited by Leander E. Keck et al., vol. 10, 393–770. Nashville: Abingdon, 2002.

Yoder, John Howard. *The Politics of Jesus: Vicit Agnos Noster.* Grand Rapids: Eerdmans, 1972.

————. *What Would You Do? A Serious Answer to a Standard Question.* Exp. ed. Scottdale, PA: Herald, 1992.

Yoder, Perry B. *Shalom: The Bible's Word for Salvation, Justice, and Peace.* Nappanee, IN: Evangel, 1987.

York, Tripp. "Conclusion: A Faith Worth Dying For: A Tradition of Martyrs Not Heroes." In *A Faith Not Worth Fighting For: Addressing Commonly Asked Questions about Christian Nonviolence,* edited by Tripp York and Justin Bronson Barringer, 207–25. Eugene, OR: Cascade, 2012.

York, Tripp and Andy Alexis-Baker, eds. *A Faith Embracing All Creation: Addressing Commonly Asked Questions about Christian Care for the Environment.* Eugene, OR: Cascade, 2014.

————. *A Faith Embracing All Creatures: Addressing Commonly Asked Questions about Christian Care for Animals.* Eugene, OR: Cascade, 2012.

York, Tripp and Justin Bronson Barringer, eds. *A Faith Not Worth Fighting For: Addressing Commonly Asked Questions about Christian Nonviolence.* Eugene, OR: Cascade, 2012.

Zahnd, Brian. *A Farewell to Mars: An Evangelical Pastor's Journey Toward the Biblical Gospel of Peace.* Colorado Springs: David C Cook, 2014.

Zarembo, Alan. "Detailed Study Confirms High Suicide Rate Among Recent Veterans." *Los Angeles Times*. January 14, 2015. http://www.latimes.com/nation/la-na-veteran-suicide-20150115-story.html.

Scripture Index

Author Index